LATIN SCRIPT AND LETTERS
A.D. 400–900

LATIN SCRIPT AND LETTERS

A.D. 400-900

Festschrift presented to Ludwig Bieler
on the occasion of his 70th birthday

EDITED BY

JOHN J. O'MEARA

AND

BERND NAUMANN

E.J. BRILL
LEIDEN
1976

ISBN 90 04 04725 5

TABLE OF CONTENTS

FOREWORD

The Board of Medieval Studies of University College Dublin, felt it appropriate that Ludwig Bieler's distinguished contribution to several of the disciplines with which it was concerned should be formally recognized by the presentation to him of a *Festschrift* on his seventieth birthday. Accordingly it established a committee which invited a number of contributions from among Ludwig Bieler's professional colleagues. These contributions are intended to represent in a general way the areas of scholarship in which Ludwig Bieler has worked so fruitfully.

The committee also appointed editors to carry out its instructions. These have not sought to impose any single system of conventions in regard to such matters as spelling, mode of reference and punctuation on this volume as a whole. Each scholar is responsible in these regards for his own contribution.

The Board of Medieval Studies of University College Dublin, counts it a special pleasure to acknowledge a generous grant towards the volume from the *Bundesministerium für Wissenschaft und Forschung in Wien*. It wishes to thank also the *National University of Ireland* for a similarly generous subvention. The Board is likewise grateful to *University College Dublin*, for its no less generous subsidy. Finally it desires to thank with special warmth those of its fellows in University College Dublin, whose early support, financial and other, made possible this presentation to an esteemed colleague.

J.J.O'M., B.N.

BIBLIOGRAPHY LUDWIG BIELER

ABBREVIATIONS

AB	Analecta Bollandiana
AfR	Archiv für Religionswissenschaft
AJP	American Journal of Philology
BEC	Bibliothèque de l'École des Chartes
BFC	Bollettino di filologia classica
BullTAM	Bulletin de Théologie Ancienne et Médiévale
CHR	Catholic Historical Review
CR	Classical Review
DLZ	Deutsche Literaturzeitung
EHR	English Historical Review
IER	Irish Ecclesiastical Record, 5th series.
IHS	Irish Historical Studies
JEH	Journal of Ecclesiastical History
JTS	Journal of Theological Studies
Med. Aev.	Medium Aevum
MIÖG	Mitteilungen des Instituts f. österr. Geschichtsforschung
OrLZ	Orientalische Literaturzeitung
ProcRIA	Proceedings of the Royal Irish Academy
RB	Revue Bénédictine
REL	Revue des Études Latines
RHE	Revue d'Histoire Ecclésiastique
RhMus	Rheinisches Museum für Philologie
RPh	Revue de Philologie
RTAM	Recherches de Théologie Ancienne et Médiévale
SLH	Scriptores Latini Hiberniae
Studies	Studies. An Irish Quarterly Review
TLZ	Theologische Literaturzeitung
WSt	Wiener Studien
ZKG	Zeitschrift für Kirchengeschichte
ZKTh	Zeitschrift für katholische Theologie
ZntWiss	Zeitschrift für neutestamentliche Wissenschaft

1929

1. Dionysii Halicarnassei Opuscula edd. H. Usener et L. Radermacher, II. 2 (Lipsiae, Teubner), pp. 389-420 (Indices).

1931

1*. Silberstäbe als Weihgeschenk—Anz. d. Akad. d. Wiss., Wien, pp. 1-12.

2. Zu Porphyrios, Vita Pythagorae 27—WSt 48, pp. 201-5.

1932

3. Die Sage von Perseus und das zehnte pythische Gedicht Pindars—WSt 49, pp. 119-28.
4. Motiverweiterung in den Vitae Vergilianae—Wissensch. Beilage z. Jahresbericht des Privatrealgymnasiums Rainer, Mauer bei Wien, pp. 1-5.
5. Psyches dritte und vierte Arbeit bei Apuleius—AfR 30, pp. 242-70. *Reprinted* in "Amor u. Psyche" (Wege d. Forschung Bd 126, Darmstadt, Wiss. Buchgesellschaft, 1967), pp. 334-69.
6. *Review:* J. P. Becker, Über eine Trilogie des Sophokles (Bonn 1932)—DLZ 1932, cols 2462-6.

1933

7. Zu Sophokles' Antigone, Vers 569—WSt 50, p. 174.
8. *Review:* H. Herter, De Priapo (Giessen 1932) — Gnomon 9, pp. 331-2.

1934

9. Σχιᾶς ὄναρ ἄνθρωπος — WSt 51, pp. 143-5. *Reprinted* in "Pindar u. Bacchylides" (Wege d. Forschung Bd 134, Darmstadt, Wiss. Buchgesellschaft, 1970), pp. 191-3.
10. Totenerweckung durch Synanachrosis: ein mittelalterlicher Legendentypus und das Wunder des Elisa—AfR 32, pp. 228-45.
11. Indices zu Weinbergers Ausgabe von Boethius, Philosophiae Consolatio (C.S.E.L., vol. LXVII).
12. *Review:* G. Richter, De mutis personis quae in tragoedia et comoedia Attica in scaenam producuntur (Diss. Halle, 1934) — DLZ 1934, cols 2415-9.

1935

13. Theîos Anér. Das Bild des göttlichen Menschen in Spätantike und Frühchristentum. Wien, Höfels. Bd I. xvi, 150 pp.
14. Kritisch-Exegetisches zur Suasoria de Alexandro des Arellius Fuscus — WSt 53, pp. 84-94.

1936

(13) Theîos Anér. (s. 1935).) Bd II. 130 pp.
    Reprinted (I and II): Darmstadt, Wiss. Buchgesellschaft, 1967.

15. Iohannes Franciscus de Pavinis, Rede auf den heiligen Leopold. Kritisch hrsg. u. übersetzt. Wien, Tyrolia. 45 pp.
16. Die Namen des Sprichworts in den klassischen Sprachen — RhMus 85, pp. 240-53.
17. Textkritische Nachlese zu Boethius' De Philosophiae consolatione — WSt 54, pp. 128-41.
18. *Review*: M. K. Flickinger, The ἁμαρτία of Sophocles' Antigone (Iowa 1935) — DLZ 1936, cols 359-61.

1937

19. Antigones Schuld im Urteil der neueren Sophoklesforschung. Wien, Höfels. 18 pp.
20. Bibliographie Ludwig Radermacher. (Herausgeber). Wien, Holzhausen. 41 pp.
21. Dynamis und Exousia — WSt 55, pp. 182-90.
22. Kulturbiologie und Literaturwissenschaft: Zu Ernst Bickels "Lehrbuch der Geschichte der römischen Literatur" — Reichspost 24-X-1937, pp. 17-18.
23. Zur Mosella des Ausonius — RhMus. 86, pp. 286-7.
24. *Review*: F. Göbel, Formen und Formeln der epischen Dreiheit in der griechischen Dichtung (Stuttgart 1935) — DLZ 1937, cols 12-17.
25. *Review*: Ruth Camerer, Zorn und Groll in der sophokleischen Tragödie (Borna 1936): *ibid.*, cols 1784-7.

1938

26. Das lateinische christliche Schrifttum — Schweizer Schule 1938, Nr. 10-13.
27. Der vollkommene Mensch im Denken der Antike — Schweizer Schule 1938, Nr. 16-17.
28. *Review*: F. Stoessl, Die Trilogie des Aischylos (Wien 1937) — DLZ 1938, cols 660-64.

1939

29. *Review*: E. Kroeker, Der Herakles des Euripides (Giessen 1938) — DLZ 60, cols 1342-6.

1940

30. Palaeography and Spiritual Tradition — Studies 29, pp. 269-80.

1941

31. Artikel "Schatten" und "Spiegel" in: Handwörterbuch des deutschen Aberglaubens, Bd 9 (1938-41), cols 126-42, 547-77.

1942

32. Codices Patriciani Latini: a descriptive catalogue of Latin manuscripts relating to St. Patrick. Dublin Institute for Advanced Studies. xvii, 72 pp.

1943

33. The Problem of "Silva Focluti" — IHS 3, pp. 351-64; cf. 4 (1944), pp. 103-5.
34. Was Palladius Surnamed Patricius? — Studies 32, pp. 323-6.

1944

34a Anecdotum Patricianum, Fragments of a Life of St. Patrick from MSS Cotton Vitellius E. vii and Rawlinson B 479 — Measgra i gcuimhne Mhichíl Uí Chléirigh (Assisi Press, Dublin), pp. 220-37.

1945

35. Codices Patriciani Latini: Addenda et corrigenda — AB 63, pp. 243-56.

1946

36. Casconius, the monster of the Navigatio Brendani — Éigse 5, pp. 139-40.
37. O'Sullevan Beare's Patriciana Decas: a modern Irish adaptation — Journal of the Galway Archaeol. and Hist. Society 22, pp. 19-33.
38. Recent Research in Irish Hagiography — Studies 35, pp. 230-38, 536-44.
39. *Review:* E. Bickel, Lehrbuch der Geschichte der römischen Literatur (Heidelberg 1937) — Anthropos 37-40, pp. 466-9.

1947

40. Der Bibeltext des heiligen Patrick — Biblica 28, pp. 31-58, 236-63.
41. Latin Manuscripts: facsimiles, editions, studies published in

Great Britain, Ireland, Canada and the United States since 1939 — Scriptorium 1, pp. 181-9, 329-54.

42. The Grammarian's Craft — Folia 2, pp. 94-105 (continued in 1948).

43. Utility and Tradition: two aspects of "simplified spelling" — Studies 36, pp. 203-10.

44. *Review:* E. A. Lowe, Codices Latini Antiquiores, vol. IV (Oxford 1947) — The Times Literary Supplement, 23-VIII-1947.

1948

45. A Viennese Schoolmaster (in memoriam Dr. Josef Pavlu) — Studies 37, pp. 440-46.

46. Exagellia — AJP 69, pp. 309-12.

47. Father Francis Nugent, Founder of the Irish Capuchins — The Irish Book Lover 30, pp. 98-99.

48. John Colgan as Editor — Franciscan Studies 8, pp. 1-24.

49. St. Patrick and the Irish People — Review of Politics 10, pp. 290-309.

50. The "Creeds" of St. Victorinus and St. Patrick — Theol. Studies 9, pp. 121-4.

51. The Grammarian's Craft (continued) — Folia 3, pp. 23-32, 47-55.

52. The Life and Legend of St. Patrick — IER 70, pp. 1087-91.

53. The Irish Book of Hymns: a palaeographical study — Scriptorium 2, pp. 177-94.

54. The Missio of Palladius: a comparative study of sources — Traditio 6, pp. 1-32.

55. The Ordination of St. Patrick — Scriptorium 2, pp. 286-7.

56. *Review:* F. Masai, Essai sur les origines de la miniature dite irlandaise (Brussels 1947) — Speculum 23, pp. 495-502.

1949

57. The Life and Legend of St. Patrick: problems of modern scholarship. Dublin, Clonmore & Reynolds. 146 pp.

58. Das Mittellatein als Sprachproblem — Lexis 2, pp. 98-104.

59. Die klassische Philologie in den Vereinigten Staaten (Edward Kennard Rand: Versuch einer Würdigung) — WSt 63, pp. 148-55.

60. Insular Palaeography: present state and problems — Scriptorium 3, pp. 267-94.

61. Manuscript Studies in Ireland, 1946-48 — *ibid.*, pp. 325-7.
62. Sidelights on the Chronology of St. Patrick — IHS 6, pp. 247-60.
63. Studies on the Text of Muirchú I: The Text of MS. Novara 77 — Proc RIA 52 C 5, pp. 178-220.
64. *Review:* A. Dold, Die Orakelsprüche im St. Gallener Palimpsestcodex 908 (Wien 1948) — Scriptorium 3, pp. 174-5.
65. *Review:* L. Radermacher, Weinen und Lachen (Wien 1947) — AJP 70, pp. 432-4.
66. *Review:* P. Walsh, Irish Men of Learning (Dublin 1947) — Scriptorium 3, p. 170.

1950

67. A Primer of Medieval Latin: the Roman Missal — The Catholic Educator (New York) 20, nos 4-5.
68. Libri Epistolarum sancti Patricii episcopi. I. Introduction and text — Classica et Mediaevalia 11, pp. 1-150.
69. The Humanism of St. Columbanus — Mélanges colombaniens (Luxeuil 1950), pp. 95-102.
70. *Review:* E. A. Lowe, Codices Latini Antiquiores, vol. IV (Oxford 1947) — AJP 71, pp. 323-7.

1951

71. A Political Slogan in Ancient Athens — AJP 72, pp. 181-4.
72. Libri Epistolarum sancti Patricii episcopi. II. Commentary — Classica et Mediaevalia 12, pp. 79-214.
73. Versus sancti Columbani: a problem re-stated — IER 76, pp. 376-82.
74. *Review:* H. Foerster, Abriss der lateinischen Paläographie (Bern 1949) — Scriptorium 5, pp. 161-2.

1952

75. Libri Epistolarum sancti Patricii episcopi. Vols I and II. (Reprint from "Classica et Mediaevalia", vols 11 and 12.) Dublin, Irish Manuscripts Commission.
76. The Nature and Meaning of Language — Studies 41, pp. 83-90.
77. The Place of St. Patrick in Latin Language and Literature — Vigiliae Christianae 6, pp. 65-98.
78. *Review:* B. Bischoff, Palaeographie (in: Deutsche Philologie im Aufriss, Bd I, Berlin 1951) — Scriptorium 6, p. 329.

79. *Review:* H. Foerster, Urkundenlehre in Abbildungen (Bern 1951) — *ibid.*, pp. 329-30.
80. *Reviews:* Liber Floridus (Festschrift Paul Lehmann, St. Ottilien 1950) — *ibid.*, pp. 161-4.
81. Wiener Studien, 1939-49 — Studies 41, pp. 255-6.

1953

82. The Works of St. Patrick; St. Secundinus, Hymn on St. Patrick. Transl. and annotated. Westminster, Md., Newman Press — London, Longmans, Green & Co. (Ancient Christian Writers, vol. XVII) 121 pp.
83. Manuscript Studies in Ireland, 1951-52 — Scriptorium 7, pp. 323-5.
84. St. Patrick a Native of Anglesey? — Éigse VII/2, pp. 129-31.
85. The Hymn of St. Secundinus — Proc RIA 55 C 6, pp. 117-127.
86. Vindiciae Patricianae: remarks on the present state of Patrician studies — IER 79, pp. 161-85.
87. *Review:* B. Bischoff — J. Hofmann, Libri sancti Kyliani (Würzburg 1952) — Scriptorium 7, pp. 326-7.
88. *Review:* E. Demougeot, De l'unité à la division de l'Empire Romain, 395-410 (Paris 1951) — AJP 74, pp. 306-10.
89. *Review:* Herbipolis iubilans (Würzburg 1952) — Scriptorium 7, pp. 327-8.

1954

90. Fernassimilation und Reimzwang — Classica et Mediaevalia 15, pp. 120-23.
91. Hibernian Latin — Studies 43, pp. 92-5.
92. Professor in Irland — Landstrasser Gymnasium, Jahresbericht 1953/54, pp. 7-9.
93. The Island of Scholars — Revue du Moyen Âge Latin 8, pp. 213-34.
94. The Notulae in the Book of Armagh — Scriptorium 8, pp. 89-97.
95. *Review:* Cassiodori — Epiphanii Historia Ecclesiastica Tripartita rec. Jacob — Hanslik, C.S.E.L. vol. LXXI (Wien 1952) — Scriptorium 8, pp. 335-6.
96. *Review:* E. A. Lowe, Codices Latini Antiquiores, vols V-VI (Oxford 1950, 1953) — AJP 75, pp. 323-6.
97. *Review:* D.D.C. Pochin Mould, Ireland of the Saints (London 1954) — Cath. Hist. Review 40, pp. 290-91.

98. *Review :* St. Irenaeus, Proof of the Apostolic Teaching. Transl. and annotated by J. P. Smith (Westminster Md. — London 1952, Ancient Christian Writers, vol. XVI) — IER 81, pp. 307-8.

1955

99. St. Severin and St. Patrick: a parallel — IER 83, pp. 161-6.
100. *Review :* Arator, ed. A. P. McKinley (C.S.E.L. vol. LXXII, 1951) — Scriptorium 9, pp. 165-7.
101. *Review :* W. Delius, Geschichte der irischen Kirche (München 1954). TLZ 1955, cols 663-4.
102. *Review :* Disticha Catonis, rec. M. Boas (Amsterdam 1952) — Scriptorium 9, pp. 154-5.
103. *Review :* H. Günter, Psychologie der Legende (Freiburg 1949) — IER 83, pp. 307-8.
104. *Review :* H. Vanderhoven — F. Masai, Regula Magistri (Les Publications de Scriptorium, III, 1953) — Speculum 30, pp. 690-2.

1956

105. Adamnan und Hegesipp — WSt 69, pp. 344-9.
106. Manuscript Studies in Ireland, 1953-55 — Scriptorium 10, pp. 319-21.
107. "Patrick and the Kings": apropos a new chronology of St. Patrick — IER 85, pp. 171-89.
108. St. Patrick and Rome — The Irish Augustinians in Rome (St. Patrick's, Rome), pp. 11-14.
109. St. Secundinus and Armagh — Seanchas Ardmhacha 2, pp. 21-7.
110. (and B. Bischoff) Fragmente zweier frühmittelalterlicher Schulbücher aus Glendalough — Celtica 3, pp. 211-20.
111. *Review :* F. Blatt, Précis de syntaxe latine (Lyon 1952) — Lingua 6, pp. 109-12.
112. *Review :* Corpus Christianorum (vols I, II, XXXVI, XLVII, XLVIII, CIII, CIV, CXXII) — Scriptorium 10, pp. 322-4.
113. *Review :* W. Delius, Geschichte der irischen Kirche (see under 1955) — JTS, N.S. 7, pp. 141-2.
114. *Review :* Itala ed. Jülicher-Matzkow-Aland, vol. III. Lucas — Scriptorium 10, pp. 137-8.
115. *Review :* J. Kirchner, Scriptura Latina Libraria (München 1955) — *ibid.,* pp. 142-3.

116. *Review:* L. Wenger, Die Quellen des römischen Rechts (Wien 1953) — *ibid.*, pp. 324-5.

1957

117. Boethii Philosophiae Consolatio (edition). (Corpus Christianorum vol. XCIV, Turnhout, Brepols). xxviii, 124 pp.
118. Hibernian Latin and Patristics — Studia Patristica 1 (Texte und Untersuchungen 63), pp. 182-7.
119. Irish Manuscripts in Medieval Germania — IER 87, pp. 161-9.
120. Vorbemerkungen zu einer Neuausgabe der *Consolatio* des Boethius — WSt 70, pp. 11-21.
121. (Contributor): S. Columbani Opera ed. C. S. M. Walker (SLH 2, Dublin Institute for Advanced Studies): Notes on the Text Tradition and Latinity lxxiii-lxxxii); Linguistic Indices 123-41.
122. *Review:* J. Carney, Studies in Irish Literature and History (Dublin 1955) — DLZ 78, cols 16-21.
123. *Review:* A. Gwynn, The Writings of Bishop Patrick, 1074-1084 (SLH 1, Dublin Institute for Advanced Studies) — MIÖG 65, pp. 139-40; TLZ 1957, p. 120.
124. *Review:* E. A. Lowe, Codices Latini Antiquiores, vol. VII (Oxford 1956) — AJP 78, pp. 448-9.
125. *Review:* G. Schreiber, Irland im deutschen und abendländischen Sakralraum (Köln 1956) — TLZ 1957, p. 117-8.

1958

126. Notes on the Durham Copies of the Psalterium iuxta Hebraeos — Scriptorium 12, pp. 282-3.
127. Römische Dichtung von Hadrian bis zum Ausgang des Altertums, 1926-35 (Literaturbericht) — Lustrum 1957/2 (1958), pp. 207-93.
128. The Grammarian's Craft. 2nd, revised edition — Folia 10/2, pp. 1-42.
129. The Lives of St. Patrick and the Book of Armagh — St. Patrick (Radio Eireann Thomas Davis Lectures, vol. 4), pp. 53-66.
130. Letter of Credence by Donatus Magrahe, Prior of Lough Derg — Clogher Record 2, pp. 257-9.
131. *Review:* M. L. W. Laistner, Thought and Letters in Western

Europe, A.D. 500-900. 2. ed. (London 1957) — JTS, N.S. 9, pp. 173-4.

132. *Review*: Corpus Christianorum (vols IX, XIV, XXXVIII-XL) — Scriptorium 12, pp. 325-7.

1959

133. Studies on the Text of Muirchú II. The Vienna Fragments and the Tradition of Muirchú's Text — Proc. RIA 59 C 4, pp. 181-95.

134. "Trias Thaumaturga" — Father John Colgan, O.F.M., 1592-1658 (Dublin, Assisi Press), pp. 41-49.

135. (Contributor) Adamnan, De locis sanctis ed. D. Meehan (SLH 3, Dublin Institute for Advanced Studies). "The text tradition", pp. 30-34; critical text; linguistic indices, pp. 124-49.

136. *Review*: Arnulfi Aurelianensis Glosule super Lucanum ed. B. M. Marti (American Academy in Rome 1958) — Scriptorium 13, pp. 134-5.

137. *Review*: N. K. Chadwick (ed.), Studies in the Early British Church (Cambridge 1958) — *ibid.*, pp. 118-21.

138. *Review*: Corpus Christianorum (vols LXXVIII, XCIV, XCVII, XCVIII, CXVII) — *ibid.*, pp. 121-5.

1960

139. Psalterium Graeco-Latinum (Codex Basiliensis A. VII. 3). Amsterdam, North Holland Publishing Co. (Umbrae Codicum Occidentalium, vol. 5) xxii pp., 196 plates. (Introduction).

140. St. Patrick's Purgatory: contributions towards an historical topography — IER 93, pp. 137-44.

141. *Review*: R. I. Best, Palaeographical Notes III: The Book of Armagh (Ériu 18, 1958, pp. 102-7) — Scriptorium 14, pp. 354-6.

142. *Review*: G. Schreiber, Die Wochentage im Erlebnis der Ostkirche (Köln 1959) — IER 94, pp. 120-22.

1961

143. Geschichte der römischen Literatur (Berlin, de Gruyter. Sammlung Göschen, Bd 52, 866). 160, 133 pp.

144. Irland: Wegbereiter des Mittelalters. (Stätten des Geistes, Urs Graf Verlag). 155 pp., 24 plates.

145. An Austrian Fragment of a Life of St. Patrick — IER 95, pp. 176-81.

146. Glimpses of St. Patrick's Spiritual Life — Doctrine and Life 11, pp. 126-32.

147. Towards an Interpretation of the so-called "Canones Wallici" — Medieval Studies presented to A. Gwynn (Dublin, Colm O Lochlainn), pp. 387-92.

148. (and G. MacNiocaill): Fragment of an Irish Double Psalter in the Library of Trinity College, Dublin — Celtica 5, pp. 28-39.

149. (Contributor): The Palaeography of the Book of Durrow. In: The Book of Durrow. Facsimile edition (Urs Graf Verlag), pp. 87-97.

150. *Review:* J. Carney, The Problem of St. Patrick (Dublin 1961) — The Irish Times, July 1, 1961, p. 9.

151. *Review:* R. B. C. Huygens, Lettres de Jacques de Vitry (Leiden 1960) — ZKG 72 (1961), pp. 391-2.

152. *Review:* J. Laporte, Le Pénitentiel de Saint Colomban. Introduction et édition critique (Tournai 1958) — JTS N.S. 12, pp. 106-12.

153. *Review:* Navigatio S. Brendani ed. by C. Selmer (Notre Dame, Ind. 1959) — ZKG 72, pp. 164-9.

154. *Review:* P. Walsh, Livy: his historical aims and methods (Cambridge 1961) — The Month 212, pp. 117-9.

1962

155. A Linguist's View of St. Patrick (a propos Chr. Mohrmann, The Latin of St. Patrick, Dublin 1961) — Éigse 10, pp. 149-54.

156. Editing St. Columbanus — Classica et Mediaevalia 22, pp. 139-150.

157. Patriciology: reflections on the present state of Patrician studies — Seanchas Ardmhacha 1961-62, pp. 9-36.

158. The Celtic Hagiographer — Studia Patristica 5, pp. 243-65.

159. Vindicta Scholarium: Beiträge zur Geschichte eines Motivs — Serta Philologica Aenipontana (Innsbruck 1961), pp. 383-5.

160. *Review:* S. Benedicti Regula ed. R. Hanslik (C.S.E.L. vol. LXXV, Wien 1960) — DLZ 83, cols 1079-81.

161. *Review:* P. B. Corbett, The Latin of the Regula Magistri (Louvain 1958) — Scriptorium 16, pp. 62-68.

162. *Review:* E. A. Lowe, Codices Latini Antiquiores, vols VIII-IX (Oxford 1959) — AJP 83, pp. 100-103.

163. *Review:* M. Seidlmayer, Currents of Medieval Thought (Engl. ed. Oxford 1960) — Med. Aev. 30, pp. 207-8.

1963

164. Ireland: Harbinger of the Middle Ages. (Engl. ed. of "Irland", see under 1961, adapted by the author, with the assistance of T. A. Bieler) Oxford University Press. 148 pp., 24 plates.

165. Irish University Education in a United Europe — The European Teacher 2, 2, pp. 32-6.

166. Patrick's Synod: a revision — Mélanges offerts à Mlle Christine Mohrmann (Utrecht, Spectrum), pp. 96-102.

167. The Irish Penitentials. With an appendix by D. A. Binchy. (SLH 5, Dublin Institute for Advanced Studies), 367 pp.

168. *Review:* Adamnán's Life of Columba, ed. by A. O. Anderson and M. O. Anderson (London 1961) — IHS 13, pp. 175-84.

169. *Reviews:* M. Bévenot, The Tradition of Manuscripts: a study in the tradition of St. Cyprian's treatises (Oxford 1961), and

170. H. J. Frede, Pelagius, der irische Paulustext, Sedulius Scottus (Freiburg 1961), and

171. A. Olivar, Los Sermones de San Pedro Crisólogo (Montserrat 1962) — JTS N.S. 14, pp. 196-202.

172. *Review:* Corpus Christianorum (volumes published 1958-60) — Scriptorium 16, pp. 324-33.

173. *Reviews:* N. R. Ker, English Manuscripts in the Century after the Norman Conquest (Oxford 1960), and

174. E. A. Lowe, English Uncial (Oxford 1960) — *ibid.* pp. 333-6.

175. *Review:* P. McGurk, Latin Gospel Books from A.D. 400 to A.D. 800 (Paris-Brussels 1961) — EHR 78, pp. 147-8.

1964

176. Christianity in Ireland during the Fifth and Sixth Centuries: a survey and evaluation of sources — IER 101, pp. 162-7.

177. Patrician Studies in the *Irish Ecclesiastical Record* — IER 102, pp. 359-66.

178. The New Testament in the Celtic Church — Studia Evangelica 3 (Texte u. Untersuchungen 88), pp. 318-30.

179. Some Remarks on the Text of St. Peter Chrysologus — Oikoumene. Studi Paleocristiani in onore del Concilio Ecumenico Vaticano II (Catania 1964), pp. 175-9.

180. Short autobiography. In: Österr. Hochschulzeitung 16, Nr. 14, p. 4.

181. *Review:* E. A. Lowe, Codices Latini Antiquiores, vol. X (Oxford 1963) — AJP 85, pp. 209-11.

1965

182. Geschichte der römischen Literatur. 2., verbesserte Auflage. (Berlin, de Gruyter. Sammlung Göschen Bd 52, 866) 160, 133 pp.
    Translations: Istoría tês Romaikês logotechnías (by A. D. Skiadas). Athens, Grigori, 1965.
    História de la literatura Romana (by M. Sanches Gil). Madrid, Gredos, 1968.

183. The Grammarian's Craft. An introduction to textual criticism. (Special issue of "Classical Folia", New York). 47 pp. (Revised).

184. (with L. Krestan) Eugippius, Life of St. Severin. Transl., with introduction and Notes. (Fathers of the Church, 55). Washington, Cath. Univ. Press X, 139 pp., 1 map.

185. The Text Tradition of Dicuil's *Liber de mensura orbis terrae* — ProcRIA 64 C 1, pp. 1-31, 1 table.

186. Die lateinische Kultur Irlands im Mittelalter in der Forschung des zwanzigsten Jahrhunderts — Hist. Zeitschr., Sonderheft 2, pp. 260-76.

187. The Chronology of St. Patrick — Old Ireland, ed. R. McNally (Dublin, Gill & Son), pp. 1-28.

188. Dank an die Alma Mater — Die Presse, Wien, 15-16 Mai 1965.

189. Manuscripts of Irish Interest in the Libraries of Scandinavia — Studies 54, pp. 252-8.

190. *Review:* Corpus Christianorum (volumes published 1961 to 1963) — Scriptorium 19, pp. 77-83.

191. *Review:* N. R. Ker, Medieval Libraries of Great Britain, 2nd ed., London 1964 — Hist. Zeitschr. 202, pp. 179-81.

192. *Review:* Eugippius, Das Leben des heiligen Severin. Lat. u. deutsch ... von R. Noll, Berlin 1963 — Scriptorium 19, pp. 135-7.

1966

193. History of Roman Literature. Condensed and adapted, with the collaboration of the author, by John Wilson. London, Macmillan. ix, 209 pp. Illustrated.

194. J. F. Kenney, The Sources for the Early History of Ireland: 1. Ecclesiastical. (1929). Revision, with Addenda and Corrigenda. New York. Octagon Books, xviii, 815 pp., 2 maps.

195. Libri Epistolarum S. Patricii Episcopi: Addenda — Analecta Hibernica 23, pp. 313-5.
196. Muirchú-Interpretationen — WSt 79, pp. 530-6.
197. The Irish Penitentials: their religious and social background — Studia Patristica 8 (Texte u. Untersuchungen 93), pp. 329-39.
198. *Review:* O. Loyer, Les chrétientés celtiques (Paris 1965) — Med. Aev. 35, pp. 85-6.
199. *Review:* B. Löfstedt, Der hibernolateinische Grammatiker Malsachanus (Uppsala 1965) — Éigse ii, pp. 300-302.
200. *Review:* E. Latham, Revised Medieval Word-List from British and Irish Sources (London 1965) — Hist. Zeitschr. 204, pp. 150-52.

1967

201. (Contributor) Dicuili Liber de mensura orbis terrae, ed. by J. J. Tierney. (SLH 6, Dublin Institute for Advanced Studies), pp. VII, 135 (Latinity and versification; textual basis; critical text and apparatus; index Latinitatis.)
202. St. Patrick and the Coming of Christianity. (A History of Irish Catholicism, I.1.) Dublin, Gill & Son. 100 pp.
203. La conversione al cristianesimo dei celti insulari e le sue ripercussioni nel continente — Settimana XIV di Studi sull'Alto Medioevo, Spoleto 1966 (publ. 1967), pp. 559-83.
204. The Book of Armagh — Great Books of Ireland (Dublin, Clonmore & Reynolds), pp. 51-63.
205. *Review:* Colophons de manuscrits occidentaux (Bénédictins du Bouveret), vol. I (1965) — JTS, N.S. 18, pp. 250-3.

1968

206. (with I. P. Sheldon-Williams) Iohannis Scotti Eriugenae Peri Physeon (De divisione naturae), vol. I (SLH 7, Dublin Institute for Advanced Studies), pp. x, 269, frontispiece.
207. St. Patrick and the British Church — Christianity in Britain, 300 — 700 ed. by M. W. Barley and R. P. C. Hanson, Leicester Univ. Press, pp. 123-130.
208. The Christianization of the Celts — Celtica 8, pp. 112-125.
209. *Review:* P. Collura, La precarolina e la carolina a Bobbio (Milano 1943, reprinted Firenze 1965) — Hist. Zeitschr. 206, pp. 117-9.

210. *Review:* A. Lesky, Gesammelte Schriften (Bern, 1966) — Journ. Hellen. Stud. 88, pp. 248 f.

1969

211. E. A. Lowe, an appreciation — The Irish Times, 30-VIII-1969.
212. *Review:* R. P. C. Hanson, St. Patrick: his origins and career (Oxford, 1968) — JTS, N.S. 20, pp. 328-32.
213. *Review:* B. Bischoff, Mittelalterliche Studien (2 Bde, 1966, 1967) — IHS 16, pp. 346-50.
214. *Review:* L. D. Reynolds and N. G. Wilson, Scribes and Scholars: a guide to the transmission of Greek and Latin literature (Oxford 1968) — JTS, N.S. 20, pp. 666f.

1970

215. "Corpus Christianorum" (Chronique) — Scriptorium XXIV, pp. 74-91.
216. E. A. Lowe (necrologue) — RIA Annual Report 1969/70, pp. 2-6.

1971

217. Four Latin Lives of St. Patrick — (SLH 8 Dublin Institute for Advanced Studies), pp. ix, 266.
218. The Classics in Celtic Ireland — Classical Influences on European Culture A.D. 500-1500 (Cambridge Univ. Press), pp. 45-49.
219. Eine Patricksvita in Gloucester — Festschrift Bernhard Bischoff zu seinem 65. Geburtstag dargebracht (Stuttgart, Anton Hiersemann). pp. 346-363, 1 plate.
220. *Review:* R. Düchting, Sedulius Scottus. Seine Dichtungen (München 1968) — Med. Aev. 39, pp. 166-7.
221. *Review:* Bede's Ecclesiastical History of the English People. ed. by Bertram Colgrave and R. A. B. Mynors (Oxford 1969) — Latomus 30, pp. 410-412.
222. *Review:* Jean Scot, Homélie sur le Prologue de Jean ed. E. Jeauneau (Sources Chrétiennes 151, Paris 1969) — Latomus 30, pp. 412-413.

1972

223. E. A. Lowe, Palaeographical Papers 1907-1965 (editor). 2 vols (Oxford, Clarendon Press), pp. xviii, 1-347; pp. x, 349-645, frontispiece, 150 plates.

224. Geschichte der römischen Literatur. 3., verbesserte, Auflage. (Berlin, de Gruyter. Sammlung Göschen Bd 4052, 4053), 153, 132 pp.
225. (with I. P. Sheldon-Williams) Iohannis Scotti Eriugenae Peri Physeon (De divisione naturae), vol. II (SLH 9, Dublin Institute for Advanced Studies), 252 pp.
226. (with James Carney) The Lambeth Commentary — Ériu 23, pp. 1-55, 4 plates.
227. Adversaria zu Anthologia Latina 676 — Antidosis (Festschrift für Walther Kraus, Wien, Hermann Böhlaus Nachf.), pp. 41-48.
228. Aspetti sociali del Pentenziale e della Regola di San Colombano — Atti del Congresso Internazionale di Studi Colombaniani, Bobbio 1965 (Amici di S. Colombano, Bobbio), pp. 119-126.
229. Towards a Hiberno-Latin Dictionary — Bulletin du Cange 38, pp. 248-255.
230. *Review:* S. Harrison Thomson, Latin Bookhands of the Later Middle Ages (Cambridge Univ. Press, 1969) — Med. Aev. 41, pp. 82-84.
231. *Review:* Migne up-to-date. (Migne P. L. Supplementum, curante A. Hamman) — Scriptorium 26, pp. 76-79.
232. *Review:* J. W. Smit, Studies on the Language and Style of Columba the Younger (Amsterdam 1971) — Latomus 31, pp. 896-901.
233. *Review:* J. M. Wallace-Hadrill, Early Germanic Kingship in England and on the Continent (Oxford 1971) — EHR 87, pp. 816-819.

1973
234. (co-editor with J. J. O'Meara) The Mind of Eriugena. Papers of a Colloquium held in Dublin, 14th-18th July 1970 (Dublin, Irish Univ. Press), xiii, 199 pp.
235. Remarks on Eriugena's original Latin prose — The Mind of Eriugena (see above, no. 234), pp. 140-146.
236. Some recent work on Eriugena — Hermathena 115, pp. 94-97.
237. Textkritisches zu Muirchú — Classica et Mediaevalia Francisco Blatt septuagenario dedicata (Librairie Gyldendal, Copenhagen), pp. 396-404.

238. St. Ignatius of Antioch and his Concept of the Christian Church — Grazer Beiträge I, pp. 5-13.
239. *Review:* T. A. M. Bishop, English Caroline Minuscule (Oxford 1971) — Med. Aev. 42, pp. 154-156.
240. *Review:* Jean Scot, Commentaire sur l'Evangile de Jean (ed. E. Jeauneau, Sources Chrétiennes 180, Paris 1972) — Latomus 32, pp. 883-885.

1974

241. Muirchú's Life of St. Patrick as a work of literature — Med. Aev. 43, pp. 219-233.
242. Bethu Phátraic. Versuch einer Grundlegung des Verhältnisses der irischen Patriciusviten zu den lateinischen — Anzeiger d. phil.hist. Kl. der Österr. Akademie d. Wissenschaften III, pp. 253-273.
243. Tírechán als Erzähler. Ein Beitrag zum literarischen Verständnis der Patrickslegende. — Sitzungsberichte der Bayerischen Akad. d. Wiss. (München), phil.-hist. Kl. 1974, Heft 6, 22 pp.
244. Zur Interpretation hagiographischer Parallelen — Sitzungsberichte d. Heidelberger Akad. d. Wiss., phil.-hist. Kl. 1974, Abh. 7, 20 pp.
245. Opera Memories of a Transplanted Viennese — The Irish Times, 11-1-1974.

1975

246. Ancient Hagiography and the Lives of St. Patrick — Forma Futuri, Studi in onore del Cardinale Michele Pellegrino (Torino, Bottega d'Erasmo), pp. 650-655.
247. Hans Pfitzner's *Palestrina* — Studies 64, pp. 66-73.
248. Did Jocelin of Furness know the writings of St. Patrick at first hand? — Corona Gratiarum: Miscellanea Patristica, Historica et Liturgica Eligio Dekkers O.S.B. XII lustra complenti oblata, II (Sint Pietersabdij, Brugge), pp. 161-167.
249. *Review:* E. A. Lowe, Codices Latini Antiquiores. Supplement. (Oxford 1971). — Part II. Great Britain and Ireland. 2nd ed. (Oxford 1972) — AJP 96, pp. 86-8.
250. *Review:* H. Scheible, Die Gedichte in der Consolatio Philosophiae des Boethius (Heidelberg 1972) — Hetairos (Galway), pp. 10-11.

Contributions to Encyclopaedias:
Encyclopaedia Britannica, Encyclopedia Americana, New Catholic
Encyclopedia, Bibliotheca Sanctorum, Lexikon für Theologie und
Kirche, u.a.

I

ROMAN ANTIQUITY
CLASSICAL AND CHRISTIAN

DIE FRÜHESTEN CHOLIAMBEN
DER LATEINISCHEN LITERATUR

FRANZ STOESSL

In seiner Erörterung über den Choliamb nennt Terentianus
Maurus 2416ff den Cn. Matius in seinen Mimiamben als Dichter von
Choliamben; und in der Tat finden wir in der lateinischen Literatur
Choliamben seit dem 1. Jh.a.C.: bei Cn. Matius (Fr. 9-17 M = 9-17
T), dann bei Varro Fr. 57, 109, 219, 293, 358, 373, 401, 549 B, bei
Laevius Fr. 12,25 M, C. Licinius Macer Calvus Fr. 3 M, Cinna Fr.
10 M; Catull, der das Versmaß recht häufig gebraucht (c. 8, 22, 31, 37,
39, 44, 59, 60) konnte also an eine reiche Tradition anknüpfen.[1] Aber
es scheint, daß die Spuren des Versmaßes in der lateinischen Literatur noch um ein Jahrhundert weiter zurück verfolgt werden
können.[2]

Hieron. Abr. 1777

Die auf Sueton zurückgehende Notiz über Ennius' frühe Lebens-
umstände hat den eigentümlich privaten, fast anekdotischen Ton,
den man in letzter Linie auf eine Satura des Ennius zurückführen
möchte.[3]: Q. Ennius poeta Tarenti nascitur, qui *a Catone quaestore*
Romam *translatus* habitavit in *monte Aventino*, parco *admodum
sumptu contentus* et unius ancillae ministerio. Ennius hat in ähn-
lichem Ton in seinen Satiren über sein Leben berichtet. Stilistisch

---

[1] Die vorcatullischen Choliamben zusammengestellt bei J. W. Loomis,
Studies in Catullan Verse, Leiden 1972, S. 103ff. Vgl. J. Pelckmann, *Versus
Choliambi apud Graecos et Romanos Historia*, Diss. Kiel 1908, S. 17.

[2] J. H. Waszink, *Problems concerning the Satura of Ennius*, Entretiens
Fondation Hardt XVII, 1971, S. 125, rechnet mit der Möglichkeit, daß es
Satiren d. Ennius in Choliamben gegeben habe, die aber durch die Ungunst
der Überlieferung verloren seien.

[3] Vgl. H. D. Jocelyn, *The Poems of Quintus Ennius. In: Aufstieg und Nieder-
gang der römischen Welt 2*, 1972, S. 1022; C. A. Van Roog, *Studies in Classical
Satire and Related Literary Theory*, Leiden 1965, S. 32; Knoche, *Römische
Satire*[3], S. 15ff. Das bekannteste Beispiel ist wohl die von Cic. De or. II 275
mitgeteilte Anekdote über Ennius und Scipio Nasica, die E. Badian, *Ennius
and his friends*, Entr. Fond. Hardt 17, 1971, S. 170 wohl mit Recht auf eine
Satura des Ennius zurückführt.

fällt an der Hieronymusnotiz die Subordination eines großen Gedankenkomplexes in einem Relativatz mit Nachhinken der beiden
Bestimmungen parco admodum sumptu contentus et unius ancillae
ministerio auf, wobei das zu beiden Aussagen gehörige contentus
statt an den Schluß oder den Anfang in die Mitte gestellt ist. Sollte
nicht in dieser Fügung die in Erzählung umgesetzte ursprüngliche
Formulierung nachklingen? Und in der Tat können einige Partien
als Reste choliambischer Trimeter gedeutet werden:

monte Aventino – ◡ – – –, Schluß eines choliambischen Trimeters.
Dieser Rhythmus ist durch die ungewöhnliche Fügung und Stellung
monte Aventino erreicht. Ennius selbst hat "in alto/quaerit *Aventino*" Aventino ohne Beisatz monte,[4] 8of. V; ebenso gebrauchen z.B.
die Historiker Aventinus ohne Beisatz: z.B. Sall. Iug. 31, 17, Hist. 1,
11, Livius 42 Mal,[5] Suet. Vi 16, Tac. Ann. 6, 45, 1, Hist. 3, 70, 1.
Wenn zu dem Eigennamen der Beisatz mons steht, dann fast immer
in der Reihenfolge Aventinus mons; das Material des Th. L. L. s.v.
Aventinus hat nur 3 Beispiele für die Stellung mons Aventinus:
Paul. Fest. 148; Val. Max. 1, 8, 3; Flor. 1, 1, 1, 6. (Kaum dazu zu
zählen Frontin aqu. 76 circa montem Caelium et Aventinum.)
Hieron. selbst bietet (Abr. 1397): Ancus Marcius, Numae ex filia
nepos *Aventinum montem* et Janiculum urbi addidit, also die gebräuchliche Junktur Aventinus mons. Die Praeposition *in* muß in
der auf Ennius zurückgeführten Wendung aus metrischen Gründen
getrennt gestanden haben, ähnlich wie Ann. 8of.

(contentus) admodum[6] sumptu[7] (– – ◡) – ◡ – – – Choliambenschluß. Contentus hat Ennius an einer berühmten Stelle der Annalen: 246, die seit L. Aelius Stilo[8] vielfach auf ihn selbst bezogen
wird. Über admodum vgl. Ter. Ad. 403.[9] parcus[10] muß von der Wortgruppe getrennt gewesen sein; es würde ein tadelloses Schlußwort
des vorhergehenden Verses abgegeben haben oder konnte auch den
gleichen oder den folgenden Vers einleiten, etwa:

---

[4] Das Wort mons als solches mehrmals bei Ennius: A.440, A.420, Sa.67 V.

[5] D. W. Packard, *A Concordance to Livy s.v. Aventinus.*

[6] Admodum in ähnlicher Verwendung z.B. Plaut. Pseud. 1219 (mit
magnus), mehrfach mit anderen Adjectiven (Lodge), ebenso Ter. (Mc Glynn).

[7] Sumptus vielfach bei Plaut. (Lodge) und Terenz (Mc Glynn).

[8] Gell. 12, 4, 5.

[9] Schon L. Aelius Stilo bei Gell. XII 4, 5.

[10] Parcus z.B. bei Plaut. von Personen: Most. 31, 237, Rud. 919, Aul. 314,
315, Stich. 555 (Lodge s.v.); Ter. Andr. 450 ...(te) nimium parce facere
sumptum.

parco ⟨quidem⟩ contentus admodum sumptu.

a Catone quaestore[11] $-\cup-\cup--\cup$.

Ennius hatte des Cato jedenfalls in den annales gedacht: Ann. XII Fr. IV.

Die Wendung Romam translatus klingt, als könne sie Ennius selbst verdankt sein; freilich bildet wohl translatus $--\cup$ Choliambenschluß, Romam aber müßte wohl aus metrischen Gründen von translatus getrennt gestanden haben.[12]

Hieron. Chron. Abr. 1838

Die wichtigste, dem Sueton verdankte Nachricht über das Leben des Komödiendichters Caecilius Statius setzt ihn in ihrem Hauptteil in Verbindung mit dem Dichter Ennius und mag sehr wohl ebenfalls auf Ennius selbst als letzte Quelle zurückgehen; dafür spricht auch ihr privater, geradezu zum Anekdotischen neigender Charakter: Statius Caecilius comoediarum scriptor clarus habetur natione *Insuber Gallus* et Ennii primum *contubernalis*. Quidam Mediolanensem ferunt. mortuus est anno post mortem Ennii et iuxta Janiculum sepultus. Nun zeigt auch diese Notiz des Hieronymus zwei sehr auffallende Wendungen: Statius Caecilius wird *Insuber Gallus* genannt. Diese Junktur im Singular hat im Lateinischen keine Parallele. Ich verdanke die folgenden Angaben dem Material des Th. L. L., die mir der Generalredaktor P. Flury liebenswürdiger Weise zur Verfügung stellte.[13] Der Singular von Insuber — auch ohne Verbindung mit Gallus — ist überhaupt selten: Cic. Pis. 34; fam. 15, 16, 1; Liv. 22, 6, 3; Ascon. Pis. p. 13, 18, Spart. Did. 1, 2. Der Plural Insubres Galli als Stammesbezeichnung kommt gelegentlich vor: Liv. 30, 18, 1; 32, 7, 5; 34, 46, 1; Flor. epit. 2, 3, 2; 2, 4, 1; Oros. hist. 4, 13, 11. Ebenso für Galli in Verbindung mit anderen Stammesnamen nur Belege im Plural und immer erst Galli, dann der Stammname: z.B. Galli Boi (Liv. 36, 40, 3; 37, 57, 8; Paul. Fest. p. 36); Galli Senones (Paul. Fest. p. 69; Fest. p. 339; 372; Flor. epit. 1, 13, 4; Gell. 5, 17, 2). Aber die speziell gebildete Junktur Insuber Gallus hat eine bestimmte metrische Eigenschaft: Insuber Gallus $-\cup--\bar{\cup}$

---

[11] Quaestor bei Plaut. Ba. 1075, Cap. 34, 111, 453 (Lodge).

[12] Regel des reinen Jambus im fünften Fuß: Bassus p. 257, Terentianus Maurus 2408, freilich von Varro nicht eingehalten: Fr. 58, 109 (?). Vgl. *Christ. Metrik* S. 362, J. W. Loomis, *Studies in Catullan Verse*, Leiden 1972, S. 102, Anm. 3; O. Massor, *Les fragments du poète Hipponax*, Paris 1962, 23f.

[13] Brief vom 24.III.1975.

wäre ein tadelloses Ende eines Choliambus; der Schluß liegt nahe,
daß die singuläre Fügung eben aus metrischen Gründen gesucht
wurde und bei Sueton — Hieronymus letztlich aus einem Gedicht in
Choliamben, also wohl aus einer Satire des Ennius stammt.

In diesem Zusammenhang wird aber noch ein weiteres Wort dieser
Hieronymusnotiz bedeutsam: contubernalis – ∪ – – ∪̄; auch dieses
fünfsilbige Wort eignet sich zur Bildung eines Choliambenschlusses
und kommt als solcher auch in einem Choliambus Catulls vor:
c. 37, 1.[14] Lucilius hat es geteilt, um es im Hexameter unterbringen
zu konnen: conque tubernalem 1137 M. Die Zurückführung auf Ennius muß hier aus verschiedenen Gründen mit größerer Vorsicht er-
folgen: Sueton selbst gebraucht das Wort auch von Varius und Tucca
(Hieron. Abr. 1994, z.J. 17 a.C.) Varius et Tucca, Vergilii et Horatii
contubernales poetae habentur inlustres. Ferner eignet es sich auch
als Schluß einer Prosaperiode (Creticus + Trochäus) und wird als
solcher auch verwendet; z.B. Colum. 12, 1, 1, Sen. ep. 47, 1 und
steht bei Hieron. in der Notiz über Statius ebenfalls am Satzschluß.
Trotzdem würde ich auch hier das contubernalis auf ein choliambi-
sches Gedicht des Ennius zurückführen.

Als Gegenprobe möge die Betrachtung anderer auf Sueton basie-
render Dichternotizen bei Hieronymus dienen: Hier. Abr. 1830
über den Tragiker Livius. Hier. Abr. 1816 über den Tod des Nae-
vius. Hier. Abr. 1817 über Plautus' Tod. Hieron. Abr. 1863 über
Pacuvius (trotz der Verbindung zu Ennius kein choliambischer
Anklang — ex filia nepos übrigens Irrtum und schon deshalb nicht
auf Ennius fußend). Hieron. Abr. 1959 über den Tod des Terenz.
Nirgends Anklang an choliambischen Rhythmus. Die gesamte
Terenzvita des Sueton, die Donat am Beginn seines Terenzkommen-
tars wiedergibt, zeigt nirgends den leisesten Anklang an choliambischen Rhythmus.

Auf Grund dieses Materials darf wohl der Schluß gewagt werden:
Ennius hat in seinen Satiren auch über sein bescheidenes Dasein
auf dem Aventin und seine dortigen Freunde berichtet und dabei
auch den Choliambus verwendet und in die lateinische Literatur
eingeführt wie den Hexameter, das Distichon, den Sotadeus; er war
auch auf diesem Gebiet der große Neuerer.

---

[14] Über die erstaunlich häufige Wiederkehr derselben Wörter in den so
geringen Resten lateinischer Choliambendichtung vgl. J. W. Loomis, a.O.
S. 108. Über fünfsilbiges Wort am Versende ebda S. 116.

THE RULE OF FAITH OF
VICTORINUS AND OF PATRICK

R. P. C. HANSON

I

The resemblances between the doctrinal formulae in Victorinus of Pettau, *Commentary on the Apocalypse*, chapter 11, and in Patrick, *Confession*, chapter 4, have long been noticed.[1] For ease of reference it is convenient to set out both formulae in parallel columns:

VICTORINUS[2]

(4) '*mensura*' *autem fidei est manda-tum*/(5) *domini nostri, confiteri omni-potentem, ut didicimus*/(6) *et huius fi-lium dominum nostrum Iesum Chris-tum ante ori*/(7) *ginem saeculi spirita-liter apud patrem genitum, factum homi*/(8) *nem, et morte devicta in caelis cum corpore a patre receptum,*/(9) *sanc-tum dominum et pignus immortali-tatis, hunc per prophetas*/(10) *praedica-tum, hunc per legem conscriptum, hunc per manum dei et*/(11) *per verbum patris omnipotentis et conditorem orbis totius mundi*/,(12) *haec est arundo et mensura*

PATRICK[3]

quia non est alius Deus nec umquam fuit nec erit post haec praeter Deum patrem ingenitum, sine principio, a quo est omne principium, omnia tenen-tem, ut didicimus; et huius filium Iesum Christum, quem cum patre scilicet semper fuisse testamur, ante originem saeculi spiritaliter apud pa-trem ⟨et⟩ inerrabiliter genitum, ante omne principium, et per ipsum facta sunt visibilia et invisibilia, hominem factum, morte devicta in caelis ad pa-trem receptum, et dedit illi omnen potestatem super omne nomen cae-

---

[1] First apparently by A. Hahn. A bibliography of this subject must include: *Victorini Episcopi Petavionensis Opera*, ed. J. Haussleiter (C.S.E.L. XXXXIX, Vienna 1916); also review in *Göttingische Gelehrte Anzeigen* 160.Jahrgang, Bd. 1 (Berlin 1898), pp. 369-371; E. Kattenbusch, *Das Aposto-lische Symbol*, Vol. 1 (Leipzig 1894), pp. 188, 212-214, 395; E. Norden, *Agnostos Theos* (Stuttgart 1956, repr. of ed. of 1923), pp. 263-276; J. E. L. Oulton, *The Credal Statements of St. Patrick*, (Dublin 1940); L. Bieler, "The 'creeds' of St. Victorinus and St. Patrick", *Theological Studies* 9 (1949), pp. 121-124; R. P. C. Hanson, "Patrick and the *Mensura Fidei*", *Studia Patristica X* (ed. F. L. Cross, Berlin 1970), pp. 109-111, an article of which this is a correction and an enlargement.

[2] Haussleiter's ed., p. 96. In future this edition will be referred to as *H*, with page and line given. The lines of Victorinus in my text above, p. 25 are indicated in brackets.

[3] L. Bieler, *Libri Epistolarum Sancti Patricii Episcopi* (Dublin 1952), pp. 58, 59.

fidei, ut nemo adoret ad aram sanc/[13] *tam, nisi qui haec confitetur*: dominum et Christum eius.

lestium et terrestrium et infernorum et omnis lingua confiteatur ei quia Dominus et Deus est Iesus Christus, *quem credimus et expectamus adventum ipsius mox futurum*, iudex vivorum atque mortuorum, qui reddet unicuique secundum facta sua; *et* effudit in nobis habunde Spiritum Sanctum, donum *et* pignus *immortalitatis, qui facit credentes et oboedientes ut sint* filii dei *et* coheredes Christi, *quem confitemur et adoramus unum deum in trinitate sacri nominis.*

It should be noted that in cap. 14 of his *Confession* Patrick describes this formula as *mensura fidei trinitatis;* also that Bieler's reading *didicimus* in Patrick's *Confession* 4 is not the best one; it is better to take the *dicimus* of the majority of MSS.

Next, we must note that we have another version of Victorinus' formula, in the recension of Victorinus' *Comm. on the Apocalypse* made by Jerome (as Oulton calculated) about the year 406. It runs thus in *H* (the odd pages of the text being devoted to Jerome's recension, while the even pages show the original of Victorinus), p. 97:

> '*mensura*' *autem filii dei mandatum domini nostri, patrem confiteri omnipotentem; dicimus et huius filium Christum ante originem saeculi spiritalem apud patrem genitum, hominem factum et morte devicta in caelis cum corpore a patre receptum effudisse spiritum sanctum, donum et pignus immortalitatis, hunc per prophetas praedicatum, hunc per legem conscriptum, hunc esse manum dei et verbum patris et conditorem orbis. haec est arundo et mensura fidei, et nemo adorat aram sanctam, nisi qui hanc fidem confitetur.*

It must also be observed that none of these formulae are creeds. They are all rules of faith, i.e. longer, ampler, looser statements than creeds, but historically related to them. Creeds were first regarded as bare, skeletonic summaries of the rule of faith, but later, in the fourth century, creeds began to be enlarged so much as to become in the end indistinguishable from the rule of faith, and gradually came to take its place.[4] We should also note that Jerome admits in his Prologue to his recension of Victorinus' work that he made three

---

[4] See R. P. C. Hanson, *Tradition in the Early Church* (London 1962), caps 2 and 3 and bibliography, and "Patrick and the Mensura Fidei", pp. 109, 110.

kinds of alteration to it: *correxisse* (i.e. he had emended readings corrupted by the carelessness of scribes), *sociavisse vel addidisse* (i.e. he had interspersed matter taken from earlier commentators), and *abstulisse* (i.e. he had removed objectionably chiliastic or literalist interpretations of Victorinus).[5]

The general resemblance in form and vocabulary between Victorinus' formula and that of Patrick is obvious, and perhaps most striking is Patrick's calling the formula by the unusual name *mensura fidei* and his echo of Victorinus' *ut didicimus* in the phrase *ut dicimus*. His only noteworthy resemblances to Jerome's version of the formula are in this phrase *ut dicimus* (J *dicimus* without *ut*, V *ut didicimus*), and in his words *et effudit in nobis habunde spiritum sanctum, donum et pignus immortalitatis*, apparently echoing Jerome's *effudisse spiritum sanctum, donum et pignus immortalitatis*. But it should be noted that Patrick places his *ut dicimus* in the same construction as Victorinus places his *ut didicimus*, differing thereby from Jerome, and that he puts his reference to the Holy Spirit at the end of his formula, thereby differing both from Jerome and (at least as far as the position of the words *donum et pignus immortalitatis* goes) from Victorinus.

II

It must now be, observed that there are some readings in H's version of Victorinus' formula which are impossible and should never have been allowed to stand. The tenth and eleventh lines of Victorinus' formula contain the words *hunc per manum dei et per verbum patris omnipotentis et conditorem orbis totius mundi*. No verb whatever is supplied for this construction, whereas it is supplied for the similar construction *hunc per prophetas praedictum, hunc per legem conscriptum* in lines 9 and 10 above. Victorinus' Latin (as Jerome condescendingly observed) was far from elegant, but it was not execrable; it was much better than Patrick's. Victorinus could not have written a totally ungrammatical and indeed obscure sentence such as that from *hunc per manum* to *totius mundi*. But much more striking is the fact that if we retain the *per* in lines 9 and 10 before the words *manum* and *verbum* we ruin the theology

---

[5] See *H*, pp. XXXVI-XLV.

of Victorinus' formula. Much has been made of Victorinus' confusion of the pre-existent Christ with the Holy Spirit, and much of his "Binitarian" faith in apparently omitting the Holy Spirit altogether from his formula. But nobody appears to have noticed that if we keep Haussleiter's reconstruction of the formula here we have a pre-existent Christ begotten as Son of God before the origin of the age (who was led or appointed or in some way dealt with) *through* the hand of God and *through* the Word of God and (the construction demands it) *through* the founder of the world. What does this imply? Two pre-existent Sons of God or Words? This would be absurd. Clearly the passage must be amended, and if we are to amend it the best authority to fall back on is Jerome's recension. Jerome added to and abstracted from Victorinus' original, but he did not completely re-write it and he tells us that in places he corrected corruptions in the text. We need not assume that all Jerome's variations from Victorinus were derived from Jerome's free fancy or from other authors. For that matter, we need not assume that the text which Jerome had before him was precisely the text which Haussleiter has reconstructed as the original. Jerome is indeed a witness (though an uncertain and biased witness) to Victorinus' text much earlier than the earliest MS of that text (which in fact is of the XVth century and very late). When Jerome reproduces Victorinus' text here as *hunc esse manum dei et verbum patris et conditorem orbis*, he not only recalls an early Patristic title of Christ ("hand of God", to be found in Irenaeus *Adv. Haer.* 4.20.1; 5.6.1; 16.1) but also makes good sense of a passage which is otherwise nonsense both grammatically and theologically. Allowing for some stylistic tidying up on the part of Jerome, we can with some confidence reconstruct the original word of Victorinus as *hunc manum dei, et verbum patris omnipotentis et conditorem orbis totius mundi.*

Emboldened by this example, we can now look at the extraordinary expression in line 9 of Victorinus' formula in *H*, *sanctum dominum et pignus immortalitatis*. In fact, the *apparatus criticus* tells us that the MS A, the most important of the three,[6] does not read *sanctum dominum;* it reads *sčm dñm.* Haussleiter assumed, not without

[6] For the MSS attestation of Victorinus' *Comm. on Apocalypse*, see *H*, XXX-XXXV.

references to justify the assumption, that *sm̄* was an abbreviation
for *sanctum* and that *dm̄* meant *dominum*, though he curiously saw
no need to justify this much more difficult assumption. First, the
expression *sanctum dominum* as applied to Christ is wholly un-
parallelled in any doctrinal formula and is peculiarly unsuitable
here, as Christ has already been called *dominus* in line 6 above and
the word is to be used for God the Father, not Christ, five lines below
in line 13. Second, it is wholly unlikely that the expression *pignus
immortalitatis* should be used in a doctrinal formula for anyone
except the Holy Spirit. For parallels to these expressions Haussleiter
adduces *Apoc.* 6.10, *domine sanctus et verus* (which clearly refers to
God the Father), and *Eph.* 1.14, *signati spiritu promissionis qui est
pignus hereditatis nostrae*. In Latin here the *qui* can only apply to
the Holy Spirit, but some MSS of the Greek read ἐσφραγίσθητε τῷ
πνεύματι τῷ ἁγίῳ ὅς ἐστιν ἀρραβὼν τῆς κληρονομίας ἡμῶν though
others read ὅ, and the evidence is pretty evenly balanced. Victorinus certainly knew Greek, yet if we assume that he here wrote
sanctum dominum and applied to Christ the expression *pignus
immortalitatis* we are assuming that he was applying to the Son an
expression which all his readers who did not know their Greek New
Testament would have associated with the Holy Spirit. Indeed in
view of the fact that there is good evidence for the reading ὅ and
the likelihood that even those readers who saw ὅς in their texts
would take it as attracted into the masculine by ἀρραβών after it
and not as referring to Χριστῷ several lines above it, perhaps most
of the readers of *Eph.* 1. 14 who knew Greek would refer the expression to the Holy Spirit and not to Christ.[7] Elsewhere in his *Commentary* Victorinus shows that he certainly thinks of the Spirit as a
gift and as given or poured out by Christ: cf 26.9, *spiritus sanctus
septiformis virtutis datus est in potestatem eius (Christi) a patre;* 26.12,
a quotation of *Acts* 2,33, *dextra igitur dei exaltatus acceptum a patre
spiritum effudit;* 46.7, (Christ) *statim spiritum sanctum effudit qui
ferturus est hominem in caelum; 76.1 acceperunt, inquit, stolas albas,
id est donum spiritus sancti*. I believe that we must be influenced here
primarily by Jerome, and more indirectly by Patrick, and assume

---

[7] The likelihood of the relative pronoun being attracted into the masculine
has been drawn to my attention by my colleague Prof. F. F. Bruce, D.D.,
F.B.A. The evidence of the MSS stands thus: ὅς-ς⁻ D° 1739 al lat ς ὅ 𝔓46
A B G pm d; R. In 2 Cor. 1.22 and 5.5. *pignus* is certainly used of the Holy
Spirit.

that the original reading here was *sanctum donum et pignus im-mortalitatis*, and that the words *effudisse spiritum* have dropped out before *sanctum*. This is either what Jerome read in his copy of Victorinus or what he restored if he found the text as corrupt as it is in Haussleiter's reconstruction. This emendation of the text has the added advantage that it places rather further apart the very difficult but apparently necessary switch in the meaning of *domi-num* = Christ in line 6 to *dominum* = God the father in line 13. Oulton (*op. cit.* p. 17) suggests that we should conclude that Jerome introduced the words *effudisse spiritum* because this would account for the difficulty of the sentence as he has it, changing awkwardly from *donum immortalitatis* to *hunc*, referring back to Christ. But it is just as likely that the corruption (if we accept that Haussleiter's text represents a corruption) first began because of the awkward-ness of the original sentence as that Jerome emended it in such a way as to make it awkward. Elsewhere Jerome's text runs smoothly, all too smoothly. The scribe of MS A (Ottobonianus latinus 3288A, which is the chief, indeed in a sense the only MS for this work) intended the reader to read *sanctum donum et pignus immortalitatis*, the words *effudisse spiritum*, as has already been argued, having fallen out before *sanctum*.

I therefore conclude that Jerome's version here, as in lines 10 and 11, represents the correct original of Victorinus, and that what we have to do with here is a rule of faith which is "Binitarian" in form but not in content. This is, after all, highly probable in an author such as Victorinus who was writing at the very end of the third or the beginning of the fourth century. Jerome left it in its "Binitarian" form (which incidentally suggests that the form was not as obsolete in his day as some scholars have made out). But Patrick received it in a different form approximating closer to the Trinitarian one. This argument also removes the main point of agreement between Jerome and Patrick against Victorinus. Further it means that Vic-torinus must be removed from the list of those Patristic writers who attest the reading of ὅς rather than ὅ at *Ephesians* 1.14.

III

When we come to determine the relation of Patrick's formula to that of Victorinus, we are now left only with Patrick's *ut dicimus* as

evidence that he derived his formula through Jerome's recension,
This is not a weighty piece of evidence. It is possible, but on the
whole unlikely, that *dicimus* is the original reading in Victorinus.
preserved in Jerome's recension. Oulton[8] refers *ut didicimus* to the
incident commented on in *H* 88.18-90.3 when a great angel, whom
Victorinus identified with Christ (88. 1-7), tells the prophet John to
annnounce *omnipotentis dei verba*. The phrase in 96.5 would then
mean that the formula is the words of God, duly announced. Even
though Patrick has *dicimus* and not *didicimus*, he places *ut* before it
and uses the expression in precisely the position in his formula in
which Victorinus put it, viz at the end of the article dealing with God
the Father, as a kind of transition between that and the Christological article, whereas Jerome's syntax attaches his *dicimus*, without
an *ut*, to the Christological article. It is better to assume that if
Patrick's formula derives indirectly from Victorinus, during the
course of transmission Victorinus' *ut didicimus*, which became
meaningless once the formula was taken out of its context, was reduced to *ut dicimus*.[9]

We can therefore be pretty confident that there is no connection
at all between Patrick's formula and the formula of Jerome's recension of Victorinus' *Commentary*. Oulton's arguments in favour of
a connection between Patrick and Jerome had already been seriously
damaged by Bieler's treatment of the subject.[10] But the resemblances
between Patrick's formula and that of Victorinus have been in-
creased if the argument of this article is accepted, and make it
impossible to deny that there was some connection between them.
What that connection was is not easy to determine. It should be
noted that Victorinus' *Comm. on Apoc.* was well known and widely
read in the ancient Christian world, as Haussleiter makes clear in
his Introduction to *H*. Tyconius, the Donatist in Africa, knew it
before the end of the fourth century, and Jerome's friend Anatolius
as well as Jerome himself in Bethlehem knew it at least as early as
the opening years of the fifth century, and the presbyter Beatus of
Liebana in Spain knew it in the eighth century. The fact that its
author had died as a martyr in the Diocletian persecution no doubt

---

[8] *Op. cit.*, p. 13.
[9] There are some parallels for the use of *dicimus* in doctrinal formulae of
the fifth century and later. See Oulton, *op. cit.*, p. 27 n. 1.
[10] For Bieler's article see the bibliography in note 1 above.

helped its circulation. The very fact that Jerome thought it necessary to issue a revised version of it suggests that it was popular, too
popular to suppress or ignore, too chiliastic to leave untouched. And
Haussleiter traces two later recensions of it besides that of Jerome.[11]
It is not surprising that a copy should have found its way to the
British Church of Patrick's day. We need not assume any further
connection between the Christianity of Britain and that of remote
Pannonia where Victorinus' see of Poetoevium lay, than simply that
this popular work by a Pannonian martyr bishop made its way to
the British Church. It is a little surprising that there appears to be
no evidence that Victorinus' work was read in Gaul. In the lack of
evidence we can draw no firm conclusions, but this may indicate
that the British Church was not wholly ruled in its tastes and choices
by the Gallic.

There is, however, plenty of material in Patrick's formula which
does not derive from Victorinus. The most valuable part of Oulton's
monograph is that in which he supplies the documentation for this.[12]
He finds several points in common with formulae associated in one
way or another with the creed produced by the Council of Ariminum
of 359, and several points which recall expressions in the work of
Hilary of Poitiers (ob. 369). He states his general conclusion thus:
"But I do not claim to have in any sense proved that Patrick read
Hilary... What does emerge is that Patrick was acquainted with the
theological phrases current in Gaul in the fourth and fifth centuries
and to be met with in Gaul's most eminent theologians".[13] This is
what might be expected of someone who was trained to be a priest
in Britain. Victorinus' formula has been enlarged by expressions
which reflect the theological controversies and interests of the fourth
century, though not in any sharp or emphatic way. Though some of
Patrick's expressions echo phrases to be found in some fifth-century
writers, no fifth-century controversy is reflected in any term used in
Patrick's formula. Again, this is what we should expect from one
whose ecclesiastical formation had taken place in a church remote
from the centres of sophisticated theological activity, a church
probably conservative and perhaps even archaic in its customs, and
since Patrick was resident in far-away Britain and Ireland when the

---

[11] See *H*, Introd. pp. XLV-LXVI.
[12] See Oulton, *op. cit.*, pp. 17-31.
[13] *Ibid.*, p. 30.

great councils of 431, 449 and 451 took place he would have been unaffected by them. One resemblance, however, in Patrick's formula demands notice. It shares two expressions with a creed of Auxentius of Milan; they are *ante omne principium and per ipsum facta sunt visibilia et invisibilia*. We know this creed because Hilary of Poitiers in his *Contra Auxentium* quotes a letter of Auxentius in which he professes this creed.[14] Auxentius says of it: *ex infantia quemadmodum doctus sum sicut accepi de sanctis scripturis*.[15] There is nothing specifically Arian in this creed, though Auxentius was Arian bishop of Milan when he uttered it. The year in which he wrote the letter quoted by Hilary was 364. Auxentius had been bishop of Milan since 355. He was a native of Cappadocia; Hilary says that he received his theological education in the church in which the Arian bishop Gregory of Alexandria had presided.[16] Auxentius himself in his letter says that he had never known Arius and never laid eyes on him and that he did not know his doctrine.[17] There is no reason to suppose that any of these statements are false, except that it is hard to believe that Auxentius did not know Arius' doctrine.

Where did Auxentius' creed come from? From Cappadocia? From Alexandria? Or from Milan? Auxentius' native language was Greek; apparently he only learned Latin when he was appointed bishop of Milan by the Emperor Constantius in 355. But before we rush to the conclusion that Patrick's rule of faith was influenced by a formula from the Eastern Church, we should consider the attitude of the theologians of the early Church, at least till the end of the fourth century, to formulae. The early Christian fathers were not wedded to nor deeply concerned with the actual verbal form of doctrinal formulae. The *homoousion* of Nicea drops out of sight for twenty years after 325. The people who composed the "Nicene" creed of 381 regarded themselves as exactly reproducing the doctrine of 325, but they appear to have adopted a formula the basis of which was not the creed of 325 and one which by no means exactly reproduced all the terms of that creed. What the theologians of that period were concerned with was not to secure a formula but to secure a doctrine, and this doctrine could be expressed rather differently in

---

[14] Migne, *Patrologia Latina* 10: 617, 618 (14).
[15] *Ibid.*, 10: 617.
[16] *Ibid.*, 614 (8).
[17] *Ibid.*, 617 (14).

different places and times and circumstances, and still remain the same doctrine.[18] Everybody who presented a doctrinal formula in the fourth century, be they pro-Nicene, Arian, Semi-Arian, or anything else, protested that they were not adding to the traditional faith but merely stating it in other words. It would therefore be perfectly possible for somebody brought up in one church to declare his faith in the words of another church and still to protest that this was the faith which he had known from childhood. Marcellus of Ancyra was quite willing to declare in the presence of Pope Julius in 330 his traditional belief in the words of the Roman creed. It is therefore unnecessary to imagine that in this document given by Hilary in which Auxentius declares his creed we are dealing with a creed of Cappadocia or Alexandria. No doubt Auxentius is quoting a creed of Milan, and declaring that this expresses adequately the faith that he has always held. Hilary never attacks this creed as Arian; his only objection to it is that it is not capable of bringing to light Auxentius' Arianism. Patrick's formula incorporates expressions from a creed which was known in Milan in 364. This is as much as we should infer from the elements common to the formulae of Patrick and of Auxentius.

It may be asked whether this was a personal formula of Patrick. Kattenbusch warns against mistaking a private document for a definite creed and then drawing a conclusion about the verbal form of the creed of the area where the theologian in question was a native or functioned as an official of the Church.[19] But it may be doubted whether this distinction between a private formula and a formula of the Church is a realistic or useful one. If by a private formula is meant an interpretation of the Christian faith wholly confined to the individual who expresses it, setting out an idiosyncratic list of beliefs that happen to appeal to him, no such thing existed or was thought of in the ancient Church. The nearest approach to a private formula would be some statement covering selected points of Christian doctrine which either a writer particularly wishes to emphasise or which have been presented to him by others who suspect his orthodoxy. Such are the statement that opens the *Dialogue with Heracleides* of Origen, and perhaps the

---

[18] For a more elaborate exposition of this point, see R. P. C. Hanson, "Dogma and Formula in the Fathers" in *Studia Patristica XIV* (Berlin 1976).

[19] *Das Apostolische Symbol*, p. 395.

Letter of Hymenaeus presented probably to Paul of Samosata about 268, and the formula submitted by Auxentius of Milan to his judges when in 364 his orthodoxy was impugned by Hilary of Poitiers: *deum verum filium ex deo vero patre*.[20] Even formulae such as these can scarcely be called personal rules of faith, because they were all probably known and used by others.

But anyway there is no evidence that Patrick's doctrinal formula in *Confession* 4 is in any sense a personal declaration of faith. He calls it *mensura fidei*, using Victorinus' unusual phrase; he does not claim that it is peculiarly his but suggests rather that its doctrinal content is what everybody should believe. Patrick, we may well agree, was not the sort of person to be, or to set himself up to be, a connoisseur of doctrine.

There are a few faint indications in chapter 4 of the *Confession* that Patrick is retailing here a traditional formula which was regularly handed on to neophytes. The first is the expression *ut dicimus*. Even if this is (as has been suggested above, p. 31) a reduction or corruption of Victorinus' *ut didicimus*, it would still suggest to those who heard it for the first time a formula expressing the Church's faith. The other is a subtler point, but an interesting one.[21] Towards the end of his formula, Patrick quotes in his own version the words of Titus 3.6 *effudit in nobis* (Vulgate, *effudit in nos*). The reading of the MSS is not certain here. *D* has *effudit in vobis*, the rest *infudit in nobis*. Bieler has chosen to follow *D* for *effudit* and the rest for *nobis*. This seems an inconsistent and unjustifiable choice, for we should surely choose the whole phrase in *D* or in the rest. If we are to choose, *D* will clearly be preferable, and we are therefore faced with the statement *effudit in vobis habunde spiritum sanctum*. There is apparently no precedent for *vobis* in MSS of the Latin New Testament. It is possible that the change from the *nobis* of the Latin Bible to the *vobis* of *D* reflects a deliberate alteration designed to impress the truth concerning the Holy Spirit upon those who were receiving for the first time this version of the Church's rule of faith,

---

[20] *P.L.* 10: 614 (8), 617 (14). It appears in his creed, but may have been specially inserted by Auxentius.

[21] This point I owe to the perspicuity of Mr. D. R. Bradley, Senior Lecturer in Greek and Latin and Classical Philology in the University of Manchester, a colleague of mine in a seminar in the University.

that doctrinal standard upon which, it is reasonable to believe, instruction leading up to baptism was usually based.

We can therefore recognise in Patrick's formula one reasonably reliable account of the rule of faith of the British Church in the first half of the fifth century. It is an adaptation of the rule of faith of a Pannonian martyr bishop as he gave it in a widely read work at the end of the third century. By the beginning of the fourth century the British Church had become firmly, though modestly, established and had been organised into a number of sees.[22] It is likely that this is the period in which Victorinus' formula was adopted as a basis of catechetical instruction. The later material in Patrick's formula reflects the history of Christian doctrine during the fourth century as it was filtered to the distant and conservative British Church through the influential churches and theologians of Italy and Gaul. This rule of faith helps us to place Patrick in the context to which most of the other evidence points, that of a Christian bishop in a remote outpost of the Christian Church in the West in the first half of the fifth century.

[22] See R. P. C. Hanson, *St. Patrick : his Origins and Career* (Oxford 1968), caps. 1 and 2; M. Barley and R. P. C. Hanson, *Christianity in Britain 300-700* (Leicester 1968).

PAULINUS NOLANUS, *CARMEN 24*

P. G. WALSH

Paulinus' twenty-fourth poem is obviously one of his more ambitious poetic creations. It contains nine hundred and forty-two lines, more than any of the other thirty poems which can indubitably be ascribed to Paulinus,[1] and it is composed in alternating iambic trimeters and dimeters, a more ambitious metrical scheme than those of the other long poems, most of which are in dactylic hexameters. Yet at first sight there is a disturbing absence of a unifying theme, which appears to contradict the evidence of length and of metrical form and to suggest a slapdash and ill-considered design. The poem is addressed to one Cytherius, a person unknown outside the evidence it adduces; from this we learn that he was an Aquitanian with a background comparable to that of Paulinus himself, for our poet reminds him that he is "splendid in the things which the world finds glorious — that is, in distinction, in literary activity, in family" (481f.). He is married, with a son whom he has committed at an early age to Sulpicius Severus, friend of Paulinus and famed author of the *Vita S. Martini*, at his new monastic foundation of Primuliacum (715ff.).

The apparently disparate topics taken up in the poem and at first sight militating against artistic unity are as follows:

1-472   Martinianus, the messenger whom you sent to me, has barely escaped with his life. The ship he sailed on from Narbo has sunk. The captain and other unbelievers perished, but the Christians and those who followed them escaped by the ship's boat which reached Marseilles. After receiving hospitality from a Christian community there, Martinianus took another ship to Ostia, rested from his journey at Rome, and completed his journey to Nola on foot and by mule.

473-900   God now selects for his service the rich and powerful as well as the poor. You are among his chosen, for you have consigned

---

[1] Of the thirty-three poems ascribed to Paulinus by G. de Hartel (CSEL 30, Vienna 1894), the authorship of IV is disputed, V is by Ausonius, XXXII is not by Paulinus, and XXXIII is of doubtful authenticity. See now the present writer's translation of and notes on the poems in ACW 40 (1974); also R. P. H. Green, *The Poetry of Paulinus of Nola* (Brussels 1971).

your son to him as Abraham consecrated Isaac. May he become
a consecrated priest and nourish you and your chaste wife.
May he expound the secrets of God as a second Joseph, and
enable you as a second Israel to share his dominion; may he
lead his family at last to heaven.

901-942   But you will not mount to heaven if inherited wealth weighs
you down, for possessions prevent men from rising. Lighten
yourselves of oppressive belongings to dwell for ever with God.

This structural analysis lays bare the bones of the problem.
Paulinus appears to handle two disparate main themes, the narrative of Martinianus' travel-adventures and the commendation of
Cytherius for consecrating his son to God; and to the second he
appends a brief exhortation to the parents to share their son's salvation by renunciation of temporal possessions. Fabre[2] suggests that
the tale of the shipwreck is a mere hors d'oeuvre to the main course
that follows, yet the "hors d'oeuvre" comprises exactly half the
poem, and this exact division into two halves can surely be no
coincidence. We must add this evidence of structure to that of length
and metrical form to demonstrate the conscious art which Paulinus
has devoted to the poem, and we must accordingly look more carefully at the inner design of the whole.

There is in fact a close interconnection between the two halves of
the poem, and a unifying theme behind both. This central message
is that God separates his elect from those who reject his dispensa-
tion. In the first section Paulinus deliberately exploits the incident
of the shipwreck to stress this distinction between those who acknowledge God and are saved, and those who reject him and are lost.
The second part of the poem depicts Cytherius amongst God's
elect, one who has demonstrated his allegiance by relinquishing his
own son to God's service. That boy will certainly attain salvation if
he remains faithful to his calling, and as a consecrated priest of God
he will become a father to his own parents and aid their salvation.
But they must play their part by lightening themselves of the
riches which are an impediment to their eternal welfare.

In this deployment of the shipwreck as a sign of God's economy of
election, Paulinus wishes us to see the literal application of the
traditionally Christian metaphor of salvation from "the shipwreck
of the world":

---

[2] P. Fabre, S. Paulin de Nole et l'amitié chrétienne (Paris 1949), 196: "C'est
donc une oeuvre assez disparate... toute la première partie est une sorte de
hors d'oeuvre."

> sed adusque portus et salus cunctis deus
>   manum paternum porrigit,
> et inter alta medii dorsa gurgitis
>   pietatis expandit sinum,
> quo abrupta mortis incidentes excipit
>   et in vado vitae locat. (67ff.)

Novatianus, the ship's captain, is representative of those whose spiritual desolation marks them out for death, and the metaphor of shipwreck is applied to his spiritual condition:

> hanc ipse navis rector et cum litore
>   in alta primo solveret,
> Novatianus ille, discissam fidem
>   in corde portans naufrago,
> homo mortis ⟨itaque⟩ et apta morti cogitans... (79ff.)

All who share his unbelief are to follow him to physical death, whereas the Christian voyagers are saved.

> ...constat perisse Christianum neminem,
>   et interisse perfidos
> namque aut maligno corde Iudaeus perit
>   reus aut superbi schismatis. (127ff.)

Then comes the explicit affirmation that this separation between Christian believers on the one side and Jews and heretics on the other is a sign of the future division. "God revealed in the persons of the few, as clear truth of the great mystery (*ut clara magni veritas mysterii*), that at the end of the world there will be a division amongst the tribes and a separation among all mankind, when the avenging angel will leave unscathed those whose faces are marked with the sign of the cross." (137ff.) This is the key-passage for the interconnection of the shipwreck-theme and the later topic of the consecration of Cytherius' son to God's service.

II

To underline this interconnected message inculcated in both parts of his poem, Paulinus compares the three protagonists Martinianus, Cytherius' son, and Cytherius himself with the great scriptural exemplars who demonstrate to us how we are to achieve salvation. Hilary and Ambrose, Jerome and Rufinus had schooled Paulinus in the various levels of meaning to be unearthed from scripture. Following the Origenist tradition, they demonstrated how the bible offers not only literal truth (*historia*) and figurative truth (*allegoria*) but also moral truth (*tropologia*) which men demonstrate in the conduct of their lives.[3] In this moral instruction the great figures of the Old and New Testaments are types for our edification and imitation, and for revealing to us how God protects those who commit themselves to him.

The obvious type of Martinianus is Jonas. Initially Martinianus sleeps soundly in the doomed vessel "untroubled in his blameless life, like Jonas of old hidden away in the belly of his ship" (168f.). And "just as the whale of old welcomed in Jonas...so the ship's boat met Martinianus and took him in" (195f.). Paulinus now embarks upon a meditation on Jonas whose three days in the whale prefigured Christ's three days in the tomb. The poet concentrates here on the motif of physical incarceration combined with spiritual freedom; the prophet who had sought to flee from God was physically imprisoned but was able to fly forth in spirit and prevail on God by prayer (205ff.). Martinianus too was secure in faith when in the ship's boat, and he too was enabled to emerge in due time; so too in the second part of our poem Cytherius is lodged in the prison of this world yet exercises freedom. Soon he will guide his fellow-passengers in the barque of the Church

> bonusque mentis vir gubernator suae
> et ecclesiae navem reget (765f.)

The second type of Martinianus is Paul. The faith of the messenger was manifest by his bearing from the wreck nothing but Paul's epistles, which he found next to his heart on arrival at Marseilles. This motif allows the poet to introduce a reminiscence of Paul's shipwreck in the *Acts*, and to suggest that Paul's presence next to Martinianus' heart allowed the apostle to save human lives on the sea a second time (263ff.; cf. *Acts* 27.13ff.). The Jonas-Paul sequence is found elsewhere in Paulinus' typology of a saintly man storm-tossed at sea.[4] But it would be an unworthy suspicion to suggest that Paulinus has invented this detail of Martinianus' carrying Paul's epistles on his person merely for apposite scriptural instruction.

Thirdly, Martinianus is depicted as a second Joseph. "As Joseph

---

[3] On this large question, see above all H. de Lubac, *Exégèse médiévale* (Paris 1959).
[4] See Letter 49.9ff. (= ACW 36, 267ff.)

of old fled the lust-maddened woman with the clothes torn off him,
so Martinianus left all behind when he escaped in naked flight from
that unfaithful ship" (191ff.; cf. *Gen.* 39.12). This comparison with
Joseph would have little point if viewed in isolation from the rest
of the poem. But the point of the typology is applicable to the whole
poem, the emphasis on separation of believers from the unbelieving
world. And we shall presently note that Joseph is also seen as the
type of Cytherius' son; as Martinianus achieves safety by leaving
the unbelievers in the doomed ship, Cytherius' son is to find his
salvation in separation from the world.

In the second section of the poem Cytherius and his son are likewise visualised as imitators of the great biblical exemplars. The
father who devotes his son to God is a second Abraham sacrificing
his son Isaac. "God demanded your son of you so that he could
compare you with that father of faith, so he enrolled your seed in the
seed of Isaac, and demanded him as a second Isaac,

> quem tu Abrahamiae caritatis aemulus
>   vivam dedisti victimam,
> deoque tradens iam peremisti tibi
>   ut salvum haberes firmius." (499ff.)

But Cytherius' son is more than a sacrificial victim, a second Isaac;
he is also a second Samuel "growing in God's temple" in the monastery of Primuliacum. Hence Cytherius is not merely a second
Abraham but is also embarking on "a partnership with Anna" (525).
This motif of Cytherius' son as future priest encourages Paulinus to
devote a long section of the poem to a description of him as a
Nazarite, a person apart (535ff.). In his reading of Ambrose, Paulinus had found an extended discussion of the Samson saga, and he
reproduces Ambrose's allegorical interpretation not only in this
poem but in greater detail in a letter to Sulpicius Severus roughly
contemporaneous with it.[5]

This section on Samson is an excellent example of the "tropologi-
cal" application of scripture for moral instruction. Samson's hair
represents the boy's faith, which the razor of heresy (see 675) must
not shave off. The boy must throttle and bring down the lion, which
connotes the devil, and pluck the sweet honey of victory from its

---

[5] See Letter 23.10ff. (= ACW 36, 13ff.) and Ambrose, *De spiritu sancto* II,
prologue.

mouth. Delilah is "the law of the flesh" which "blinds the eyes of the mind and shaves the head, plundering and disarming faith". Though the later incidents in the Samson story are not applicable to the status of Cytherius' son, Paulinus recounts the climax of Samson's vengeance to pray that the boy may imitate Samson's death in destroying the enemies which are the flesh. These sins of the flesh are subsequently personified first as Amalek and then as that Goliath which this second David must lay low.

Cytherius' son is next depicted as a second Joseph; this overt connection with Martinianus likewise, as we have seen, a second Joseph, is notable, and the common typology assists in fusing the two sections into a unity. But the figure of Joseph is much more appropriate to the consecrated child who Paulinus prays "may feed his parents and brothers during their period of hunger in this world"; who is "sold to a eunuch" because he is a slave to chastity and is a eunuch for God's kingdom (701ff.); who like Martinianus will flee from the shameless woman who represents the enticing pomp of this world:

> inretientis saeculi pompam inlicem
> ut impudentem feminam
> casto superbus respuet fastidio
> nudaque vitabit fuga (719ff.).

Like Joseph, Cytherius' son will sit in solitary confinement so that later he may attain royal status with God. Then as one free and as his own master he will be teacher and guardian of others. Paulinus continues to apply the details of Joseph's appurtenances and achievements to the youthful aspirant of Primuliacum; appropriate interpretations are offered for Joseph's long linen garment, the golden chain, the ring, the royal chariot. But above all the theme of Joseph in Egypt is exploited to depict Cytherius' son as an exile in this world awaiting deliverance to his true *patria*.

III

The overall theme of *Christiana salus* from worldly shipwreck, into which both main parts of the poem are subsumed, closes with a direct exhortation to Cytherius and his wife to merge their course with that of their son, and sounds a sombre warning that those whose inherited wealth weighs them down will fail to rise at the Parousia,

> quia sarcinatos et graves rebus suis,
> mundi caduci divites,

portare tenera non valebunt nubila
   ad regis occursum dei;
sed haesitantes in luto faecis suae
   opumque pressos molibus,
meridiano incendio mundi repens
   ruina mortis opprimet (911ff.).

There follows the appeal direct: "So do you...lighten yourselves in preparation for Christ, and now free from the luggage which causes pain shake the shackles from your feet. Become naked in this world to be clothed in abundance of light..." (923ff.).

Thus in the final section Paulinus indicates that the whole poem is to be read as a *protreptikon*, a poem of exhortation to Cytherius and his wife to detach themselves from the possessions of this world. The shipwreck of Martinianus, which foreshadowed that those marked with the cross will be saved, and the commitment of Cytherius' son, whose self-dedication will ensure his salvation, are themes now seen to point forward to the final exhortation. Just as Martinianus "left all behind when he escaped naked" (193), and just as Cytherius' son "will avoid the enticing pomp of the enmeshing world by fleeing naked from it" (719ff.), so Cytherius and his wife must strip themselves of possessions to attain salvation.

It is instructive to note that this poem is one of three extant *protreptika* in the poetry of Paulinus. Poem 22, addressed to an intellectual friend in Aquitania, urges Jovius to abandon the cultivation of secular literature. The verses sent to Licentius, ex-intimate of Augustine at Cassiciacum but now slackening in his religious commitment, are a warning against aspirations for secular position in Roman life.[6] This third *protreptikon*, as I have sought to demonstrate, advocates the abandonment of secular wealth. The trinity of secular position, wealth, literature represents the three facets of the secular world from which he has prised himself and from which he seeks to prise others. His success was an important factor in the decline of the Roman state and in the growth of monasticism in the West.[7]

---

[6] They are enclosed with Letter 8. See ACW 35, 78ff.

[7] See my paper "Paulinus of Nola and the Conflict of Ideologies in the Fourth Century", *KYRIAKON : Festschrift J. Quasten* (Munster 1970), 565ff. The broader question of the political outcome of Paulinus' retirement from the world is well treated by W. H. C. Frend, "Paulinus of Nola and the last century of the Western Empire", *JRS* 59 (1969), 1ff.

PATRICK'S *CONFESSIO* AND
AUGUSTINE'S *CONFESSIONES*

J. O'MEARA

Pierre Courcelle, in *Les Confessions de saint Augustin dans la tradition littéraire*,[1] writes:

"Cette *Confessio* a suscité récemment des recherches attentives, mais contradictoires dans leurs conclusions sur le rapport avec les *Confessions* d'Augustin. M. Bieler a cru remarquer divers emprunts textuels aux *Confessions*.[2] M. O'Meara, au contraire, nie que les rapprochements allégués par M. Bieler soient probants.[3] Il faut lui concéder que bon nombre sont peu sûrs. Même le fait que Patrick, comme Augustin, joigne à la confession d'action de grâces l'auto-défense et la confession des péchés, peut sembler insuffisant. Pourtant, certains des parallèles établis par M. Bieler me semblent valables, même s'il est vrai, comme objecte M. O'Meara, que le passage augustinien repose lui-même sur un texte scripturaire, qui risque ainsi d'être leur source commune. De telles rencontres sont, en réalité, plus nombreuses et plus précises que ne le signalait M. Bieler."

Courcelle then quotes and examines a number of parallels which I shall discuss presently. His final conclusion is:

"L'influence des *Confessions* sur Patrick me semble d'ailleurs ne pas être seulement d'ordre littéraire, mais toucher plutôt à la formation spirituelle intime."[4]

Again he writes:

"Patrick.... semble avoir été touché intimement par le maître."[5]

The intervention of Courcelle in this debate invites a brief assessment of his contribution which may suitably be done here.

It must first be stated that Ludwig Bieler in the article in question was mainly quoting the views of P. Grosjean and H. Misch, which he

---

[1] Paris 1963, p. 211.
[2] "The Place of Saint Patrick in Latin Language and Literature," *Vigiliae Christianae*, vol. VI, 1952, pp. 69f.
[3] "The *Confession* of St. Patrick and the *Confessions* of St. Augustine," *Irish Ecclesiastical Record*, LXXXV, 1956, pp. 190⁻197.
[4] *Op. cit.*, p. 213.
[5] *Op. cit.*, p. 217; cf. p. 541.

describes as "certainly *suggestive* of literary dependence." He manifests his detachment, however, not only by drawing attention in the same article to the difference between the two works,[6] but also when he reports the matter as an hypothesis:[7] "*If* Patrick did study St. Augustine..." Accordingly at the beginning of my discussion of the matter I drew attention to Bieler's clear reserves.[8] Since then Bieler has dismissed the case first put forward seriously by Misch.[9]

Although Courcelle does refer in a note[10] to Professor Christine Mohrmann's *The Latin of Saint Patrick*,[11] he does not manifest any appreciation of how she widened and strengthened the attack on the thesis that literary dependence of the *Confessio* on the *Confessiones* could be proved. She draws attention to the fact that *confessio* may well not be a title for Patrick's letter; that in any case it does not cover the same range of meaning as does the title (real and contemporary) of Augustine's work; that the use of the Bible in both works may seem superficially similar, but is in fact quite different; and finally that "there is not a single passage which can be proved to be a quotation from or an allusion to Augustine's *Confessions*."[12] But her whole characterization of Patrick's Latinity is such as to make the literary dependence of the one on the other almost, if not quite,[13] impossible.

---

[6] P. 93.

[7] P. 98.

[8] *Art. cit.*, p. 190: "Dr. Bieler was careful not to advance his findings with any show of confidence."

[9] *Eigse* X, Dublin 1962, p. 150: "It is, in fact, impossible to establish any literary connection between Augustine's spiritual autobiography and the 'Confession' of St. Patrick." Cf. *Irish Ecclesiastical Record*, CII, 1964, p. 363: "O'Meara shows how little foundation there is for this assertion."

[10] *Op. cit.*, p. 211, n. 4: "Il (O'M.) est suivi sur ce point par C. Mohrmann."

[11] Dublin 1961. The topic had been studied already by F. R. Montgomery Hitchcock, *Hermathena*, 47 (1932), pp. 202-233; 51 (1938), pp. 65-76; 54 (1939), pp. 93-109; and, of course, by L. Bieler, *Libri epistolarum sancti Patricii episcopi*, Introduction, Text and Commentary, *Classica et Mediaevalia*, 11 (1950), pp. 1-150; 12 (1951), pp. 82-214 — reprinted by the Irish Manuscripts Commission, 1, 2, Dublin 1952.

[12] *Op. cit.*, pp. 7, 4ff., 34f. Cf. D. Binchy, "Patrick and his Biographers Ancient and Modern," *Studia Hibernica*, no. 2, Dublin 1962, p. 88 and n. 237.

[13] She believes (*op. cit.*, p. 47) that Patrick's language shows elements which "cannot possibly belong to early British Latin. They bear all the marks of living fifth-century Continental Latin." Binchy, who quotes (*art. cit.*) K. Jackson, *Language and History in Early Britain*, Edinburgh 1953, p. 80 (the significant lack of mention of which by Mohrmann is noted by both Binchy and Bieler: *Eigse* X, 1962, p. 149) in relation to the problem, does not follow Mohrmann here.

It can be seen, then, that Courcelle misrepresents the extent of
Bieler's advocacy of Misch's thesis; did not perhaps have the
opportunity of noting Bieler's withdrawal from Misch's point of
view; and did not draw sufficient attention to the seriousness of the
further attack by Mohrmann. In these circumstances, doubtless, he
did not forbear to use the technique of comparing parallel passages
to improve on Misch. I had indicated the "possibility" and likely
fruitlessness of this.[14]

The great uses and equally great abuses of employing the comparison of parallel passages to establish literary dependence were
fairly comprehensively expounded, for example, by A. Mandouze[15]
and discussed by others and by Courcelle, Mohrmann and myself[16]
(but in another context) at the Congrès International Augustinien
in 1954. There is much that one could recall from that discussion
that would be useful in the present context, but brevity compels me
to give one excerpt only — but one indispensable here — from
Mohrmann's contribution on that occasion:

> "1. Là où il s'agit de textes techniques, rédigés dans la langue
> spéciale et technique d'un groupe bien défini, une identité de mots
> et de tournures nous donne, en général, le droit de conclure à un
> emprunt. Mais il s'agit d'un emprunt au groupe, on n'a pas encore
> prouvé, sans plus, un emprunt à tel ou tel auteur de ce groupe."
> "2. La situation change foncièrement dès que l'on quitte le domaine
> technique. Si l'on constate des ressemblances, voire des identités
> textuelles là où il s'agit d'éléments de la langue courante qui décri-
> vent des situations générales de la vie de tous les jours, il faut être
> très prudent. Une dépendance réelle, un emprunt est loin d'être
> établi par le seul fait d'une ressemblance ou d'une identité des mots
> employés. Voyons la chose de plus près.
> "Il ne faut jamais oublier que telle ou telle situation suscite pres-
> que invariablement tels ou tels mots. Les possibilités de l'expression
> linguistique sont loin d'être illimitées, comme d'ailleurs les res-
> sources créatrices de l'esprit humain. Une situation définie inspire
> des mots définis et l'identité des mots ne présuppose pas, dans ce
> cas, une dépendance, une relation de source.

---

[14] *Art. cit.*, p. 195: "As it would be exceedingly pedantic to mention
phrases which occur to one as possible echoes, only to dismiss them immediately, I shall confine myself to the suggestions of others." On this occasion
I do not propose to repeat my former arguments or those put forward by
Professor Mohrmann.

[15] "'L'extase d'Ostie,' Possibilités et limites de la méthode des parallèles
textuels," *Augustinus Magister*, I, Paris 1954, pp. 67-84.

[16] *Ibid.* III, pp. 35-38, 41-50.

"Il faut encore ajouter que dans chaque langue existent des tour-
nures toutes faites s'appliquant à telle situation, des clichés qui
s'emploient presque automatiquement. La phraséologie toute faite
des faits divers de nos journaux n'est pas une innovation des nos
jours. Les procédés de la rhétorique antique aboutissaient également à une langue banale où abondaient les clichés.

"Dans le domaine de la langue littéraire, de la prose et de la poésie,
la situation est encore plus compliquée par la relation qui existe
entre langue poétique ou littéraire et langue courante. Les jeux de
mots de la langue populaire par example, sont repris à des époques
très diverses par des auteurs de caractère très différent..."

..."D'innombrables mères répètent chaque jour à leur enfant:
Sois sage. Des centaines de maîtres d'école, à tel élève: tiens-toi
tranquille. Il suffit de trois petits mots, intercalés entre ces expressions, et voici le vers de Baudelaire:

"Sois sage, ô ma Douleur, et tiens-toi plus tranquille."

"Il y a ici une différence à la fois minime et capitale qui distingue
de l'idiome courant celui de la poésie, mais qui montre combien
devient délicate cette science des sources dès qu'on se trouve dans
le domaine de la littérature et de la langue courante.

"Le danger est particulièrement grand pour nous autres qui tra-
vaillons dans le domaine du monde antique: nos connaissances de la
langue courante latine sont extrêmement restreintes. Presque tous
les textes qui sont parvenus jusqu'à nous sont d'un caractère nette-
ment littéraire. Que savons-nous du latin parlé dans la vie de tous
les jours?"[17]

Armed with the sobriety that is indispensable let us scrutinize the
additional parallel texts between the *Confessio* and the *Confessiones*
now advanced by Courcelle.[18]

AUGUSTIN, *Conf.*, X, 3, 4, 16,
p. 243:
"Indicabo me talibus (= animis
fraternis)... Tu autem, domine...,
consumma *imperfecta* mea. Hic est
fructus confessionum mearum, non
qualis fuerim, sed *qualis sim, ut* hoc
confitear non tantum coram te se-
creta exultatione *cum tremore* et se-
creto maerore cum spe, sed etiam in
auribus credentium filiorum hominum... Hi sunt servi tui, *fratres* mei."
X, 27, 38, 1, p. 268:
"*Sero* te amaui, pulchritudo tam
antiqua et tam noua! Et ecce intus

PATRICK, *Conf.*, 6, p. 60, 1:
"Tamen etsi in multis *imperfectus*
sum, opto, *fratribus* et cognatis meis
scire *qualitatem meam, ut* possint per-
spicere uotum animae meae... Vnde
autem uehementer debueram *cum*
timore et *tremore* metuere hanc sen-
tentiam."

2, p. 57, 14:
"Et ibi dominus aperuit sensum
incredulitatis meae, ut uel *sero* reme-

---

[17] *Ibid.* III, pp. 36f.
[18] *Op. cit.*, p. 212.

eras et ego foris et ibi te quaerebam
et in ista formosa, quae fecisti, defor-
mis inruebam."

IV, 1, 1, 25, p. 67:
"Sed *invideant*[1], nos fortes et po-
tentes, nos autem infirmi et inopes
confiteamur tibi."

IX, 4, 12, 2, p. 218:
"Nec oblitus sum *nec silebo* flagelli
tui asperitatem et misericordiae tuae
mirabilem celeritatem[2]."

IV, 16, 31, 4, p. 88:
"Sed sic eram *nec erubesco*, Deus
meus, *confiteri tibi* in me misericor-
dias tuas."

XI, 25, 32, 8, p. 319:
"Ecce, Deus meus, coram te, quia
non mentior (*Gal.* 1, 20.)"

morarem delicta mea et ut conuer-
terem toto corde ad Dominum deum
meum."

45, p. 83, 13:
"*Rideat* autem et insultet qui
uoluerit, ego *non silebo* neque abscon-
do signa et *mirabilia* quae mihi a
Domino monstrata sunt."

44, p. 83, 9:
"Sed *confiteor Domino meo* et *non
erubesco* in conspectu ipsius, quia
non mentior (*Gal.*, 1, 20)."

The first of these sets of parallels is concerned with the inescapable
task of an autobiographer: he must tell what manner of man he is
(*qualis sim, ut; qualitatem meam, ut*) if he has a purpose (*ut*) to
achieve. Furthermore while he may have to address himself to his
enemies he is likely also to address himself to his friends ("brothers")
around him (*fratres* and *animis fraternis* — a phrase fabricated with
possible, but not total, justification from a long paragraph preceding
— *fratribus*). The recurrence of *cum timore* from the New Testament
in both texts in this context would be natural in authors at all
familiar with the Scriptures. I would regard all of these parallels in
the contexts of the works as, in Mohrmann's term, banal and without any significance in relation to proving literary dependence. The
suggestion, however, of a connection between *imperfecta* and *imperfectus* is quite unacceptable: the first refers to God's completion
of things yet unperfected in Augustine (*nequaquam deserens coepta
tua consumma imperfecta mea*); the second refers to Patrick's failings
(Bieler translates: "although I am imperfect in many things").[19]

The second instance depends entirely on the recurrence of the one
word *sero* in Patrick. In Augustine's case it refers to his *loving* God
late. In Patrick's case, (Bieler: "that I might at last remember my
sins and be converted with all my heart to the Lord my God") it
refers to a late *repentance* and (probably) *conversion* to God. (Courcelle fails to draw attention to the idea common to both texts that
God had care of the authors, who were themselves unaware of this).

---

[19] *The Works of St. Patrick*, ACW 17, 1953, p. 22.

While the word *sero* can have for those who know Augustine's *Confessiones* a special association which they apply (but only, of course, from time to time), when occasion offers, it is an almost inevitable word when one sets out to describe doing anything late, or too late. Any good Latin dictionary gives instances of its use in the sense of "too late" and this, inevitably, has its own sense of regret quite independently of its use in one place in Augustine's *Confessiones*. Virgil (to give but one example) too has his own haunting use of the word:

> *Libertas, quae sera tamen respexit inertem,*
> *candidior postquam tondenti barba cadebat,*
> *respexit tamen et longo post tempore uenit.*[20]

And there is an old proverb: *sero sapiunt Phryges* which sums up the banality and universality of the experience implied in *sero*.

The next item is made up of two quotations from Augustine and one from Patrick. The Augustine quotations are taken from books of the *Confessiones* as far apart as IV and IX, which destroys the notion of *a* parallel text. In any case the recurrence of *inrideant* and *rideat* has Biblical reference. There are some 18 instances of *irrideo* and 20 of *rideo* in the Bible, a number of them, in both cases, in the Subjunctive mood and with the meaning "scoff". Patrick's *non silebo … mirabilia* is referred by Bieler, properly, to Psalms 71, 17. Augustine's text from *Confessiones* IX *could* indeed have the same reference — but this would be no proof that Patrick depends on Augustine: there are over 100 uses of *mirabilis* and associated words in the Bible, and 35 of *mirabilia* in the *Psalms* alone. There are over 40 uses of *sileo* in the Bible, and several similar to *non silebo* — e.g. *Ezech.* 24.27: *et loqueris et non silebis ultra;* 33.22: *non silui amplius; Ps.* 39.12: *ne sileas;* 49.3: *Deus . . non silebit.*

The final instance given by Courcelle, likewise, has such strong Biblical reference that it is without use to prove dependence of the one text on the other: I have already indicated that *confiteor* occurs over 160 times in the Bible, *erubesco* 52 times, and that both words are connected in meaning.[21]

Courcelle concludes: "Quelle que soit la distance entre la culture d'Augustin et l'inculture de Patrick, il me paraît comme à M. Bieler que la *Confessio* de l'un suppose les *Confessions* de l'autre. J'incline-

---

[20] *Ecl.* 1.27ff.
[21] *Art. cit.,* p. 196, n. 1.

rais même à croire que Patrick conçoit et décrit ses "voix" à la manière et sous l'influence d'Augustin.[22] Enfin, l'emploi d'un registre analogue de citations scripturaires est tout de même un indice sérieux de parenté littéraire. L'influence des *Confessions* sur Patrick me semble d'ailleurs ne pas être seulement d'ordre littéraire, mais toucher plutôt à la formation spirituelle intime."[23]

The reader should note carefully the escalation that occurs in this final conclusion. It is implied that Bieler felt that the *Confessio* of the one *supposes* (that is, has demonstrable literary dependence on) the other: this is, as we have seen, untrue. Courcelle's daring *inclinatio (J'inclinerais même)* to connect the description of the voices is, on the face of it, an admission that he has not proved it.[24] The use of

---

[22] The evidence alleged on p. 213 n. 1 to support this is, by implication, considered by Courcelle as less convincing than that already examined. While, as always, the dependence *could* exist it is not *proved*.

[23] *Op. cit.*, pp. 212f.

[24] The evidence alleged by Courcelle is given in *op. cit.*, p. 213, n. 1:

1. AUGUSTIN, *Conf.*, III, 11, 20, 4, p. 61 (à propos du songe de Monique):
"Non, inquit, *non* enim *mihi dictum est:* 'Vbi ille, ibi et tu', *sed:* 'Vbi tu, ibi et ille.' Confiteor tibi, Domine, recordationem meam, quantum recolo, quod saepe non tacui amplius me isto per matrem uigilantem *responso tuo*... etiam tum fuisse conmotum, quam ipso somnio... Et dedisti alterum *responsum* interim, quod recolo."

VIII, 12, 29, 1, p. 199:
"Flebam amarissima contritione cordis mei. Et ecce *audio uocem* de uicina (diuina *S*) domo cum cantu dicentis et repetentis *quasi* pueri an puellae nescio: 'Tolle, lege'... *Et legi* in silentio capitulum quo *primum* coniecti sunt oculi mei... *Nec ultra uolui legere* nec opus erat."

PATRICK, *Conf.*, 29, p. 74, 14:
"Ad noctem illam uidi in uisu noctis (cf. *Dan.*, VII, 13) scriptum erat contra faciem meam sine honore, et inter haec audiui *responsum diuinum* (cf. *Rom.*, XI, 4) *dicentem mihi:* 'Male uidimus faciem designati nudato nomine.' *Nec sic praedixit:* 'Male uidisti', *sed:* 'Male uidimus' quasi sibi se iunxisset."

23, p. 70, 16:
"Et ibi scilicet uidi in uisu noctis uirum uenientem quasi de Hiberione, cui nomen Victoricus, cum epistolis innumerabilibus, et dedit mihi unam ex his. *Et legi principium* epistolae continentem: 'Vox Hiberionacum', et cum recitabam principium epistolae, putabam ipso momento *audire uocem* ipsorum, qui erant iuxta siluam Vocluti, quae est prope mare occidentale, et sic exclamauerunt *quasi* ex uno ore (cf. *Dan.*, III, 5): 'Rogamus te, puer, ut uenias et adhuc ambulas inter nos', et ualde compunctus sum corde (cf. *Act.*, II, 37) *et amplius non potui legere* et sic sum expertus."

the same Biblical texts in the *Confessio* and the *Confessiones* can certainly indicate that both authors depend on the Bible, or on readings (liturgical, for example) from it, or common quotations from it — but practically all ecclesiastical writers and preachers of every age depend on the Bible in this way. It could not possibly be proved that Patrick got his quotations from the Bible from Augustine's *Confessiones only*. Finally, it *seems* to Courcelle that the influence of the *Confessiones* on Patrick is *rather* in the area of intimate spiritual formation. At this point this idea is confessed to occur to Courcelle himself only — later in the book, however, it is implied that it is entertained as likely by others.[25]

While it must remain *possible* that Patrick read the *Confessiones* before he wrote the letter now called *Confessio*, and that consciously or unconsciously he could in a literary or spiritual sense be dependent on that work, there is no proof within the documents that this is so.

Up to this point, as on the previous occasion when I examined this topic, I have confined myself narrowly to the two works involved. I might now, however, be allowed to make some few remarks on the implications for the Patrick question in general of the negative results here indicated.

Courcelle himself[26] gives us sufficient guidance as to the extent to which Augustine's *Confessiones* were known and used in the century which, on any reading of the Patrick question, is relevant, that is the fifth century A.D. — and in the geographical areas again most relevant, that is Gaul and, to a lesser extent, Italy and Africa.

Although it might seem surprising that St. Jerome implies that he had not known of the *Confessiones* some four to seven years after they were written around 400, we have sufficient evidence that they were known and used before 422 by some people closely associated

---

On notera qu'il s'agit ici et là d'une "vocation". Le *responsum* divin est fréquent chez Patrick, *Conf.*, 17, p. 65, 24; 21, p. 70, 4; 35, p. 77, 6; surtout 42, p. 81, 12: "Insinuauit nobis responsum accepisse a nuntio Dei, et monuit eam ut esset uirgo Dei et ipsa Deo proximaret: Deo gratias, sexta ab hac die optime et auidissime arripuit illud quod etiam omnes uirgines Dei ita hoc faciunt."

Bearing in mind the comments of Mohrmann on parallel texts given in the body of this article, I can discover no *solid* ground to support Courcelle's inclination here.

[25] P. 217: "Patrick seul semble avoir été touché intimement par le maître;" p. 541: "Patrick seul semble avoir été touché intimement par l'ouvrage."

[26] *Op. cit.*, pp. 201-221.

with Augustine — Paulinus of Nola, Evodius of Uzala (near Hippo), the Spaniard Orosius (who was at Hippo in 417), Paulinus of Milan and Augustine's biographer Possidius.

Of people not so immediately connected with Augustine Prosper of Aquitaine, who lived at Marseilles up to 440, mentions Germanus and Palladius, and died after 455, is of clear interest in a Patrician context. His *Liber Sententiarum ex operibus sancti Augustini deliba-tarum* affords incontrovertible proof of his use of the *Confessiones*. The relevance of Paulinus of Pella (died after 459) to the present topic is not proved, and in any case would at most but confirm that the *Confessiones* were known in Marseilles at a possibly relevant date. Claudianus Mamertus, a priest from Vienne in Gaul who died about 474, appears to know the *Confessiones*. Ennodius of Pavia (who however was writing at the end of the century and from Italy) definitely knew the *Confessiones* and indeed wrote in their manner what Courcelle calls "un pastiche assez mediocre." Eugippius (who was also writing from Italy even later in the century, if not in the next) clearly knew the *Confessiones* since he published excerpts (doctrinal, however, rather than autobiographical) from them. Finally Fulgentius of Ruspe (in Africa), who died in 533, cites the *Confessiones*.

The hard evidence given by Courcelle, therefore, of the knowledge of the *Confessiones* in Gaul in the fifth century can be reduced to, perhaps significantly, Prosper at Marseilles. We could possibly add Paulinus (also at Marseilles) and Claudianus Mamertus from Vienne, about 150 miles to the North. This is not to say that it is unlikely to have been known to others in that area of Gaul or elsewhere — especially because of Augustine's prominence in relation to all aspects of Pelagianism. Nevertheless, whatever *our* views of the fame of the *Confessiones*, our certain knowledge of its fame in Gaul in the fifth century seems disappointing.

The conclusion that Patrick's *Confessio* shows no reliable indication of literary dependence on Augustine's *Confessiones* could be interpreted (though I do not do so) as confirmation that the latter work was not after all very famous. One would then be free to suppose that Patrick could have spent a lengthy sojourn in Gaul without showing evidence of dependence on the *Confessiones* in his *Confessio*. This may be so. But it would seem to the present writer that, so far as literary[27] (as distinct from linguistic and other)

---

[27] Cf. C. Mohrmann, *op. cit.*, p. 8: "There are, as far as I can see, in Patrick's works no traces of quotations or borrowings from any other book than the

evidence is concerned, the testimony of the *Confessio* is almost decisively against Patrick (who was clearly no dullard) having been exposed over a long period, not only to the *Confessiones*, but to any literary influence in any relatively cultured ecclesiastical centre such as existed at the time in Gaul. In coming to this conclusion I am not ignoring irony and both traditional and personal humility in Patrick's references to his own rusticity.

Bible. We can assert that Patrick was, so far as we can gather from his works, a man *unius libri*. His only book was Holy Scripture." An authoritative assessment of the unrelated pronouncements of Jackson and Mohrmann (see n. 13 above) on the *linguistic* aspect of the problem would be valuable.

SOME REMARKS ON THE LANGUAGE OF BOETHIUS, *CONSOLATIO PHILOSOPHIAE*

CHRISTINE MOHRMANN

Since the boethian authorship of several theological treatises is proved by the discovery of the so-called *Anecdoton Holderi*, being an abstract of a note of Cassiodorus concerning Boethius, there can be no doubt any more that the man, who was called the last of the Romans, was a Christian.[1] It is the more surprising that in his last work, the *Consolatio Philosophiae*, his spiritual, or rather philosophical, testament, written in prison shortly before his execution, hardly any traces have been found of Christian faith or piety. The work is a sort of Protreptikos of Neoplatonic inspiration, mixed with certain elements belonging to the more or less popular philosophy of late antiquity. There seems to be in the *Consolatio* hardly any place for Christian thought, nor for biblical quotations. Professor Bieler was perfectly right, when in the Index Locorum Sacrae Scripturae on p. 109 of his edition of the *Consolatio*,[2] he marked all supposed bible quotations but two with an asterisk, thus defining them as more or less vague allusions, or as coincidental parallels. The God whose name occurs so many times in the *Consolatio* is much more the abstract God of the philosophers than the personal God of the Christians. Moreover, the name of Christ does not occur in this essentially neoplatonic work: an absence which confirms what saint Augustine had once said with regard to the neoplatonic writings he had been reading: *sed quia verbum caro factum est et habitavit in nobis, non ibi legi* (Conf. 7, 9, 14).

On the other hand there are, in the *Consolatio*, hardly any elements openly contrary to Christian doctrine. The apparent pagan elements, such as the Muses in the beginning of the treatise, the frequent use of *Phoebus* in the poems, written in a highly traditional poetic style, and even the part played by Dame Fortuna, particularly in the first books, are hardly more than purely literary devices. By way of his language Boethius evidently tries to create a certain philosophi-

---

[1] H. Usener, *Anecdoton Holderi, ein Beitrag zur Geschichte Roms in ost-gothischer Zeit*, Leipzig 1877.

[2] *Anicii Manlii Severini Boethii Opera*, Pars I, Turnholti 1957, *Corpus Christianorum*, Series Latina, vol. XCIV.

cal atmosphere, mixed with traditional poetic elements. In this way he aims at a certain linguistic "neutrality", trying to exclude all words and formulas belonging to Christian language. As a matter of fact he was not the first Christian who, in this way, tried to adapt his literary form to traditional Roman standards.

Though nobody denies, nowadays, the general non-christian, neoplatonic character of the *Consolatio*, the question has repeatedly been raised, whether there are not in this work some, more or less latent, features betraying the Christian faith of its author. The existence of any such elements has recently been denied by several scholars, such as P. Courcelle, O. Gigon, and V. Celeto.[3] On the other hand, Prof. Dr. C. J. de Vogel, raising this question once more, has by way of a very fine-strung analysis of some passages concluded that there are quite a few clearly Christian elements in the *Consolatio*.[4] Without testing all the texts quoted by Dr. de Vogel, I propose to examine once more a few passages, looking at them particularly from a linguistic angle. I hope, in this way, to confirm certain conclusions drawn by de Vogel and — at the same time — to specify the sources from which Boethius is drawing in some of the texts where he gives himself away as a believing Christian.

There is, first of all, the noteworthy passage in the last book of the *Consolatio*, viz. 5, 3, 33 ff., where Boethius, in the discussion about divine prescience, spontaneously advances that, if things which will happen in the future, shall happen necessarily because they are foreknown by God, there is no freedom for man, virtue and vice will be nothing, and "there is no room left for hope and prayer": *Igitur nec sperandi aliquid nec deprecandi ulla ratio est; quid enim uel speret quisque uel etiam deprecetur quando optanda omnia series indeflexa conectit?* (*ib.* 33). I agree fully with de Vogel, *o.c.*, p. 4, that what is said in the passage on prayer which follows these words, is quite different from what Socrates and Plato thought about prayer. It seems to me evident that Boethius speaks here much more as a Christian than as a neoplatonic philosopher. But let us consider in detail this emotional outburst— for that it is — where Boethius the philosopher seems to commit himself as a Christian, fully aware of the spiritual value of prayer. The full text runs as follows: *Auferetur igitur unicum illud inter homines deumque commercium, sperandi*

[3] See for bibliographical details p. 2 of the Study of C. J. de Vogel, quoted in the following note.

[4] C. J. de Vogel, "Boethiana II", *Vivarium* 10, 1972, p. 1ff.

scilicet ac deprecandi, si quidem iustae humilitatis pretio inaestima-
bilem uicem diuinae gratiae promeremur; qui solus modus est quo cum
deo colloqui homines posse uideantur illique inaccessae luci prius
quoque quam impetrent ipsa supplicandi ratione coniungi. Quae si
recepta futurorum necessitate nihil uirium habere credantur, quid erit
quo summo illi rerum principi conecti atque adhaerere possimus?
(*ibid.* 34 and 35). I might give here a literal, and far from elegant,
translation: "For then will be eliminated that only way of intercourse (exchange) between men and God, consisting in hope and
prayer, in so far we, by the price of right humbleness, obtain in
return the inestimable gift of God's grace; and this is the only manner, it seems, by which men can talk with God and — by the way of
prayer — can be joined to that inaccessible light, even before they
share it. If these things (= prayers) will be believed to have no
force, because it is admitted that future things are preordained,
what means shall we have to come into contact with Him, who is
the sovereign principle of all things and how can we adhere to Him?"

This text is not only of undeniable Christian inspiration, but there
can be found in it several elements which seem to betray a certain
influence of liturgical language and thought.

There is first of all the verb *deprecari*. I am not so sure that it has
here the classical meaning of "to ask", or "to pray, that something
may not happen".[5] There is, I think, not so much an antithesis:
"hope for something (good) — pray that something (bad) may not
happen", but a sort of climax: "hope for something and — what is
more — pray in order to obtain it". The principal reason why I
vote for this interpretation is, that in this passage as a whole there is
no question of evil and good future things, but of contact with God
in order to obtain the gift of grace. Now this *deprecari* (in which,
according to a general tendency in Late Latin, the force of the prepo-
sitional suffix is weakened) is extremely frequent in liturgical Latin,
particularly for prayer of petition. Often the meaning of *deprecari*
"to pray" is emphasized, in liturgical Latin, by the addition of
supplices, or *suppliciter*.[6] This brings us to another liturgical prayer-
term in our text: *supplicandi ratione*. This *supplicare*, a very usual
term for prayer in the Roman liturgy, does not occur in the ancient

---

[5] In classical Latin *deprecari* is also used with the meaning "to ask" or
"to pray".
[6] See M. P. Ellebracht, *Remarks on the vocabulary of the Ancient Orations
in the Missale Romanum*, Nijmegen 1963 (LCP vol. XVIII), p. 114f.

orations of the Missale Romanum as a finite verb, but it is used regularly in the present participle form, or, though seldom, as a gerund, as it is used here.[7]

The keyword of this passage seems to be the term *commercium*, intercourse, traffic, exchange.[8] I cannot go into details concerning the role of this word in Christian theology and in Roman liturgy. For all details the reader is referred to: Martin Herz, *Sacrum Commercium*, Eine begriffsgeschichtliche Studie zur Theologie der Römischen Liturgiesprache, München 1958.[9] A few remarks can throw light on the background of this word, which Boethius uses here with regard to prayer.

Commercium is used in Late Latin for any exchange of goods, and especially for exchange of gifts, particularly New Year's gifts. In early Christian and in liturgical Latin this colloquial term has become a keyword of Christological theology. In patristic tradition the incarnation of the Son of God is considered as a sort of exchange, *commercium*, between God and man, exchange which has lead to a certain deification of human nature.[10] Towards the middle of the 5th century *commercium* is already used with this meaning in the Roman liturgy. To quote an example:[11] the first antiphon of Vespers on the octave of Christmas runs as follows:

o admirabile commercium: creator generis humani, animatum corpus sumens, de virgine nasci dignatus est: et procedens homo sine semine, largitus est nobis suam deitatem.

But *commercium* described also, in liturgical language, an other form of exchange. It is used in relation with the offerings in the Eucharistic liturgy, and as such it appears particularly in the Secrets of the roman missal.[12] To quote an example: in the secret of the first Mass of Christmas: *ut .. per haec sacrosancta commercia, in illius inveniamur forma, in quo tecum est nostra substantia.* Here *commercium* means the human ritual action in and through which supernatural effects are produced, thanks to — and through — the incarnation. Cf. also the secret Dom. IV p. Pasch.: *Deus, qui nos per*

---

[7] See Ellebracht, *o.c.*, p. 149; cf. also André Pflieger, *Liturgicae orationis concordantia verbalia*, Prima Pars, Missale Romanum, Rome etc., 1964, s.v.

[8] See C. J. de Vogel, *o.c.*, p. 5.

[9] See also Ellebracht, *o.c.*, p. 53 and 97. — Pflieger, *o.c.*, s.v.

[10] See Herz, *o.c.*, p. 308.

[11] See Herz, *o.c.*, p. 24.

[12] See Herz, *o.c.*, p. 318; Ellebracht, *o.c.*, p. 97.

huius sacrificii veneranda commercia unius summae divinitatis participes effecisti.

As Herz clearly has pointed out, the offering of gifts by men and their receiving by God considered as a sacred exchange, makes God, so to say, a partner of man.[13] But there is always the working of divine grace which makes this exchange possible.

Let us go back now to Boethius' *Consolatio*. Prayer is clearly considered as an exchange between God and man, in the same way as the offerings are.

It is clear that the parallel of our text with the liturgical prayers is only partial. There is an exchange between God and man, but this takes place, not by offerings, but by means of prayer: the price (*pretium*) paid by man being *iusta humilitas* (a purely Christian formula), the reward (*uicem*) divine grace (*divina gratia*, once more a Christian formula). But, if this parallel concerning *commercium* is partial, there is in this passage such a concentration of Christian and particularly liturgical terms (and thoughts), that it is not only beyond doubt that Boethius speaks here as a Christian, but also that he had in mind certain liturgical texts.

There is still one formula in the passage we are examining which needs a comment: *Quid erit quo summo illi rerum principi conecti atque adhaerere possimus?* (ib. 35). What is one to think of: *summo illi rerum principi?* Dr. de Vogel translates: "that sovereign *Lord* of all things", adding: "If one prefers 'Prince' for 'principi', I have nothing against it. But I think 'Lord' is a correct rendering."[14] The author thinks that she can discover behind: *summus ille rerum princeps* the biblical-Christian Greek term Κύριος. Here I can hardly agree with my learned colleague. As she herself points out, the formula, with *princeps* or *principium*, occurs several times in the *Consolatio*. There is first 3, 10, 7: *Deum, rerum omnium principium*, but here Philosophy refers to: *communis humanorum conceptio ... animorum*. A few lines further on 3, 10, 12 she speaks, in the same line of thought, of: *rerum omnium patrem*, a formula which, de Vogel remarks, had a good tradition in Greek philosophy and was also used by Plotinus.[15] *Ibid.* 14 there occur the words: *de rerum principe loquamur deo.* And a few lines later Philosphy shifts from "princeps" to "principium". Dr. de Vogel comments: "This is

[13] See Herz, *o.c.*, p. 318.
[14] *O.c.*, p. 6.
[15] *O.c.*, p. 7.

characteristic of philosophy". There is a certain tendency to shift from the impersonal "principium" to the more personal *princeps* or even *pater*. But, notwithstanding this tendency, we are far away from the biblical-Christian Κύριος. In itself it could be possible that in a clearly Christian context Boethius used a philosophical term with a biblical Christian meaning. Nevertheless, in this particular case, there is strong evidence against such a supposition. In biblical and early-Christian Latin Κύριος is always rendered by *dominus*, this being one of the most "stable" terms in Christian usage. On the other hand *princeps*, by preference in the plural form, is constantly used, in biblical and early Christian texts, in quite a different semantic context: *principes sacerdotum, principes populorum, principes* = ἄρχοντες. Both words, *dominus* as well as *princeps*, have their traditional, and stable, place in Christian usage. Therefore I am of the opinion that with *summo illi rerum principi* Boethius backslides into philosophical language ... though by using *princeps*, and not *principium* he makes, perhaps, a certain concession to the Christian conception of a personal God. Thus the God of Grace imperceptibly draws near to the "First Principle" of the philosophers.

Are there, in the *Consolatio*, any other traces of liturgical influence? I could agree with Klingner who, commenting on the last words of the famous metrum 3, m. 9, 26ff.: *"tu namque serenum tu requies tranquilla piis, te cernere finis principium, uector, dux, semita, terminus idem"*, remarks that with *namque* Philosophia passes on from supplication to glorification of God.[16] This doxological element could point to Christian liturgical influence, notwithstanding the verbal classical parallels quoted by the editors.[17] If this supposition is true, there could be concealed behind *semita*, the *via* of John 14, 6, ... though applied, not to Christ, but to the God of the philosophers... or to God the Father.

In 3, 9, 32 Philosophy refers to the *Timaeus* of Plato: *Sed cum, ut in Timaeo Platoni, inquit, nostro placet, in minimis quoque rebus diuinum praesidium debeat implorari, quid nunc faciendum censes ut illius summi boni sedem repperire mereamur?* Nevertheless there occurs in this passage the formula *diuinum praesidium: praesidium* is a very usual term in liturgical prayers, it occurs e.g. very frequently in the *Sacramentarium Veronense*.[18] In the ancient orations

---

[16] See de Vogel, *o.c.*, p. 10.
[17] See Bieler, a.l.
[18] See L. C. Mohlberg, L. Eizenhöfer, P. Siffrin, *Sacramentarium Veronense*,

of the roman missal it indicates supernatural, divine help or support in general.[19] As to *diuinum* in this formula, the use of this adjective, with genitive meaning, is very frequent in early Christian Latin.[20] More interesting is the fact that the sentence quoted ends with a clausula, consisting in the form *mereamur* preceded by an infinitive: *repperire*. The use of *mereamur* with an infinitive is extremely frequent in liturgical prayers. In the ancient orations studied by Ellebracht, *mereri* occurs 45 times; it rarely has the meaning of "to merit" in the strict sense of the word. It has either the meaning of "to be judged worthy", or — and this is the most frequent function of the term — it has become a term of reverence which implies the reception of a "free gift" for which one depends on the favour of God.[21] In our text one can hesitate as to the exact meaning of "mereamur"; the essential thing is however that a very traditional liturgical formula seems to be used in this context spontaneously ... and, perhaps, unconsciously.

In 3, 12, 22 Philosophy says: *Est igitur summum, ... bonum quod regit cuncta fortiter suauiterque disponit.* The last words of this sentence have been the object of several speculations as to the source from which Philosophy-Boethius is drawing here:[22] is it an allusion to Sap. 8, 1? Is Boethius drawing here from Augustine? Or, have we, once more, to vote for a liturgical source (Antiphona ad Magnificat, Dec. 17)? These three suggested sources can be, and are probably, closely related, the primary source being Sap. 8, 1. Whether these words had for Boethius a biblical or a liturgical flavour, we hardly can define. But what is interesting, is the enthusiasm with which Boethius hails these words of Philosophy: *Tum ego: Quam, inquam, me non modo ea quae conclusa est summa rationum, uerum multo magis haec ipsa quibus uteris uerba delectant* (3, 12, 23). Is it the biblical or the liturgical flavour which pleases him so much in these words?

And then, to conclude, I might draw the reader's attention to the end of the *Consolatio*, viz. 5, 6, 46, where there is a clear allusion to Boethius' own words on prayer, 5, 3, 33ff.:[23] *Nec frustra sunt in*

Rome 1956. (Rerum Ecclesiasticarum Documenta, Ser. Maior, Fontes I). Wortverzeichnis s.v. The formula *divina praesidia* occurs twice.

[19] Ellebracht, *o.c.*, p. 176f.; cf. also Pflieger, s.v.

[20] See Jos. Schrijnen-Christine Mohrmann, *Studien zur Syntax der Briefe des hl. Cyprian*, I, Nijmegen 1936 (LCP vol. V), p. 90f.

[21] Ellebracht, *o.c.*, p. 199.

[22] See Bieler, a.l.

[23] Cf. p. 55 ff.

deo positae spes precesque, quae cum rectae sunt inefficaces esse non possunt. There can be no doubt that *spes precesque* in this passage has the same meaning as *sperandi — deprecandi* in the preceding text. Then follows an exhortation: *Auersamini igitur uitia, colite uirtutes, ad rectas spes animum subleuate, humiles preces in excelsa porrigite.* (5, 6, 47). That *preces* and *in excelsa* have a certain liturgical flavour, but that the verb *porrigere* is, in this context, quite unusual, needs hardly any comment. More interesting is the Christian meaning of *humilis* (cf. *iustae humilitatis pretio*, 5, 3, 34); whereas there is a slight play on words: *humiles preces — in excelsa, humilis* having its spiritual meaning, but at the same time suggesting, by means of *excelsa* in the context, its concrete meaning "low".

The conclusion to be drawn from this short investigation could be, first of all, that Prof. de Vogel is right when she is of the opinion that there are certain Christian features in the *Consolatio*. But this statement can be completed: these Christian elements concern Christian piety and they seem to find their source particularly in the liturgy. Boethius has been rather successful in his attempt to ban Christian theology from his philosophical dialogue, but he failed to conceal that he was a pious Christian.

ME QUOQUE EXCELLENTIOR
(BOETHII *CONSOLATIO* 4.6.27)

ANTONY E. RAUBITSCHEK

Meine Absicht war, dem verehrten Jubilar und dem alten Freunde die Erklärung einer Boethiusstelle vorzulegen, über die ich mir seit Jahren Gedanken gemacht habe; ich muss aber gestehen, dass ich der Lösung der Frage nicht näher gekommen bin, wen Philosophia als *me quoque excellentior* bezeichnet, und aus welchem Gedicht der von ihr zitierte griechische Hexameter stammt: ἀνδρὸς δὴ ἱεροῦ δέμας αἰθέρες ᾠκοδόμησαν. Dabei habe ich nicht nur die einschlägige Litteratur eingesehen, sondern auch eine Reihe von Freunden um Rat gefragt, denen auch hier mein Dank ausgesprochen werden soll.

Ich bin überzeugt, dass die griechische Quelle sich auf denselben "heiligen Mann" bezieht, von dem Philosophia kurz vorher spricht: cunctis virtutibus absolutus sanctusque ac deo proximus. Die (göttliche) Vorsehung hat bestimmt, dass unser Heiliger von keinerlei Unglücksfällen getroffen werden darf, so sehr, dass er nicht einmal von körperlichen Krankheiten beunruhigt werden darf. Er ist demnach aus einem anderen Stoff gemacht als die gewöhnlichen Menschen.

Solche Vorstellungen entsprechen weder klassischem noch biblischem Denken, aber sie mögen dem Boethius, als er die Consolatio verfasste, vertraut und genehm gewesen sein. Die genaue Bestimmung dieses Begriffes des Heiligen würde demnach auch zur Lösung des Hauptproblems der Consolatio beitragen: was hat diese Schrift mit dem Christentum zu tun, d.h. mit der Religion seines Verfassers?

Mein Freund und Kollege Edwin M. Good zeigt uns die Richtung, die wir verfolgen sollten; er teilte mir mit: "does Boethius ever use Gnostic materials or extra-canonical early Christian ones (which might have Gnostic flavoring)? The line strikes me as having that sort of flavor to it."

LUPUS OF FERRIERES ON THE METRES OF BOETHIUS

VIRGINIA BROWN

Famous for his activities as scribe and textual critic, Lupus of Ferrières is credited with a work on the metres of Boethius which is often referred to but has yet to be examined. Brief though this treatise is — it comprises pp. xxv-xxix of R. Peiper's edition (Leipzig, 1871) of the *Consolatio philosophiae* — it is nevertheless of some interest for the picture it gives of Lupus as metrician.

Then, too, the treatise's preoccupation with metre may make it something of a rarity as well as an authority on the subject so far as medieval commentaries on the *Consolatio* are concerned. Granted, of course, that much if not most of this vast material remains at present unstudied or inaccessible, yet, to judge from those glosses or commentaries which have been examined and published, Lupus' observations did indeed circulate to some extent. They appear, for example, in excerpted form in the anonymous commentary of Einsiedeln MS. 179 (s. IX) and in the commentary of Remi of Auxerre (s. X), and further sifting of the notes amassed on the *Consolatio* by medieval scholars will doubtless reveal other occurrences. Hand in hand with their use by commentators goes the survival of Lupus' remarks in not a few manuscripts. In addition to the eight codices mentioned by Peiper (p. xxiv), there are the six listed by E. T. Silk and the Heiligenkreuz copy noted by N. M. Haring; since the "anonymous" treatise on the Boethian metres of Balliol College MS. 10 noted by R. A. B. Mynors is actually that of Lupus (to line 132), this brings to at least sixteen the number of codices which contain the work.[1]

---

[1] P. Courcelle, *La consolation de philosophie dans la tradition littéraire* (Paris, 1967), p. 12 nn. 1-6 lists medieval commentaries on the *Consolatio* that have been studied and at least partially edited; to these should be added N. M. Haring, "Four Commentaries on the *De consolatione philosophiae* in MS Heiligenkreuz 130", *Mediaeval Studies* 31 (1969) 287-316. For the Oxford manuscript see R. A. B. Mynors, *Catalogue of the Manuscripts of Balliol College Oxford* (Oxford, 1963), p. 8. I have to thank Mr. John F. R. Coughlan for calling my attention to this witness and for examining Parisinus lat. 15090 which contains Remi's commentary. As in Einsiedeln 179 and the first commentary (ff. 6-76) of Heiligenkreuz 130, the metrical glosses of

For all these reasons, and not merely because it was compiled by one of the most outstanding ninth-century humanists, does the commentary of Lupus deserve study, and I propose here to give an analysis and consideration of its contents.

By way of a prefatory statement, it would be well to note that the treatise does not signify a hitherto unsuspected interest on Lupus' part in either metre or related matters. Witness the passages in *Letters* 5, 8, 9, and 21 in which he discusses questions of pronunciation and declares that he has consulted the "poets" for his evidence. *Letters* 5 and 8 offer, perhaps, the clearest indication that he continued to ponder such problems until he found a satisfactory solution. In the former (dated to May 836 by L. Levillain in his edition of the *Letters*), Lupus admits to Einhard that he is uncertain, in the case of words like *aratrum* and *salubris*, as to whether the penult is pronounced long (since it is long by nature) or short (since the vowel in the penultimate syllable is followed by a mute plus a liquid). However, by April 837 (Levillain's date) Lupus had decided that the penult in such instances was to have the accent, for in *Letter* 8 he writes to Alcuin that "*salubris, aratrum* et similia accentu paenultimo indubitanter moderanda". Whoever the "docti et studiosissimi viri" were who assisted Lupus in reaching this conclusion, one result of their joint deliberation is obvious: while working on the metres of Boethius, he was to insist on the precedence of nature over position ın penultimate syllables composed of a mute and a liquid, and his scansion of these words does not reflect the teaching of Donatus whose dictum had puzzled him in *Letter* 5.

To turn now to the commentary itself. It consists of a short introduction wherein Lupus asserts that his task required a great deal of diligence ("non mediocri diligentia"), and then there follows a listing (in the numerical order of the poems) of the 27 metres according to which Lupus has classified all *carmina* in the *Consolatio*, together with a brief explanation of each metre and citation of the first or the first two line(s) from each poem.[2] As Peiper has pointed out (p. xxiv),

---

Parisinus lat. 15090 are not attributed to Lupus, and they appear at the head of each poem, occasionally spilling over into the margin.

[2] His quoting of the first line(s) might suggest that he scanned only this portion of the poem, and see below p. 75 f. where he appears to have examined only the opening lines. However, it seems to me that, for the most part, this is an undeniably handy way of indicating which poem is under discussion, and I base this inference on metres nos. 1, 4, 15, 22, 25, 27 where the citation is preceded by "quorum initia haec sunt" or "cuius initium hoc est".

his source is the *De centum metris* of Servius and, in fact, Lupus himself mentions this work (metre no. 18). It is probable that Servius was his principal and perhaps his only authority. Even though other metrical grammarians occasionally put forward similar statements, Lupus never refers to them (either in the commentary or in the *Letters*), nor does he include any portion peculiar to any of them. This is not true when it comes to Servius, for he generally quotes him verbatim (and several times at some length) besides giving definitions that are unique to the latter.[3]

In order to demonstrate this evident dependence and also to provide an abbreviated version of Lupus' commentary for convenience of discussion, I give below the parallel passages for both texts. The Servius sections are from H. Keil, *Grammatici latini* IV (reprint Hildesheim, 1961) 456-467 and, for Lupus, I have used Peiper's edition. An asterisk preceding the number of a poem designates an instance of an erroneous judgment by Lupus or mistake in terminology or other notabilia having some bearing on his method and metrical ability.

Boethius	*Lupus*	*Servius*
I. 1	Primum itaque genus car-	(465. 19-20) elegiacum
V. 1	minis elegiacum est quod	constat de penthemimeri
	constat primo uersu heroico,	prima heroica, secunda
	secundo prima pentemimere	dactylica... (457. 9-10)
	heroica, secunda dactilica.	penthemimeren esse, cum
	pentemimeris autem est	duos pedes sequitur syl-
	post duos pedes sillaba de	laba quae partem termi-
	verbo remanens.	nat orationis...
*I. 2	Secundum dactilicum tetra-	
*IV. 5	metrum quod constat spon-	
	deo dactilo catalecto item	
	dactilo spondeo...	
I. 3	Tertium quod constat pri-	(457. 15-16) acatalec-
	mo heroico secundo alcma-	tum... qui legitimo fine
	nio dactilico tetrametro aca-	concluditur... (460. 11-

---

[3] For definitions given correctly in the commentary, I have been able to locate similar passages in the *De centum metris* in every case except for the "heroic hexameter" (metre no. 21). The explanation which he gives, however, is not found in the grammarians to whom he refers in the *Letters*, namely Caper, Donatus, Priscian, and Servius, commentary on the *Aeneid*.

talecto id est quattuor pedibus dactilicis nulla remanente sillaba. acatalectus enim uersus est qui legitimo fine clauditur. Metra autem dactilica principaliter dactili constant, recipiunt tamen spondeum et non numquam in fine trocheum.

12) Metra dactylica principaliter constant dactylo, recipiunt tamen et spondeum et interdum ultimo loco trochaeum.

*I. 4
*III. 10

Quartum ponit falleutium constans spondeo dactilo tribus trocheis.

(465. 31) phalaecium constat spondio, dactylo, tribus trochaeis...

I. 5
III. 2

Quintum anapesticum pindaricum constans dimetro acatalecto. metra uero anapestica principaliter constant anapesto, recipiunt tamen frequenter spondeum, raro proceleumaticum apud comicos autem etiam dactilum saepiusque ultima cum superest syllaba in duas soluitur breues.

(462. 8) pindaricum constat dimetro acatalecto... (461. 27-29) Metra anapaestica principaliter constant anapaesto; recipiunt tamen frequenter spondeum, raro proceleumaticum, apud comicos autem etiam dactylum, saepiusque ultima cum superest syllaba, in duas solvitur breves.

I. 6
II.8
*III. 12
*IV. 3
*V. 4

Sextum gliconium quod constat spondeo choriambo pyrrichio...

(465. 10) glyconium constat spondio choriambo pyrrichio...

I. 7

Septimum dactilicum dimetrum catalecticum cui est nomen adonio. catalecticus autem uersus dicitur cui una syllaba deest.

(460. 14) adonium constat dimetro catalectico ... (457. 13-14) catalecticum versum dici, cui syllaba una deest...

II. 1
III. 11

Octavum genus iambicum est hyponactium constans trimetro acatalecto claudo. iambica uero metra imparibus quidem locis possunt recipere iambum tribra-

(458. 22) hipponactium constat trimetro acatalecto claudo... (457. 25-458. 3) Metra iambica locis inparibus quinque recipere possunt pedes,

chum spondeum dactilum anapestum. In paribus iambum tantum uel tribrachin et frequenter apud comicos anapestum ita tamen ut multarum breuium iunctura uitetur.

iambum tribrachum spondeum dactylum anapaestum, locis autem paribus tantum iambum vel tribrachum, et apud comicos frequenter anapaestum, ita tamen ut multarum brevium iunctura vitetur.

*II. 2 Nonum est asclepiadeum quod fit spondeo duobus coriambis pyrrichio siue iambo cui et ferecratium subiecit constans spondeo dactilo spondeo.

(465. 13-14) asclepiadium constat spondio, duobus choriambis, pyrrichio...
(465. 7) pherecratium constat spondio dactylo spondio...

*II. 3 Decimum est saphicum quod constat trocheo spondeo dactilo duobus trocheis. miscuit autem huic secundum semper uersum gliconium de quo superius dictum (cf. sup. I. 6).

(466. 2-3) sapphicum constat trochaeo, spondio, dactylo, duobus trochaeis...

II. 4 Vndecimum genus iambicum anacreontium est quod constat dimetro catalectico cuius secundum uersum supposuit ferecratium quod paulo ante memoraui (cf. sup. II. 2)...

(458. 10) anacreontium constat dimetro catalectico...

II. 5
III. 5 Duodecimum anapesticum parhemiacum est quod constat dimetro catalectico.

(462. 6) paroemiacum constat dimetro catalectico...

II. 6
IV. 7 Tertium decimum saphicum continuatum...quamuis id (sc. IV. 7. 35) dimetro adonio terminauit ita: Sidera donat.

II. 7 Quartum decimum iambicum archilochium quod constat trimetro acatalecto

(458. 20) archilochium constat trimetro acatalecto... (458. 12) archilo-

habetque subiectum iambi-
cum archilochium constans
dimetro acatalecto...

chium constat dimetro
acatalecto...

II. 8   *cf. sup.* I. 6

cf. sup. I. 6

III. 1   Quintum decimum faliscum
constans tribus dactilis et
pyrrichio...

(465. 5) faliscum constat
tribus dactylis et pyrri-
chio...

III. 2   *cf. sup.* I. 5

cf. sup. I. 5

III. 3   Sextum decimum iambicum
archilochium quod constat,
ut supra memoraui (*cf. sup.
II. 7*), trimetro acatalecto
cui mixtum est elegiacum
ita ut supra exposui (*cf. sup.
I. 1*) constans.

cf. sup. II. 7, I. 1

*III. 4   Septimum decimum et fal-
leucium posuit subiecitque
illi dactilicum archilochium
tetrametrum catalecticum
.... In quo tamen pro spondeo siue dactilo imparibus
locis trocheum reperies.

(460. 27) archilochium
constat tetrametro cata-
lectico...

III. 5   *cf. sup.* II. 5

cf. sup. II. 5

*III. 6   Duodeuicesimum dactili-
cum alcmanium constans
trimetro ypercatalecto. y-
percatalectus uero est uersus cui una syllaba superest habetque subiectum sibi
ferecratium quod, ut supra
memoraui (*cf. sup. II. 2*),
spondeo constat et dactilo
et spondeo. Sed in hoc loco
pro primo spondeo est ubi
anapestum contra regulam
in *centimetro* traditam in-
uenimus.

(460. 25) alcmanium con-
stat trimetro hypercata-
lecto... (457. 14-15) hy-
percatalectum, cui una
(*sc.* syllaba) superest...
(465. 7) pherecratium
constat spondio dactylo
spondio...

*III. 7   Vndeuicesimum iambicum
anacreontium constans di-
metro catalectico...

(458. 10) anacreontium
constat dimetro catalec-
tico...

III. 8   Vicesimum asclepiadeum cuius supra regulam posui (*cf. sup. II. 2*) habetque subiunctum sibi iambicum archilochium dimetrum acatalectum.

(458. 12) archilochium constat dimetro acatalecto...

III. 9   Primum et uicesimum est heroicum exametrum qui locis omnibus aliis dactilum siue spondeum, quinto solum modo dactilum recipit, sexto spondeum siue trocheum.

*III. 10   *cf. sup.* I. 4

cf. sup. I. 4

III. 11   *cf. sup.* II. 1

cf. sup. II. 1

*III. 12   *cf. sup.* I. 6

cf. sup. I. 6

IV. 1   Secundum et uicesimum dactilicum alcmanium constans tetrametro acatalecto subpositumque sibi habet iambicum archilochium de quo paulo ante dixi (*cf. sup. II. 7*).

(460. 30) alcmanium constat tetrametro acatalecto...

*IV. 2   Tertium et uicesimum trochaicum alcmanium constans dimetro acatalecto. Sane metra trochaica locis imparibus trocheum tribrachin et nonnumquam dactilum paribus uero cum supradictos, tum etiam spondeum et anapestum recipiunt. huic autem generi subdidit Boetius de quo supra dictum est (*cf. sup. II. 2*) ferecratium quod pro spondeo interdum recipiunt anapestum.

(459. 17) alcmanium constat dimetro acatalecto...
(459. 5-7) Metra trochaica locis inparibus hos recipiunt pedes, trochaeum tribrachum et non numquam dactylum, locis vero paribus cum his quos memoravi spondeum et anapaestum.

*IV. 3   *cf. sup.* I. 6

cf. sup. I. 6

IV. 4   Quartum et uicesimum fal-

leutium habens subiectum
elegiacum...

*IV. 5   *cf. sup*. I. 2

*IV. 6   Quintum et uicesimum ge-

*V. 3   nus est mixtum uariis pedi-
bus quod incertum quo po-
tissimum debeat censeri
uocabulo. Aut enim dactilicum adonium erit quod pro
dactilo siue pro spondeo
anapestum recipiat aut dactilicum archilochium tetrametrum quod idem pro
spondeo siue dactilo anapestum indifferenter admittat.
Nam anapesticum sentire
ratio dissuadet quando
spondeo uel dactilo quam
anapesto compositum sit.

IV. 7   *cf. sup*. II. 6

V. 1   *cf. sup*. I. 1   *cf. sup*. I. 1
                                     (460. 27) archilochium
                                     constat tetrametro cata-

V. 2   Sextum et uicesimum dac-   lectico...
tilicum archilochium quod
constat tetrametro catalectico...

*V. 3   *cf. sup*. IV. 6

*V. 4   *cf. sup*. I. 6   *cf. sup*. I. 6

V. 5   Septimum et uicesimum ar-   (466. 23-24) archilochi-
chilochium constans tetra-   um constat tetrametro
metro bucolico et tribus   bucolico et tribus tro-
trocheis. tetrametrum uero   chaeis... (461. 12-13) bu-
bucolicum est, cum quartus   colicum constat hexame-
pes dactilus est qui partem   tro catalectico, ita ut
finiat orationis...   quartus dactylus partem
                                       determinet orationis...

Obviously Lupus' purpose was simply the identification of the
metre of each poem; there is nothing whatever on such points as
the Boethian use of the caesura, his predilection for the number of
syllables with which to end the hexameter, or the metrical practice

of other poets for purposes of comparison. Lupus' own observations relieve the stark simplicity of the commentary only three times, namely when he notes that IV. 7. 35 consists of an adonic (no. 13) and comments on metrical peculiarities in III. 4 (no. 17), IV. 6 (no. 25) and V. 3 (no. 25). We shall probably never know precisely why Lupus settled on the design of his treatise as we now have it, but speculation on his reasons for doing so may include the following suggestions: first, there is the fact that Servius in the *De centum metris* does no more than give the skeletal framework of each metre and Lupus may have followed the pattern of this and other metrical works; next, since Lupus himself wrote little poetry (and this only in hexameters and elegiacs), he may have been interested in the metres of the *Consolatio* for strictly antiquarian and grammatical motives instead of their use as possible models for his own compositions.[4] The apparent sparseness of his commentary may be a disappointment, but it is hardly fair and certainly useless to censure him for what he did not do, especially as he does not appear to have been concerned with any feature pertaining to the oral recitation of verse.

It is perhaps also unfair that most of the discussion of the commentary will be concerned with Lupus' erroneous identifications, for this will tend to give a onesided picture of his abilities. The overall figures, however, will serve to dispel any impression of incompetence. Of the nearly 60 occurrences of various metres (either singly or in combination) in the *Consolatio*, Lupus was actually *wrong* in 9 instances; add to these another 6 instances where he "slipped" rather than erred, and the result is that Lupus achieves almost a 75 per cent record for correctness. To give him just due, we must further concede that some of the trouble could be owing to a faulty manuscript of Boethius. I think, nevertheless, that the kinds of errors to be enumerated will indicate that inaccuracies which can be blamed on a badly transcribed codex, or one with variant readings, are few and far between.

The modern edition of Boethius which I have used is that of Professor Bieler, published in volume 94 of the *Corpus Christianorum*, Series latina (Turnhout, 1957).

---

[4] J. Szövérffy, *Weltliche Dichtungen des lateinischen Mittelalters* (Berlin, 1970), p. 598 gives a list of Lupus' poems and observes "als Dichter ist er anscheinend ziemlich unbedeutend."

Alcaics

Only once does Boethius use this type of Aeolic verse, namely in
III. 4 where the alcaic decasyllabic (– ᴗ ᴗ – ᴗ ᴗ – | ᴗ – ᴗ̄) occurs in
even lines. Lupus correctly identified the phalaecian hendecasyllabic
as the metre of the odd lines but mistook the alcaic form for the
dactilicum archilochium (tetrameter catalectic). Since he understood
the latter to consist of 4 feet, of which the last was a spondee (cf. V.
2: – ᴗᴗ – ᴗᴗ | – ᴗ ᴗ – ᴗ̄), his dactylic tetrameter catalectic (without
spondaic substitutions in the first two feet) would indeed resemble
the alcaic in nearly every particular. The exception is the third foot
where the alcaic demands a trochee, and Lupus, to his credit,
pointed out this anomaly in the alleged dactylic metre. Although it
was certainly not unknown to the Middle Ages, the alcaic was not
commonly employed by medieval poets, and it is possible that, apart
from III. 4, Lupus had never, or very seldom, encountered this
type.[5]

Anapestic metres

Used in II. 5 and III. 5, the anapestic dimeter catalectic presented
no difficulty to Lupus. As for the anapestic dimeter acatalectic, he
identified it correctly at I. 5 and III. 2 but wavered when grappling
with IV. 6 and V. 3, finally concluding on the basis of the large
number of spondees and dactyls contained therein that the metre of
the latter instances was not anapestic. If he hesitated to classify the
metrical scheme of IV. 6 and V. 3 as anapestic dimeter acatalectic
(which it actually is) because of an apparent scarcity of anapests,
then his reluctance is all the harder to understand, for a comparison
of these poems with I. 5 and III. 2 shows throughout a consistent
pattern regarding the occurrence of anapests. For example, I. 5 and
IV. 6 both consist of 48 lines, with the total number of anapests

---

[5] There are few examples of alcaics in the MGH, *Poetae aevi Carolini*; the
index to vol. III places this metre among the "metra rariora" (p. 816). A
number of hymns composed in the alcaic hendecasyllabic are mentioned by
D. Norberg, *Introduction à l'étude de la versification latine médiévale* (Stock-
holm, 1958), p. 83. With regard to III. 4, P. Klopsch points out that Lupus'
erroneous identification may have prompted his pupil Heiric of Auxerre to
combine the phalaecian with the dactylic tetrameter catalectic in the preface
to the *Vita Germani*; see Klopsch's *Einführung in die mittellateinische Vers-
lehre* (Darmstadt, 1972), pp. 96-97. It should be noted, however, that Heiric's
tetrameter follows the usual rules of prosody and does not admit a trochee
in uneven feet.

amounting to 42 and 45 respectively. They are distributed among the four feet that make up the two metra as follows: (I. 5) 13, 16, 6, 7; (IV. 6) 14, 24, 4, 3. III. 2 (38 lines) and V. 3 (31 lines) have respectively a total of 37 and 21 anapests which are allocated thus: (III. 2) 12, 13, 7, 5; (V. 3) 5, 8, 3, 5. Two of the conclusions which can be drawn from these statistics are directly relevant to the problem at hand: IV. 6 and V. 3 are in no way deficient in anapests since the former contains more than I. 5 does, and the latter, though 7 lines shorter than III. 2, still contains a goodly number; both IV. 6 and V. 3 display the greatest frequency of anapests in the second foot of the first metron, agreeing in this feature with I. 5 and III. 2. In dealing with the metre of I. 5 and III. 2, Lupus himself had already pointed out that the anapestic dimeter acatalectic allows the substitution of spondees and dactyls, and it is puzzling that he should adopt such a cautious approach to IV. 6 and V. 3.

In any case, his allegations in no. 25 are false, namely that the adonean permits an anapest to take the place of a dactyl or spondee and the dactylic tetrameter admits an anapest for a spondee or dactyl. These are probably Lupus' own deductions since similar statements are not put forth by Servius or other metricians, and they represent doubtless an attempt to explain the facts as he found them. He has reversed the relationship between the adonean and the anapestic dimeter acatalectic as the adonean may be one variant of the anapestic metron, but not vice versa. And while grammarians have noted the similarity of the anapestic to the dactylic metre, provided that the first syllable of the first dactylic foot is removed, nowhere do they affirm that the dactylic metre can receive an anapest for a dactyl or spondee.

Dactylic metres

These are the metres most frequently used in the *Consolatio*. Their number varies, depending on the method of classification, but they encompass approximately ten different forms of which Lupus recognized correctly the following: adonean (I. 7), alcmanian (I. 3, IV. 1, V. 5), hexameter (I. 1, I. 3, III. 9, V. 1), elegiac pentameter (I. 1, III. 3, IV. 4, V. 1), tetrameter catalectic (III. 6, V. 2), and trimeter acatalectic (III. 1).[6] On the debit side are his erroneous sug-

---

[6] Lupus refers to III. 6 and V. 5 as the dactylic trimeter hypercatalectic and bucolic tetrameter respectively; I am following Peiper's terminology in the Index metricus (pp. 220, 221) to his edition of the *Consolatio*.

gestion that the metres (anapestic dimeter acatalectic) in IV. 6 and
V. 3 were either the adonean or archilochean, the identification of the
alcaic (III. 4) as a dactylic tetrameter catalectic, and his belief that
the metre of I. 2 and IV. 5 was the dactylic tetrameter. The metrical
scheme of IV. 5 will be discussed below under *Iambic and Trochaic
metres*, and it is convenient to treat here the question of I. 2.

Lupus defined the "dactylic tetrameter" in which this poem is
supposedly written as consisting of a "spondee, dactyl catalectic,
likewise a dactyl, spondee". The metre, however, is actually the
dactylic trimeter catalectic coupled with the adonean, thus forming
the pattern $- \overset{\smile\smile}{} - \overline{\smile\smile} - \mid - \smile\smile - \smile$. I think that it is possible to follow
his reasoning if we look at this scheme from another angle and
understand the "spondee, dactyl catalectic" to refer to the dactylic
trimeter catalectic and the "dactyl, spondee" to refer to the adonean. The difficulty, of course, with Lupus' statement is that it would
be an odd dactylic tetrameter indeed which allows a catalectic foot
in the middle of the line. This, then, is an example similar to II. 4,
III. 6, IV. 2, IV. 6 and V. 3 of his introducing an anomaly to explain
the metrical facts. Finally, because he writes "*spondee*, dactyl
catalectic", it may not be too wide of the mark to infer that he was
aware of the predominantly spondaic bases (lines 1, 4, 6, 8-12, 15-19,
21-23, 25, 26) of I. 2.

Glyconics

The sixth metre treated in the commentary is the glyconic, and
under this heading Lupus rightly groups I. 6, II. 8, III. 12, IV. 3,
and V. 4, explaining that the metrical scheme is composed of a
spondee, choriamb, and pyrrhic. The even lines of II. 3 (the tenth
metre) are also in the glyconic, and Lupus notes here that he has
spoken previously of this metre, thus affirming, it would seem, his
earlier definition. Consequently, since he has stated so clearly his
notion of the components of the glyconic, it is rather surprising that
he did not point out such irregularities as the iambic base in II. 3. 16
(*bonis*), III. 12. 29 (*stupet*), V. 4. 11 (*nihil*), V. 4. 13, 38 (*notis*, from
nota, -ae) and the trochaic base for the whole of IV. 3 (with the exception of the last line).

Perhaps these aberrations on the part of Boethius failed to catch
Lupus' attention or perhaps, given the summary nature of the
treatise, he felt there was no need to expatiate on anomalies. It

seems unlikely, however, that in the case of two of the iambic bases he could have obtained a spondaic first foot unless he was deliberately inconsistent, for he apparently scanned as short the first syllables of *bon-* and *not-* elsewhere in the *Consolatio. nihil* and *stup-* figure in other erroneous identifications, and Lupus may have had some doubt regarding their vowel quantities. For *stup-* see *Iambic and Trochaic metres;* as for *nihil,* he would have had to scan a long first syllable at IV. 3. 25 since he included the poem among those glyconics beginning with a spondee.

This brings us to the question of why Lupus considered the bases in IV. 3 to be spondaic when, in fact, 38 of the 39 lines have a trochaic first foot. Further metrical analysis shows that lines 1, 3-7, 9, 11-12, 14-16, 18-20, 22, 24, 26-28, 31-34, 36-37 begin with a word of two syllables or more, and that the rules of position do not allow the second syllable to be scanned as long. The base in lines 2, 4, 8, 10, 13, 17, 21, 23, 25, 29-30, 35 comprises a monosyllabic word plus the opening syllable of another word; except for *aper* at IV. 3. 10 (whose first syllable is also long at IV. 4. 5), the quantity of the first syllable of the second word is always short elsewhere in the work. Clearly Lupus could have obtained a spondee in the first foot of IV. 3 only by contravening the rules of prosody which he had already successfully applied. Did his recognition of the metre as glyconic derive from the choriambic and pyrrhic elements in the line?

Iambic and Trochaic metres

Lupus correctly identified eight of the nine occurrences of iambic verse, namely the dimeter acatalectic (II. 7, III. 8, IV. 1), dimeter catalectic (II. 4),[7] trimeter acatalectic (II. 7, III. 3), and limping trimeter acatalectic (II. 1, III. 11). With regard to trochaic types, he was right in designating IV. 2 as the dimeter acatalectic, and he described the ithyphallic of V. 5 simply as "three trochees". His score would have been perfect except for a slip at IV. 5. The metre is a trochaic tripody catalectic followed by an adonean (odd lines) alternating with an iambic tripody catalectic plus adonean (even lines),[8] but Lupus classified it as a dactylic tetrameter and, curiously

---

[7] In his "La metrica di Boezio", *Giornale italiano di filologia* 7 (1954), L. Pepe shows (pp. 238, 239 n. 38) that the metre of II. 4 is iambic rather than ionic (Peiper, p. 222).

[8] I follow Pepe (p. 238) here rather than Peiper who considers (p. 219) the

enough, grouped the poem with I. 2 (dactylic trimeter catalectic with adonean).

As with I. 2, if considered in a certain way, the metrical scheme of IV. 5 ($- \cup - \overset{\cup\cup}{-} \overset{\smile}{} \mid - \cup\cup - \bar{\cup}$ and $\overset{\smile}{} - \cup \overset{\cup\cup}{-} \overset{\smile}{} \mid - \cup\cup - \bar{\cup}$) does resemble an odd kind of dactylic tetrameter, but one encounters even more problems in trying to force the latter into this mould. For example, in the trochaic tripody (usually five syllables), the second syllable is always short and the third always long; Lupus needs a long second syllable for an opening spondee or a short third syllable (if the pattern is dactyl, spondee). However, none of the rules of position would have permitted him to make the necessary adjustments, nor, in comparison with occurrences of similar forms in the rest of the *Consolatio*, are there changes in the quantity of vowels which would account for such a scansion. Besides, even if circumstances did allow him to scan two successive spondees and a long syllable (which would generally be the case since two shorts for the long fourth syllable are found only in line 5), this would hardly explain why he thought the metre to be composed of a "spondee, dactyl catalectic".

The matter of the iambic tripody catalectic is equally as complicated. A long first syllable occurs in every instance except in lines 2 (*prŏpinqua*) and 20 (*stŭpetque*). If Lupus were here to scan the first syllable as long, he would be inconsistent in the case of *propinqu-* at least, for he has scanned it as short in III. 10. 9 and IV. 4. 3. It might be possible to argue that he regarded the first syllable of *stupetque* as long since in III. 12. 29 *stupet* must, according to his definition, comprise the spondaic base of a glyconic line. On the other hand, *stŭpebit* occurs in line 6 of IV. 5 where it constitutes the third syllable of the tripody and fits perfectly into the scheme. Lupus is also in trouble in various other ways: he needs the second syllable short (which is always long) to scan an opening dactyl; and he needs the third syllable long (which is always short) to scan a second spondee (or dactyl in the case of line 20 with the tribrach *subitis*).

The adonean at the end of every line in IV. 5 seems to be the "dactyl, spondee" referred to in his treatment of the metre, and its occurrence in a similar position in I. 2, together with approximately the same number of syllables in the first half of the line, may have

---

metre to consist of a trochaic penthemim (first part of the sapphic) and iambic penthemim (first part of the alcaic hendecasyllabic) combined with the adonean.

prompted Lupus to associate the two poems metrically. But even with the greatest good will, the task is hopeless for any one who tries to scan either poem as any kind of "dactylic tetrameter".

Ionics

If a "minor ionic" dimeter opens with a long syllable rather than two shorts, it would be a simple matter to mistake the pattern (‿‿ – – ‿ ‿ – –) for a pherecratic (– – – ‿ ‿ – –). This is what Lupus has done for III. 6 and IV. 2 where an apparent spondaic first foot occurs in lines 2, 5-8 and 2, 4, 7-9 respectively. The metre, however, is the ionic since genuine pherecratics do not normally display an anapestic base (Peiper, p. 222); this irregularity in his "pherecratic" was noted by Lupus for both poems. It should be mentioned, too, that he identified correctly the dactylic tetrameter catalectic (= his dactylic trimeter hypercatalectic) and the trochaic dimeter acatalectic as the respective metres combined with the "minor ionic" in III. 6 and IV. 2. The ionic anacreontic of III. 7 he took to be the iambic anacreontic.

Phalaecian hendecasyllabics

At I. 4, III. 4, III. 10 and IV. 4 Lupus has properly identified the metre and explained that the phalaecian consists of a spondee, dactyl, and three trochees. What he has not told us is that Boethius substituted an iambus, dactyl, and spondee for the first trochee in I. 4. 2, 6, 11 respectively. Nor did he let us know that, in III. 10, lines 1-3 are phalaecian but thereafter this metre (odd lines) alternates with the sapphic (even lines). His assumption that the poem is composed entirely in phalaecians was to be expected if he scanned merely the first two lines, for in III. 10 we have the only instance where Boethius did not introduce the alternating metre in the second line.

Pherecratics

A similar situation exists in his treatment of this metre. Lupus observed that even lines in II. 2 and II. 4 are in pherecratics consisting of a spondee, dactyl, spondee. Curiously enough, he did not point out that the bases in II. 2. 14 (*alios*), II. 2. 18 (*sitis ar(descit)*) and II. 4. 8 (*bibulas*) are anapestic although he remarked on a similar phenomenon in III. 6 and IV. 2 (see above under *Ionics*) which he also considered to be in "pherecratics". Some manuscripts offer the reading *altos* for *alios;* this variant would constitute the spondaic base of the pherecratic and could, of course, have appeared in Lupus' own copy of the *Consolatio.*

Sapphics

II. 3, II. 6, III. 10 and IV. 7 are written in the sapphic hendecasyllabic. The metrical irregularities evident in the phalaecian are not present in this type of aeolic verse, and there is nothing for which Lupus may be called to task apart from his failure to notice that from line 4 on the even lines in III. 10 are in sapphics (see above under *Phalaecian hendecasyllabics*). His remark that IV. 7. 35 consists of an adonean is correct.

* * *

To sum up. Although Lupus did not compile a detailed commentary on the metres of the *Consolatio*, nevertheless his little treatise is sufficiently full to allow us to form an opinion regarding his abilities as metrician.

The overall impression must, I think, be distinctly favourable. As noted on p. 71, Lupus has a score for accuracy of nearly 75 per cent. The metres which caused him the most trouble were the alcaic (III. 4), anapestic dimeter acatalectic (IV. 6, V. 3), dactylic trimeter catalectic with adonean (I. 2), iambic tripody catalectic with adonean (IV. 5, even lines), "minor ionic" dimeter (III. 6, IV. 2), sapphic (III. 10), and trochaic tripody catalectic with adonean (IV. 5, odd lines), for he was unable to identify properly their metrical arrangement. On several other occasions Lupus correctly identified the metre but failed to report certain irregularities which would have invalidated his definition of the metre; such aberrations occur in Boethius' employment of the glyconic (II. 3, III. 12, V. 4), phalaecian (I. 4), and pherecratic (II. 2, II. 4).

How to explain Lupus' errors? Since there appears to be only one instance (II. 2. 14) where a textual variant may be adduced as an explanation, we must look to his methodology. It seems to me that the faulty identifications can be described as "intelligent" mistakes, and that they originate in his attempt to force the metre into another scheme which it resembles closely, but is not identical with (as he often notes) in every particular. As for those individual lines where he would have been wrong according to the rigid Servian formula, it may be that he based his conclusions on the general metrical scheme, being constrained simply to overlook Boethian peculiarities.

If these suggestions are anywhere near the truth, then it is necessary to assume that the changing quantity of vowels in the medieval period had little to do with the matter. And, indeed, we have evidence that only *stup-*, *nihil*, and *aper* may have been a problem. Until more substantial proof of Lupus' own poetic practices is discovered, there seems to be little chance of showing that the phenomenon of vowel changes lay behind his metrical blunders in the commentary.

II

HYMNODY AND LITURGY

HYMNOLOGICA PARTIM HIBERNICA

WALTHER BULST

Paulinus hymnographus

Das Zeugnis des Gennadius *Paulinus, Nolae Campaniae episco-pus, ... fecit ... et hymnorum* stand bisher allein; daß kein *hymnus* unter seinem Namen unseres Wissens erhalten ist, berechtigte nicht, an der Mitteilung des Gennadius zu zweifeln. Jedoch ist auch ein authentisches Zeugnis dafür bewahrt. Auf einen verlorenen Brief des Alypius, derzeit schon Bischofes zu Tagaste, an Paulinus ist seine Antwort erhalten (ep. iii ed. Hartel); Rauschen[1] und Reinelt[2] haben sie in das Jahr 396 datiert, als Paulinus schon sich nach Nola zurückgezogen hatte. Darin schreibt er im vorletzten Satz, ohne die Bitte mit einem Worte weiter einzuführen, *et hoc rogo scribas mihi, quem hymnum meum agnoueris.*[3] Also hat Paulinus zugleich mit der von Alypius erbetenen *de cunctis temporibus historia* des Eusebius ihm Hymnen übersandt, unter welchen einer von ihm selbst ver-faßt war, und ist sich seiner kenntlichen Verschiedenheit von den übrigen bewußt gewesen. Das Unvermittelte der Bitte macht es höchst wahrscheinlich, daß auch sie von Alypius erbeten waren.

Bedeutender noch als die neue Bewährung des Zeugen Genna-dius, ist, auch wenn es um ein unerbetenes Antidoton für die von Alypius übersandten *libri quinque* eines augustinischen *opus*[4] sich handelte, das in jedem Fall vorauszusetzende, — gewiß nicht, zum wenigsten nicht vorwiegend literarische — Interesse eines Bischofes der Africa an *hymni*. Ihre Namenlosigkeit sollte keine literarischen Rätsel aufgeben und entspricht ihrer Namenlosigkeit in Hymna-rien; die Bitte des Paulinus bezeichnet ihn als "homme de lettres",

---

[1] G. Rauschen, *Jahrbücher der christlichen Kirche unter dem Kaiser Theo-dosius d. Gr.*, Freiburg i. Br. 1897, S. 464.

[2] P. Reinelt, *Studien über die Briefe des hl. Paulinus von Nola*, Diss. theol. Breslau 1903, S. 10; J. Brochet, *La correspondance de saint Paulin de Nole et de Sulpice Sévère*, Thèse Paris 1906, p. 95 (cf. p. 22) ist nicht eindeutig: 395?

[3] In meinen *Hymni latini antiquissimi* LXXV, Heidelberg (1956), unter den Testimonia vor dem des Gennadius einzureihen.

[4] Zur Frage, welche *libri*, s. P. Courcelle, *Recherches sur les Confessions de saint Augustin*, Paris 1950, p. 29 ann. 3.

der er auch gewesen ist. Von Hymnen des Ambrosius hat wohl
Alypius wie Paulinus wissen müssen;[5] besaß aber Alypius sie
schriftlich in ihrem Wortlaut? Hilarius oder sein "liber hymnorum"
ist in den erhaltenen Schriften des Paulinus überhaupt nicht genannt. Daß er "Cathemerinon" und "Peristephanon" des Prudentius
gekannt habe, ist aus Hartel's Index auctorum kaum zu erweisen.
So läßt sich auch kaum vermuten, welche Hymnen Paulinus nach
Tagaste übersandt hat. —

Die abwegige Vermutung, Gennadius habe unter den von ihm
genannten *hymni* des Paulinus die dreizehn carmina natalicia, insge-
samt über 5000 Verse, verstanden, ist von G. M. Dreves, der sie
geäußert hat,[6] selbst nicht ernstlich vertreten worden. Er hat von
carmina des Paulinus die Paraphrasen des 1., des 2. und des 136.
Psalmes und die von Hartel als carm. iiii eingereihte, inzwischen
von P. Courcelle an Paulinus Pellaeus zurückgegebene Oratio, inc.
Omnipotens genitor, rerum cui summa potestas,[7] in den "Analecta
hymnica" abgedruckt,[8] die freilich den Begriff der "Hymnendichtung" so weit ausgedehnt haben, daß er einschließt, was weder zum
Gebrauch als Hymnus verfaßt noch in solchem Gebrauch gewesen ist.

Um soviel mehr wäre unter Paulinus' Namen ein anderer Text
aufzunehmen gewesen. Ein Cluniacenser Brevier vom Jahre 1686,
desgleichen eines vom Jahre 1693 und eine Victoriner-Handschrift
aus demselben Zeitraum enthalten als Vesper-Hymnus in der Octave
der Epiphanie *Hic reparandarum generator fons animarum* in sechs
Strophen.[9] Als der Verfasser ist Paulinus genannt; jedoch man sucht
sie vergebens unter seinen Carmina (CSEL.XXX ii). Der Text findet
sich, wie auch J. Mearns später gewahr geworden ist,[10] in einem
Schreiben von Paulinus an Severus aus dem Jahre 402,[11] das unter

---

[5] Über Alypius, Paulinus, Ambrosius und Augustinus in ihrem Verhältnis
s. Courcelle, p. 29ss. 216s. 256.

[6] *Analecta hymnica*, L, 1907, p. 47.

[7] *Vigiliae Christianae*, I, 1947, 101-113.

[8] *Analecta hymnica*, L, 1907, p. 48sqq.; in *Ein Jahrtausend Lateinischer
Hymnendichtung*, I, Leipzig 1909, 26ff. nur mehr die Paraphrasen des 1. und
des 2. Psalms.

[9] J(ames) M(earns) in J. Julian, *A Dictionary of Hymnology*, London 1892
(Rev. Ed. 1907), p. 521 s.v. *Hic reparandum* [sic] etc.; U. Chevalier, *Reperto-
rium hymnologicum*, nr. 7828; *ib.* t.V, p. 184; Ch. Kohler, *Catalogue des
manuscrits de la Bibliothèque Sainte-Geneviève*, I, 1893, p. 614 nr. 1326.

[10] J. Julian, *l.c.* (1907) p. 1570.

[11] ep. xxxii ed. Hartel p. 279, von P. Fabre, *Essai sur la chronologie de
l'œuvre de Saint Paulin de Nole*, Paris 1948 (Publications de la Faculté des
lettres de l'Université de Strasbourg. 109) p. 39s.45 datiert 404.

anderen zwei Reihen Disticha enthält, die Paulinus als Tituli für das
Baptisterium des von Severus errichteten Martins-Heiligtumes zu
Primuliacum verfaßt hat. Die ersten drei Disticha sind in ebensoviele vierzeiligen Strophen verwandelt worden, indem, wie auch
sonst gelegentlich verfahren worden ist, ein jeder Vers durch Tei-
lung nach der Penthemimeres in zwei Verse zerlegt wurde:

> Hic reparandarum
> generator fons animarum
> uiuum diuino
> lumine flumen agit. *etc.*

Eine andere Handschrift, aus der ersten Hälfte des XVIII. Jahrhunderts, "Offices et prières relatives aux offices de S. Augustin",
enthält als Hymnus zu den Laudes *Mira dei pietas: peccator mergi-
tur undis, mox idem emergit* etc. in drei Strophen.[12] Der Text ist kein
anderer als die zweite Hälfte (v. 7-12) desselben Titulus, *Hic
reparandarum* etc. Die Lesung *idem* anstelle *eadem* findet sich in
keiner alten Handschrift; sie ist metri gratia hergestellt; *eadem* ist
gesichert.[13]

Beide Hymnen wären vielleicht noch in anderen Drucken oder
Handschriften zu finden, aber wohl nicht vor 1686. Im Jahre 1685
waren, von J.-B. Le Brun herausgegeben, S. Pontii Meropii Paulini
Nolani Episcopi Opera zu Paris erschienen; der vor dem Cluniacenser Brevier vom Jahre 1686 bisher nicht in liturgischem Gebrauch be-
zeugte Text ist mit Wahrscheinlichkeit auf diesen Druck zurückzuführen.[14] Wie dem aber auch sei, er ist ein Beispiel, wie der Gebrauch
eines Textes ihn in ein anderes Genus zu überführen vermag.

*

Mediae noctis tempus est und *Rex aeterne domine*

Caesarius, Bischof zu Arles vom J. 502 bis zu seinem Tode im
J. 542, hat in seiner den 22.VI.534 unterzeichneten "Regula sanc-
tarum uirginum"[15] als *ordo, quo modo psallere debeatis, ex maxima*

---

[12] Chevalier, nr. 29647, der die Doxologie als 4. Strophe zählt; *ib.* t.V,
p. 426; Kohler, I, p. 102s. nr. 163.
[13] A. Huemer, *De Pontii Meropii Paulini Nolani re metrica* (Diss. philol.
Vindobon. VII 1), 1903, p. 21.
[14] *Idem* anstelle *eadem* ist als Lesung Poelmans darin z. St. vermerkt.
[15] Ed. Morin, 1933 (*Florilegium Patristicum* XXXIII), p. 26.

parte secundum regulam monasterii Lyrinensis, vorgeschrieben *ad primos nocturnos ... in fine* Rex aeterne domine *... alia nocte ad primum nocturnum dicendum est* Mediae noctis tempus est.[16] Die Regel des im Anfang des V. Jahrhunderts gegründeten Klosters Lerinum (Lérins) ist selbst nicht erhalten. Caesarius' zweiter Nachfolger Aurelianus, Bischof vom J. 546 bis zu seinem Tode im J. 550, schrieb eine Mönchs- und eine Jungfrauen-Regel mit beinahe gleichlautenden Vorschriften beider für das Officium, aufgrund jener des Caesarius, hat aber als *hymnus ad primos nocturnos* allein "Rex aeterne domine" vorgeschrieben.[17]

Der ungewöhnlichen Formen beider Texte ist Wilhelm Meyer 1882 gewahr geworden und hat sie aufgeführt unter den "jambischen Achtsilbern mit unreinem (fallendem) Schlusse",[18] ohne näher auf sie einzugehn, ist aber nie wieder auf sie zurückgekommen. Als ich die Texte herauszugeben hatte, ergab sich mir, daß ihre "unreinen Schlüsse" Regeln unterliegen.

"Mediae noctis" besteht aus 13 Strophen (ohne die Doxologie).[19] Unter den 52 Zeilen schließen fallend neun: 1, 3 *deo*, 3, 1 *habet*, 4, 3 *erat*, 6, 1 *sumus*, 6, 3 *malum*, 10, 3 *Iesu*, 12, 2 *deus*, 12, 3 *peccatorum*, 13, 3 *mereamur*. Man ersieht, 1) daß alle fallenden Schlüsse, ausgenommen das nomen sacrum *deus*, in ungeraden, und außer 3, 1 und 6, 1 in dritten Zeilen stehn; 2) daß, ausgenommen *peccatorum* und *mereamur*, alle diese Zeilen mit einem zweisilbigen Wort schließen; 3) daß, ausgenommen das nomen sacrum *Iesu* und wiederum die viersilbigen, die vorletzten Silben dieser Wörter Kürzen sind.

Die ungleiche Bildung der Zeilen, indem fallende Schlüsse in ungeraden erlaubt, in geraden verboten sind, erweist Langzeilen, die aus je zwei Achtsilbern bestehn. Dem Verhältnis dritter und erster Kurzzeilen, die fallend schließen (6 : 2), entspricht Sedulius' "A solis ortus cardine" in der Stellung der Reime, indem, anstelle aaaa oder aabb, in fünf Strophen (BEFTV) der dritte Dimeter nicht mitreimt (aaxa).

---

[16] *Ib.* p. 24; Bulst, p. 164.

[17] *Ib.* p. 165.

[18] *Gesammelte Abhandlungen zur mittellateinischen Rythmik*, I, 1905, S. 220f. (VIII 12. 14).

[19] Edd. A. S. Walpole, *Early Latin Hymns*, Cambridge 1922 (Repr. Hildesheim 1956), p. 207ff.; Blume, *Anal. hymn.*, LI, p. 3sq.; Bulst, *l.c.* p. 91; aus dem "Antiphonarium" von Bangor allein: Warren, fol. 11v; E. Franceschini, Padova [1941], p. 25sqq.

Die so bedingte Zulassung zweisilbiger Schlüsse mit vorletzter Kürze (*habet*, nicht *morem*) unter sonst steigenden Achtsilbern läßt ihre metrischen Vorbilder, jambische Dimeter und jambische Quaternare, noch durchscheinen, die vorletzte Kürze im Versschluß unabdingbar fordern, sei er zwei- oder mehrsilbig, *sonat* oder *peruigil*, *uiantibus*, — sodaß alle jambischen Verse mit mehr-als-zweisilbigem Schluß, accent-rhythmisch gelesen, "steigend" schließen.

Unter den 52 Zeilen zählen zwei, 10, 1 *quare uigilemus sobrii* und 11, 1 *noctisque mediae tempore*, neun Silben; auch sie nach dem Vorbild jambischer Dimeter, zumal des Ambrosius, die in thesi und in arsi die Auflösung einer Länge in zwei Kürzen zulassen.

"Rex aeterne domine", in 16 Strophen (ohne die Doxologie),[20] gewährt einen anderen Befund. Unter den 64 Zeilen schließen fallend 6, 1 *baptismum*, 9, 1 *uires*, 10, 1 *semper;* sechs Zeilen, 1, 1.3; 5, 3; 6, 1; 14, 1; 15, 3, zählen sieben Silben; zwei (3, 1; 13, 1) neun. Wiederum aber verteilen sich alle Abweichungen vom steigenden Achtsilber auf ungerade, hier überwiegend (7) erste Zeilen. Wie in "Mediae noctis" besteht also die Strophe aus zwei Langzeilen.

Anders aber als in "Mediae noctis" sind in den drei fallenden Schlüssen die vorletzten Silben lang; auch die beiden zweisilbigen (9, 1 und 10, 1) sind also nicht auf das Vorbild jambischer Dimeter und Quaternare zurückzuführen, außer vielleicht ihre Zweisilbigkeit überhaupt. Von den neunsilbigen Zeilen gilt vielleicht das zu "Mediae noctis" Ausgeführte; hingegen für die siebensilbigen Zeilen gibt es kein Vorbild in Dimetern und Quaternaren.

Die erwiesene Langzeiligkeit beider Texte entspricht einem von W. Meyer erhobenen Befund an den Strophen des Ambrosius und Jüngerer, daß nämlich zwischen dem 2. und dem 3. Dimeter "fast immer eine stärkere Sinnespause steht als zwischen dem 1. und 2. oder zwischen dem 3. und 4." "Allein es ist nur eine Wohlklangsregel, d.h. aus wichtigen Gründen (sic) kann sie verletzt werden",[21] nicht ein metrischer Befund. Aber es gibt auch einen metrischen, von ihm nicht erhobenen Befund: in den 104 Strophen der 13 Hymnen des Ambrosius[22] zähle ich 17 Auflösungen einer Länge in zwei Kürzen

---

[20] Edd. Walpole, p. 212ff.; Blume, *Anal. hymn.*, LI, p. 5sqq.; Bulst, p. 92.
[21] *l.c.* III, S. 7; "Wohlklangsregel" gesperrt von W. M.
[22] Ed. Bulst, p. 37-51.

(wie *fidei repleuit ueritas* in thesi, *martyribus inuentis cano* in arsi),
davon aber 12 im 1. oder 3. Dimeter, nur 5 im 2. oder 4. Das starke
Überwiegen der ungeraden Dimeter gleicht formal dem Vorwiegen
der 1. und 3. Halbzeilen der beiden accent-rhythmischen Texte in
den beschriebenen Freistellungen. Also sind auch die Strophen des
Ambrosius vielmehr als je zwei Tetrameter denn als vier Dimeter zu
verstehn; so hat Beda ihr *metrum* als *iambicum tetrametrum* bezeichnet[23] (indem zwei Jamben *ein* metrum, ῡ – ᴗ –, sind).

—

Christe caeli domine

Mit "Mediae noctis" und "Rex aeterne" wäre auch "Christe caeli
domine"[24] von W. Meyer *l.c.* anzuführen gewesen. Die ungleichen
Schlüsse hat Cl. Blume wortlos hingenommen; auf "die Unebenheiten
in der Silbenzahl der Verse" ist er nicht eigegangen. A. S. Walpole
sah die weniger- oder mehr-als-achtsilbigen Zeilen für "defective
lines", wie auch die fallenden Zeilenschlüsse (darunter zehn Tro-
chäen), für ihn "spondees", für beinahe ebensoviele Verderbnisse an.
Der Text besteht aus 12 vierzeiligen Strophen. Unter ihren 48
Zeilen sind acht Siebensilber, fünf Neunsilber und je ein Sechs- und
Zehnsilber; die übrigen 33 sind Achtsilber. Die Sieben-, Acht- und
Neunsilber schließen steigend oder fallend, Sechs- und Zehnsilber
beide fallend, ohne daß die Anzahl der Silben und steigender oder
fallender Schluß einer Zeile einander ersehbar bedingen.
Die Regel der Unregelmäßigkeiten ergibt sich aus der Verteilung
der acht verschiedenen Zeilenformen auf ungerade (1. und 3.) und
gerade Zeilen.
Unter den 24 geraden Zeilen stehn drei Siebensilber; alle anderen
sind Achtsilber mit steigenden Schlüssen (*maxime, legibus,* etc.).
Dagegen sind unter den 24 ungeraden Zeilen alle acht verschiedenen
Zeilenformen vertreten, am stärksten, durch neun Zeilen, Achtsilber mit fallenden Schlüssen (*aeterni, terra, inmaculatus,* etc.). Die
ungeraden Zeilen sind also nicht weiter geregelt als in der Anzahl
der Silben, von sechs bis zehn: die geraden, ausgenommen drei,
sind es hinsichtlich sowohl der Anzahl der Silben wie ihrer Schlüsse.

---

[23] De arte metrica, cap. xxi, ed. Keil VII, p. 256.
[24] Edd. Blume, *Anal. hymn.,* LI, p. 12sq. (9, 3/4 lies *Qui in nomine dei
uenisti / de excelsis, domine*); Walpole, p. 234ff.; Bulst, p. 108, cf. p. 192sq.
(VIII 4).

Wie "Mediae noctis" und "Rex aeterne" besteht also auch "Christe caeli domine" aus Strophen zu je zwei Langzeilen.

—

Clare sacerdos clues und Mundus iste transibit

Die vom Verfasser der Vita s. Columbani gedichteten und nach Bobbio übersandten *Versus in eius festiuitate ad mensam canendi* hat er selber am Ende des Liber I der Vita mitgeteilt.[25] Wilhelm Meyer hatte gesehen, daß "— wenn die Ueberlieferung verlässig ist — von den 60 Langzeilen nicht weniger als 21 mit einer Kurzzeile von 6 Silben (Sic virtutum décus *oder* Te sofum próceres) beginnen." In der lateinischen Dichtung der Iren ist sonst "die gleiche Silbenzahl der sich entsprechenden Zeilen durchaus sorgfältig gewahrt; denn die Ueberlieferung des Gedichtes des Jonas ist mir sehr verdächtig; es scheint mir ein unvollendeter Entwurf zu sein."[26]

Nun war Ionas, von *Sigusia* (Susa), *quondam Taurinatum colonia*,[27] gebürtig, nicht Ire. Er hätte auch nicht als *uersus canendi* einen "Entwurf" zu solchen übersandt, noch ihn hernach tel quel in seine Vita des Heiligen aufgenommen. Endlich wären in einem Entwurf schwerlich 21 erste Halbzeilen um je eine Silbe zu kurz ausgefallen, zufällig aber keine zweite. Zudem finden sich alle acht steigenden Schlüsse in ersten Halbzeilen; die zweiten schließen sämtlich fallend. Die Überlieferung ist nicht anzuzweifeln.

Die Bestimmung des Textes als *uersus canendi* besagt eine strophische Form. Sie ist auch innerhalb der Vita noch erhalten in Kruschs cod. A 1 a,[28] sein Druck in 60 Langzeilen verdunkelt sie: daß 30 Strophen vorliegen, ist nurmehr an den Reimen abzulesen. Wie verschieden die Reimstellungen auch sind, so ergibt sich doch, daß zweimal zwei Siebensilber, bezw. Sechs- und Siebensilber eine Strophe bilden; jedoch ohne daß alle vier zu reimen brauchen. Die Reime sind ein- oder zweisilbig, auch innerhalb einer Strophe, mit gleichen oder ungleichen intervocalischen und auslautenden Consonanzen oder auch ohne auslautende Consonanz: *-ecus : -euum; -aput :*

---

[25] *Ionae Vitae sanctorum Columbani, Vedastis, Iohannis.* Recogn. Br. Krusch. 1905 (Scr. rer. Germ.), p. 224sqq.

[26] l.c. III, 1936, S. 305. 307.

[27] V. s. Columbani, ed. cit., p. 237.

[28] Ed. cit., p. 224: primus versus littera miniata incipit ac deinceps quartus quisque A 1 a.

-arum; -is : -allis : -anctis : -actis; -a : -a : -as : -a; anstelle Reimes stehn *Omerus : Maro; Ambro : Sicamber.*

Vorbild für Ionas war vielleicht "Mundus iste transibit, cotidie decrescit" des Columbanus,[29] in ebensovielen Strophen, die sämtlich aus zweimal zwei Siebensilbern bestehn. Ihre Form ist von Wilhelm Meyer beschrieben worden als fallende Siebensilber "gemischt" mit steigenden.[30] Jedoch die 63 steigenden und 56 fallenden (27, 1 b ist verderbt) sind nicht in dem Sinne "gemischt", daß ihre Stellung gleichgültig wäre: 11 Langzeilen-Paare schließen in beiden Zeilen fallend, 17 in beiden Zeilen steigend, nur eines (18) "gemischt" *bibere : ridére.* Dagegen von den ersten Langzeilen-Hälften, den ungeraden Siebensilbern, schließen 12 Paare fallend, 9 steigend, 9 ungleich, indem je der zweite fällt (*labitur : seducit*). Also ist gleicher oder ungleicher Halbschluß innerhalb eines Langzeilen-Paares freigestellt, während mit einer Ausnahme beide Langzeilen eines Paares fallend oder beide steigend schließen. Die beiden Siebensilber einer Langzeile schließen weit überwiegend gleich, beide fallend oder beide steigend, ungleich nur in 16 unter den (ohne 27, 1) 59 Langzeilen; in 13 darunter steht am Ende der steigende Schluß, wie in 13, 1 *arescit : deperit* 2 *iuuentus : defecerit.*

Unter den Langzeilen- und Halbzeilen-Paaren zusammen überwiegen die (17 und 9) steigenden Schlüsse die (11 und 12) fallenden im Verhältnis 26 : 23, das ungefähr dem der einzelnen Siebensilber, 63 : 56, entspricht.

Die steigenden Langzeilen-Schlüsse reimen, mit gleichen oder ungleichen intervocalischen Consonanzen, *-edibus : -erimus,* auch *florida : gloria,* dreisilbig, wenigstens "oft" nach Wilhelm Meyer,[31] vielmehr sämtlich; er hat in 3 *subripit : corripit,* 7 *colligere : credere,* 16 *species : pernicies,* 20 *libidinem : dulcedinem* den von ihm selbst in vielen Texten seit Venantius Fortunatus nachgewiesenen "Reim mit den drei Vocalen",[32] a + (e = i) + (o = u) übersehen.

Die fallenden Langzeilen-Schlüsse reimen "meistens" zweisilbig,[31] nämlich 9 unter den 11 (in 25 *retinetur : sititur* mit e = i).

---

[29] Edd. Gundlach, MGH., Epp. III, p. 188sq. Blume, *Anal. hymn.* LI, p. 352sqq.; G. S. M. Walker, *Sancti Columbani Opera,* Dublin 1957 (Scr. lat. Hiberniae. II), p. 182sqq. 28,2 ist zu emendieren *Quam nec mortis meroris metus...;* cf. 3, 2 *meror mortis.*

[30] *l.c.,* III, S. 305.

[31] *ib.* III, 317.

[32] *ib.* III, 284-302.

Die Ausnahmen sind 1 *decrescit* : *remansit,* und 5 *uix audent* : *-is habent;* reimen hier in Vertretung der vorletzten Silben die drittletzten?

Columbanus' Verfasserschaft an "Mundus iste peribit" ist unmöglich mit J. F. Kenney[33] darum anzuzweifeln, daß die vier übrigen Dichtungen metrisch verfaßt sind; unter den mehr als einhundert Carmina des Sedulius Scottus stehn als einzige Ausnahme die *rithmici uersiculi,* II lviii,[34] auch sie in Strophen zu je zweimal zwei Siebensilbern.

"Die Beobachtung der gleichen Schlußcadenz ist bei den Iren lange nicht so streng wie die Beobachtung der gleichen Silbenzehl."[35] Das Umgekehrte gilt von Ionas: er hat in "Clare sacerdos" sowohl in ungeraden Halbzeilen auch 6 anstelle 7 Silben zugelassen, wie den fallenden Schluß der Langzeilen ohne eine Ausnahme durchgeführt.

Einander gegenüber stehn mit ungleicher Silbenzahl, aber gleichen Schlüssen auf der einen Seite "Rex aeterne domine" und Ionas' "Clare sacerdos clues", auf der anderen "Mediae noctis tempus est" und Columbanus' "Mundus iste transibit', mit gleicher Silbenzahl, aber ungleichen Schlüssen.

Nach der angeführten Regel Wilhelm Meyers steht "Mediae noctis" auf der irischen Seite. Den Text überliefert als älteste der erhaltenen Handschriften das "Antiphonar" von Bangor; seinen liturgischen Gebrauch bezeugt schon im J.534 Caesarius für Arles. Über das Jahrhundert irischer Kirchengeschichte von ihrem ältesten Datum, der Bestellung und Entsendung des Bischofs Palladius *Ad Scottos in Christum credentes* im J.431[36], bis zum J.534 sind wir weitaus zu unwissend, um den Weg eines *hymnus* vom Continent in die irische Kirche für wahrscheinlicher anzusehen als den umgekehrten. Von den übrigen *hymni,* die Caesarius und Aurelianus vorgeschrieben haben, ist keiner in irischem Gebrauch nachgewiesen.

—

[33] J. F. Kenney, *The Sources for the Early History of Ireland,* New York 1929 (Repr. Shannon 1968), p. 194f.

[34] MGH., Poetae III, p. 215sq. Dazu R. Düchting, *Sedulius Scottus. Seine Dichtungen,* München 1968, S. 166f.

[35] Wilhelm Meyer, III, S. 307.

[36] Prosper Tiro, Epit. chron., a. 431, ed. Mommsen, MGH., Auct. ant. IX, p. 473.

Ignis creator igneus und *Sancti uenite*

"Ignis creator" ist erhalten im Antiphonar von Bangor (A) und einer Bobbieser Handschrift (B).[37] Blume hat ihn als "wohl irischen" Ursprunges in die Hymnodia Hiberno-Celtica eingereiht und ihn in das "6. oder gar 5. Jahrhundert" datiert. Entschieden widersprochen hat Wilhelm Meyer: "irisch kann er nicht sein. Denn er ist noch quantitirend gebaut".[38] Das Metrum der Strophen hat er beschrieben als "eine überhaupt noch nicht erkannte Spielart:" "jambische Dimeter mit altlateinischem Bau; von 32 Zeilen haben 18 [vielmehr 21] in der 2. Senkung eine Länge." Die "Spielart" war schon sonst erkannt und auch benannt, nämlich als jambische Quaternare, die sich von wirklichen Dimetern unterscheiden wie jambische Senare von jambischen Trimetern, indem in allen Jamben, ausgenommen je den letzten, also auch dem 2. und, im Senar, auch dem 4., Länge der ersten Silbe erlaubt ist, also nicht je zwei Jamben ein *metrum* bilden wie in Dimetern und in Trimetern.

Noch finden sich drei Längen-Auflösungen, in arsi oder in thesi, sogar eine Elision. Gegen das Metrum verstoßen allein die Kürzen *hŏminem, ălitus* (A; *hālitus* B) und *quŏd inluminas.* Die Anzahl der Strophen, acht, ist ambrosianisch.

Nur fünf unter den 32 Quaternaren schließen mit einem zweisilbigen Wort, davon vier in ungeraden, 1. oder 3. Zeilen. Nun bewirken mehr-als-zweisilbige Schlüsse jambischer Verse[39] *eo ipso,* daß dieselben Verse, accent-rhythmisch gehört (*cónditor, fastídium*), "steigend" schließen. Wenn auch von "Ignis creator" anzunehmen ist, daß je zwei Quaternare eine Langzeile bilden, so ergeben sich 15 "steigende" Schlüsse in 16 Versen.

Der im Antiphonar von Bangor voraufgehende Hymnus "Sancti, uenite, corpus Christi sumite"[40] scheint ebenso gewiß dem jambischen Senar "rythmisch nachgebildet",[41] wie "Ignis creator" "noch" metrisch ist; in den 22 zweizeiligen Strophen sind nicht weniger als 22 (2., 6., 8., 10.) Silben in arsi kurz. Davon sind fünf entschuldigt: *dominus* (5, 1; 9, 1; 11, 1, je im Versschluß) als nomen sacrum,

---

[37] Edd. Walpole, p. 346ff.; aus A: Warren, I, fol. 11r/v, Blume, *Anal. hymn.*, LI, p. 266sq., Franceschini, p. 23ff.

[38] III, S. 325.

[39] Einbegriffen *maior est* oder *commota sit.*

[40] Edd. Warren, I, fol. 10v/11r; Blume, *Anal. hymn.*, LI, p. 298sq.; Walpole, p. 344ff.; Franceschini, p. 22f.

[41] W. Meyer, III, S. 304.

esŭrientibus, sĭtientibus (11, 1.2) als biblisches Citat (Ioh.vi 35). Von
den übrigen 17 metrisch "falschen" Kürzen sind nicht weniger als
14 letzte Silben eines Wortes bezw. einsilbige Wörter (3, 1 *ab*, 10, 1
dat) oder einsilbiges Praefix (6,2 *ad-*). Daß damit ebenso viele Zufälle
vorliegen, ist unwahrscheinlich. Hier ist, kaum zum ersten oder einzigen Male, von der *productio finalium in arsi* in einem jambischen
Metrum sogar erweiterter Gebrauch gemacht. Gegen das Metrum
verstoßen, wie in "Ignis creator', drei Kürzen in arsi, *săluti, quoque,
hominum.*

Daß keine productio auch vierter Silben stattfindet, ergibt sich,
indem die Caesur des Trimeters und Senars nach der 5. Silbe, wenn
sie überhaupt wie von Prudentius in Cathem. VII durchgeführt
wird, kaum ein einsilbiges Wort als 5. Silbe zuläßt.[42] Daß keine productio 10. Silben stattfindet, ergibt sich, indem, ausgenommen 2, 2
-us dei und 4, 1 *-us dei*, 20 unter 22 Versen mit einem drei-oder-
mehrsilbigen Wort, accent-rhythmisch also "steigend" schließen.

Die *productio finalium* hat als solche metrischen Sinn. Für die
unter dem Ictus gedehnten Silben ist es gleichgültig, ob auf sie der
"natürliche" Accent (oder Neben-Accent) fällt oder, wie öfter,
nicht. "Steigende" Schlüsse sind, wie schon gesagt, vollkom-
men vereinbar mit metrischem Vers-Schluß. "Sancti uenite" ist
nicht weniger als "Ignis creator" "noch" metrisch, auch in einem
anderen als dem von W. Meyer gemeinten chronologischen Sinn.
Die Strophe besteht aus zwei Senaren.

Auf die von W. Meyer zu "Ignis creator" ohne ein begründendes
Wort vorgetragene These "quantitirend, also nicht irisch" hat schon
J. F. Kenney entgegnet: It is at least possible, however, that there
were clerics in Ireland as well as on the Continent in the fifth or sixth
century who could write simply classical verse.[43] Ein Grund, für
"Ignis creator" (und "Sancti uenite") continentale Herkunft zu
vermuten, besteht nicht.

—

Precamur patrem. Celebra Iuda. Audite fratres

Die Strophe zu zwei Senaren ist, indirect oder direct, auf Hilarius' "Liber hymnorum" zurückzuführen, wo sie in "Fefellit saeuam

---

[42] Die verschwindenden Ausnahmen in Cathem. VII (220 v.) sind 171 *et*,
180 *est*, 206 *sic*.
[43] P. 262.

uerbum factum te caro"[44] zuerst begegnet. In der lateinischen Dichtung der Iren ist sie "rythmisch nachgebildet" auch weiterhin vertreten. Solche Nachbildungen sind erhalten in drei Texten: "Precamur patrem regem omnipoténtem",[45] "Celebra Iuda festa Christi gaudia",[46] "Audite fratres facta sine crimine".[47]

W. Meyer hat seine Bemerkungen dazu beschränkt auf ihre Reime und Alliteration;[48] ihre Rhythmik wäre mit seinem schon angeführten, allgemein "irischen" Befund: strenge Einhaltung der Silbenzahl, nicht aber der Accent-Rhythmik der Schlüsse, nur zu "allgemein" beschrieben. Die Nachbildung des Trimeters und Senars besteht in einer zwölfsilbigen Zeile, die vor dem Einschnitt nach der 5. Silbe fallend und am Ende steigend schließt, wie die angeführten "Celebra" und "Audite".

"Precamur patrem" besteht aus 84 Zeilen in 42 Strophen. Davon schließen 23, mehr als ein Viertel, fallend, somit "falsch" (darunter beinahe die Hälfte (10) mit einem zweisilbigen Wort[49]). Diese unregelmäßigen Schlüsse verteilen sich auf 1. und 2. Zeilen im Verhältnis 15 : 8. Jedoch indem davon 5 mal je 2 auf eine Strophe entfallen, entscheiden über den Vorzug der 1. oder 2. Zeile die übrigen 13 Schlüsse; sie verteilen sich auf 1. und 2. Zeilen im Verhältnis 10 : 3. Es ergibt sich, daß unregelmäßige Schlüsse zweiter Zeilen zwar nicht vermieden, aber deutlich gemieden sind.

Die relative Anzahl der fallenden Schlüsse in "Celebra Iuda", 44 Zeilen in 22 Strophen, ist nicht ebenso hoch (9). Sie verteilen sich auf 1. und 2. Zeilen im Verhältnis 6 : 3. In zwei Strophen schließen beide Zeilen fallend; von den 5 übrigen, entscheidenden Schlüssen

---

[44] Ed. W. Meyer, III, S. 158ff.; Bulst, p. 33sq. — carmina epigraphica, die aus zwei oder drei oder mehr Senaren bestehn, sind nicht Strophen. Die continental verbreitete Strophe zu fünf Senaren (seit Cathem. VII und Perist. X des Prudentius und Orientius' "Orationes", CSEL.XVI 1, p. 251sqq.) ist in der lateinischen Dichtung der Iren nicht vertreten.
[45] Edd. Warren, fol. 4v-6v; Blume, *Anal. hymn.* LI, p. 271sqq.; Franceschini, p. 10ss. — Kenney, p. 262: not later than the sixth century.
[46] Edd. Bernard and Atkinson, *The Irish Liber Hymnorum*, I, p. 18ff.; Blume, *l.c.*, p. 308sqq. — Kenney, p. 266: hardly of earlier date than the seventh century.
[47] Edd. Blume, *l.c.*, p. 337ff.; Esposito, *Proc. of the Royal Irish Academy*, XXVIII, C, p. 242ff. 1, 1 *sine crimine* scr. Bl.; *sine ullo crimine* cod., cf. 2, 1. — Kenney, p. 371: composed... in the eighth, or possibly seventh, century.
[48] III, S. 316f., 321f., 324f., 327.
[49] Solche zweisilbigen "falschen" Schlüsse sind also nicht so "selten zu finden", wie W. Meyer (III, S. 319) gemeint hat.

entfallen 4 auf 1. Zeilen, einer auf eine zweite. Das Ergebnis entspricht "Precamur patrem".

In "Audite fratres", 48 Zeilen in 24 Strophen, schließen, wie in "Celebra Iuda", 9 Zeilen fallend, davon 8 in 4 Strophen gepaart; die allein übrige ist eine zweite Zeile. Aber anders als in "Precamur" und "Celebra", wo die Verhältnisse 10 : 3 und 4 : 1 eine Regel der Unregelmäßigkeit besagen, ist aus dem Verhältnis 0 : 1 *eo ipso* eine (umgekehrte) "Regel" nicht mehr zu entnehmen.

—

metrum iambicum tetrametrum

Wie schon angeführt, hat Beda die herkömmlich als vier Dimeter angesehene (und in vier Zeilen gedruckte) sogen. "ambrosianische" Strophe als zwei Tetrameter verstanden.[50] Es wäre von jeher nahe gelegen zu fragen, ob die 206 "ambrosianischen" Strophen seiner eigenen hymni[51] nicht selbst sich als aus je zwei Tetrametern bestehend erweisen.

Unter den 416 Dimetern des Ambrosius schließen 138 mit einem zweisilbigen Wort, unter den 36 Senaren des Hilarius (inc. *Fefellit saeuam*) 14, unter den 1140 Trimetern in Prudentius' Perist. X zählte ich 341 solche Schlüsse, — ersichtlich zufällige Verhältnisse. Unter den 824 jambischen "Dimetern" Beda's endigen 56 zweisilbig, sodaß alle übrigen (768) zugleich accent-rhythmisch "steigend" schließen, — ersichtlich sind accent-rhythmisch "fallende" Schlüsse in Beda's "Dimetern" zwar nicht vermieden, aber gemieden. Aber 46 unter den 56 "fallenden" Schlüssen finden sich in ungeraden (1. und 3.) "Dimetern". Indem in ihnen sechs Mal soviel solche Schlüsse zugelassen sind wie in den geraden, erweisen sie sich als erste Tetrameter-Hälften, und ihre Schlüsse als entsprechend freier gestellte Halb-Schlüsse.

—

Die aus den untersuchten Texten, ausgenommen "Sancti uenite" und "Audite fratres", erhobenen Befunde haben gemein, daß ihre Unregelmäßigkeiten sich vielmehr als Freistellungen der Silben-

---

[50] Oben S. 88.

[51] Ed. Fraipont, CC., CXXII 405sqq. Nicht von Beda verfaßt sind I 29sqq. IV. V. VI 17a; vgl. W. B., *Zeitschrift für deutsches Altertum*, LXXXIX, 1959, 83ff.

Anzahlen und Schlüsse erster Halbzeilen oder erster Zeilen zweizeiliger Strophen erweisen, die in zweiten Halbzeilen oder zweiten Zeilen zweizeiliger Strophen selten oder überhaupt nicht begegnen. Diese Freistellungen sind nicht ableitbar als mögliche Consequenz aus den Formen der Texte.

Die Texte selbst haben gemein ihre Bestimmung und ihr längst verstummtes Da-Sein als geistliche Gesangs-Dichtung, *hymni* und *uersus canendi*, nicht Lese-Literatur, ausgenommen vielleicht "Mundus iste" des Columbanus,[52] an einen darin angesprochenen *amicus*, *filiolus*, *carissimus* (*noli*, *scito*, *conspice*, etc.). Die Frage nach der *ratio* der Freistellungen, aber auch der accent-rhythmischen Schlüsse überhaupt, ist an die historische Musik-Wissenschaft zu richten, als Frage nach ihrer *ratio musica*.

—

Iam dulcis amica uenito

Der chronologisch vorgesehene Umfang unserer Beiträge, A. D. 400-900, würde nicht übertreten sein, wenn die Datierung des "most famous of all the Cambridge Songs"[53] in das IX. Jahrhundert[54] Recht behält. G. M. Dreves hat "Iam dulcis amica uenito" in die "Analecta hymnica" aufgenommen;[55] man mag es mit seinem liebenswürdigen Mißverständnis entschuldigen, daß die folgende Untersuchung diese "Hymnologica" beschließt.

Die Handschriften des Liedes unterscheiden sich in Anzahl und Folge der Strophen, dargestellt im Verhältnis zu ihrer Zählung in K. Streckers Edition der "Carmina Cantabrigiensia",[56] wie folgt (und werden weiterhin danach angeführt):

   ed. Str.   1. 2. 3. 5. 4. 6. [6a]. [6b][57]. 7. 8. 9. 10

---

[52] In gleichen Strophen verfaßt sind Anal. hymn. LI, p. 328: *Martine*; p. 351: *Pro peccatis*; p. 326: (*Benchuir bona regula*) *Munther Benchuir beata*.

[53] F. J. E. Raby, *A History of Secular Latin Poetry in the Middle Ages*, II, Oxford 1934, p. 310f.

[54] Fedor Schneider, *Fünfundzwanzig lateinische weltliche Rhythmen aus der Frühzeit*, Rom 1925 (Texte zur Kulturgeschichte des Mittelalters. 1), S.X.

[55] XI, 1891, p. 57sq. ("Ad Beatam Mariam V."), zufolge der Eintragung des Textes in ein Troparium (S. Michaelis Lemovic., Paris. lat. 1118).

[56] Ed. sec., Berolini 1955 (MGH. Scr. rer. Germ. XL), p. 69sqq. (zuerst 1926); in meiner Ausgabe, Heidelberg 1950 (Ed. Heidelbergenses. 17), p. 52sqq.

[57] Die allein in den beiden älteren Handschriften, nicht in C erhaltenen Strophen 6a und 6b hat Strecker darum unter den var. lect. gedruckt.

C saec. XI   1. 2. 3. 4. 5. 6. 7. 8. 9. 10
V saec. X   1. 2. 3. 5. 4. 8. 10. 6. 6b. 9
P saec. X ex. 1. 2. 3. 5. 4. 6. 6a

Die Form der Strophen ist weder von W. Meyer noch von K. Strecker eingehend untersucht worden. W. Meyer sprach davon als einem Gedicht, "dessen Rythmus ich noch nicht erkannt habe. ... Die Einmischung daktylischen oder anapästischen Tonfalls scheint regelmäßig zu sein."[58] Er ist nicht mehr darauf zurückgekommen. K. Strecker äußerte: "Die rhythmische Form ist sonst nicht belegt. ... Eigenartig ist der Tonfall, mir scheint, daß es rhythmische Anapäste sein sollen."[59]

Nachdem Str. 7 ganz, 6, 4 und 10, 2 nicht mehr herstellbar sind, verbleiben zur Untersuchung 42 Zeilen. Unter ihnen sind 33 Neunsilber, 7 Zehnsilber,[60] 2 Achtsilber.[61] Ihre Schlüsse fallen (wie 1, 1 *uenito*) oder steigen (wie 1, 2 *diligo*) unabhängig von der Anzahl der Silben einer Zeile; daß beide Achtsilber fallend schließen, besagt noch nicht eine "Regel". Unter den Zehnsilbern überwiegen die steigenden Schlüsse, unter den Neunsilbern die fallenden, in den Verhältnissen 5 : 2 und 28 : 4.[62] So besteht "Iam dulcis amica" aus fünferlei Zeilen; in der vierzeiligen Strophe finden sich bis zu dreierlei, ohne Regel ihrer Folge.[63]

Die sogen. accent-rhythmischen Strophen sind geregelt hinsichtlich der gleichen Anzahl der Silben einer Zeile und ihres gleichen, sei es fallenden oder steigenden Schlusses, nicht hinsichtlich des Falles der Accente *vor* dem Zeilen-Schluß; daß die für den Übergang von der metrischen zur accent-rhythmischen Dichtung gerne angenommene "sostituzione dell'accento all'*ictus*" gar nicht stattgefunden hat, ist längst erwiesen.[64]

Hingegen der Fall der Accente in den fünferlei Zeilen des "Iam dulcis amica" ist schon *vor* ihren verschiedenen Schlüssen gleich geregelt: der vorletzte Accent einer "fallend" schließenden Zeile

---

[58] I, 1905, S. 228 (1882).
[59] Ed. cit., p. 72, mit Verweisung auf W. Meyer.
[60] 5, 1.2.3; 6a, 3; 6b, 3.4; 8, 1.
[61] 4, 4; 10, 3.
[62] Zu 4, 3 s. unten Anm. 65.
[63] Über die hinsichtlich der Anzahl ihrer (gleichen) Zeilen "ungleichen Strophen" vgl. W. B., in der *Festschrift Percy Ernst Schramm*, I, Wiesbaden 1964, S. 434ff.
[64] Vgl. W. Meyer, III, 1936, S. 1ff. (1906).

fällt auf ihre fünftletzte Silbe (*dócta puélla*), der einer "steigend"
schließenden auf ihre sechstletzte (*áltius tíbie*).

Diesen fünf oder sechs accent-rhythmisch geregelten Silben gehn
voraus 3 oder 4 oder 5 Silben, jedoch ohne daß eine Zeile mehr als
zehn Silben zählt; also nicht 5 vor sechs:

4, 4 diuersis | poculis plenas
2, 2 atque uelis | domus parata
5, 3 ibi puer et | docta puella
3, 1 est ibi | mensa apposita
8,1 non me iuuat | tantum conuiuium.

Der Fall der Accente in diesen 3 oder 4 oder 5 Silben befolgt keine
Regel; daß auf die je letzte kein syntaktischer Accent fällt, ist bei
der Seltenheit, daß lateinisch zwei syntaktische Accente nebeneinander stehn, nicht als eine "Regel" anzusprechen.

Die Accent-Fälle der fünf oder sechs folgenden Silben sind bekannt als die des cursus planus und cursus tardus der Prosa,
(*prod-, inter-)esse uidetur* und *.. uidebitur*.[65]

Die so oft nicht befolgte Regel des strengen planus und tardus,
daß ihre erste Senkung die letzte Silbe eines Wortes sein soll, wie in
esse, ist auch hier in einem Viertel der 42 Zeilen nicht eingehalten:
4, 4 *poculis plenas* (so acht Mal), 1, 2 *cor meum diligo*, 9, 2 *post
facienda*, 8, 4 *familiaritas*.

Die von W. Meyer, der den Cursus nicht erkannt hatte, genannten
"eingemischten" Accent-Daktylen und -Anapäste lassen beide sich
finden, Daktylen, indem die tardi aus zwei Daktylen zu bestehn, die
plani mit einem Daktylus zu beginnen scheinen, und wo immer unter
den vier dem Cursus vorausgehnden Silben der erste Accent auf die
zweite Silbe fällt, wie in *Iam dúlcis a|mica*, 2, 3 *florésque in | domo*, 9,2
que súnt tamen | post, und Anapäste entsprechend, wo immer unter
vier vorausgehnden Silben er auf die dritte Silbe fällt, wie in 1, 4
ornaméntis, 2, 2 *atque uélis*, 6, 2 *et diléxi*, 6b, 3 *sine té non;* wo aber
fünf Silben vorausgehn, wie in 5, 3 *ibi puer et | docta puella* und 6a, 3
philomena iam | cantat in alto, lassen sich ebensowohl drei Anapäste
wie zwei Daktylen zählen.

---

[65] Der Accent-Fall des planus scheint nicht eingehalten in 4,2 *illa melos
cum lira pangit* und 4,3 *portantque ministri pateras*. Der Text (PVC) ist nicht
anzuzweifeln. In 4, 3 ist sehr wahrscheinlich zu lesen *patēras* (nach *cratēras* ?).
4,2 *cum lira*, mit einem zweisilbigen Wort in der Senkung des cursus, wie
sonst nur *cór meum diligo*, ist vielleicht hienach entschuldbar, zumal im
gesanglichen Verlauten, das nicht "scandiert", wie ein Leser.

K. Strecker hörte keine Daktylen heraus, oder hinein; "mir scheint, daß es rhythmische Anapäste sein sollen". Worin sah er "sein sollende" Anapäste ? indem es dem Verfasser nicht gelungen wäre, Anapäste durchzuführen ? oder er sie durchzuführen nicht "beabsichtigte" ?[66]

Die Anzahlen der Daktylen oder Anapäste schwanken beinahe von Zeile zu Zeile: ein bis zu drei Daktylen, oder ein bis zu drei Anapäste, innerhalb einer und derselben Zeile aber, je nachdem ob man Daktylen oder Anapäste zählt, 2 D. oder 2 A., wie in *iam dúlcis amica uenito*, 3 D. oder 2 A., wie in *iam décet amorem perficere*, 1 D. oder 2 A., wie in *uniuérsis cibis honusta*, und so weiter in wieder anderen Verhältnissen. Ersichtlich ist es auf Daktylen oder auf Anapäste nicht abgesehen und nicht angekommen.

Alle Zeilen aber haben gemein *drei Hebungen*, die beiden des cursus planus oder tardus, und eine ihnen vorhergehende. Der ersten Hebung geht keine oder eine oder zwei Senkungen voraus, wie 1, 3 *intra in cubiculum*, 5,4, 6a,2, 8,2; *Iam dúlcis;* 1, 4 *ornaméntis;* zwischen die ersten und zweiten Hebungen fallen ein bis drei Senkungen, wie 1, 2 *quam sícut cór*, 1, 1 *Iam dúlcis amica*, 6a, 2 *fólium et hérba;* zwischen der zweiten und dritten, gemäß dem cursus planus und tardus, regelmäßig zwei; nach der dritten, gemäß dem planus oder tardus, eine oder zwei, *amíca* oder *díligo*.

Von den sonst, nach ihren entweder steigenden oder fallenden Schlüssen, "accent-rhythmisch" genannten Zeilen gleicher Silbenzahl unterscheidet sich "Iam dulcis amica" von Grund auf durch die Zählung der Hebungen und, aus der "Senkungsfreiheit" erfolgende, ungleiche Silbenzahl der Zeilen.

Den Reim der Zeilenpaare hat K. Strecker nicht näher beschrieben denn als "einsilbig, zuweilen auch zweisilbig" (S. 72). Es fällt auf, daß die zweisilbigen, anders als 6a, 3.4 *in alto : in antro*, "reimen", auch consonantischen Reime, ausgenommen 6b, 3.4 *uiuere : perficere*, in sieben ersten Zeilenpaaren (der Strophen 2, 4, 5, 6a, 6b, 8, 10: -*ata*, -*ie*, -*angit*, -*escit*, -*are*, -*ium*, -*ecta*) stehn, als hätten sie zunächst einmal unüberhörber ins Ohr fallen sollen.

Als W. Meyer seine alte Frage nach "Anfang und Ursprung der lateinischen und griechischen rythmischen Dichtung"[67] noch einmal

---

[66] Cf. ed. tit. p. XXII l. 23.
[67] II, 1905, S. 1ff. (1885).

aufnahm, hat er als "Eintritt des rythmischen Schlusses in die rythmische Dichtung" sich vorgestellt, "daß die rythmischen Dichter ... bestimmte Cadenzen annahmen, wie solche in der Prosa allgemein üblich waren",[68] — ohne etwa den steigenden Schluß als Reduction eines cursus tardus (*esse vi|débitur*), den fallenden als eine des planus oder velox anzusehen. Jedoch auch die von ihm angenommene Vorbildlichkeit des cursus überhaupt ist ganz unwahrscheinlich; keinesfalls aber wäre "Iam dulcis amica" dafür anzuführen, nachdem der Übergang von metrischen versus zu accentrhythmischen Zeilen vor Jahrhunderten schon vollzogen war. "Iam dulcis amica" steht für sich allein, wie andere Texte desgleichen.

---

[68] III, 1936, S. 26 (1906).

STUDIES IN THE VOCABULARY OF THE
SACRAMENTARIUM VERONENSE

JOHN HENNIG

Whatever may have been their status, their source(s) or the date and place of their compilation, whoever may have been their author(s) or compiler(s) and whatever part(s) of the Church they may represent or originate from, the libelli in ms. Verona, Bibl. Capit. LXXXV, formerly known as *Sacramentarium Leonianum*,[1] are *eine unschätzbare Sammlung*.[2] This fact has become even more obvious since the collapse of the tradition of which they have been the earliest collective record.[3]

The importance of this collection, henceforth referred to as V, has been recognised by the compilation of a word-index. In fact, this word-index has been compiled twice: In P. Bruylant's *Concordance verbale du Sacramentaire Léonien (Archivum Latinitatis Medii Aevi* 18 (1945) 51-376 and 19 (1948) 39-405), also separately in one volume (Louvain, s.d., 679 p.), based on C. L. Feltoe's edition (Cambridge 1896), and in C. Mohlberg's edition of *Sacramentarium Veronense (Leonianum)* in *Rerum Ecclesiasticarum Documenta, Series major: Fontes* I (Rome 1956) 235-438. This duplication is the more remarkable as the further volumes in *Rerum Ecclesiasticarum Documenta: Fontes*, in particular the edition of *Sacramentarium Gelasianum* (1960),[4] contain only lists of liturgical formulae, as did H. Wilson's *Classified Index to the Leonine, Gelasian and Gregorian Sacramentaries according to the texts of Muratori's Liturgia Romana Vetus* (Cambridge 1892). H. Lietzmann's edition of *Sacramentarium Gregorianum nach dem Aachener Urexamplar* (Münster 1921, reprint 1958) contained a *Wortregister* (p. 132-176), but in the absence of a word-index to the Gelasianum it is hard to link together the existing indexes to Veronense and Gregorianum.

---

[1] For literature see K. Gamber, *Sakramentartypen* (Beuron 1958) 48f. and *Codices liturgici latini antiquiores* (Freiburg 1963) 110f.

[2] A. Baumstark, *Missale Romanum* (Eindhoven 1929) 30.

[3] C. Mohlberg (see below) p. xvi.

[4] Also P. Siffrin, *Konkordanztabellen zu den römischen Sakramentarien* (Rom. 1959).

The indexes to V are the basis of any investigation into the history
of Latin liturgical terminology. The present study rests upon the
conviction that studies in the history of liturgical terminology must
take into account — at least implicitly — the entire tradition, because they come into their own only when one considers their subject
as a living tradition. The present paper continues earlier studies of
mine in the vocabularium proprium of the Missale Pauli VI with
reference to that of its predecessor[5] and of the latter with regard to
the Vulgate[6] (Vulg.). In my list, words still found in Missale Romanum 1963 (R) (according to A. Pflieger's Concordance)[7] or in other
liturgical books still in use at that time (so far as I could establish
from my own indexes) will be italicized. Each entry will show how
many times the word occurs in V, and if this figure is italicized, the
word in question does not occur in Gelasianum/Gregorianum (G/Gr).

It would have exceeded the space available to quote for each
word the context in which it occurs. Contexts are stated — different
in extent though — in the indexes to V, to Gr and to R; I have
confined myself to instances which I considered as relevant to the
history of terminology apart from the strictly technical one.
Thesaurus started quoting V from the word exuberantia; it has not
advanced beyond letter O.[8] Italicization of the abbreviation ThLL
means that the instance in question is quoted in ThLL. A. Souter,
Glossary of later Latin (Oxf. 1949) lists words or meanings appearing
after 180 A.D. In my list, words prefaced by an asterisk are words
listed by Souter. With very few exceptions (adcumulo, adscisco,
atrocitas, calliditas etc.), words in my list are found in A. Blaise-
H. Chivat, *Dictionnaire Latin-Français des auteurs chrétiens* (Paris
1954). The lists of sources in both Souter and Blaise-Chivat mention V. For indiffidenter, V is the only source quoted by ThLL and

---

[5] *Heiliger Dienst* 35 (1971) 156-161.
[6] *Ephemerides Liturgicae*, 81 (1967) 131-135.
[7] (Rome 1964). Texts from Pontificale Romanum have always been
specified in my list, e.g., Cons. Episc. or Ord. Diac.
[8] ThLL, of course, has all the words listed by me. In my list I have referred
to ThLL only in special instances. Among the sources of F. Arnaldi, *Latinitatis Italicae Medii Aevi Lexicon imperfectum* (Brussels 1939, addenda 1967),
sacramentaries are not listed. J. F. Niermeyer, *Medii Latinitatis Lexicon
novum* (Leiden 1954ff.) — available up to letter V — is excellent for legal
terms, such as *actio, censura, credulitas, documentum, interdictum, legalis,
patronus, praesul, provisio, regimen, relaxo* and *tenor*; in these articles and
others on words found in our list, only in that on *impetitor*, so far as I can
see, reference is made to V.

by Blaise-Chivat (this word is not listed by Arnaldi, Souter, and Niermeyer). After letter O I occasionally refer to Georges's Latin dictionary. Outside technical terms, such as apostolicus, commercium is, to my knowledge, the only word in my list on the liturgical use of which a monographical study is extant.[9] A. Blaise's *Vocabulaire Latin des principaux thèmes liturgiques* (Turnhout 1966) is a systematic study in liturgical terminology (drawing also on sacramentaries other than V, G and Gr).

Where Blaise (B) quotes V, the number relating to the paragraph in his work has been italicized in my list.

Blaise referred to the Vulgate only. The card-index to Vetus Latina at the Beuron Institute has not yet progressed beyond Genesis. My thanks are due to that Institute for assisting me in culling from its Index the few instances relevant to my list, i.e., of words occurring in both Vetus Latina and V but not in Vulg. A few further Vetus Latina instances were obtained from ThLL. In all these respects the fragmentary character of my investigation reflects the state of studies in this field at large. The purpose of my paper is to encourage studies in the position of V within the history of Latinity and in the theological and philosophical contents[10] of V of which the vocabularium proprium is an expression.

So far as some general conclusions can be drawn at this stage, they corroborate conclusions drawn from earlier investigations in this field.

The words listed by me may be grouped by
a) their meaning

---

[9] M. Herz, *Sacrum commercium. Eine begriffsgeschichtliche Studie zur Theologie der römischen Liturgiesprache* (München 1958). P. 226 index of terms incl. actio, deitas, essentia, insolentia, paschalis, restauratio and spiritalis. See however also M. P. Ellebracht, *Remarks on the vocabulary of the ancient orations of the Roman Missal* (thesis Nymegen 1964, with valuable bibliography), where actio, apostolicus, catholicus, commercium, credulitas, dispositor, expedio, frequentatio, glorificatio, immolatio, incarnatio, incessanter, intercessio, intercessor, interventio, (in)visibiliter, largitor, martyrium, medicatio, medicinalis, natalicia, perceptio, pontificalis, sacro, salubriter, salutifer, suffragium and vitiosus are dealt with.

[10] C. Callewaert, *S. Léon le Grand et les textes du Léonien* (Bruges 1948) contains only an index of liturgical formulae, see however M. M. Mueller, *The vocabulary of Pope Leo the Great* (*Patristic Studies* 67, Washington D.C., 1943). By incorporating into his booklet *Sursum Corda* (Salzburg 1954) texts and German translations of 13 prefaces from V, A. Dold tried to draw attention to this source of Christian thought.

1. words denoting ecclesiastical persons or derivations from such words: apostolicus, diaconium, episcopalis....

2. theological and ecclesiological terms: catholicus, coaeternus, consempiternitas....

b) their formation

1. abstracts ending in -tio: abolitio, actio, admonitio...., -tas: adversitas, atrocitas, calliditas..., and -um: adjumentum, collegium, commercium....

2. terms denoting factor: adsertor, captor, conlator... (see, however, already the Vulgate words: liberator, miserator, redemptor...)

3. adverbs, in particular those derived from present participles: affluenter, competenter, congruenter..., those the basic adjective of which occurs in the Vulgate: fallaciter, (in)visibiliter... and the comparatives: decentius, desiderabilius, enixius...

As 4. we may add the large number of negatives formed by the prefix in-.

Groups b 1-4 represent mental developments of which we may now become more conscious as they are no longer a matter of course.

75% of the words in my list occur but once and of these again the vast majority is found in the *praefationes;* the large number and the wealth of original ideas are an outstanding feature of V.

Does there exist a study of words occurring but once in the Hebrew, Greek or Latin texts of the Bible? A few words occurring but once are not found in Gelasianum/Gregorianum but appear again in the Missale Romanum up to 1963 (immoderantia, pontificatus, ullatenus), an illustration of the importance of V to the tradition living right up to our time. The words most frequently used are

apostolicus 60, supplico 55, intercessio 49, natale 46, fragilitas 44, natalicia 32 and actio 23 — this list alone is an interesting cross-section through the basic mentality of V.

The liturgy, however, does not present systematic teaching, but the use of individual terms and the history of their use (frequency and connotation) throughout the ages is a lesson of its own. The few general conclusions we could draw from our list are less relevant to the specific field of liturgical terminology than are the single points to which attention can be drawn. The significance of such points may be illustrated by the following random samples:

1. The only instance in which the words bestialis and funestus occur in V is its first Preface for the feast of the Holy Innocents, to this day the one used in the Ambrosian liturgy (which liturgy has

most faithfully preserved — in its many prefaces — the tradition of V). The piling up of words (saevitia is not used by the Vulgate in this context) expressing horror at Herod's deed illustrates a specific interpretation of the event, an interpretation derived of course from the period of persecutions.

2. In the tradition under consideration it was not until the Gelasianum that the word perfidus was applied to the Jews in particular. V clearly shows that the translation of this word (in the Good Friday supplications) by "perfidious" was indeed perfidious. The continuous assertion that in the liturgy perfidus ever had the meaning of perfidious shows inexusable ignorance.

3. Also in connection with present-day reforms in the liturgy, the use of concelebrare calls for attention. In V this word has the general meaning comparable to that of collaudare in the Vetus Latina version of Ps. 116 or of confiteri and consonare (V).

In the light of such material points, the questions mentioned in the beginning of this paper seem to decrease in importance. In fact, due to the uncertainty of its historical position and its status V is of special interest. Baumstark thought that this collection originated from "the broad stream of creative formation".[11] However, creativeness is obviously not the highest aim of V or indeed of liturgical terminology in general. V illustrates the special meaning which auctoritas has in matters liturgical: V is naturally indebted to Biblical and Patristic terminology, but as accents in the liturgy are not the same as in Scripture[12] and in theology, traditional terms occasionally mutate in weight or in connotation and new terms are introduced. Already from its vocabulary V shows a high level of achievement which has set a standard for all times.

*abolitio 3 (B 250)
absurdum 1
actio 23 (Vulg. only gratiarum a.)
adcumulo 3 (also Gr[egorianum])
adflatus 1 (= G[elasianum])
*adjumentum 6 (also in Gr, G: Praef. Ord. Presbyt.)
admonitio 1
*adnisus 1
adscisco 1

adsero 1 (R 2 different, modern: assero) (B 429)
adsertor 3 (R 2 different, modern: assertor)
*adstruo 1
adulo 1 (adulantes and adulatio)
*adversitas 7 (sing. and plur., 3 = R; B 398)
affluenter 1
alternatio 1 (= Gr)

---

11 See above note 2.
12 W. J. Gocher, "The Latin liturgical text: a product of Old Latin and Vulgate textual interpretation", Cath. Bibl. Quart, 35 (1975) 206-220 deals with adaptation of Biblical texts for liturgical use.

anterior 1 (= G, Cons. Episc.)

apostolicus 60 a: connected with Apostles (B 384), b: connected with Holy See (B 349f.); never in the general sense now prevalent

atrocitas 1

*bestialis 1 (the same Praefatio in natale; Innocentium; also in Muratori's Gr)

caducus 1 (= G) (s.B 404, also R 1 — modern — and — new — Missale Pauli VI: Postc. s. Marthae and Commune Virginum II)

calliditas 1

candidatus 1 (noun rather than adjective as in the Te Deum)

*captiosus v. adulo

captor 1: captores piscium (from Vulg.: piscium captio) (B 172; ThLL)

*castigatius 1 (v. restrictius). Castigatior in the sermons of Leo the Great.

catholicus 1 (B 349; adject. since Tertullian)

*cautela 1 (same text as indiscretus)

*celsitudo 1 (not mentioned B 125; in ThLL only secular meaning)

*censeo 2 (different from instances in G, R and B 388 and 469)

*censura 2 and = Ordin. Presbyteri

cessatio 1

*claresco 1 (Consecr. Episc., as in Gr)

claritudo 1 (otherwise claritas)

*coaeternus 1 (= Gr, B 215 f.; ThLL: Tertullian)

collegium 2 (= Gr) (ThLL: Tertull., but not in A. Michels' Index Verborum Tertulliani (Steenbrugge 1960)

commendatio 1: sanctorum (Commendatio Animae)

*commercium 6 (of which 2 = R). Vetus Latina Gen 42, 1 (Vulg.: venditio). Sing. — in V and Gr- no longer in R. See my note 9.

*compensatio 1

*compenso: 1

*competenter 5 (MR only: c. annunties Evangelium; not in G)

*complex 1: nullum errorem tuae vis complicem fieri veritatis (ThLL: Ambrosius)

*concelebro 3: plebs, ecclesia, familia

tua (G, R only: angeli) (B 9, 312)

concors 1 = G, R: pietate (as in most instances in R), 1: lege (B 477)

*congruenter 1: exhibere officium (G, R: tendere)

*conlator 2, once even as the first word of a Collect

*consempiternitas 1 (a definitely dogmatic term) (ThLL: Patristic)

consensio 1

*consideratio 1: consideratione devotus

consono 1: fide consonante (Vulg.: voce consona) (v. dissono)

conspicuus 8 (mostly in Prefaces e.g. Ascens.: visu c. tactuque palpabilis (q.v.). Already in Gr this word does not occur anymore.

constructio 1: ecclesiae spiritalis, the technical sense emphasized by preceding words: ...fundamenta posuisti... lapidibus solidata

contactus 1 (R: Nuptial Mass, B 341)

conveniently 15 (some = Gr R)

corporeus 5: alimentum. conspectus, delectatio, gustus, subsidia; B 213 only: assumptio

*credulitas 1 (= Gr, R)

*crementum 1 (incrementa ?)

cymeterium 8 (only in headlines with reference to Roma cemetries). ThLL: cimeterium ex corrupta vocabuli apud vulgus pronunciatione.

*debitrix 1: natura (comp. Tertullian: omnium delictorum d. anima est)

decenter 1: aptius et decentius celebrare (the comparative e.g. in the rubrics of Consecr. Altaris)

*deceptor 1

*dedicator 1 (v. adsertor)

dedisco 1 (in one of the most intellectual prefaces of V)

deditus 3 (1 = G, V ms.: debita; Gr)

*deitas 3 a: general: tua deitate succurreris, b: specifically monotheistic: confessio deitatis unius, c: Trinitarian: unam cum filio deitatem (this only B 186, 189)

delibo 1 (ms delivat; s. praelibo) (Vulg., however, delibor)

deposco 2 (B 81)

depromo 5 (R 1 derived from V: mea voce depromitur; B 78, 80)

*desiderabiliter 1: desiderabilius capiamus (ThLL only positive)

desideranter *1* (ThLL: Cassiodorus)

devote *1*: devotius (ThLL: comparative Maxim. Taur. about 470)

*diaconium 2 (= Gr, Pontificale; B 363)

difficulter 2 (1 = G)

*dignanter 14 (B p. 147 last 4 lines)

digredior *1*

discrepo 2 (of which 1 = R, not Gr) (B 503)

*discutio 1: noxia discutias (R only: judex discussurus = B 203)

dispenso: 12 (3 in Gr, none of these in R)

dispositor *1*: officiorum (B *366*), 1: conjugii (R; B *139*)

*dissimulatio 3 (of which 1 in G)

*dissono 2 (ThLL: Vetus Lat.: Ex 24, 11, Jos 23, 14; Vulg. deest; primarily Patristic)

*distributor 2: ordinum (Gr, see dispositor, B *366*), dignitatum (Gr, Ord. Presb.). R: caelestium donorum (B 267)

diuturnitas *1*

divello *1*

*documentum 1 (= Gr, Consecr. Ep.: indumenta caelestis documenta culturae)

*eatenus 2

*ecclesiasticus 3 (of which 1: gubernatio = R; not Gr)

*editio *1* (v. virginalis)

efficientia *1*

eluceo 1 (= Gr, Ord. Presbyt.)

enigma 1 (= Gr, Consecr. Episc.)

eniteo 1 (= G). R with regard to a modern Saint

enixe *1*: enixius supplicandum

*episcopalis 2 (of which 1: cathedra = Gr, Cons. Episc.)

essentia *1*: nec a nostra divisus natura nec a tua discretus e.

evangelicus 6 (R 4 different; not in Gr)

eveho *1*

evidenter 3

*evinco 1 (Consecr. Virg.)

examinator 1 (same text as captor), a Patristic term

*excellenter 1 (= Gr)

excellentia 3

*excello *1*: glorificatione (q.v.) membrorum excellit pars in compage ecclesiae (comp. Praef. Ord. Diaconi, v. imus)

excidium *1*

*excusabilis *1*

*exiguitas *1*

exorno *4*

expedio 13 (in contexts very much the same as R, see B 74; Vulg. only expedit, expediunt)

experientia *2*

exposco *1*

*exsecutor *2*: divinitatis (Joh. Bapt.), dispensationis (Laurentius)

exultanter 3

exuberantia 1 (Gr ed. Muratori 336; Vetus Lat. Lk. 21, 4, Vulg.: abundanti) (*ThLL*)

facundus *1*: facundos et ineruditos (q.v.)

fallaciter *1*

*falsitas 3 (*ThLL*)

familiaris 1 (= Gr, Consecr. Episc.). Vulg. however has 1* familiariter.

familiaritas *1*

fastidio *1* (in marg. fastidiosus); 1 = Bened. Virg.

faveo 1: (sancti) oratio poscat nobis favere (ms: fore) placatum (Christum) (B 81)

*favor 3 (of which 2 also G, practically = R, B 265)

*fecunditas *1*

*fecundo 3 (Gr; R 12: foecundo)

fecundus 1 (= Gr, R: Nuptial Mass) and 3, e.g.,: justis operibus f.

*felicitas 6 (Gr, R)

*feralis *1*

fido 6 (mainly: fidentes; Gr)

fidus *1*: humani generis fida societas

*figuralis *1*: legis oservatio f. (B 420; *ThLL*)

*flagellatio 1 (= Gr, R; B 443; *ThLL*)

fluor *1*: unguenti fluore, where Praef. Consecr. Ep. says: unguenti rore (*ThLL*) (Vet. Lat. Lev. 15, 2 where Vulg.: *fluxus)

fortassis *1* (Vulg. Sap. 13, 6: fortasse)

fragilitas 44, some = Gr, R 12; B 401

freno *1*

*frequentatio 1: caelestium rerum (comp. Gr.: mysterii), 1: frequentationes sanctorum (see also B 4)

*fundamen 1: in veritatis fundamine soliditata (v. constructio)

funestus v. bestialis

gemino 1: geminata laetitia Johannis et Pauli glorificatione (q.v.), 1: geminata gloria (virginitas et passio, v. triumphus), 2: (sanctorum honore geminantur salutifera (q.v., R)

*generalis 1: munere generali vivimus (Vulg. only 1 generaliter)

genetrix 3: of Elizabeth and Felicitas (R 39 only of *B.V.M.; s.B)

*glorificatio 1: sanctorum (v. excello; as in R 1; B 107) and 8: of God Saints and Church (also: ornamenta glorifications = Consecr. Episc.; glorificationis amore devotior) (ThLL)

*gratanter 3, once first word of a Collect (ThLL)

hortamentum 1 (= Gr, R; B 103, 172)

*hostilitas 2 (note: Romanis auxiliare principibus, ne h. praevaleat) (ThLL)

humanitus 1 (Simplicius, in G a general prayer for the Dead: humanitatem (in R humanitas only with regard to Christ (B 185))

ignarus 3 and: divini sensus ignari (Ord. Diac.)

imbuo 6 of which one each also in G and Gr

imitatio 3 (R 16), of which 1 Ord. Diac (B 106)

imitatrix 1 (ms: emitatrix) (= Gr, R; B 106)

*immergo 1

immeritus 8 of which 1 in G, Gr (Murat.), R; B 287

*immoderantia 1 (= R) (ThLL)

*immolatio 2 of which 1 = R (Vet. Lat. Gen. 4, 3 (Vulg.: offeret) (B 32 n. 1)

impar 1

imperturbatus 1

*impetitor 1 (ThLL), in the same text:

impeto 2 (as hostilitas once political, once theological) (ThLL)

*impossibilitas 1 (ThLL). In the same prayer:

improvidus 1

*impugnatio 1 (in contrast to securitas, B 75, 327 v. 12)

imus: In the same text where excello: superioribus ima connexa, comp. Altar. Consecr.; qui summa, et media imaque custodis

*incarnatio 1 (no less than 6 further instances in the smaller related texts embraced by Mohlberg's index; Gr 3, R 5).

*incessabiliter 7 (ThLL)

*incessanter 3 (Gr 3, R 2, of which B noted only the negative one: i. affligimur) (ThLL: Patristic; Vet. Lat. Act. 12, 5 where Vulg.: sine intermissione)

incoho: 3 possibly influenced by Vet. Lat. Gen. 2, 3, also 1: i. jejunium (= Gr, R)

incommodum 3 e.g. in the same prayer as impetitor: (Roma) incomodis laboratura.

incommutabilis (misprint in Pflieger 307; Pflieger informed me that i. occurs in R Sabb. S. or. II p. Proph.) 1 (one of the most beautiful prefaces proper to V) (Gr; ThLL: Patristic); also 1: adverb (ThLL: Patristic)

incuria 1 (= Consecr. Virg.)

indebitus 1

indiffidenter 1 (Mur.: indifferenter) intellegere (v. essentia) (ThLL)

indiscretus 1: indiscreta non subripiat (q.v.) facilitas caritati (same text as cautela; B 215 n. 8)

indo 1 (= Cons. Virg.): virtutes; 2: jejunia, hostias

*indubitanter 2 (only passive meaning, ThLL)

*ineffabilis 18 (Gr 3, R 11; B 129; ThLL: predominantly Patristic)

ineruditus 1: v. facundus

infesto 1 (= Cons. Virg.) and 2, all in connection with hostes

infestus 4

inhaereo 12 of which 10 (Gr, R 11; B 106, 430, 433, 500)

initialis 1 (where Cons. Virg has nuptialis) (ThLL)

*initiator 1 (*ThLL*)

*inluceo *1*

*innocuus *1* + 1 (Laurentius = Gr, R: Stephanus)

*inoffensus *1*: inoffensa unanimitas (societatis humanae)

inordinatus *1* (but Vulg.: inordinate 2. Thess. 3, 6 quoted in V)

inrepo *1*

*insimulo *1*

insolens *1*

*insolentia *1*

instinctus *1*: populus instinctu devotus

*institutor 1 (= Gr, R) and *3* with rector, reparator, conditor, genitor with regard to God (B 147); in R also with regard to St. Francis (B 380) (ThLL: Patristic)

*instructio *1*

insuperabilis *1*

intemerata 1: caelestio eruditio i. (Gr, R with regard to virginitas)

*intercessio 49 (R 33; B 99)

*intercessor 2 + 2, of which one now Collect of All the Saints (B 99)

*interdictus 1 (= Bened. Virg.)

*intersero 2

*interventio 14 (R 5, never plural) (B 100; *ThLL*)

interventus *1* (B 100)

*intimo *1*

intrepidus *1*

inviolabilis 1: i. fidei firmitas (comp. Gr. R: caritas; B 46), *1*: inviolabi constitutum

*invisibiliter *1* (contrast to visibiliter q.v.) (R 1, B 128, ThLL: Cassiodor., Patrist.)

invitatio *1*

largitor 3 of which 1 = Gr, R (R 11; also Altar. Conscr.; B 152)

laudabiliter 1 (also G; B 2), 1 (= Consecr. Virg.; B *425*)

*legalis a: agnus l. (Abel), b: instituta legalia (Veteris Testamenti; B 234, 429), c: erudiamur legalibus institutis (all in G). ThLL distinguishes between ad legem pertinens and legi conveniens (the latter Patristic)

letaliter *1*

*machinamentum 2 (B *325*)

magister (adj.) *1*: magistra fides (Petri)

marita *1*

*martyrium 18 (R 12; B 109; *ThLL*: Vet. Lat. Ps. 118, 2)

maternus *1* (Joh. Bapt.; R: B.M.V.; B 122)

*medicatio 2 (*ThLL* mentions V for special Christian meaning)

*medicinalis 1 (= Gr, R; B 253; ThLL: spiritual meaning Patristic)

mixtus *1*

*moderamen 5 (of which *3*; B 139)

*moderatio 6 (of which: ecclesia potenti moderatione directa = R; B *139*; note also: m. gubernantium and m. nostra)

moderator *1* (B *139*) s. provectus

modulus 2

mortalitas 13, except perhaps in: ab anno mortalitatis incursu nos protegas, not in the meaning of *epidemy (B 75) but only as contrast to immortalitas (B 405)

*multimodus 1 (= Cons. Episc.)

*munificentia *3*

mutalibilis *1*

*mystice *1*: quod in nobis m. geritur veraciter impleatur (cf. m. designetur in facto, B 342)

*natalicia 32 (R 24)

*natale 46 (B 108)

necessario 3 (of which 1 also G)

*nitor (subst.) 1 (= Cons. Episc.)

*nullatenus 4 (of which 1 in R; also in Gr); v. ullatenus.

nutabilis *1*

*obfusco *1* (see B 9: Augustinus)

*obloquium 1 (also G; *ThLL*)

*obreptio 1 (also Gr Muratori) (*ThLL*)

obstaculum 2 (B *401*; ThLL: Vet. Lat. Eph. 2, 14)

*obtutus 1 (= Cons. Episc.)

*omnipotentia *1*

paco *1*: nos pacati (G: placati) (B *483*)

*palpabilis: v. conspicuus

*parsimonia 3 (of which 1 = R, v. medicinalis) (B 450)

*paschalis 7 (R 15)

patronus 4 (R 1, not Gr)

peculiarius *1*

*penso *3*

*perceptio 10 (R 14; B 261: with

reference to sacramentum)

perfector *1*

perfidus 3 only: ecclesia nulla recipiat consortia perfidorum

*permisceo *1**

perniciosus *1* (Vet. Lat. Gen. 47, 9,
where Vulg.: mali)

perpendo *4* (of God and of men)

perpes *2* (Feltoe p. 62 n. 5: the rare
form of the adj. is noticeable; G
reads perpetua, so does Gr; again
Feltoe 126)

perpetuitas *2* a: absolute (sine initio),
b: concrete (justitiae)

perpetuo 2

perseveranter *1*

persolvo *2* (B 26)

*personalis *1*: distinctio p. (v. perpetuitas a and deitas b) (4th c.)

*perversitas *2* (of which 1 also G)

*pervigil *2* (also G; B *138*)

*placidus *1*: p. aspice, *1*: secura (ms.:
placida) mente

plerumque *1*

*poenaliter *1* (Georges: in particular
Augustine)

polleo *2* (B 492)

pontificalis 5 (of which 1 = R,
B *382* and 1 = Cons. Episc.)

*pontificatus *1*: Xystus, 1: Clemens
(B 382; not Gr)

*postpono *1* (not Gr)

praeconium 9 (*8* in Prefaces) always
in plural: nostra, praestitorum,
angelorum, prophetarum (B 173,
429), martyrum (B 27), evangelii

*praefigo *1**

*praejudico *1* (contrast to praevinces
(q.v))

*praelibo *2* (1 ms: praelivavit)

praenoto 1 = Bened. Virg. (B *342*)

praepedio 3 (Gr = R, B 411)

praerogativa 2

*praerogo *1* (same text as desiderabiliter)

*praescius *2* (1 also G, Gr)

praesul 12: te solo praeside, otherwise of bishops, e.g., nobis consti-
tuisti praesules; fideles tui diligant
praesules suos et ab eis| mutuo
diligantur; corda fidelium et de
ecclesiae praesulum (ms.: aeclesia
praesolum, G: ecclesiae praesule)

*praetestor *1*: apostolo praetestante
(Feltoe: "Edd. protestante, which
seems more appropriate" to Eph.
5, 32) (Georges: Tertullian)

praevinco 3 (not in Georges)

precatio 1 (also Gr)

primitus *1*

primordium 3: sacerdotalis, sacrificii,
dignitatis (episcopi), but not (as
GR = R): mundi (Vet. Lat. Gen.
1, 1)

principaliter 3 (not Gr = R: p. ordinata societas)

profanitas 4 (once: prophanitas)
(Georges: Tertullian)

profundo 5 (= Gr, R): profusis gau-
diis; *1*: precibus; 3: sanguis profu-
sus (also Gr, v. Vet. Lat. Gen. 38,
9, where Vulg.: fundebat (semen))

profusius *2*

progigno *3* (progenitus = Christus;
also Gr)

promo 2

promptius 4: p. caelestis vitae novi-
tate gaudere, temporalibus solaciis
incitati p. aeterna desiderant (this
phrase was dropped by G) (R only
promptior, but p. in Rituale Rom.,
Blessing Aeroplane)

propagatio 1 = R (Nuptial Mass, not
Gr)

propensius 13 (Gr, R; B 458)

*protoplastus *1* (as deceptor; B *223*)
(Georges: Ambrosius)

provectio 2

*provectus *1*: cum provectu temporis
bonorum mihi operum des profec-
tum; 1: foves crementum provectuum (ms. proventuum; Ben. Abb.:
justorum provectuum moderator)

*provisio *1**

puerperium *1* (Vet. Lat. Gen. 25, 22)

quadriformis 1 (= Gr: Evangelia)
(Georges: Macrobius; missing in
Souter)

quamlibet *1*

*quantuslibet *1**

quatenus 2 (R 10)

rabies *1*

ratiocinatio *1*

rationabiliter *2*: r. et convenienter
exposcit; r. et prudenter credimus;
1: r. exsequi (also G, Gr)

*rationalis *1*: cum summa sis ratio nosque rationales effeceris (Gr: natura r.)

reatus 2 = R: sacramentum non sit nobis reatus ad poenam, 6 of which one plural: nostris reatibus absolvi

*receptio *1*: Clemens inquisitione vel receptione mirabilis (B 224; not in the Eucharistic sense, see B 261 n. 3)

*reciproco *1* (same text as deceptor and protoplastus)

*rectitudo *2*: fidei, praeceptorum (B 430), 2: semitarum Joh. Bapt., tua (Georges: primarily Patristic)

*recursio *1*: annua

*recursus *1*: mensis

redundantia *1*

refercio *1* (not Gr)

reformator *1*: conditor et r. (B 231) (Georges: moral sense: Augustinus)

refoveo 14 (of which 9, e.g.: refoventur corpus et mens hac temperie in the Preface on conditio humana)

*refuto 4 (of which 3)

regimen 2 (B *385*) and 1 = Bened. Virg.: munimen et r.

*relatio *1*: evangelica

relaxo 3 (of which 1 B *228*), 1: poscimus relaxari (also G; Gr: r. delicta = R)

remunero 1 (also G)

reparatio 1 = R: praesumptio et r. primi hominis, *1*: substantia reparationis (sacramentum), *1*: nostrae reparationis commercium (q.v.) (B 257)

reparator 3 (B *231*: Georges: Ambros.: auctor et r.)

repenso 2

*resero 2 (= Gr)

*resipiscentia *1* (Georges: Lactantius)

*resolvo *1* (Vet. Lat. Gen. 3, 19 where Vulg. revertaris) (but B 280 and 98: peccata)

*restauratio *1*

restrictius *1* v. castigatius

*restringo *1*

*rimor *1* (after immergo: pelagi profunda rimari (ed.: profundari mari)

*rudimentum *1* (Velatio Nuptialis), 1 (Gr 3)

sacro incl. *sacrat(issim)us* 32 (Gr; R 32; B 234)

*sacrosanctus 8 (Gr; R 22)

saevitia 4

*sagino *1*: anima jenuniis saginatur (Gr: JChri corpore saginati (Vet. Lat. Gen. 18, 7)

salubritas *1* (Gr)

salubriter 6 (s. sentiamus also Gr, R)

*salutifer 2 (different from 2 Gr = R; B 285)

saucio 3 (of which L = Gr, R; B 419)

*secretum 4 (of which 3 plural) (different from Gr 2, which again is different from R 2)

*septiformis *1* (= Cons. Diaconi) (Georges: Isidor., Cyprian.; one of the very few instances where Blaise-Chivat quotes V)

*series *1*: cum conjuge

*serus *1*

*soliditas 2 of which 1 = R: ecclesiae (Gr: apostolica)

solemniter 2 (1 = Gr; R 3; B 3)

solor 3

*specialis 2

*specialiter 2

*spiritaliter *1*: contrast to corporaliter (B 397), *1*: contrast to temporaliter (Gr only spiritalis, originally meaning: belonging to air; religious meaning Patristic; R always spiritualis)

suboles 5 (of which: in subole sit fecunda = Gr)

*subreptio 2 (different from Gr = R)

*subripio 3

subrogo 3 (different from Gr 1 = R)

subsicivus *1* fidelis ut Sara nihil ex hac s. (ms: subsicibus), where R: nihil in ea ex actibus suis ille auctor (Ben. Nuptial.); *1* facultas subsiciva laedendi

succurro 6 (of which 1 also G, Gr; R 6) (B 71)

suffragator *3* (B 102)

suffragium 34 (R 24), of Saints, but *1*: quod nobis ad immortalitatis pignus esse voluisti ad salutis aeternae tribuis provenire s.

supplico (but Vulg. has suppliciter

and supplicium) 53 R 22

*sustentaculum *1*

*sustentator *1* (not in Georges)

*_temperies_ 1 (not in Gr, in R only Sequ. Pentec.)

*_temporaliter_ 9 (R 6) v. spiritaliter, also contrast to aeterna, perpetua vita, sine fine (also G, Gr); *1*: quidquid t. est acerbum (Georges: Tertull., Augustin.)

*temptamentum *1*: inter hujus mundi temptamenta constantia (Vulg. tentamentum not either)

*tenor *2*: justitiae, evangelii

*torpesco *1*

transitorius *2*

*_trinitas_ 1: before quadriformis (q.v.) (not Gr; R 16)

trinus 1: trini gradus ministrorum (= Gr; Ord. Diac.; R only in Trinitarian meaning)

triumphus 19 (Gr 1, R 5)

*turbido 1 (also Gr) (Mohlberg, ed.

cit. no. 1113, but not in wordindex)

uberius *1*: multipliciter u., 1: securius u.que

*_ullatenus_ 1 (a 4th century coinage?) v. nullatenus

*unanimitas *1*

*unitio *1* (Patristic)

vegetatio 2 (also G, Gr; B 456)

*velatio *1* (Georges: Augustin.; B 376)

*veneranter 1 (also Gr Muratori)

*_virginalis_ 1 (different from 2 R of which 1 = Gr)

*_visibiliter_ 3 (different from Gr and R) (Georges: Ambros.)

*_vitiosus_ 1 = R

votivus 19 (Gr 6, R 11): dies, dignitas, donum, festivitas, gaudium, munus, mysterium, natalicia, oblatum, officium, promordium, prosperitas, sacramentum, subsidium

MONSTERS AND ODYSSEAN ECHOES IN THE EARLY HIBERNO-LATIN AND IRISH HYMNS

W. B. STANFORD

There are nine references to classical mythology in these hymns.[1] These (ignoring eccentric spellings) are Cocytus, Charybdis,[2] Scylla, and Tethys in the *Altus Prosator;* the Sirens and Tartarus in the *Lamentation of St. Ambrose;* "the daughters of Orcus" in the *Eulogy of St. Columba;* and Phoebus and Numa in the *Hymn in praise of St. Brigid.* Two of these, Tethys[3] and Phoebus, are hardly more than ornamental synonyms, often used elsewhere, for the ocean and the sun. Numa is mentioned merely for his connection with the calendar. But the contexts of the other six suggest that they carried more emphasis.

The early commentators on the hymns add some details. The commentary on *Altus* 56-61 mentions the giants imprisoned under Etna (as, e.g., in Virgil, *Aeneid* 3, 571-80 and Ovid, *Metamorphoses* 14, 1). It also names the three other rivers of Tartarus, Styx ("Strix"!), Phlegethon and Acheron, and offers etymologies for Cocytus, Styx and Phlegethon (*absque gaudio, tristitia, flammeus*), adding a suggestion that they were all names of the same river. Then the story about Scylla (described as 'daughter of "Porcus"': Porcus occurs as a variant for Phorcys as early as Hesychios *s.v.* Nereus) and Circe, as related in *Metamorphoses* 14, is briefly told and is tidied up genealogically by making Charybdis the mother of Scylla, a relationship unrecorded in classical sources. The classical tradition is also abandoned in a note in Irish on 1.61 by placing Scylla on the Sicilian side of the straits (against, e.g., Virgil, *Aen.* 3, 420, and Ovid, *Met.* 13, 730). Probably a false etymological connection between Scylla and Sicilia prompted this departure.

---

[1] J. H. Bernard & R. Atkinson, *The Irish Liber hymnorum* 2 vols (London 1898), 1, 75, 79; 139; 182 (see 2, 227 n. on l. 60); 161.

[2] Charybdis is used for "whirlpool" in Adamnán's *Life of St. Columba* 1, 5, *in undosis charybdis Brecani aestibus.* Cf. *loc. cit.* in n. 12 below.

[3] "*Tithis*" is a hesperic word. See M. W. Herren, *Hisperica famina* i (Toronto 1974) 232. It also occurs in the *Navigatio Brendani*.

The commentary on the *Eulogy of St. Columba* is even more idiosyncratic in its remarks on "the three daughters of Orcus". Presumably conflating Orcus, god of the underworld, with "Porcus", it states that "in the sky" the three daughters of Orcus were Stheno, Euryale and Medusa (i.e. the Gorgons, daughters of Phorcys in classical myth), "on earth" Clotho, Lachesis and Atropos (the Fates, daughters of Night and Erebos), and "in the underworld" Allecto, Megaera and Tisiphone (the Furies, of various ancestry, but not daughters of Phorcys, in classical myth). It omits other alleged daughters of the philoprogenitive Phorcys, notably the Graiae and Scylla.

The commentary on the *Lamentation of St. Ambrose* presents rather more problematical eccentricities in the following passage:

> vivam et mort... ara flumen in montem Hispericum; cenophali sunt, id est, homines man(ibus) ambulantes vel scenopodi. *i. ind oin-chosaig. i. traig-lethain* (Bernard and Atkinson translate "i.e., the one-legged men; i.e., the broadfooted men") ... ul et occeanum sunt labrosi *dosreggat a mbel n-ichtarach dar a...* (B. and A.; "their lower lip they thrust out beyond their (chin)").

The note in general seems to have no connection with the *Lamentation;* and the references in the first clause have not been explained. The rest obviously refers to the topic of monsters which recurs in classical literature from Homer and Hesiod downwards and is treated at some length by Pliny (*Natural history* 7, 2), Aulus Gellius (*Attic Nights* 9, 4), St. Augustine (*City of God* 16, 8) and Isidore of Seville (*Etymologies* 11, 3). But the names *Cenophali* and *Scenopodi* have no classical equivalents.

Du Cange quotes a bestiary as evidence that *Cenophali* meant a kind of ape in Ethiopia, adding a cross-reference to *Cenocephali* which he identifies with the *Cynocephali*, the dog-headed monsters of Greek and Roman legend. But the gloss *homines manibus ambulantes* does not fit in with that interpretation. On the other term *Scenopodi* Du Cange only quotes from Odo's *De varia fortuna* which describes them as wearing no shoes, having eight toes on each foot, and covering their limbs with their feet over them (*plantis sua membra supernis/Involvit*). This seems rather far removed from the Irish gloss "the one-legged men, the broadfooted men", but a connection will be suggested later.

It may be worth while to sort out the classical sources of this peculiar menagerie. First let us consider the *Dog-heads*.[4] The terms κυνοκέφαλοι and *cynocephali* are used of three different creatures in classical Greek and Latin: dog-headed apes, the Egyptian god Anubis, and dog-headed men. It is the third meaning that concerns us here, though the notion of dog-headed men may have been derived from either or both of the other two. References to such creatures are to be found in Hesiod (fr. 153, Merkelbach-West), Aeschylus (fr. 431), Herodotus (4, 191) and many subsequent classical authors. Pliny (*N.H.* 7, 2, 23), Solinus (52, 27) and Isidore of Seville (*Etym.* 11, 3, 15 and 13, 2, 32) describe their dogs' heads and dogs' bark.

There seems to be no doubt that the *Cenophali* of our text and Du Cange correspond to these *Cynocephali*. (The haplography in *Cenophali* for *Cenocephali* is paralleled in similar Greek words.[5]) But a difficulty remains. While the first gloss "men walking on their hands" (which does not appear to be derived from any of the sources mentioned) can be explained as meaning that they walked on all fours like animals (cf. Isidore 11, 3, 20, on the Artabatitae who *proni, ut pecora, ambulare dicuntur*), why are these Dog-heads equated with the *Scenopodi* who, to judge from Du Cange, are the *Sciapodes*, the *Shade-feet?* These creatures are in origin apparently monsters of quite a different kind.[6] They first occur in a fragment of Alcman as Στεγανόποδες (lit. "foot-covered", fr. 148 Page). The earliest author to call them Σκιάποδες, "Shade-feet" is Aristophanes (*Birds* 1553). They are described by Pliny (*N.H.* 7, 2, 23) St. Augustine (*City of God* 16, 8) and Isidore (*Etym.* 11, 3, 23), as having one foot large enough to serve as a sunshade in hot weather, and as being able to move with remarkable speed. The Irish glosses in our text record their one-leggedness[7] and their large-footedness, but miss the unique use of their foot. Despite this last omission, it seems clear

---

[4] See the article on *Kynokephaloi* in Pauly-Wissowa's Realencyclopädie; Liddell and Scott's *Greek Lexicon* (1940) on κυνοκέφαλος, κυνοπρόσωπος, ῾Ημίκυνες, and on the words cited below; Lewis and Short, *Latin dictionary*, on *cynocephalus*; the *Thesaurus Linguae Latinae* on *cynocephali* and *cynophanes*; Diefenbach, *Glossarium Latino-Germanicum* on *cynocephalus* (with varied spellings, including *cenophali*); and the index to Goetz-Loewe at *Cynoscephalus* (with variant spellings in the mss, one of which is from St. Gall).

[5] See Liddell-Scott on κυνοφάλιον and Κυνόφαλοι and Diefenbach as cited in previous n.

[6] See Pauly-Wissowa on *Skiapodes*.

[7] "One-legs", *na haenchosaich*, are mentioned in the *Sex aetates* in the Book of Lecan: see J. Carney, *Studies in Irish literature and history* (Dublin 1957) 102ff.

that the Irish commentator or commentators as quoted had gained
a confused knowledge of both the *Dog-heads* and the *Shade-feet* from,
perhaps, those familiar authors among the Irish, Isidore or Pliny.
How the confusion between these different kinds of monster originally arose is not clear. (Possibly some confusion between *Scenopodi*
and the "wedge-headed Pans", Πᾶνες σφηνοκέφαλοι mentioned in
Strabo 2, 1, 9, is involved: cf. St. Patrick's Irish nickname "Adze-
head").

The *labrosi* remain to be considered. The word itself occurs only
once in classical Latin according to Lewis and Short.[8] Du Cange
quotes an unspecified Greek-Latin glossary giving πρόχειλοι as its
equivalent. A similiar equation occurs in the Irish Codex Laudunen-
sis 444. Another glossary in Goetz-Loewe gives "χιλας (presumably
for χειλίας) *labrosus*", and a third has "*labrosus, grandia labia
habens*"[9] But these may be taken from medical or ethnographical,
rather than teratological contexts. Similarly when Strabo (2, 2, 3),
citing Posidonius' treatise on the Ocean, mentions that people with
prominent lips (πρόχειλοι) and flat noses lived in the tropics, he
presumably means negroid Africans, not monsters, since the content is not teratological. These *Big-lips* however became fully
fledged monsters in Isidore (*Etym.* 11, 3, 18), who states that they
use their jutting lips as sunshades — an extrapolation, it would seem,
from the *Sciapods*. (Isidore seems to have had a *penchant* for anatom-
ical parasols: in *Etym.* 11, 3, 19, he says that the Scythian *Panotii*
used their very large ears in the same way.) He does not use the
word *labrosus*, so presumably our text and the glossaries already
cited derived this word from another source. Nor does he (or the
glossaries) say that the *Big-lips* lived near the ocean: so the mutilated
fragment in our text... *ul et occeanum* (perhaps from *procul ad
oceanum*) also suggests a source other than Isidore.

One general feature of these mythological references deserves
attention. Most of them go back originally to Homer's *Odyssey*.
Obviously they could have been taken from Latin sources. Yet it is
curious that out of all the creatures of classical mythology so many
of those chosen by the Irish hymnists were Odyssean. Early secular
Irish literature also shows incidents and details that strikingly recall

---

[8] Celsus 7, 26, 2 (in a medical context).
[9] See Goetz-Loewe *Corpus Glossariorum Latinorum* ii, 424, 585, and iii,
330. The word *labrosus* also occurs here as a gloss on *brocchus*.

parts of the *Odyssey*,[10] especially in the voyages of Brendan and Mael Duin, and in the remarkable version of the wanderings of Ulysses called *Merugud Uilix Maic Leirtis*, which shows surprisingly close analogies with Homer's narrative not to be found in any earlier Latin author.[11] Further, Cormac's *Glossary* on *Coire Brec(c)ain* has some striking parallels with *Odyssey* 12, 235ff.[12] Two references by ninth-century Irish scholars abroad also deserve to be noticed. Johannes Eriugena[13] mentions the dog Argos met by Ulysses in *Od.* 17, 292ff. — an incident which, so far as the present writer can discover, was not to be found in Latin writers accessible to Eriugena. Secondly Martin of Laon included the following entry in his Latin-Greek glossary *Odissia, liber Homeri ubi continentur gesta Odissei, id est Ulixis qui Graece Odisseus dicitur.*[14] That was in an era when the *Odyssey* was generally forgotten in western Europe.

But is there any likelihood that the early Irish could have known about the *Odyssey* and its contents from Greek sources? Literary acquaintance with a text of the poem is almost entirely incredible. Where could an Irishman have seen a copy of the *Odyssey* and what Irishman could have read it? (There is one possible exception — Johannes Eriugena who, according to William of Malmesbury, visited Athens.[15])But there is another possible source of information. If Greek merchants coming to Ireland from Spain or Gaul, or Irish travellers to a Greek colony on the continent of Europe, could have overcome the linguistic barrier, then it would not be surprising if, when their business was done, they exchanged stories of fabulous voyages and strange monsters such as both the Gaels and the Greeks loved to relate.[16'17]

---

[10] Cf. W. B. Stanford, *Proceedings of the Royal Irish Academy* 70 C 3 (1970) 31-3.

[11] See the editions of K. Meyer (London 1886), and R. T. Meyer (Dublin 1958) and the same scholar's article in *Modern Philology* 1 (1952) 73-8.

[12] See further in J. Rendel Harris "Scylla and Charybdis", *Bulletin of the John Rylands Library* 9 (1925) 94-5.

[13] *De divisione naturae* 738.

[14] For the connection between this part of Laudun. 444 and Codex Vaticanus Reg. 215 (Goetz-Loewe 5, 585) see M. L. W. Laistner in *Bulletin of the John Rylands Library* 7 (1923) 423 and cf. 440 for the gloss quoted above.

[15] *De gestis pontificum Anglorum* 5, 240.

[16] For this and other views on the possibility of Greek contacts in early Ireland see the authors cited in *loc. cit.* n. 10 above, 23-4.

[17] I gratefully record my thanks to D. A. Binchy, J. Carney, J. K. Killeen, J. J. O'Meara, E. G. Quin, and especially to Professor Bieler himself, for improvements in this excursus into unfamiliar fields *amicitiae causa*.

III

HIBERNO-LATIN
AND INSULAR LATIN

THE PSEUDONYMOUS TRADITION IN HIBERNO-LATIN: AN INTRODUCTION

MICHAEL HERREN

In recent years the subject of Hiberno-Latin has received a great deal of competent attention. Those writing after World War II have approached the subject with a good deal more caution than did their predecessors. The great editors of the *Monumenta* — Traube, Winterfeld, Ehwald — and other pioneers such as Hellman, in their enthusiasm for discovering *Scotticae consuetudines*, listed numerous features as peculiar to Irish Latinity which in fact could be found in Vulgar Latin generally. This enthusiasm led to the inevitable reaction: the tendency to regard "Hibernicism" as a philological "will-o-the-wisp", or worse, as another aberration of "Celticizing". Now, I think, we can state with some confidence that the balance has been restored. In the area of linguistics, we can single out the contributions of William Most, Ludwig Bieler, and Bengt Løfstedt.[1] These scholars have generally agreed that the number of "pure Hibernicisms" is quite small. (In orthography, for example, there is the so-called "glide-vowel" that can be attributed to Irish influence in such spellings as *staitim* for *statim*, or *ambulaire* for *ambulare*. As to lexical matters, one can cite a number of examples of Irish words with Latin forms, such as *tollus* or *tullus* from tolae, *arreum* from *arre*, *orgo* from *orgim*.) Rather, one must look for a *combination* of factors, especially the spellings of *individual words*, certain grammatical constructions, and employment of idiom (e.g. *dixit contra eum* in imitation of Irish *asbert fris*). Only a few such features, taken in isolation, can be termed Hibernicism.

In taking up the question of Hiberno-Latin pseudonymy, there is renewed danger of opening the *arca Pandorica*, — albeit here we are dealing with a literary technique as well as with linguistic features. One might well ask, was not pseudonymy employed widely in Antiquity and in the Middle Ages, especially as a means of gaining greater

---

[1] W. G. Most, *The Syntax of the Vitae Sanctorum Hib;erniae* (Diss., Washington, 1946), esp. pp. 281-337. L. Bieler, ed., *The Irish Penitentials* (Dublin, 1963), pp. 27-47. B. Løfstedt, *Der Hibernolateinische Grammatiker Malsachanus* (Uppsala, 1965), pp. 81-161.

authority for one's work? It will therefore be necessary to show what is peculiarly Hibernian about the use of pseudonymy in Ireland in the Latin treatises of the sixth to eighth centuries.

It is now well known that the Irish employed pseudonymy in their Latin writings of that period. Some famous examples are the Pseudo-Augustinian *De Mirabilibus Sacrae Scripturae*, the Pseudo-Isidorian *De Ordine Creaturarum*, and the *Cosmographia* of the so-called "Aethicus Ister", ascribed by H. Löwe to Virgil (Fergil), an eighth-century Irish bishop of Salzburg.[2] Professor Bischoff notes a number of Irish exegetical works written under the names of Augustine, Jerome, and Gregory.[3] In the first three examples the use of pseudonymy is more elaborate than the simple borrowing of a famous name. Virgil of Salzburg professes to excerpt the work of a Greek cosmographer that has been translated and edited by St. Jerome. One of the MSS of the *De Ordine Creaturarum* contains a dedication *ad Braulium episcopum Urbis Romae*, thereby strengthening the fiction of Isidorian authorship. The author of the *De Mirabilibus S.S.* calls himself "Augustinus" in his dedication and addresses his work to *presbyteris... maxime Carthaginensium*. As Père Grosjean wondered, does such elaboration of the fiction indicate a serious attempt to deceive some readers?

Another distinguishing feature of Hiberno-Latin pseudonymy is the use of bi-lingual word plays on the names of writers and places, or, in some instances, the use of cryptograms. Some writers chose Latin names for themselves that might conceal their identities from the uninitiated, but reveal it to the *cognoscenti*. Some of these names could be "decoded" by a knowledge of Irish; a few, by unscrambling a cryptogram; others, possibly, by recognizing some obscurantist allusion. This "tradition" is apparently quite different from that of the Carolingian circle, in which the poets, as a kind of game, arbitrarily took on the names of various classical writers with whom they identified themselves. In Ireland, the pseudonym was rather often determined by the "punonym" — at least in certain "schools".

The following study is by no means intended to be exhaustive. It

---

[2] H. Löwe, "Ein literarischer Widersacher des Bonifatius", Mainz: Akademie der Wissenschaften und der Literatur, *Abhandlungen der Geistes- und Sozialwissenschaftlichen Klasse*, 1951, esp. pp. 928-37.

[3] B. Bischoff, "Wendepunkte in der Geschichte der lateinischen Exegese im Frühmittelalter", *Sacris Erudiri* 6 (1954) = *Mittelalterliche Studien* I (1966), nos. 11A, 11B, 27, 32, 34B, 36, 37, 38.

is meant, rather, as an introduction to what may later develop into a longer study. I have chosen a few egregious examples to show how, in my opinion, the tradition of pseudonymy was employed in Hiberno-Latin treatises. I expect that not all will agree with my interpretations. It is after all a risky business to attempt to explicate the *Wortspiele* of men who lived around thirteen hundred years ago and used languages which are today imperfectly understood. However, if any parts of this study are successful, we shall not only gain some insight into the workings of an interesting literary tradition, but we might also learn the identities of men and places hitherto concealed from us.

1. *Columba : Colum : : Columbanus : Columban*

St. Columba the Younger, as he is called by J. Smit, in his monograph *Studies on the Language and Style of St. Columba the Younger* (Diss., Amsterdam, 1971), did not, as far as we know, use a pseudonym. However, he was the first Hiberno-Latin writer whose works we can positively authenticate — despite recent controversies over some of them. Moreover, he did enjoy making word plays on his own name, some of them more elaborate than previously supposed. In a famous passage, he states his name in the *tribus linguis sacris*, giving special emphasis to the Hebrew version on account of its personal associations. *Epist.* 5.16 (Walker):

> Sed talia suadenti, utpote torpenti actu ac dicenti potius quam facienti mihi Ionae hebraice, Peristerae graece, Columbae latine, potius tantum vestrae idiomate linguae nancto, licet prisco utor hebraeo nomine, cuius et pene subivi naufragium, veniam, quaeso, sicut saepe rogavi, date, quia necessitate magis quam cenodoxia scribere coactus sum,...

In another passage (also cited by Smit), St. Columba makes this series of associations: *Ionae* (Old Testament figure), *columba* (meaning of *Iona* and name of writer), *Ionam vestrum* (= St. Columba, the new Jonas). Thus, *Epist.* 4.8 (Walker):

> Si in mare proiciar more Ionae qui et ipse in hebraeo columba dicitur, orate, ut vice ceti sit quidam felici revocans remigio tutus celator, qui Ionam vestrum terrae reddat optatae.

Note that the primary word play *Ionae : columba* is enhanced by the secondary *mare : more* and *ceti : celator*. The play *mare : more* is further embellished by Irish "resonances". *Mór* and *már-* are variant stems of the OI genitive of *muir*, "sea".

Smit has uncovered yet another ingenious name play that occurs at the end of *Epist.* 1.1: "... *ego, Bar-iona (vilis Columba), in Christo mitto Salutem*" Smit comments, p. 151:

> The game that Columba is here playing with his name is extremely refined. The combination *vilis Columba* (Columba often uses *vilis* of himself) leads Columba, via a sound-play with *filius columbae*, to call himself *Bar-iona*, just as in EPIST. V, 18 he compares himself with the prophet Jonah by means of the Hebrew equivalent of his name.

Finally, there is the question of the longer form of Columba's name: *Columbanus*. According to Smit, Columba never uses the name of himself in any of his authentic writings. We need not here debate Smit's thesis that only the Letters can be ascribed to Columba the Younger, and that the poems under the long form of the name were written by another Columbanus, possibly a Carolingian. Smit, of course, was well aware that Columba's biographer, Jonas, referred to his subject as Columbanus. Several reasons are advanced: (1) Jonas may have preferred the more masculine-sounding form of the name in Latin; (2) he may have wished to distinguish his subject clearly from the other famous Columba (Columcille); (3) the name *Columbanus* might render the Irish Columbán, "White Dove", an allusion to Jonas' description of the saint's *corporis candor*.

All of this goes to suggest that both Columba and his biographer were well aware of the possibility of word plays in the use of names. As it is now generally agreed that Columba's intellectual formation was Irish,[4] one can posit (at least hesitantly) an Irish interest in word and sound plays in Latin writings dating from the late sixth century onward. It is not possible to show that Columba the Younger was responsible for the forcefulness of that tradition in his native island after his death. The textual tradition of his letters is a purely continental one, and we are not certain as to the date when they were known in Ireland. However, as we shall see, a number of Hiberno-Latin texts dating mainly from the mid-seventh century and coming from Ireland proper combine pseudonymy with word

---

[4] For a summary of the arguments, see L. Bieler, "The Island of Scholars", *Revue du Moyen Âge latin* 8 (1952), 213ff.

play. Thus Columba the Younger might be seen in this light as a "precursor" — if you like — of an important feature of Hiberno-Latin literature.

2. *Virgilius Maro*

Virgili Maronis Grammatici *Epitomae* ad fin. (Huemer, p. 92):

> Erant praeterea tres Lucani, unus in Arabia, alius in Endia, tertius in Africa: quos Aeneas meus praeceptores habuit, quorum libros meditante notaria arte in lucidam discripcionem transtulit. in quibus repperit quod uir quidam Maro fuerit prope diluuium, cuius sapientiam nulla narrare seculas potebunt. unde Aeneas cum me uidisset ingeniosum hoc me uocabulo iussit nominari dicens: *hic filius meus Maro uocabitur, quia in eo antiqui Maronis spiritus rediuiuit.*

Some may object to my listing Virgilius here as a Hiberno-Latin writer, since opinion has been sharply divided on the questions of his origin and place of activity.[5] However, there are indications that certain scholars now favour an Irish locale — if not origin — and, indeed, no less an authority than Bernhard Bischoff has suggested in print that Virgilius spent at least part of his career in Ireland[6]. That scholar has also placed Virgil's dates in the seventh century, on the basis of his acquaintance with the *Etymologiae* of Isidore. I should state here that the present paper incorporates the results of three years' labour on Virgil, which should appear in published form quite soon.[7] In that paper I hope to have shown the arguments for a French origin to be entirely unconvincing. On the other hand, Virgil's indications of knowledge of Irish syntax, his use of Irish-based words and proper names, and most especially, his exhibition of Irish-Latin puns and riddles establish him as a "Scottophone" for all practical purposes. For the aims of this study, then, I regard Virgilius as a Hiberno-Latin writer at least in the sense that he writes a kind of Latin that can only be fully understood and appreciated by one with some knowledge of the Irish language.

In the passage cited above, Virgilius reveals how he came to be called "Maro". It is quite possible that his actual name was Fergil, which the writer latinized to Virgil for literary reasons (the same

---

[5] For a summary of the scholarship to 1928, see D. Tardi, *Les Epitomae de Virgile de Toulouse* (thèse, Paris, 1928), p. 12ff.

[6] B. Bischoff, *Mittelalterliche Studien: Ausgewählte Aufsätze zur Schriftkunde und Literaturgeschichte* (Stuttgart, 1966), I, 288.

[7] In the C-Section of the *Proceedings of the Royal Irish Academy*, 1977.

may be true of Virgil of Salzburg). In an earlier passage, our writer
tells us that he is the third of a series of famous grammarians named
Virgil.[8] His *praeceptor* was named "Aeneas", and the writer heard
many debates among the grammarians at "Roma". According to
Virgil, his teacher "Aeneas" named him "Maro" because he was a
kind of re-incarnation of a certain *Maro* who lived *prope diluuium*,
whose wisdom surpassed that of all ages. *Prope diluuium* can be
taken to mean "at the time of the flood", with *prope* in its rather
rare temporal sense. But if we take *prope diluuium* to mean "near
the tide" (understanding *prope* spatially), we have a good Latin
gloss on *uir... Maro*, understood as Irish *fer (ind) maro*, "man of the
sea". *Maro*, in Old Irish, is found alongside *moro*, *mora*, and *mara*,
as a genitive singular of *muir*. Hence, Virgil is called "Maro" because he lives by the tide — a nice folk etymology. But this is not
quite the end of the word play. By a neat metathesis *maro* can be
transformed into *móra* — an Irish word for "greatness". *Móra*, then,
"explains" the phrase *cuius sapientiam nulla narrare secula potebunt.*
Moreover, *mutatis mutandis*, we can produce *Roma:* "This my son
shall be called *Maro* because in him the spirit of ancient *Roma* (or
Romani) re-lives." This bit of lexical magic is not my own. It comes
directly form Virgil's own book, in his doctrine of the *scinderatio
fonorum:* the breaking up and rearranging the letters of a word,
phrase, or sentence (Huemer, pp. 76-82). One of the purposes of *scinderatio* is to conceal the mysteries of wisdom from the profane (Huemer, p. 76): *tertia ne mystica quaeque, et quae solis gnaris pandi debent,
passim ab infimis ac stultis facile repperiantur, ne secundum antiquum
sues gemmas calcent.*" Virgil provides the example of changing *dono*
into *nodo* (parallel to *Maro/Roma*). We can imagine a semantic play
to accompany the sound play: "gift"/"knot"/"riddle". As to the "semantic connection" between *Roma* and *móra*, Irish tradition provides
corroboration, as *móra* is glossed by *Roma* in the *Félire Húi Gormáin.*
Róm- becomes an Irish adjectival element meaning "chief, pre-emi-
nent". It doubtless did not escape Irish grammarians that *mór*
spelled backwards is *Róm*. We shall see in the next section if *Roma*
gives us any clue as to the location of Virgil's activity.

---

[8] Huemer, p. 88: "fuit itidem apud Troiam quidam Virgilius eiusdem
Donati auditor, qui in discribendis uersibus diligentissimus erat, qui LXX
uolumina de ratione metri scribens et epistolam ad Virgilium Assianum
missam de uerbi explanatione. tertius Virgilius EGO."

3. Augustinus, Carthago, Roma

Ps. Augustinus, *De Mirabilibus Sacrae Scripturae*, inc. (P.L. 35, col. 2149):

> Venerandissimis urbium et monasteriorum Episcopis et Presbyteris, maxime Carthaginensium Augustinus per omnia subiectus, optabilem in Christo salutem.

Père Paul Grosjean, in an article now famous,[9] has shown that *Carthaginensium* can hardly refer to the famous North African city, and that such proposed emendations as *Cantuarensium* and *Cambrensium* are scarcely convincing. Rather, *Carthaginensium* refers to the monks of one of the foundations of the Irish St. Carthach, or *Carthagus*, in Latin. Grosjean argues convincingly that the settlement was Lés Mor, or Lismore, in County Waterford. That scholar also thought it probable that the author was a member of that community (the address to the *presbyteris Carthaginensium* being only a literary pretext) and that he chose the pseudonym "Augustinus" as a natural complement to the word play *Carthach/Carthagus/Carthaginensium*. The date of the treatise, as established earlier by Esposito,[10] is 655, a year that in all probability coincides with the *floruit* of Virgilius Maro. I conjecture that the author of the *De Mirabilibus* may have used the pseudonym "Augustinus" in another treatise, namely in the *Ars breviata* that was taken by Angelo Mai to be the lost *De Grammatica* of St. Augustine of Hippo (*Patrum Nova Bibliotheca* I, 165ff.).[11] Huemer, in his edition of Virgilius Maro (p. 45), cites Clemens Grammaticus: *Augustinus ait quod infinita pronomina per quae generaliter de omnibus interrogatio fit id est cuius cuia cuium secundum praedictorum pronominum regulam per omnes casus declinantur*. Clemens then proffers the contradictory opinion of Virgilius. It is interesting that Clemens cites "Augustinus" and Virgilius Maro in close juxtaposition. Clemens, an eighth-century Irish grammarian working on the continent, cites a number of Irish authorities. The *explicit* of the *Ars Breviata* given by the

---

[9] P. Grosjean, "Quelques exégètes irlandais du VIIe siècle", *Sacris Erudiri* 7 (1955), 67-98.

[10] M. Esposito, "On the Pseudo-Augustinian Treatise, 'De Mirabilibus Sanctae Scripturae'", *Proceedings of the Royal Irish Academy*, Vol. 35, Section C, No. 2 (March, 1919), 197-98.

[11] The *Ars* is classed among the *spuria* of St. Augustine in the *Clavis Patrum Latinorum*.

Vatican MS points at least to the Irish transmission of the work: *Heic* (sic) *revera Augustini ars grammatica explicit.*

Another possible reference to the "Carthaginians" is made by Virgilius Maro. It has been argued that Virgilius invented the names of his "authorities", but I think it more probable that he used "disguise-names" to conceal real personages. Most of these, admittedly, we shall never identify. An interesting case is that of *Sibyllae Carginiensis* (Huemer, p. 48): *legi in quodam Sibyllae Carginiensis libello templis inque parietibus dium innumeris ille.* *Sibyllae* is Huemer's conjecture, placed in the text. In the apparatus our editor has after *carginiensis:* fort. *Carthaginiensis.* I think that both his conjectures are right. It is part of Virgil's teaching that syllables can be added or removed from words in some cases (cf. p. 66). Hence, the reading of the Paris MS, *Sibae Carginiensis*, may be right, but is to be understood as a type of "Virgilian contraction" for *Sibyllae Carthaginiensis.* Although I shall not attempt to guess the identity of our writer's "oracle", it is noteworthy that a female writer is cited here in connection with the foundation of St. Carthach. Les Mór, as is well known, was a double monastery.

There is one other mention of *Carthago* in Virgil's work (p. 27): *proprie ergo nomina dicenda sunt ut Roma Carthago* (*chartago* P). Is it possible that the two examples are linked for any other reason than to exemplify proper nouns, here names of cities? I have found other cases in Virgilius where lists of grammatical examples display a thematic relationship. This case is particularly interesting: Rome and Carthage were ancient rivals. If *Carthago* in the work of Virgilius (as in Ps. Augustinus) stands for Les Mór, what was *Roma* intended to represent? One tradition has the Irish Rome at Temair. However, our "circle" appears to be based in Munster. Besides Les Mór in County Waterford, there is also Clonfert-Molua in County Laois, the seat of activity of Laidcenn, who wrote the *Ecloga de moralibus in Iob* and the Hisperic hymn, *Lorica*, attributed to Gildas.[12] Is it possible that *Roma* refers to Caisel? Caisel, like Rome, and unlike either Temair or Armagh, was a centre of both civil and ecclesiastical jurisdiction. There is also a tradition of Caisel's laying claim to the kingship of all Ireland. Moreover, Caisel, and Munster generally, sided with Rome in the Paschal controversy at

---

[12] See my article, "The Authorship, Date of Composition, and Provenance of the So-Called *Lorica Gildae*", *Ériu* 24 (1973), 35-51.

the synods of Mag Lena and Mag nAilbe about 632. That the Munstermen, at least in one instance, thought of Caisel as a new Rome is indicated in the tradition that Patrick baptized Oengus and his sons at Caisel *super petram Cothrigi*, i.e. on the rock of Patrick:[13] *Caisel*, borrowed from Latin *castellum*, means "stone fortress" in Irish. Thus Patrick is seen as a new Peter and the rock of Caisel becomes the *petra* on which the new church is built.

Do we now conclude that Virgil's *Roma* is Caisel, the rival of Carthage (Les Mór)? This seems improbable for three reasons: (1) we have no certain knowledge of scholars or writers who emanated from Caisel in the seventh century; (2) it is unlikely that the monks of Les Mór (Carthage) would create even a symbolic rivalry with Caisel (as another Rome), with whom they were so closely allied spiritually and theologically; (3) Caisel scarcely answers to the description of *prope diluuium*.

I noted at the beginning of this paper that one of the MSS of the Ps. Isidorian *Liber de Ordine Creaturarum*, an Irish work composed after the middle of the seventh century,[14] addresses the composition *ad Braulium episcopum urbis Romae*.

M.C. Díaz y Díaz, who has recently brought forth a new edition of that work (Santiago, 1972) has argued cogently that *Braulium* cannot be a mistake for the name of Isidore's friend and editor, nor is it a mistake for *Bonifatium*, as some have suggested. Díaz y Díaz conjectures that the recipient of the treatise was an abbot-bishop of an Irish *urbs* (monastic community) called *Roma*. The author of the treatise, who relied upon the *De Mirabilibus* of Ps. Augustine, in a number of places (according to Díaz y Díaz) was clearly employing the same tradition of pseudonymy (if we accept the authority of the subscription of codex *A* as providing the *ipsissima verba* of the author). If we grant that Virgilius Maro belonged to an Irish community known as *Roma* just after the middle of the seventh century, is it not likely that it is identical to the *urbis Romae* mentioned by Ps. Isidore, a close contemporary?

Where, then, was *Roma?* Díaz y Díaz speculates that it might be the *Tech na Róman*, or *Domus Romanorum*, a foundation of Palladius, mentioned in the *Four Latin Lives of St. Patrick* (ed. Bieler;

---

[13] See now F. J. Byrne, *Irish Kings and High-Kings* (London, 1973), p. 192.
[14] M. C. Díaz y Díaz, "Isidoriana I: Sobre el 'liber de ordine creaturarum'", *Sacris Erudiri* 5 (1953), 147-66.

1971, p. 77). The fact of Palladian foundation argues for South Leinster although, to my knowledge, the exact site is not known. What seems clear, however, is that "Roma", "Carthago", and perhaps some other names mentioned by Virgil (e.g. *Troia*, *Africa*) refer to monastic schools in Southern Ireland (mainly Munster). These schools appear to be in competition, especially in the seventh century, as centres of Latin education, with their emphases on grammar and biblical studies. It was apparently a popular pastime to identify various schools and scholars with great centres and writers of classical antiquity (gleaned, no doubt, from the pages of Isidore). In a curious passage of Virgil's *Epistolae* (p. 152), a certain "Virgilius Troianae scolae" is described as *doctor contra Romanos scribens eosque falsitatis arguens*. Our Virgil attributes to him the statement: *O Romani, cur uestrae inmemores ueritatis, quae credidistis, transgredi uoluistis?* This kind of invective and interscholastic rivalry is somewhat reminiscent of certain passages of *Hisperica Famina*, for which I have pleaded elsewhere a seventh-century date and Irish locale.[15] One wonders if the writers of those compositions were not also centred in Munster. We have already noted that the Munsterman Laidcenn was responsible for the *Lorica*, a hymn written in Hisperic Latin. It is instructive that the *faminatores* used such epithets as *Hispericus*, *Ausonicus*, and *Italicus* to describe elegant Latinity. Did they think of *Hibernia* as the new *Hisperia?* I think it a fair assumption that they did.

Was there such a thing as a "Carthaginian circle"? Grosjean thought that there was, although he admits that not all the members were active at Les Mór. Perhaps one could speak more accurately of a "Munster Circle" that included both grammarians and biblical exegetes. A minimum list of the members would comprise Ps. Augustinus (who may have written a grammatical work in addition to the *De Mirabilibus*), Ps. Isidore, Laidcenn, Virgilius Maro, Manchianus, Banbanus, and perhaps Berchán, son of Áed, who was active near Les Mór. To these one might tentatively add the writers of *Hisperica Famina*.

A small point to conclude this section. Grosjean wondered if the "Bregandus Lugenicus" mentioned by Virgilius (p. 162) might not refer to either Berchán, son of Áed, or Brecannus, alias Mo-Bríccu, both of the Dési Muman and of the seventh century. Although I

---

[15] M. Herren, *The Hisperica Famina* (Toronto, 1974), I, 32-9.

have no reason for declaring in favour of one or the other, I find the suggestion quite plausible, given the time and place of activity of Virgilius Maro.

4. Olimbrianus

Rubisca 77-80 (ed. Jenkinson, p. 58):

> Tuus monarchus per has ut fatur
> olimbrianus totum rimatur
> molosi rerum res dominatur
> bellique uigil cloca solatur (sonatur, Jenk.)

I discussed this passage at some length in *Ériu* 25. I shall deal with it briefly here as an example of the kind of pseudonymy employed by Virgilius Maro: the choice of a "classical" type of name that contains a clue to the author's identity. The name *Olimbrianus* reminds us of *Olimpianus*. Moreover, as my *Ériu* article noted, it contains the elements *olim* and *Brianus* — formerly Brian! It is just possible that our poet can be identified with Máel Dub, who, according to the *Félire Óengusso*, may have sprung from the race of Brian. Máel Dub was the Irish teacher of Aldhelm, who in all likelihood transmitted the text of Virgilius Maro to England. The "punonym" in this case yields a clue to the writer's identity and plays on the classical-sounding *Olimpianus*.

5. Conclusion

Pseudonymy enjoyed considerable popularity among Latin writers in Ireland, especially in the seventh century. The rather elaborate techniques employed (bi-lingual word plays, cryptograms, and the use of pseudonymous place names) indicate that the tradition had as much to do with erudite games as with the concealment of identity or the enhancement of authority. Bi-lingual word plays on names in Hiberno-Latin texts go back at least as far as Columba the Younger in the late sixth century. The pseudonymous tradition (as distinguished from forgery) in Hiberno-Latin writing reached full bloom in the middle of the seventh century and was centred mainly in Munster. Virgilius Maro brought the art to its state of advanced perfection.

ZUR GRAMMATIK DES ASPER MINOR

BENGT LÖFSTEDT

In seinen *Grammatici Latini* Bd. 5 S. 547ff. hat H. Keil eine
"Aspri grammatici ars" veröffentlicht, die einen Abriss von Donatus' grösserer Grammatik (Donatus Maior) darstellt. Im Vorwort
S. 529f. bemerkt er aber, dass es eine andere unter Aspers Namen
überlieferte Grammatik gibt, die er in mehreren Handschriften gefunden hat (Bern 207 und 611, Sangerm. 1180, Frising. 81, Tegerns.
181, Sangall. 876). Hier wollen wir uns nur mit der letzteren Grammatik beschäftigen. Da sie sich auf Donatus' kleinere Grammatik
(den Donatus Minor) gründet,[1] mag sie Asper Minor genannt werden,
im Gegensatz zum erstgenannten Asper Maior.

Keil gab den Asper Minor nicht heraus; warum er darauf verzich-
tete, geht aus seiner Bemerkung S. 530 klar hervor: "Eruditionis...
nulla in hoc libro sunt vestigia, neque ulla veterum scriptorum
exempla adscripta sunt." Aber H. Hagen hat in seinen *Anecdota Helvetica* (= *Gramm. Lat. suppl.*, Leipzig 1870) S. 39ff. diese Grammatik
ediert, und zwar auf Grund der Berner Hs. 207 (8.-9. Jh.; = A)[2]
und unter Vergleich mit cod. Bern 611 (8. Jh.; = B);[3] die letztere
Handschrift ist also freilich älter, hat aber nach Hagen im allgemei-
nen einen schlechteren Text.[4]

Obgleich Keil darin recht hat, dass unser Asper kein sehr ge-
lehrter Mann war, war eine Edition durchaus am Platze. *Erstens*
handelt es sich um einen unserer ältesten grammatischen Texte
insularer Herkunft. Der insulare Ursprung geht aus den vielen
Parallelen und Ähnlichkeiten mit insularen Grammatiken hervor:
so habe ich im *Arctos* 7 (1972), 62 nachgewiesen, dass Tatwine

---

[1] Der Abschnitt über das Pronomen ist sogar in einigen Handschriften
(BPV) wörtlich dem Don. Min. entnommen; in anderen (ACGM) wird nur
auf den Donat verwiesen. Es sei hier auch bemerkt, dass in G der Abschnitt
S. 49, 1-50, 9 Hagen durch Don. Min. S. 359, 13-360, 5 Keil ersetzt worden
ist. (Zu den Handschriften-Sigeln s. unten.)

[2] Nach Lowe, CLA 7 Nr. **568 vielleicht aus Fleury.

[3] Nach Lowe, CLA 7 Nr. **604 saec. VIII[1], wahrscheinlich aus Ost-
frankreich.

[4] Im folgenden wird Asper Minor nach Seite und Zeile von Hagens Ausgabe zitiert.

(Erzbischof von Canterbury zwischen 731 und 734) in seiner Grammatik[5] den Asper Minor benutzt hat (im Abschnitt über die Präpositionen); Hagen erwähnt in seinem Vorwort S. LXXX zwei Zitate aus unserem Texte in der hibernolateinischen Ars Bernensis;[6] in der anonymen hibernolateinischen Grammatik, die dem Cuimnanus gewidmet ist, heisst es (St. Paul, Kärnten, 25.2.16)[7] f. 41[ua] *De hisdem autem praepossitionibus utriusque casus quando in bonam malamue partem diriguntur uel motum stabilitatemue ostendunt satis Asporius (sic) et ipse Donatus ostendunt* (Asper S. 59, 5ff.); auch ib. f. 23rb wird Asper zitiert. Der Terminus ante quem des Asper Minor wird durch seine eben erwähnte Benutzung durch Tatwine sowie durch seine Überlieferung in zwei Handschriften aus dem 8. Jh. (s. unten) gegeben.

Zweitens haben wir überhaupt sehr wenige mittelalterliche Kommentare des Donatus Minor, und es lohnt sich, diejenigen, die überliefert sind, näher zu studieren. Zu erwähnen sind ausser unserem Texte in erster Linie die Kommentare des Iulianus Toletanus (ed. Maria A. H. Maestre Yenes, Toledo 1973), des (Pseudo) Erchanbertus (ed. W. V. Clausen, Chicago 1948), des Remigius (ed. W. Fox, Leipzig 1902) sowie des Sedulius Scottus (in der Hs. Tours 843; meine Ausgabe im *Corpus Christianorum*, cont. med. 40 C ist im Druck). Es gibt auch einige bisher unedierte anonyme Kommentare: einer steht am Rande der Hs. Orléans 295, und ein anderer ist im Vatic. Lat. 3318 f. 41[r]-58[u] überliefert.[8]

Hagens Ausgabe kann natürlich schon deswegen heutigen Ansprüchen nicht genügen, weil er nur zwei der damals bekannten Handschriften benutzt hat; ferner hat er — wie bei den anderen Ausgaben in den Anecdota Helvetica — keinen Quellenapparat beigegeben. In der Hoffnung, dass sich bald jemand der Aufgabe annimmt, uns eine moderne kritische Ausgabe des Asper Minor zu schenken, seien nun einige vorläufige textkritische und sprachliche Bemerkungen meinem Freunde Ludwig Bieler als ein kleines ἀντίδωρον gewidmet.

Kollationiert wurden die folgenden mir bekannten, von Hagen nicht benutzten Handschriften:

---

[5] Hrsg. v. Maria de Marco, 1968 (*Corpus Christianorum* 133).

[6] Zur irischen Herkunft dieser Grammatik vgl. Verf., *Der hibernolateinische Grammatiker Malsachanus* (Uppsala 1965) 20.

[7] B. Bischoffs Ausgabe dieser Grammatik wird bald erscheinen; vgl. vorläufig seine *Mittelalterlichen Studien* I, 282ff.

[8] L. Holtz (Nantes) bereitet eine Untersuchung dieser Grammatiken vor.

Angers 493 saec. IX[1] aus Tours,[9] f. 104[r]-115[r] (nur von S. 43, 29 an); = C

München Clm 6281 saec. IX[1] aus Freising[10] (= Frising. 81), f. 114[u]-126[r]; = M

München Clm 18181 saec. XI (= Tegerns. 181); = T

Paris BN lat. 13025 saec. IX in. aus Corbie[11] (= Sangerm. 1180), f. 16[r]-23[u]; = P

Sankt Gallen 876 saec. VIII/IX aus Sankt Gallen,[12] S. 3-29: = G

Sankt Gallen 907 saec. VIII[2] aus Sankt Gallen,[13] f. 230[r]-237[r] (nur bis S. 42, 30); = S

Vatikan Palat. lat. 1746 saec. IX in. f. 153[r]-161[u] (nur bis S. 61, 12); = V

Da das Incipit des Asper Minor mit dem des Donatus Minor übereinstimmt, ist est wahrscheinlich, dass unser Text in Handschriften-Katalogen mehrmals unter dem Donat steht und dass weitere Textzeugen ans Licht kommen, wenn das Handschriftenmaterial des Donatus Minor durchgearbeitet ist.

Dass T eine Kopie von M ist, hat bereits Keil a.O. bemerkt; s. weiter etwa C. E. Eder, *Die Schule des Klosters Tegernsee im frühen Mittelalter* (Studien und Mitteilungen zur Geschichte des Benediktinerordens Bd. 83) 1972, S. 87.

Die Handschriften C und P sind nahe verwandt. Von gemeinsamen Auslassungen seien erwähnt z.B. 50, 5 *ut* — 7 *est* om. CP, 54, 8 *cursim* — 9 *sparsim* om. CP; 51, 5 bieten beide *remittor* statt *imitor*,[14] 56, 25 *participium est* statt *facis participium praeteriti temporis*. Dass aber P keine Kopie von C ist, geht aus Auslassungen und Fehlern in C hervor, die in P kein Gegenstück haben, z.B. 47, 13 *quod uiri habent* om. C; 45, 25f. hat P *ab his gladiis ab his ecclesiis ab his fabulis ab his maculis* (ähnlich die anderen Hss.), aber C bietet: *...gladiis et cetera;* der Abschnitt über Präpositionen 58, 26-59, 4 ist in C stark abgekürzt. Ich habe keine gleichartigen Fehler in P ge-

---

[9] Nach freundlicher Mitteilung von B. Bischoff. — Gleich nach dem Asper Minor steht in dieser Hs. der Asper Maior, f. 115[r]-120[r] (von Keil nicht bemerkt).

[10] Vgl. B. Bischoff, *Die Südostdeutschen Schreibschulen* (1960) 117.

[11] Vgl. B. Bischoff, *Mittelalterliche Studien* 1, 60.

[12] So B. Bischoff brieflich; nach A. Bruckner, *Scriptoria medii aevi Helvetica* 2, 80 f. VIII[2]-800.

[13] Nach Lowe, CLA 7 Nr. 952. — Auf diese Hs. hat mich L. Holtz aufmerksam gemacht.

[14] Dem Fehler dürfte eine — nicht ungewöhnliche — Schreibung *emitor* statt *imitor* zugrundeliegen; so hier M.

funden, die die Annahme, C sei eine Kopie von P, verbieten würden, aber andrerseits lässt sich eine solche Abhängigkeit nicht positiv beweisen, und ich betrachte vorläufig C und P als Geschwisterhandschriften.

Was die anderen Handschriften betrifft, lässt sich eine Verwandtschaft zwischen G und S feststellen; 40, 12 z.B. lassen beide *hic et haec sacerdos* unter den Beispielen für communia duobus generibus aus, und 41, 21 haben beide *osculum* statt *otium*.

Der durch Vergleich aller mir bekannten Handschriften zu rekonstruierende Archetyp ist mit dem Original nicht identisch. Der Fremdkörper 47, 5-7 wird z.B. einhellig überliefert und stand offenbar im Archetyp.

Es seien nun einige Stellen erwähnt, an denen die von mir kollationierten Handschriften erwägenswerte oder wahrscheinlich bessere Lesarten als die von Hagen in seinem Texte gedruckten bieten.

40,1 fügen alle Hss. (ausser cod. A, der Hagens Text zugrundeliegt) ein *tamen* nach *est* hinzu.

40, 6 *Superlatiuus casus cui casui seruit?* Statt *casus* ist mit GSMV *gradus* zu schreiben (das Wort ist in P ausgelassen; Druckfehler bei Hagen?).

40, 30 ist *seruus* zu streichen: es fehlt in den von mir benutzten Hss. sowie in Hagens cod. B, und es hat unter lauter Adjektiven keinen Platz. Wahrscheinlich ist es ursprünglich eine Dittographie des unmittelbar vorhergehenden *seuerus*.

41, 25 ist nicht einzusehen, warum Hagen die von allen Hss. (auch von A) gebotene normale Orthographie *tonitruum* durch *tonitrum* ersetzt hat.

44, 23 ist das einhellig überlieferte *toregma* statt Hagens *toreuma* wiederherzustellen. Zur Erklärung der in vielen insularen Texten begegnenden Form *toregma* s. Verf., *Arctos* 7 (1972), 52f.

45, 10ff. *Nam equabus et mulabus et reliqua in hoc casu ideo contra rationem artis ponuntur, ne masculini potius quam feminini generis nominentur.* So Hagen, aber A ebenso wie die von mir eingesehenen Hss. lassen *generis* aus, und dieses Wort braucht nicht hinzugefügt zu werden: entweder ist mit CM *masculina...feminina* oder mit G *masculi...femine* zu schreiben; die letztere Alternative finde ich ansprechender, vgl. Don. 378, 9 *ab his deabus, ne, si deis dixerimus, deos, non deas significare uideamur.*

46, 14. Zwischen *ab hoc agili horum agilium* und *ab hoc difficili horum difficilium* ist mit allen von mir kollationierten Hss. *ab hoc*

stabili horum stabilium hinzuzufügen, vgl. die Dative/Ablative Z.
15f. *agilibus stabilibus difficilibus.*

46, 24f. *Item feminini generis saepes nubes dies: haec saepes et hae
saepes,* † *nuptiae dies: nam singularem numerum non habent.* Ein
wahrscheinlicher Text lässt sich mit Hilfe von MV und CP rekon-
struieren; M hat: ...*sepes nubes dies nuptiae. Haec sepes et hae sepes.
Nam nuptiae singularem non habet numerum* (ähnlich V); C hat:
...*sepes dies nubes. Dicis enim haec sepes et hae sepes. Similiter dies
et nubes. Nam singularem numerum non habent* (ähnlich P); ich
vermute: ...*sepes nubes dies nuptiae. Dicis enim haec sepes et hae
sepes; similiter dies et nubes. Nam nuptiae singularem numerum non
habent.* Zum plurale tantum *nuptiae* vgl. Don. 376, 28, zur Verwendung derselben Form *dies* und *nubes* im Sing. und im Plur. vgl.
Char. 195, 5f. (Barwick). Die Konstruktion *nuptiae...habent* ist
beizubehalten, s. z.B. U. Hahner, *Cassiodors Psalmenkommentar*
(München 1973) 150ff. über Ausdrücke wie *oues significant* bei
Cassiodor.[15]

47, 9 ist nach *conspectus* mit allen von mir eingesehenen Hss.
hinzuzufügen: *hic fluctus et hi fluctus.*

47, 16 haben alle meine Hss. *quia* statt des von Hagen gedruckten
quod; dasselbe gilt für 55, 8; 56, 26; 61, 7.

47, 21f. *dicis nominatiuo casu hic currus mugitus sensus, similiter
per u scribendum erit.* Es liegt eine Auslassung propter homoioteleuton in A (der einzigen von Hagen hier benutzten Hs.) vor. Zu
schreiben ist mit den anderen Kodizes: *dicis nominatiuo casu hic
currus mugitus sensus; per u scribendum erit. Et si dixeris plurali
numero accusatiuo hos currus mugitus sensus, similiter per u scribendum erit.*

47, 24. Die von Hagen eingeklammerte Glosse *locus secretus* wird
in allen von mir kollationierten Hss. ausgelassen.

48, 4ff. *Rogo, ut legas et uehementiam animi tui, sicut in utilitate
aliqua, sic etiam in adsaeculitate rarum claritata demonstres, quod non
in uanitate dico, quod hoc nec apertius nec rationabilius alibi inuenies.*
Es fällt auf, dass Hagen dem sinnlosen *sic* – Satz kein Korruptel-
zeichen beigefügt hat. Zu schreiben ist mit den von mir kollationierten Hss.: ...*sicut in utilitate reliqua, sic etiam in adsecuta
litterarum claritate demonstres, quia...*

---

[15] In V wird ursprüngliches *habent* von einer 2. Hand in *habet* korrigiert.

48, 18-20. Die Andeutung der Lücken und das hinzugefügte *ut* sind zu streichen.

48, 24f. *inchoatiua ab incipiendo*. Besser scheint die Lesart von CP *inchoatiua ab inchoando, id est ab incipiendo* zu sein. Vgl. gleich vorher *meditatiua a meditando* und *frequentatiua a frequentando*. *Inchoatiua dicta est ab inchoando* heisst es in der von mir im Corp. Christ. zu edierenden Ars Laur. (cod. Vatic. Palat. lat. 1754 f. 23ᵘ). Dennoch macht der Umstand, dass sämtliche anderen Hss. die Worte *ab inchoando id est* auslassen, die Lesart von CP etwas verdächtig.

49, 20f. *Haec enim uerba es habent in fine declinationis personae secundae, et ideo secundae declinationis sunt*; so A. Zu schreiben ist mit CPV *coniugationis* statt *declinationis* (M und B lassen das Wort aus und G hat einen anderen Text). Offensichtlich liegt in A ein Perseverationsfehler vor.

49, 32. Die Wörter *confringor — laedor* werden in allen von mir eingesehenen Hss. ausgelassen.

50, 12. Das von Hagen hineinkonjizierte *de* ist von allen meinen Hss. überliefert.

50, 23. Die in allen Hss. (auch in AB) überlieferte Schreibung *degeo* (statt Hagens *dego*) ist beizubehalten; zu dieser Form s. meinen *Malsachanus* 93. Die Form *degeo* ist auch im Kapitel über die Präpositionen überliefert (s. Hagens Apparat zu S. 59, 16).

53, 28 ist mit allen Hss. (ausser B) *paruum* statt *parum* zu schreiben. Diese Schreibung des Adverbs ist auch an den entsprechenden Stellen von Donatus (386, 13), Clemens (hrsg. von Tolkiehn 1928) S. 86, 25 u.a. von einigen Handschriften überliefert, s. *Arctos* 7 (1972), 57. Smaragdus zitiert in seiner Grammatik sowohl *paruum* wie *parum* (cod. Paris. lat. 7551 f. 86ᵘ).

55, 10. Das von Hagen hinzugefügte *sunt* ist in allen von mir kollationierten Hss. überliefert.

56, 28ff. *si dicatur "questus est mihi contentum comitem suum"* et *"flexus est ad misericordiam", participia facis praeteriti temporis.* Statt *contentum comitem suum* haben GMV *contemptum suum*, B (nach Hagens Apparat) *comitum suum*, CP dagegen *comitem suum uel contemptum suum* (das letztere *suum* von C ausgelassen). Offensichtlich gab es zwei alte Varianten, die der Schreiber von A, dem Hagen wie gewöhnlich folgt, nebeneinander schrieb statt eine Auswahl zu treffen. Wahrscheinlich schrieb Asper *questus est mihi contemptum suum* "er beklagte sich bei mir über die Verachtung, die er gelitten hatte".

60, 1 *bene in ablatiuo.* Mit allen von mir eingesehenen Hss. (und B) ist ein Prädikat *ponitur* hinzuzufügen.

60, 2f. *"deduc me, domine, in uia tua et ambulabo in ueritate tua"* ;[16] *licet "ambulabo" motum uidetur habere,* ... *Licet* ist eine Emendation Hagens; seine Hs. A hat *dicet* (B hat einen anderen Text). Zu schreiben ist mit den von mir kollationierten Hss. *"deduc" et "ambulabo" motum uidentur habere.*

60, 7f. *"induxisti nos in refrigerio"* ;[17] *"induxisti" motus esse uide-tur, sed quod in refrigerio, merito in ablatiuo conplicatur.* So Hagen mit A. Die Lesart von A ist wohl an sich nicht unmöglich; zur Ver-wendung von *conplicare* im Sinne von 'iungere' vgl. Beda, orthogr. (gramm. 7) S. 279, 19 *maiestas cum scribis aut dicis, s secundae syllabae complicari debet.* Aber BGCP bieten *ablatiuo casui applica-tur (casui* von G ausgelassen; V hat *in ablatiuo applicatur,* M *in ablatiuo amplectitur),* und für die Authentizität dieser Lesart spricht die Parallele 61, 1f. *Quaelibet ergo nomina uerbis istis...uolueris applicare:* so alle von mir kollationierten Hss.; A hat *ampliare,* während B die Stelle auslässt; Hagen vermutet auch hier *complicare,* eine m.E. wenig wahrscheinliche Emendation.

60, 19. Alle von mir kollationierten Hss. bieten mit B *etiam* statt *enim.*

61, 4 *Accusatiuo enim casui cum haec uerba nominibus iunguntur, sine praepositione declinationi seruiunt, ut est egredior foras, Romam uado.* Erstens ist mit allen von mir benutzten Hss. (+ B) zu schrei-ben *forum* statt *foras:* die letztere Form kann ja als ein Adverb die Verwendung des Akkusativs nicht exemplifizieren. Zweitens muss mit GV eine Umstellung gemacht werden: *Cum haec uerba nomini-bus iunguntur, sine praepositione accusatiui casus declinationi seruiunt* (G hat *ablatiui* statt *accusatiui;* ACP bieten: *accusatiuo etiam [enim A] casui cum haec uerba nominibus iunguntur sine praepositione accusatiui casus declinationi seruiunt [accusatiuo casui* statt *declinationi* A; *declinatione* C]); vgl. oben Z. 2 *ablatiui casus declinationi seruiunt.*

Es folgen einige sprachliche Bemerkungen zum Text.

42, 20 druckt Hagen unter den Neutra auf *-men* mit A *lamen.* In BM begegnet dafür *iamen,* und in den anderen von mir eingesehenen Hss. fehlt das Wort (in C ist der betreffende Abschnitt nicht erhal-ten). Unsere Stelle ist die einzige im ThLL für das Wort *lamen* ange-

---

[16] Psalm. 85, 11.
[17] Psalm. 65, 12.

59, 1of. *in proditionem et in proditiones mittor.* Zu schreiben ist mit allen von mir kollationierten Hss. *perditionem...perditiones*, vgl. 60, 5 *deduc me in perditionem.*

führte; es wird als Nebenform zu *lamentum* aufgefaßt. Die Lesart *iamen* dürfte ein Schreibfehler für *lamen* sein, aber es ist in Anbetracht der schwachen handschriftlichen Bezeugung unwahrscheinlich, dass Asper *lamen* in seinem Nominalkatalog aufführte; entweder ist es ein ursprünglicher Fehler für *lumen* oder *limen*, die beide in allen Hss. vorkommen, oder ist es ein späterer Zusatz: in einigen Hss. — besonders in V — ist das Streben ganz deutlich, die Nominal- und Verbalkataloge zu erweitern. Im letzteren Falle ist wohl *lamen* mit dem von Blatt, *Novum Glossarium* und Latham, *Revised Medieval-Latin Word-List* s.v. in englischen Texten aus dem 13.-16. Jh. belegten *lamen* im Sinne von *lamina* "Blech" identisch; dieses *lamen* ist eine neutrale Rückbildung aus dem als einem Plural aufgefassten fem. *lamina* (so Blatt. a.O.).

42, 29f. (unter Neutra auf *-r*) *robur de arbore, robor de uirtute, rubor coloris.* Der Umstand, dass jedes der drei Wörter eine Bestimmung hat, zeigt, dass sie ähnlich oder gleich ausgesprochen wurden. Die Farbe *rubor* wird auch von Tatwine (ed. De Marco) S. 36 Z. 1138 und in der insularen Ars Ambian.[18] (cod. Ambian. 426 saec. IX) f. 53[u] als ein Neutrum bezeichnet.

43, 3 (unter Neutra auf *-e*) *aplare cochleare.* Die Form *aplare* begegnet ausser in A auch in G, während MPV *amplare* haben (in C fehlt der betreffende Abschnitt, und in B wird das Wort ausgelassen). Das Wort kehrt S. 47, 12 wieder; hier haben AB *aplare*, G *apulare*, CP *appellare* und MV *amplare*. Dies ist ein Glossenwort, das u.a. in den angelsächsischen Glossarien Affatim (CGL 4, 472, 35) und Corpus (ed. Lindsay 1921 S. 17 Nr. 706) begegnet; s. weiter Thesaurus Glossarum emendatarum s.v. *applare*. In mehreren Glossen wird das Wort durch *coc(h)lear* erklärt, und es ist sicher kein Zufall, dass Asper *aplare cochleare* nebeneinander verzeichnet; zum Einfluss der Glossarien auf insulare Grammatiken vgl. meinen *Malsachanus* 74ff. In den Glossen wird das Wort gewöhnlich *ap(p)lare* geschrieben, aber es gibt auch die Form *amplare* (Thesaurus Glossarum a.O.). Zu diesem dunklen Wort s. weiter ThLL 2, 295, 2ff.

49, 20 bieten codd. MV *erudio* unter den Verben der 2. Konjug. Das ist ein durch Zusammenfall der Endungen *-eo* und *-io* und

---

[18] Zu dieser Grammatik vgl. meinen *Malsachanus* 23f.

daraus folgenden Konjugationswechsel leicht zu erklärender Fehler; Belege aus anderen insularen Grammatiken in meinem *Malsachanus* 116f.

54, 21 *ab scholastico* G (die anderen Hss.: *a scholastico*). Die Lesart von G hängt mit der romanischen Aussprache mit prothetischem Vokal vor dem *s* impurum zusammen. Eine gleichartige und ebenso zu erklärende Verwendung der Form *ab* (*ab spiritu* usw.) lässt sich bei Hermae pastor und Gregorius von Tours belegen, vgl. M. Bonnet, *Le latin de Grégoire de Tours* (Paris 1890) 147 mit Lit.

59, 14 begegnet die Schreibung *uascem* statt *fascem* in M. Wie in meinem *Malsachanus* 103 bemerkt, begegnet *f-* für *u-* und umgekehrt *u-* für *f-* in insularen Texten, aber auch anderswo; den dort angeführten Belegen und Literaturhinweisen füge ich hinzu z.B. Gil, *Habis* I (1970), 71 (Belege aus Spanien), Jonah W. D. Skiles, *The Latinity of Arbeo's Vita Sancti Corbiniani* (Diss. Chicago 1938) 83 (*uulgorem* statt *fulgorem* bei Arbeo); in *Vitae sanctorum Danorum* (ed. M. Cl. Gertz, Kopenhagen 1908-12) 159, 12 ist *ueritate* statt *feritate* überliefert.

SYNODUS II S. PATRICII

KATHLEEN HUGHES

The canons of the Second Synod of S. Patrick were edited and translated by Professor Bieler in 1963. J. T. McNeill and Helen Gamer had provided a translation in 1938 and J. B. Bury discussed the canons briefly in an appendix to *The Life of St Patrick*.[1] Bury notes that the *Collectio Canonum Hibernensis* ascribes most of the canons of Pa. II to the *Romani*, or the *Sinodus Romana*. This compilation of the *Collectio* was begun between 704 and 725 and completed before 747.[2] It is generally agreed that the canons of Pa. II were not passed by Patrick.

As I have shown elsewhere, many of the native Irish canons in the eighth-century *Collectio* belong to two distinct groups, the *Romani* and the *Hibernenses*. The *Romani* were concerned with a church administered by bishops and clinging to Roman and continental usage: the *Hibernenses* were dealing with a church normally administered by abbots, a church concerned with native legal institutions, trying to fit the Irish church into the structure of native law.

By the early eighth century, when the *Collectio* was compiled, Pa. II was seen as emanating from the *Romani*. There is one canon (Pa. II. 30) which specifically says that business transactions are to be confirmed by signature, ⟨more⟩ *Romanorum*. This seems to be saying that the native law of contract is not enough, and it firmly labels the canons as "Roman".

In a "Roman" church the position of the bishop is one of supreme administrative importance. The First Synod of Patrick, which I have argued dates from the second quarter of the sixth century,[3]

---

[1] L. Bieler, *The Irish Penitentials*, Dublin 1963, pp. 184-97. J. T. McNeill and H. Gamer, *Medieval Handbooks of Penance*, Repr. New York 1965, pp. 80-86. J. B. Bury, *The Life of St. Patrick*, London 1905, pp. 235-41.

[2] It is discussed by K. Hughes, *The Church in Early Irish Society*, London 1966, pp. 123-42, and edited by H. Wasserschleben, *Die irische Kanonensammlung*, Leipzig 1885.

[3] My discussion, Hughes, *Church*. p. 44-52 and Hughes, *Early Christian Ireland, Introduction to the Sources*, London 1972, pp. 68-73. There is a controversy over the date. See bibliography cited in Hughes, *Church*; also L. Bieler, *St. Patrick and the Coming of Christianity*, Dublin and Melbourne,

does not mention the abbot until the final chapter. This set of canons shows a church under bishops, each with his own *paruchia* and
plebs.

The administration of the church depicted in Pa. II is not quite so
clear. It is still definitely a church under episcopal jurisdiction. One
incomplete canon (Pa. II. 20) reads:

> De Parrochias: Cum monachis non est dicendum, quia malum est
> inauditum; qui unitatem uero plebis non incongrue suscipimus...

Here it is *we*, as distinct from the monks, who uphold the unity of
the plebs. There are clerics in this church with a *ministerium*
(Pa. II. 10): the clerics, not the monks, are the people administering
the church. Heretics are to be absolved and re-admitted by the
bishop's imposition of hands (Pa.II.8).

All the same, abbots and monks are important. When the canonist
enumerates the seed of the gospels he ranks both bishops and *doc-
tores* and monks and virgins as a hundredfold. Monks may dwell
under either a bishop or an abbot (Pa. II. 17). The person in charge
of penance seems to be the abbot (Pa.II.3). The monastery is,
however, completely separate from the world (Pa. II. 20). Monks are
to dwell in solitude without worldly resources under a bishop or
abbot (Pa.II.17). They cannot leave their own monastery without
the abbot's permission (Pa. II. 21): this is substantially a repetition
of the last sentence of Pa. I.

This looks like the church depicted in the Penitential of Vinnian,
which probably dates from about the third quarter of the sixth
century. In Vinnian's Penitential the people who minister to the
population are priests and deacons, and the monks seem to have no
duties in the *paruchia*, for they are forbidden to baptize or receive
alms. But monks certainly existed, living under an abbot's control,
and the régime which Vinnian imposes is an ascetic one. Pa. II
seems to fit in with the conditions which we know existed in the
second half of the sixth century, when diocesan bishops still existed
but when the monastic movement was gaining power.

There are other canons in the collection which support this dating.
The church is still making adult converts; there are pagans who have
been baptized some time after accepting the Christian faith (Pa. II.

1967, pp. 16-18, D. Binchy, *Studia Hibernica* VIII (1968) 63 and *Indo-
European and Indo-Europeans: Papers presented to the Third Indo-European
Conference, 1963*, Philadelphia 1970, pp. 355-67.

31). Evangelism is still a priority (Pa. II. 15). The church is not yet a rich institution (Pa. II. 2). The First Synod of Patrick had insisted that Christians were to keep themselves separate from the world, not resort to pagan courts. In Pa. II they are told to be careful with whom they associate (Pa. II. 1), to reject the excommunicate and to avoid heretics.[4]

Canon 12 says that no *oblatio pro defunctis* is to be made at mass for those who in their lives have not taken part in the mass. It reads:

> De oblatione pro defunctis. Audi apostulum dicentem: *Est autem peccatum ad mortem*: *non pro illo dico ut rogit quis*. Et Dominus: *Nolite dare sanctum canibus*. Qui enim in uita sua sacrificium non meretur accipere, quomodo post mortem illi poterit adiuuare?

In the early church the faithful brought to the eucharist their own *oblationes* of bread and wine and any other offerings in kind which they wished to make. The Stowe Missal shows that at the mass, immediately after the chalice was uncovered (*landirech sund*, "full uncovering here") the oblation was offered, and then there was a prayer in which the names of the dead were recited (*carorum nostrorum ·n· et cararum nostrarum quorum nomina recitamus*).[5] This is the *oblatio pro defunctis* of which our canon speaks.

Pa. II. 12 is paralleled by a canon in the *Collectio* (XV. 2c) which says that for those who have been neither thoroughly evil nor thoroughly good, but who have professed Christianity, *oblatio* and prayer and alms and fasting are to be given. This canon says that for really bad people no such action must be taken, unless they have made donations to the church. In Irish civil law an offering to the church (*edpart*) is often made in return for intercession (*écndairc*), though the gift here seems to be more substantial than the offering brought to mass.[6]

There is another reference to the *oblatio* in the Penitential of Cummean XI. 11. This says:

> Diaconus obliuiscens oblationem adferre donec auferatur linteamen quando recitantur pausantium nomina similiter peniteat.

---

[4] Does Pa. II.11 imply that clerics may still continue to live in the same house with their wives, provided they maintain continence? If so this suggests a date contemporary with Vinnian.

[5] G. F. Warner, *Stowe Missal*, London 1915, II.9ff.

[6] *Ancient Laws of Ireland* V.212, 316, 500.

The *linteamen* here is the covering of the chalice, which we met in the Stowe Missal rubric, and when the covering is removed the "names of the dead" are recited. The Penitential of Cummean and the Stowe Missal thus complement each other.

Pa. II. 14 presents an interesting attack on a too rigorous asceticism. It reads:

> De abstinentia insolubili[que] a cibis. Statuunt ut Christi aduentus sponsi nullas nostras legis inueniat ieiunii. Quid autem inter Nouatianum et Christianum interest nisi quod Nouatianus indesinenter, Christianus uero per tempus absteneat, ut locus et tempus et persona per omnia obseruitur?

The Novatians were a schismatic sect which started in the third century as a protest against the ease with which the church was allowing her lapsed members to be reconciled after the Decian persecution. They continued as a rigorist group, with a very severe penitential discipline. They spread throughout the west in the third and fourth centuries, losing ground in the fifth and gradually dying out. Gildas, writing about 540, has a biting reference to them (c. 67). He likens to the Novatians those Britons who have returned from pilgrimage, full of spiritual pride, who direct their gaze up to heaven and pretend to be creatures of a new mould (*sese noua quaedam plasmata*). Our canonists are afraid of their fanatical asceticism: Christians are rather to observe *locus*, *tempus* and *persona* in their fasting. Perhaps the *Romani* who framed our canons were a little nervous of the extreme asceticism of the monastic movement, which, in the second half of the sixth century, was at the height of its enthusiasm.

Pa. II. 16 may be glancing in the same direction. It reads:

> De falsis episcopis. Qui non secundum apostulum electus est, ab altero episcopo est damnandus; deinde ad reliquam plebem declinandus, et degradandus.

There is nothing in the Epistles of the New Testament about how a bishop should be elected, though Paul describes what sort of a man he must be. Various early church canons require a number of bishops to be present at the consecration of a new bishop. The first of the *Canones Apostolorum*, included in Dionysius' collection c. 500, requires a bishop to be consecrated by two or three bishops. The Council of Nicaea had forbidden a bishop to be consecrated by one bishop, and the Council of Arles (314) asked for the presence of seven bishops, or at least three. (*Si tamen non potuerit septem, infra tres non audeat ordinare.*) At this last synod three British bishops were present, so knowledge of the ruling must have reached Britain. So presumably an "apostolic" election to the *Romani* meant consecration by several bishops.

The Life of St Samson has some interesting things to say about the election and consecration of bishops. This Life contains material which must go back to the sixth century, and it was written probably in the seventh century. It says that a synod met on an accustomed day each year to consecrate bishops, on the Feast of St. Peter's Chair. It is clear that a number of bishops attended this gathering. Samson himself was consecrated in a vision, by the three disciples, Peter, James and John, *seundum morem*. The British bishops accepted this consecration as valid, and placed him in the episcopal chair. It is clear from the Life of Samson that the synod not only consecrated but determined who was to be consecrated. So when the writer of our canon speaks of "election", election and consecration may well have seemed to him part of the same process.

P. II. 16 is a puzzling canon, but I take it to mean that the *Romani* were insisting on election and consecration by several bishops. We know that the monastic church a century later was not following continental usages in consecration, and that the manner of consecration was one of the points at issue in England between the "Roman" and "Celtic" parties. After the Synod of Whitby Tuda, who had been consecrated in southern Ireland (presumably by *Romani*), became bishop of Northumbria. Wine, bishop of the West Saxons, consecrated Chad as bishop of York with the help of two British bishops because there were no others available. Wilfrid went to Gaul to obtain consecration.

Consecration by several bishops, among the *Romani* probably by a synod, provided a check on who was appointed. This was necessary to prevent abuses. Adamnán has a passage describing how a bishop in Findchán's monastery was pressed by the abbot into ordaining as priest a very unsuitable man whom the abbot loved.[7] This sort of thing was less likely to happen under the Roman system. It may well have been some of the monastic bishops whom *Romani* in the later sixth century regarded as *falsi episcopi*.

---

[7] *Life of Columba*, I.36, ed. A. O. and M. O. Anderson, London 1961, p. 280. The text says the abbot loved him *carnaliter*.

There are four canons in Pa. II about the marriage law. A man
may not marry his dead brother's wife (Pa. II. 25): this is in accordance with earlier rulings of the continental church. A man may
not break a first marriage to enter on a second, unless the marriage
vows have been annulled by adultery (Pa. II. 28). This contradicts
a canon in the *Collectio* which is attributed to Patricius (XLVI. 32)
which says that if a man has a first wife who is a fornicator he cannot
take another wife while the first wife is living. The Penitential of
Vinnian (cc. 43-4), in the ninth-century St Gall MS, says the same
thing. Pa. II. 26 begins by quoting that the man joined to a harlot
is made one body, but goes on to quote: "It is not permitted to a
man to put away his wife, except for fornication" *hac si liciat ob
hanc causam*. Thus he may marry, for it is as if his wife had died.
This is a more relaxed marriage law than that of Vinnian, or of the
"Patrician" canon in the *Collectio*, or of the Council of Agde (506)
canon 25.

Pa. II. 29 deals with consanguinity. It reads:

> De consanguinitate in coniugio. Intellege quid lex loquitur, non
> minos nec plus; quod autem obseruatur apud nos, ut quattuor
> genera diuidantur, nec uidisse dicunt nec legisse.

I take *lex* here to mean the canon law of the church. The marriage
law of the church was at first far from clear. The Emperor Theodore
the Great had prohibited marriage between first cousins, and so had
the Emperor Honorius in 409: this is the fourth degree of consanguinity reckoned according to the Roman system. The Germanic
peoples had a different system of reckoning degrees of kindred,
based on *genicula*, counting the joints of the body from the head to
the finger nails. According to this system first cousins stand in the
second degree of consanguinity to each other. Early in the sixth
century, at the Councils of Agde (506) and Epaon (517) the church
prohibited marriage between second cousins and all nearer relations.
This, according to the reckoning of Roman law, is prohibition up to
and including the sixth degree.

It looks as if, in our canon, the *Romani* are following the Roman
reckoning, and are adopting the rulings of these early sixth century
councils. But some of their contemporaries were saying that married
couples needed only be divided by four degrees of kin (i.e. the four
degrees of Roman law): thus marriage between first cousins would
be forbidden by them, but after this there were no restrictions of
consanguinity.

The Irish were not the only people who were allowing marriage nearer than the sixth degree. Pope Zachary, in the Acts of the Roman Council of 743, said that there were men *de Germaniae partibus* who claimed that Pope Gregory the Great had given them leave to marry in the fourth degree (*licentiam illis dedisset in quartam sese copulari generationem*).[8] Zachary says he can find no trace of this writing. (It was not until the ninth century that the Church prohibited marriage up to seven canonical degrees, reckoned according to the Germanic system which the church ultimately adopted.)

The canons of the Second Synod of Patrick extend our knowledge of the Irish church in the second half of the sixth century. They are canons of the *Romani*, and the *Romani* still uphold a church governed by bishops, whose dioceses are coterminous with the *plebs*. But abbots and monks play an important part in the church. The church is still making adult converts from paganism. It is very much aware of the continental church, trying to enforce Gaulish rulings on consanguinity. The Novatian schism still has meaning in the sixth-century Irish church. It also looks as if the *Romani* may have regarded the extreme asceticism of the new monastic movement with some reserve. They may also have regarded the monastic bishops, often consecrated by only one bishop, as improperly ordained; and they were determined to keep to the practice of consecrating bishops at synods, or where several bishops were met together. The text is therefore an interesting commentary on a period of transition from diocesan bishops to monastic *paruchiae*.

---

[8] *M. G. H. Conc.* II.i. p. 20.

SOBRE LAS SERIES DE VOCES DE ANIMALES

MANUEL C. DIAZ y DIAZ

No deja de ser curioso observar cómo una serie no desdeñable de textos literarios en la tardía Antigüedad y Alta Edad Media se ha ocupado de recoger y organizar el léxico referente a los distintos sonidos animales. Estos textos plantean pequeños problemas de sentido y aun de relación entre ellos que me parecen dignos de una sucinta atención. Y pues probablemente las escuelas insulares han jugado en esto cierto papel, he decidido brindar a nuestro homenajeado estas nótulas que descubren pocas cosas pero quieren llamar la atención sobre algunas más.

En principio, el problema de los sonidos animales aparece como una dificultad lingüística, ya que se trata de *uoces confusae* en la denominación antigua, o de *uoces illitteratae*, es decir, no reproducible por las grafías usuales, en la terminología de Prisciano.[1] Del problema de la dificultad de análisis y reproducción se pasa a la curiosidad por definir estos sonidos, intentando seriamente hallar mecanismos onomatopeicos suficientes. A su vez este problema se hace lexicográfico cuando se ensaya la distinción entre ellos de los sonidos animales y se reunen como palabras curiosas. De aquí se pasa a otra cuestión cuando a alguien se le ocurre resolver el difícil empleo de estos términos, a menudo imprecisos o de fijación vacilante, dentro de un esquema métrico.

Pondré de lado cuanto se refiere a los orígenes y constitución del repertorio *de uocibus animalium* que quizás se remonte a Suetonio.[2] Me importa subrayar que la primera lista tardía, muy sucinta todavía, se debe a Polemio Silvio en cuyo Latérculo aparece constituyendo un capítulo.[3] De Suetonio, salvo el entusiasmo de Reifferscheid, contagioso pero poco probante, nada sabemos. En Polemio Silvio aparecen 19 voces animales y 5 confusas no procedentes de

---

[1] Por ejemplo Don. gramm. IV 367 K. o Mar. Vict. gramm. VI 4 K. oponen *confusa* a *articulada*, y éste ejemplifica con *equi hinnitus, anguis sibilus*. Prisciano, en cambio, al establecer dos planos de distinciones incluye estos sonidos entre las voces *illiteratae quae nec scribi nec intellegi* pueden como *crepitus, mugitus et alia* (prisc. gramm. I₂.II, 6 K.).

[2] *Suetonii fragmenta* ed. Reifferscheid, 1860, 247 ss.

[3] Pol. Silv. nom. anim., chron. I 548 Mommsen.

animales: de aquéllas 9 corresponden a mamíferos, 8 a pájaros, 1 a un insecto y otra a un anfibio. Como en la serie entran el oso y el león resulta evidente que ha habido una investigación, al no limitarse a animales domésticos o locales.

En el mundo de la poesía es Ausonio el que una vez más registra entre tantas curiosidades también su composición *in hominem uocis absonam*,[4] poema de cuatro dísticos, en que se recogen poco más de cuatro términos; subrayo que hay en él una alusión a las voces de aves.

Dentro del siglo VII comenzamos a encontrar nuevos ejemplos, variados y frecuentes, de nuestras listas, lo que ya exige una cierta explicación por la época y el tipo de textos en que aparecen incluidas. Hagamos el elenco de éstos. En Hispania, el poema 41 de Eugenio de Toledo;[5] en Irlanda el poema *de cantibus auium*;[6] en Gran Bretaña, la serie incluida por Aldhelmo de Malmesbury en su tratado *de metris et enigmatibus ac pedum regulis* que debió ser compuesto sobre 680,[7] y finalmente en Germania quizá, y no sin alguna probabilidad en el siglo VIII o mejor en el siglo IX, y en ambientes insulares, el poema misceláneo *de uolucribus et iumentis de filomela*.[8]

Aunque el primero de los textos, el hispano, aparece atribuido en el manuscrito León Catedral 22 a Eugenio de Toledo, tengo vehementes sospechas de que se trata de un pseudepígrafo: que andaba este poema por Córdoba, de donde es originario aquel códice,[9] lo prueba el que en el siglo IX med. haya sido imitado por Albaro de Córdoba, pero nada nos garantiza la autoría eugeniana. Téngase presente que la colección de supuestos poemas de Eugenio de Toledo que nos trasmite este manuscrito tiene un carácter muy especial: se trata de un conjunto de "poemas" con clasificaciones y juegos etimológicos no isidorianos,[10] que muy probablemente hayan de ser atribuidos a ejercicios de escuela. Pero no es de este lugar el proceder

---

[4] AVS. epigr. 72, p. 216 ed. Schenkl, *MGH auct. ant. V 2*.

[5] EVG. TOL. carm. 42, (*de uoce hominis absona*), p. 257 ed. Vollmer, *MGH auct. ant. XIV*.

[6] *Anthologia latina* 733, p. 218 ed. Riese.

[7] ALDHELM. metr. 131, ed. Ehwald, *MGH auct. ant. XV* 179-180.

[8] Anth. lat. 762, p. 246-248 ed. Riese.

[9] He trazado una historia amplia del manuscrito y estudiado los textos que contiene en un artículo aparecido en *Archivos Leoneses* 45-46 (1969) 133-168.

[10] Art. cit. 139: a los poemas, de origen toledano muy verosímil acompañan curiosos extractos de pasajes de los *Origenes* de Isidoro.

a un detenido estudio de su autenticidad, toda vez que en cambio podemos garantizar, a partir del conjunto de materiales en que van insertos, que proceden del siglo VII med. y con altísima probabilidad de Toledo. Desde nuestro punto de vista, sí es de recalcar que el autor del poema se ha limitado a las llamadas voces de fieras, con exclusión de las aves,[11] un poco al modo de Ausonio del que indudablemente depende, como ya había señalado Vollmer.[12]

El poema *de cantibus auium* es de indudable origen irlandés,[13] o por lo menos de región o ambiente con indiscutibles conexiones irlandesas, a lo que no parece oponerse la tradición manuscrita. Aunque en la última edición, la de A. Riese, aparece partido reclamando para los últimos versos un tratamiento distinto, como si hubiera de suponerse un primer poema en que habría perfecta coincidencia entre el epígrafe y el primer verso y su contenido, en tanto que el final pertenecería a otra pieza distinta referente a las voces de las fieras,[14] la comparación con el otro poema, también incluido en la *Anthologia latina* nos hace rechazar tal distribución y las conjeturas que implica. Lo que sí es erróneo y falsamente aplicado es el epígrafe *de cantibus auium* que, por otro lado, no aparece en absoluto en el manuscrito más antiguo y mejor, el Augiense 10, 3, de fines del siglo IX o comienzos del X. En efecto, todas las series de voces animales que conocemos por diversos repertorios comprenden indiferentemente sonidos de aves, de mamíferos o de otras clases de animales, sin excluir sonidos de seres inanimados, justamente todo lo que incluían bajo la denominación de *uoces confusae* los antiguos gramáticos.

De este poema deriva el poema *de uolucribus et iumentis de filomela*. Quizá pueda verse fácilmente la razón de esta dependencia literaria. Digamos, en primer lugar, que el poema posterior, probablemente del siglo IX, ha conocido listas más ricas que la que ha dado pie al poema *de cantibus auium*. La presencia del término *drosca* en este poema nos sitúa verosímilmente en un ambiente germánico,

---

[11] V. 8: *estque feris socia non nostrae uocis amica.*
[12] No sólo es el título el que establece este contacto. Incluso parte del texto depende de Ausonio como trama y presupuesto. Este indudable conocimiento justifica, a mi entender, contra Vollmer, la necesidad, por ejemplo, de corregir en el v. 1 *rugitum... aselli* por *ruditum aselli*, error que Vollmer quiere atribuir no a la tradición manuscrita sino al propio Eugenio.
[13] En el v. 13 se lee *Nunc cuculus cantans Scottos iter ire perurget.*
[14] Ya Riese supone, además de una laguna entre el verso 13 y el 14, que los versos 14-20 son un aditamento (app. ad loc.)

lengua de la que parece derivar este vocablo.[15] La dependencia se prueba por frases idénticas o análogas situadas en la misma posición del verso: así *gallina caccillat* forma la cláusula del hexámetro en c. 733 v. 10 y c. 762 v. 25; *accipites pipant* de c. 733 v. 6 conviene en iniciar verso (primer hemistiquio de hexámetro y pentámetro respectivamente) con c. 762 v. 24; *longoque ciconia collo|glottorat* de c. 733 v. 6|7 conviene en diversos detalles con *glottorat*[16] *inmenso maerens ciconia rostro* de c. 762 v. 29; y, lo que aun es más significativo, *improbus anser*[17] constituye cláusula a pesar de que la voz que se le atribuye en cada poema difiere del otro (*trinnit* con Aldhelmo| *graccitat*). Por otra parte creo ver en el v. 31|32 *psittacus humanas depromit uoce loquelas|atque suo domino "chaere" sonat uel "aue"* un eco de Isid. orig. 12, 7, 24.[18]

Este segundo poema posterior añade 19 voces de "fieras" y 25 de aves que no están en el primero. Ciertos datos parecen propios al no aparecer en ninguna otra serie, lo que prueba una vez más que nos encontramos ante un proceso creciente de búsqueda infatigable.

Posición definitiva adopta Aldhelmo. Su tratado *de metris et enigmatibus ac pedum regulis* fue compuesto con toda probabilidad después de 680. Al tratar del metro jónico *a minore*, el gran erudito aduce, segun su costumbre, una retahila de vocablos, en este caso ocho, el último de los cuales es *rudibundi*, que explica diciendo: *nam ruditus proprie asellorum est.* A partir de aquí añade, tomando pie en tal dato de manera arbitraria y quizá de modo deliberado, *et quia se uocis occasio praebuit non modo propter structuram pedum et rationem metrorum uerum etiam ob differentiam uocum et discretionem sonorum non absurdum arbitror quadripedum et uolucrum et reptilium uoces cum generalitate pluralitatis et specialitate singularitatis subtiliter dirimere.* En la enumeración se apoya en la *maiorum auctoritas* pero no da ninguna pista cierta que nos permita profundizar más en sus fuentes. Lo que me importa subrayar es que Aldhelmo ofrece por primera vez la lista no sólo muy enriquecida, sino lo que es más

---

[15] Cf. *ThLL* V 2070, donde se explica como denominación para una variedad de "tordo". La relación con el poema anterior exige segun parece un ambiente insular en un medio germánico, lo que sería el caso en algun centro de la misión irlandesa, o en algun centro posterior que tuviera algo que ver con un centro de aquel tipo.

[16] Nótese idéntica posición inicial del verso.

[17] C. 733 v. 12 y c. 762 v. 19.

[18] Psittacus... articulata uerba exprimit ita ut si eam [auem] non uideris, hominem loqui putes. Ex natura autem salutat dicens "haue" uel χαῖρε.

importante, por orden alfabético.[19] Es curioso que en la larga lista,
que abarca nada menos que 74 lemas, se entremezclen sonidos de
aves, mamíferos, anfibios e insectos con ruidos de la naturaleza y de
objetos inanimados. Pero es más curioso todavía que Aldhelmo se
haya sentido autorizado a incluir su lista como tal en uno de los
capítulos de su Métrica; y aunque pueda oponerse el hecho de que
la presente en el dedicado al Jónico *a minore*, no es de olvidar que al
final de la serie añade: *haec genera uocum non ad ionicum pertinebunt
sed discretionis gratia prolata sunt,*[20] con lo que queda patente la intención informativa del autor.

Si se compara, empero, la lista aldhelmiana con las otras, lo
cual no es de este lugar ni mi intención,[21] se observa que hay coinci-
dencias parciales muy interesantes, pero en ningun caso pueden
darse por idénticas distintas listas. A menudo se corresponden
exactamente, pero alguna añade o suprime referencias a animales
bien conocidos.

Volvemos a encontrarnos largas series en diversos manuscritos,
generalmente los que contienen glosarios o isagoges gramáticas. Ya
Goetz[22] editó las colecciones trasmitidas por el denominado *Liber
glossarum*, al que pronto prestaremos atención, por Oxford Bodl.
Libr. *Digby 151*[23] y por Paris Bibl. Nat. *latin 1750*, del siglo X.[24]
Debemos señalar que estas dos listas coinciden completamente con
la de Polemio Silvio, de la que a no dudar derivan, si se tiene en
cuenta que incluso es coincidente el orden de los animales y sus
voces.[25] La larga lista del *Liber Glossarum*[26] presenta ciertas carac-
terísticas: está dividida en dos grandes grupos, el de los animales
que vuelan (aves a insectos) y el de las *ferae* que *etiam proprias
uoces habere ita pronuntiant,* aunque entre estas fieras se incluya los

---

[19] En el sentido usual en los glosarios, es decir con orden basado en la
primera letra y como máximo en la primera y segunda.

[20] *Discretio* significa aqui, naturalmente, "conocimiento".

[21] Véase, como recuerdo, los estudios de W. Wackernagel, *Voces variae
animantium*, Basel 1869; C. Zangemeister en *Wiener Sitzungsb.* 84 (1876);
G. Goetz en *Corpus Glossariorum Latinorum*, I, 90, etc. No parece haber des-
pertado especial interés en tiempos modernos este retazo léxico, al menos que
yo sepa.

[22] *CGlL*, I 91 ss.

[23] *Ibid.*, 91-92.

[24] *Ibid.*, 91.

[25] Unicamente en la serie de Paris se intercala después del león la mención
elefans barrit, que aparece en muchas otras series pero no en Polemio Silvio.

[26] Goetz, *CGlL*, I 92.

cerdos, ratones, musarañas, ranas y otros animales bien poco fieros. La lista no está en ningun caso en orden alfabético. De esta colección de términos parece depender, aunque muy incompleta pero en la misma disposición que en el *Liber glossarum*, el *Vocabulista* de Papías,[27] que sólo ofrece 26 de los 53 lemas del *Liber glossarum*, o sea la mitad. En el manuscrito de la Biblioteca Catedral de Toledo *99, 30*, del siglo IX-X, probablemente copiado en Toledo mismo, aunque sobre una buena cantidad de materiales llegados de la Galia, quizá por intermedio de Cataluña, encontramos otra lista, que es la del *Liber glossarum* tal como editada por Goetz, aunque ligeramente incrementada, pues ofrece 61 términos frente a los 53 de aquél. Por el interés del códice,[28] y las condiciones de los varios materiales que encierra, me permito incorporarla a estas notas.[29] La lista aparece en un recuadro en el fol. 26r y la letra del escriba ya menuda, se achica para dar cabida a la larga serie. Hela aquí:

Toledo 99.30 f. 26r

Aquilas	clangere
accipitres	plipiare
uultures	pulpare
coruos	caraxare uel socitare
miluos	lupire uel lugere
olores	densare
grues	grbere (*sic* = gruere)
ciconias	crotallare
ansares	gliccere uel sclingere
pauones	paupulare
gallos	cucurrire uel cantare
abates (*sic* = anates)	tecircitare
turtures	gemere
palumbes	paucitare
perdices	caccabare
gragulos	fringulire
nostuas (*sic*)	cuccubire
merulos	frindire uel ziziare
turdos	traciare uel socitare
sturnos	rapsitare
irundines	minurrire
passares	tittiare
*ranas	blattarare
apes	uobire uel uombilare

---

[27] *Papías Vocabulista*, ed. anast. Torino 1966, s. *uoces*.

[28] Analizado en su rico contenido gramatical por C. Codoñer, *Archivum* [Oviedo] 16 (1966) 67-90, que ha podido establecer el carácter compósito de su varia doctrina.

[29] Antepongo un asterisco a los elementos nuevos.

cicadas	frittinnire
leones	fremere
*maucios	piare
*upupas	ponpinare
*cuculos	soccare
tigrides	racare
pardos	felire
panteras	Caurire
ursos	seuire uel uncare
apros	frendere
linches	urcare
lupos	ululare
serpentes	siuilare
eleuantos	uarrire
onagros	mugilare
ceruos	suggire
tauros	mugitare
equos	innire
asinos	rudire
porcos	grunnire
uerres	quiritare
arietes	obretare
obes	balare
yrcos	micure (*sic* = miccire) uel micere
edos	uebare
canes	latrare uel baubire
*gattos	meolare
uulpes	gannire uel lannire
catulos	glattire
lepores	uagire uel mutire
mustelas	trinorare
mures	mintare
surices	denticare
ranas	rauire uel cox⟨are⟩
*melones	merullire
*fasianos	crocitare
*trullitas	turualire

Como final, pues, de estas notas quisiera poner de relieve un hecho literario que me parece importante. Las voces de animales debieron introducirse en las escuelas como elemento léxico que proporcionaba a la vez un caudal de vocablos de variada forma y valor y una serie de correlaciones — sujetos-verbos — de difícil acoplamiento en el verso. Que hubieron de utilizarse como mecanismo para prácticas métricas no sólo lo comprueba la presencia de una lista y las observaciones de Aldhelmo, sino el hecho mismo de que se nos hayan conservado tres poemas, derivados sin duda de ejercicios de clase, y procedentes de lugares tan distintos como Hispania, Irlanda y Germania. Es probable que las variantes entre las distintas series obedezcan precisamente a las técnicas y exigencias del "agon" escolar, lo que explicaría que ciertas voces de animales bien conocidos aparezcan en algunas colecciones y falten, en cambio, en otras.[30] A los numerosos problemas que suscita el estudio pormenorizado de la escuela tardolatina y sus métodos, habría que añadir los que derivan de la intención con la que se utilizaron las voces de animales, y los caminos de su difusión en el que tan importante papel jugó, una vez, el mundo insular.

---

[30] Sería interesante, no obstante, estudiar por qué en las series de glosarios, salvo en las alfabéticas, hay una tendencia digna de nota a figurar en último lugar las ranas y su croar.

THE HISTORICAL POSITION OF
JOHANNES SCOTTUS ERIUGENA[1]

PAUL OSKAR KRISTELLER

Johannes Scottus Eriugena, born and educated in Ireland, and active in France under Charles the Bald between 850 and 870, has been generally admired and praised as a great scholar and thinker, and his historical position has often been recognized as unique in more than one way. In an age when Ireland occupied a predominant place in Western learning, Johannes came to be the greatest Irish scholar of the Middle Ages. In a century when the knowledge of Greek was rare and elementary in Western Europe, he was the best, or at least one of the two best, Hellenists of his time. He has been called a "solitary phenomenon" as a metaphysician and speculative philosopher in the Carolingian age,[2] and also "the most considerable philosopher in the Western world between Augustine and Thomas Aquinas and the greatest Irish philosopher (with the possible exception of Berkeley) ever".[3] I tend to agree with these and many similar judgments, but should like to express the matter in slightly different terms: Eriugena was the only Western philosopher worthy of the name between Boethius and Anselm; as a Greek scholar, he was superior to all his Western contemporaries (with the possible exception of Anastasius Bibliothecarius); and the two points are closely related. For there was no philosophical instruction, literature or tradition in the Latin West between Boethius and the rise of scholasticism, and it was only through a close study of Greek sources that it was possible for Eriugena to become a philospher. He was of course a man of great talent and intellectual vigor, but he could not have developed and expressed his thought in a philosophical form without some access to the philosophical tradition and terminology developed by the Greeks. He did not read or know the Greek philosophers of classical antiquity, but he found the traces of

---

[1] This article does not pretend to make a new contribution to its subject. I was invited to write on a topic of interest to the present Festschrift.

[2] M. L. W. Laistner, *Thought and Letters in Western Europe A.D. 500 to 900* (Ithaca, 1957), p. 322.

[3] John J. O'Meara, *Eriugena* (Cork, 1969), p. VII.

their thought and language in the Greek Christian authors whom he read and translated: Gregory of Nyssa, Epiphanius, Maximus Confessor, and above all, ps. Dionysius the Areopagite.

Eriugena's exceptional position becomes fully apparent when we realize that the philosophical poverty of the Latin West as compared with the Greek East was not only characteristic of the early Middle Ages but had its roots in Roman antiquity.[4] When the Romans appropriated the heritage of Greek civilization, they became its successful imitators and pupils in poetry, oratory and historiography, in grammar and in rhetoric. This is amply attested by a widespread educational system and a large body of writings, extant as well as lost but attested. In the field of law, the Romans made an independent and lasting contribution, as they did in military affairs and in political administration. Yet in the sciences, their contribution was negligible.[5] In philosophy, the Romans made some respectable contributions, but they were modest both in volume and originality when compared with the Greeks. Many educated Romans learned Greek, studied for a while in Greece, or kept Greek scholars as tutors in their household, and some of them even wrote in Greek on philosophical and other subjects.[6] Yet there never were any lasting centers of philosophical instruction in Rome or other Western cities, as there were in Athens or Alexandria, or as there were schools of grammar, rhetoric and law in the West. What there was of philosophical literature in Latin, was popular rather than original in nature and intent, and tried to reexpress Greek ideas in a new language rather than to formulate new ideas. This literature includes Lucretius and Cicero, Seneca and Apuleius, and later Macrobius and Boethius. It was important as a transmitter of Greek philosophy, and it laid the foundations, but not more than that, for a philosophical terminology in Latin, a language not originally as well suited for abstract thinking as classical Greek had been. Also the number of Greek philosophical writings translated into Latin before the end of antiquity was small, presumably because the educated Latin reader who was interested in philosophy had access to the Greek originals: some treatises of Plotinus, a part of Plato's *Timaeus*, and

---

[4] P. O. Kristeller, *Renaissance Thought* (New York, 1961), 2-30; *Renaissance Concepts of Man* (New York, 1972), 118-119.

[5] William H. Stahl, *Roman Science* (Madison, 1962).

[6] A notable example is Marcus Aurelius.

some logical works of Aristotle with Porphyry's introduction.[7] The picture is similar when we turn to Christian literature. Whereas the Greek patristic writers were thoroughly imbued with philosophical thought and terminology and reflected a good deal of it in their theological writings, many of the early Christian writers of the Latin West had a grammatical, rhetorical and legal but not a philosophical training or interest. Those who did show philosophical concerns demonstrably drew on Greek sources, such as Tertullian and Lactantius, Ambrose and above all Augustine who might be called the most original philosopher of Latin antiquity. Moreover, the chief work of a strongly philosophical Greek Christian, Origen's *de principiis*, was translated into Latin by Rufinus, and actually survives only in this translation.

Boethius was the last Latin writer who had a genuine interest in philosophy and a full command of its Greek sources. In the period following his death (525), the political and cultural separation of the Latin West from the Greek East meant in the field of philosophy that the West was cut off from the rich Greek literature on the subject and entirely thrown back on its own meager resources. As a result, early medieval education and learning was restricted to the seven liberal arts, exemplified by the work of Martianus Capella, and to certain branches of theology that might be characterized as exegetical and controversial. The seven liberal arts did not include any philosophy except some elementary logic, and the study of theology did not include the kind of dogmatic or speculative theology that in earlier or later periods had such close connections with philosophy and metaphysics. The classifications of the arts and sciences that have come down to us from the early Middle Ages, the introductions to grammatical and other commentaries, as well as other literary and historical documents make it quite clear that the very word and concept "philosophy" was not understood in its ancient Greek or later medieval and modern sense but was confused with the content of the liberal arts and with the sum total of secular learning.

Within the general limits by which the world of Western learning was restricted in the period between 500 (or 525) and 900 and even later, Ireland played an important role that has been at times

---

[7] These translations were due, respectively, to Marius Victorinus (now lost), Calcidius and Boethius.

exaggerated or minimized, but generally recognized by the most authoritative scholars.[8] To describe this role in precise terms is often difficult, for the evidence is fragmentary, and since many Irish scholars including Johannes were active on the continent, it is hard to decide how much of their work may be attributed to their Irish education or to their continental experience. The missionary activities of the Irish on the Continent are well known, and their contributions to religious and theological literature have been fully recorded. Their interest in the seven liberal arts and especially in grammar seems to be beyond doubt, although it is better attested for the continent than for Ireland. There is no doubt that they copied, read and studied a number of classical Latin authors, some of them rare, but I do not think it has been proven for any one Roman writer that he was preserved exclusively through Irish scribes.[9] Still more difficult is the question of the study of Greek in Ireland. I have no doubt that some Greek was studied in Ireland at a time when that study was neglected on the Continent except for Southern Italy or possibly at Rome. Yet I readily accept what Bischoff remarks on the nature and limitation of these studies: they were elementary, and they did not lead to a coherent understanding of a Greek classical text.[10]

This point is also important for a proper understanding of Eriugena and of his development. We have by now a precise list and rough chronology of his authentic writings.[11] His earliest work, *De*

---

[8] The "detractors" include M. Esposito, M. Cappuyns, and more recently E. Coccia (*Studi Medievali* III 8, 1967, 257-420). I tend to accept the balanced views of B. Bischoff (see below) and L. Bieler (*Ireland, Harbinger of the Middle Ages*, London, 1963 and 1966). For a rich inventory of the literary remains and testimonies, see James F. Kenney, *The Sources for the Early History of Ireland*, vol. I (New York, 1929). This must of course be supplemented by the palaeographical evidence (for the mss. up to 800 see E. A. Lowe, *Codices Latini Antiquiores*, 11 vols., Oxford, 1934-66, and Supplement, 1971).

[9] L. Bieler, "The Classics in Celtic Ireland," in *Classical Influences on European Culture A.D. 500-1500*, ed. R. R. Bolgar (Cambridge, 1971), 45-49. Id., "The Island of Scholars, *Revue du Moyen Age Latin* 8 (1952), 213-234.

[10] B. Bischoff, "Das griechische Element in der abendlaendischen Bildung des Mittelalters", *Byzantinische Zeitschrift* 44 (1951), 27-55; reprinted in his *Mittelalterliche Studien* 2 (Stuttgart, 1967), 246-275.

[11] I. P. Sheldon-Williams, "A Bibliography of the Works of Johannes Scottus Eriugena," *The Journal of Ecclesiastical History* 10 (1959), 198-225; "A List of the Works doubtfully or wrongly attributed to Johannes Scottus Eriugena," *ibid*. 15 (1964), 76-98. The list should be corrected or supplemented on a few points, see below. The only complete edition of Eriugena's works, though defective and partly superseded, is in volume 122 of the

praedestinatione (851) fits into the contemporary pattern of controversial theological treatises. It is interesting for some of its sources
and teachings, but it does not yet reflect the mastery of Greek and
of philosophy that was to distinguish the later works. His next work,
the *Annotationes in Martianum* (859-60) belongs to the study of the
seven liberal arts and thus again follows a traditional pattern, although it may be the earliest extant commentary on Martianus, and
hence have started rather than followed a literary genre.[12] Again
there is no startling display of Greek scholarship or of philosophical
speculation. Commentaries on Boethius' *Consolatio* and *Opuscula
Sacra* were long attributed to Eriugena, but recent]scholarly con-
sensus seems to reject these attributions, although some of the later
commentaries on these texts reflect some ideas and interpretations
that go back to Eriugena.[13] Next in sequence is Eriugena's transla-

---

Patrologia Latina (1853). The standard monograph is M. Cappuyns, *Jean
Scot Erigène* (Brussels, 1964). For his place in the history of literature, see
Laistner and Kenney (see above) and M. Manitius, *Geschichte der lateinischen
Literatur des Mittelalters* I (Munich, 1911 and 1959), 323-339. In addition to
the standard histories of philosophy and of medieval philosophy, see esp. *The
Cambridge History of Later Greek and Early Medieval Philosophy*, ed. A. H.
Armstrong (Cambridge, 1967), ch. 34 (by I. P. Sheldon-Williams) and 36 (by
H. Liebeschuetz). There is a large number of books and articles dealing with
Eriugena's philosophical and theological doctrines.
[12] Iohannis Scotti *Annotationes in Marcianum*, ed. Cora E. Lutz (Cam-
bridge, Mass., 1939). Cf. Cora E. Lutz, "Martianus Capella," in *Catalogus
Translationum et Commentariorum* II, ed. P. O. Kristeller and F. E. Cranz
(Washington, 1971). 367-371. L. Labowsky, "A new version of Scotus Eriugena's Commentary on Martianus Capella," *Medieval and Renaissance
Studies* I, 1943, 187-193.
[13] For the commentary on the *Opuscula Sacra*, see: Edward K. Rand,
"Johannes Scottus", *Quellen und Untersuchungen zur lateinischen Philologie
des Mittelalters* I 2 (Munich, 1906), 1-84; M. Cappuyns, "Le plus ancien
commentaire des "Opuscula Sacra" et son origine," *Recherches de Théologie
ancienne et médiévale* 3 (1931), 237-272; E. K. Rand, "The supposed commentary of John the Scot on the "Opuscula Sacra" of Boethius," *Revue néo-
scolastique* 36 (1934), 67-77. For the commentary on the *Consolatio: Saeculi
noni auctoris in Boetii Consolationem commentarius*, ed. E. T. Silk (Rome,
1935); P. Courcelle, "Etude critique sur les Commentaires de Boèce," *Archives d'histoire doctrinale et littéraire du moyen âge* 14 (1939, 5-140), at 21-26
and 80-81; E. T. Silk, "Pseudo-Johannes Scotus, Adalbolt of Utrecht, and
the early commentaries on Boethius," *Mediaeval and Renaissance Studies* 3
(1954), 1-40; G. Mathon, "Le commentaire du pseudo-Erigène sur la Consolatio Philosophiae de Boèce," *Recherches de théologie ancienne et médiévale*
22 (1955), 213-257; P. Courcelle, *La Consolation de Philosophie dans la tradition littéraire* (Paris, 1967), 248-254. H. Silvestre attributed to Eriugena a
commentary on *Consolatio* III 9 ("Le commentaire inédit de Jean Scot
Erigène au mètre IX du Livre III du 'De consolatione philosophiae' de

tion of the writings attributed to Dionysius the Areopagite (860-62). This translation was commissioned by Charles the Bald, and it made use of an earlier version by Abbot Hilduin of St. Denis. The translation which covered the four treatises and ten letters of the Dionysian Corpus, was criticized, supplemented and revised by Anastasius Bibliothecarius, and it is now believed that the text available to us represents Anastasius' revision rather than Eriugena's original version. Nevertheless, it is through this translation that Eriugena outgrew the elementary knowledge of Greek that he had acquired in Ireland and developed his mastery of the language. This work also familiarized him with the philosophical terminology and speculation which is embodied in the Dionysian Corpus and which is in part derived from Proclus and ultimately from Plotinus.[14] This translation was followed by that of a few shorter Greek works: the *De hominis opificio* of Gregory of Nyssa, the *Ambigua* and *Ad Thalassium* of Maximus Confessor, and perhaps the *De fide* of Epiphanius (862-864).[15] After having finished his translations, Eriugena composed his great work, *De divisione naturae*, in 5 books (864-866), an independent and systematic treatise on speculative theology and philosophy, on which his fame as a philosopher primarily rests.[16] During his later years, he wrote a commentary on the *De coelesti hierarchia* of ps. Dionysius, showing his continued interest in the

---

Boèce," *Revue d'Histoire ecclésiastique* 47, 1952, 44-122), but later abandoned this attribution (*Sacris Erudiri* 9, 1957, p. 398).

[14] G. Théry, "Scot Erigène traducteur de Denys," *Bulletin Du Cange* 6 (1931), 185-278; id. "Scot Erigène introducteur de Denys," *New Scholasticism* 7 (1933), 91-108; H. F. Dondaine, *Le Corpus dionysien de l'Université de Paris au XIIIe siècle* (Rome, 1953). Eriugena's preface to Charles the Bald was edited by E. Duemmler, *Epistolae variorum inde a saeculo nono medio usque ad mortem Karoli II (Calvi) Imperatoris collectae* (Monumenta Germaniae Historica, *Epistolae Karolini Aevi* 4, Berlin, 1925, 127-206), at p. 158-161, no. 14.

[15] Gregory of Nyssa: M. Cappuyns, "Le 'De imagine' de Gregoire de Nysse traduit par Jean Scot Erigène," *Recherches de théologie ancienne et médiévale* 32 (1965), 205-262 (with full text). Maximus Confessor, *Ambigua*: The preface is given by Duemmler, *l.c.*, p. 161-162, no. 15. Maximus, *Ad Thalassium*: Paul Meyvaert, "The Exegetical treatises of Peter the Deacon and Eriugena's Latin rendering of *Ad Thalassium* of Maximus the Confessor," *Sacris Erudiri* 14 (1963), 130-148. Passages from Epiphanius are cited in the *De divisione naturae*, but the complete translation has not been found.

[16] For the first two books, see now the critical edition: Johannis Scotti Eriugenae Periphyseon (*De divisione naturae*), *Liber primus*, ed. I. P. Sheldon-Williams, with the collaboration of L. Bieler, (Dublin, 1968) and *Liber secundus* (1972).

work he had translated,[17] a homily on the prologue to the Gospel of St. John,[18] and a commentary on the same Gospel.[19] A few poems, some of them in Greek, complete the list.[20] It is quite evident from this list, that his earlier works, however interesting and original in detail, remain within the typical framework of his time, whereas his later works, especially his version of Dionysius and his *De divisione naturae*, fall outside this framework and represent his unique contribution. Critical editions of these works are badly needed, and have now been supplied at least for the first books of the *De divisione naturae*, and for the two works on the Gospel of St. John, as well as for the *Annotationes in Martianum*. A critical edition of the translations, especially of Dionysius, would be most desirable, but it is clearly a difficult task, complicated by the intervention of Anastasius. A critical edition of the Dionysius and of the complete *De divisione* should then be followed by an index or glossary of philosophical and theological terms, for only in this way would Eriugena's contribution, his sources and his influence become tangible in detail.

Eriugena's influence has often been underestimated, and we must distinguish between the textual tradition of his writings, the continued effect of specific concepts or interpretations, and the conscious repetition or transformation of his larger philosophical and theological doctrines. His *De divisione naturae* had no tangible following in the centuries after his death, and it was condemned in the thirteenth century, long after the revival of philosophical studies in the West. Yet I doubt very much that this important work failed to attract readers and admirers before or even after its condemnation. Eighteen manuscripts of the text, not all of them complete, are now known, and at least one of them was copied after the thirteenth century.[21] I doubt very much that all quotations or doctrinal influences of this work in later thinkers have been identified or collected. On the other hand, the translation of Dionysius enjoyed a

---

[17] H. F. Dondaine, "Les 'Expositiones super Ierarchiam Caelestem' de Jean Scot Erigène", *Archives d'histoire doctrinale et littéraire du moyen âge* 25-26 (1950-51), 245-302, with additions to the text in Migne.

[18] Jean Scot, *Homélie sur le prologue de Jean*, ed. E. Jeauneau (Paris, 1969, with an excellent introduction on the life and works of Eriugena).

[19] Jean Scot, *Commentaire sur l'évangile de Jean*, ed. E. Jeauneau (Paris, 1972).

[20] Monumenta Germaniae Historica, *Poetae Latini Aevi Carolini*, Tomi III Partis alterius fasciculus II, ed. L. Traube (Berlin, 1896), 518-556.

[21] Sheldon-Williams, *Journal of Ecclesiastical History* 10, p. 206-211 and 224; *Periphyseon* I (introduction).

wide and continuous diffusion through manuscripts and early printed editions and held its own alongside with a number of later versions. The commentary on Martianus appears in several manuscripts and influenced later commentators, and several medieval commentators on Boethius' *Consolatio* and *Opuscula Sacra* reflect Eriugena's influence, although there is no evidence that he commented himself on these texts. Thus we must conclude that his influence in the broader sense was considerable, though he failed to have any immediate disciples in what was undoubtedly his own greatest achievement: his mastery of Greek, and his effort as a speculative philosopher and theologian.

Eriugena's example seems to show that an individual scholar and thinker may surpass the intellectual limits of his century, but that he will not perpetuate his best achievements unless they are transmitted through his pupils and embodied in the curriculum of a school that constitutes a kind of institutional tradition. It is the lack of such a school tradition before and after him, that makes of Eriugena a great but isolated figure. It took several more centuries before the acquaintance with Greek sources, this time especially with Aristotle, and the continued struggle with philosophical problems became a wide concern in the Western world. The narrow limits of the seven liberal arts were finally overcome. New institutions, the cathedral schools and universities, attracted a large number of teachers and students and thus assured a continuity and expansion of learning in a variety of subjects. Medicine and jurisprudence, philosophy and the sciences as well as dogmatic theology were constantly and widely taught, discussed and written about, and in the course of the discussions, the problems and the terminology became more and more refined. This tradition, nourished in many ways by Arabic and Latin as well as by Greek sources, has continued through many changes and transformations up to the present day. It is the everlasting glory of Eriugena that through him, and through him alone, the period from 500 to 900, interesting for a variety of political, artistic and scholarly contributions, also deserves a prominent mention in the history of philosophy.

Addendum

As I learn from Charles B. Schmitt, Marie Thérèse d'Alverny will prove in a forthcoming paper that the anonymous Latin translation of Priscianus Lydus, *Solutiones ad Chosroem*, must be attributed to Eriugena or to a member of his immediate circle. This adds to the number of Greek texts translated and utilized by Eriugena a philosophical work by a pagan Neoplatonist, and the fact has further significance because the Greek text was subsequently lost and the work has been preserved only in this Latin translation.

IV

CELTICA

SEMANTIC INFLUENCE OF LATIN IN THE OLD IRISH GLOSSES

D. A. BINCHY

Thanks to the tireless researches of Ludwig Bieler the main characteristics of "Hiberno-Latin" must now be familiar to all medievalists. The present brief note on aspects of the converse phenomenon — what we may call "Latino-Irish" — is in no sense offered as an ἀντίδωρον but simply as δόσις ὀλίγη τε φίλη τε from one who was originally trained as a medievalist in the same admirable school (Munich University) but afterwards switched to a more restricted field.

So far as Hiberno-Latin writers are concerned, the influence of their native language on what they wrote was essentially peripheral. They introduced some minor phonological and syntactical variations based on the vernacular they used in everyday life. Yet on the whole their "Hibernicisms" so carefully collated by Bieler are few and far between. Even their orthography seldom reflects the peculiarly British pronunciation of Latin that characterizes most of the loan-words in Irish, And the reason is not far to seek. From its introduction in the wake of Christianity Latin, though invested with great prestige, remained an esoteric language, confined to the ministers of the new religion. No layman, even the most powerful, needed it, for it was never, as it had been in Britain for centuries, the official language of administration and doubtless also of commerce. And even those early native clerics who may well have had to use it as a *lingua franca* to communicate with their British evangelizers, and probably took over from them all their phonetic peculiarities, were trained by the same mentors to *write* "correct" Latin after biblical and patristic models.

But this must not be allowed to obscure the profound revolution which a knowledge of Latin, even if confined to a comparatively small caste, effected in the linguistic and cultural life of Ireland. For it signalled the end of what Vendryes has aptly termed "une civilisation anépigraphique" and the transition from oral to written culture. Though the ogam script is doubtless older than the first Christian missions, its use (like that of the Nordic runes) for quasi-magic and quasi-legal purposes was so limited, and the number of those who could decipher it so few, that its invention cannot be regarded as the dawn of literacy. Literacy in Ireland began with the Latin alphabet; later, reading and writing spread from Latin to the native language. Accordingly the Irish "learned their letters" in every sense of the word from Rome, and practically every term connected with reading or writing is a loanword from Latin; the only exception I can think of is the word for ink (*dub*, lit. "black").

And not just those concerned with reading and writing. Over several centuries the Irish language received a constant stream of loanwords, most of them direct from the vulgar Latin used by the early British missionaries, others at one remove through the spoken British of the same missionaries; a third class, which came somewhat later, consisted of "learned" borrowings from Latin acquired as a *Schulsprache*. Today few scholars would accept every item in the long list compiled by Vendryes, or even all the examples cited by Pedersen, as genuine; nonetheless the total amount remains extremely large. Certain phonological tests enable us to distinguish between an earlier and a later stratum, but what is more interesting to the historian is the nature and purview of the words borrowed as revealing the gaps, material, spiritual and intellectual, they were designed to fill. There was surely no shortage of mere words in the language of pre-Christian Ireland. (Fifty years ago the monoglot native speakers from whom I had the good fortune to learn West Munster Irish, though "illiterate" in the modern sense, possessed a far more extensive vocabulary than their English-speaking and English-reading neighbours). The need for new words arose rather from the impact of so many unfamiliar objects and ideas upon a society which had remained primitive and static despite the rich oral culture of its "learned" caste.

The basic structure of that oral culture, doubtless druidic in origin like that of Gaul in Caesar's time, is now difficult to discern from the isolated fragments of it that were ultimately congealed in writing. But one can dimly perceive a fascinating amalgam of magic, myth, poetry, law and leechcraft, all of them embodied in formal and deliberately obscure language, a "Mandarin" Irish which was understood only by the privileged members of the learned class. It has been suggested that the language of the ordinary people first came into its own with the introduction of writing. Certainly the cryptic passages of mnemonic verse in the older stratum of the law-tracts, whose antiquity is proved by (*inter alia*) a total absence of Christian Latin loanwords, are much harder to interpret than the bulk of the "canonical" texts compiled in the seventh century. But even this later stratum, though decidedly more straightforward, is, I believe, very far from reflecting "ordinary" speech. On the contrary, throughout the entire Old Irish period we find a uniform "standard" language common to all the educated minority and surprisingly free from dialectal variation.

Again, while Latin made a massive contribution to the vocabulary of classical Old Irish, its influence on morphology and syntax was comparatively small. It supplied, for example, two new suffixes for nouns of agency -*aire* and -*óir* (both from -*ārius*), which eventually ousted the inherited suffixes -*em* and -*ith* (-*id*). And in the domain of syntax it was responsible for the independent use of the preposition *de, di* (later often confused with *do*) in titles, modelled on "De Senectute", etc. I had been taught to regard this as a Latinism, hence it came as a shock to find some of the most archaic law-tracts in the official edition (*Ancient Laws of Ireland*) bearing titles like *Din Techtugud* "On Taking Possession", etc. When I consulted the relevant manuscripts, however, I found that invariably these "titles" had been added in the margin by some later scholiast.

The need for loanwords was particularly acute for the monastic scribes who contributed glosses in Old Irish on Latin texts, whether religious or grammatical. For they were confronted with a whole series of abstract concepts formulated in a language immeasurably more sophisticated than their own. My great teacher Thurneysen more than once commented on the ingrained tendency of the Irish jurists to substitute enumeration for definition; it would seem that the capacity to formulate abstract principles came only after contact with Latin civilization. The native scholiasts of the eighth and ninth centuries displayed remarkable ingenuity in adapting their own language to these unfamiliar ideas. Not only did they borrow directly from Latin on a wide scale, they also constructed numerous calques.

Linguists have drawn a useful distinction between two types of calque. The more usual type is a new native word constructed entirely on the foreign model. Nearly all of the so-called "Irish grammatical terminology" (on which I shall have more to say later) belongs to this category of *Übersetzungslehnwörter*, and the individual terms correspond exactly to F. G. Möhl's general description:

"locutions formées ... d'éléments indigènes calqués avec une fidélité souvent servile sur les éléments du terme étranger correspondant."[1] The second and more subtle type of calque involves what German linguists call *Lehnprägung*: where an inherited word is invested with an additional meaning based on that of a foreign word, occasionally even with the result that this semantic interloper supersedes the old primary meaning.

Hitherto very little attention has been devoted to the Latin calques of either type in Irish. But recently Professor Enrico Campanile has given us a study of thirteen "calchi irlandesi di voci latine"[2] which he describes as "frutto di occasionali e varie letture". Unfortunately some of his examples do not carry conviction. Thus the very existence of an Irish word *ám* (6) meaning either "mano" or "gruppo di uomini" is more than doubtful: if it were really a borrowing of *agmen*, then indeed the vowel would be long and the *m* lenited (cf. Thurneysen, *Grammar* §125), but the only example that can be tested metrically shows short *a* and unlenited *m* (see R.I.A. *Contributions* s.v. 2. *amm*). The secondary meaning of "envy, illwill" assigned to *meirg* (7) "rust, corrosion" is a mere guess by Stokes from the context of one example in *Saltair na Rann;* more probably the word is used here, as elsewhere in the same poem, in the general sense of "stain, decay", and comparison with the secondary meaning of *aerugo* in Horace and Martial seems out of place. Again, Professor Campanile would hardly have based the still common meaning of O. Ir. *oíbel(l)* (12) "heat in animals", now *uíol* in spoken Irish, on Lat. *calor* had he read O'Rahilly's article on this Common Celtic word in *Ériu* XIV. 1ff.; besides, in a pastoral civilization, a word to denote this very frequent phenomenon is unlikely to have been borrowed. Again, the primary meaning of the adj. *mer*, from which *merugud* (vb. n. of *meraigid*) is formed (9), is "lively, impetuous, wild", with no suggestion of "erring", and *merugud* itself, apart from "wandering", means "distraction, confusion" rather than "error" in the sense of "mistake". And the examples of *taman* "trunk, stump" in the sense of "dullard" are all doubtful, and in any case exactly the same metaphor is found in Eng. "blockhead"; does this, too, go back to Cicero's specialized use of *truncus?*

Other items in Dr. Campanile's list are possible but by no means

---

[1] *MSL* VII. 429, quoted Knobloch, *Sprachwissenschaftliches Wörterbuch* (1971), 403.

[2] *SSL* X (1970) pp. 5-13.

certain. While *i maigin* "invece" (5) may be due to the influence of *in loco*, as is (indirectly) Eng. "instead of", *maigen* itself "punto, passo di un libro" is no more indebted to *locus* for this secondary meaning than are *baile, inad* and *á(i)tt*, all three of which are also used in this sense. The feminine noun *óg*, from the adj. *óg* "whole, complete", used for a virgin (11) is found in archaic law-tracts, and the jurists (who were active long before the arrival of Latin) would surely have needed a word for her, if only in order to fix the abnormally high penalty for rape committed on her; would they really have waited for *(filia) integra?* A similar fem. noun *mael* (1) from the adjective "shorn, blunt", etc. is undoubtedly used for a closely cropped head, thus suggesting *calvus/calva* "cranio", but it also occurs in placenames (usually a sign of antiquity) meaning a bare, treeless summit, so I find it hard to decide whether or not it is a calque on the Latin word. On the other hand *ball ferda(e)* (4) is beyond all doubt a calque on *membrum uirile*, but since *ball* itself is the Irish congener of φαλλός, its use alone in the sense may well be inherited.

The remaining calques studied by Professor Campanile belong, with one important exception, to the first type, being *Übersetzungslehnwörter*, and all would appear to be genuine. The construction of *soscéle* (2) to reproduce εὐαγγέλιον as interpreted by Christian Latin writers was made clear over a century ago in Zeuss-Ebel p. 863, but the Irish surely obtained this information from their universal *vade mecum* Isidore's *Etymologiae* (VI ii 43) rather than from Augustine as Dr. Campanile suggests. *Feóldénmaid* (8) is certainly a calque on *carnifex*; in the essentially rural Irish economy there was no room for the trade of butcher, and after the development of towns the Irish word for him, *búistéar*, was borrowed from English. A more curious example of this kind is the gloss on *opifex* which appears twice in the Milan glosses (25ª19, 42ᵇ17) as *ana(e)-dénmid* "maker of riches", showing that the glossator mistakenly analysed the word as *opum factor*!

An illuminating example of *Lehnprägung* is contained in Dr. Campanile's analysis of *folud*. His argument that this word originally meant "property, assets" is supported by its Welsh congener *golud* "wealth, property", In the Old Irish law-tracts it already shows considerable semantic development, from "assets" to the property-qualifications of the various social grades, the objects of an agreement (the "consideration" of English law), finally performance of one's legal duties (see Thurneysen, *ZCP* XIV. 374). The glossators who pressed it into service to render *substantia* (one of those unfamiliar abstract concepts) must have been acquainted with the later meaning of the Latin word. And the fact that this meaning is given pride of place in the R.I.A. Dictionary stems from a mistake which is all too common among Irish lexicographers: the notion that the occurrence of a word in the Old Irish glosses attests not merely its earliest appearance in manuscript form but also its primary meaning. We shall meet another example of this illusion presently.

The St. Gall glosses on Priscian are full of slavish calques on Latin grammatical terms, and Dr. Campanile rightly traces *áinsid* (lit. "accuser") to the Latin misinterpretation of αἰτιατικὴ (πτῶσις) as *accusativus (casus)*. But his introductory statement to this note (13) — "La terminologia grammaticale irlandese è, direttamente o indirettamente, tutta di origine latina" — may give rise to a complete misunderstanding. For, as Bergin stressed at the opening of his admirable Rhys Lecture to the British Academy in 1938 ("The Native Irish Grammarian"), the work of these scholiasts "has nothing to do with Irish grammar"; it was simply an attempt (not always very successful) to interpret the grammar of a foreign language. Accordingly all the calques they constructed with a scrupulous (and at times ludicrous) fidelity to the original term — *tuisel* ("falling") for "casus", *cam-thuisel* ("crooked *tuisel*") for "casus obliquus", *briathar* ("word") for "uerbum", *do-briathar* for "ad-uerbium", *rann-gabál* for "parti-cipium", *diuscartach* (adj. from **diuss-scart-* "puts aside, removes") for "deponens (uerbum)", etc. — are purely transitory creations, surviving only in a few exotic texts like *Auraicept na n-Éces*, that strange blend of Latin and native Irish linguistic lore.

For in the native schools of poetry, which were flourishing long before the advent of Christianity and led an independent existence after it, the students continued to receive oral instruction, not in formal grammar, but in "poetics", which included training in "correct" language as well as prosody. In keeping with the national tendency noted by Thrneysen, they were taught by means of concrete examples rather than abstract definitions. This agglutinative and empirical method of teaching (which remained largely oral long after all members of the poetic order had mastered writing) eventually culminated in an impressive series of grammatical tracts, most of which have now been published by Bergin and Rev. L.

McKenna, though a great deal of spade-work remains to be done before they can be satisfactorily evaluated. In them the standard language of Bardic verse was effectively congealed for at least four centuries. Inevitably their framers were driven to use some grammatical terms, but it is significant that only a very small fraction of these are found in the St. Gall glosses: the loanword *consain* "consonant" and the calques *ainm* ("name") for "noun", also for "nominative" (but *ainmid* Sg.), *briathar* ("word") for "verb", *guthaighe* (from *guth* "uox") for "vowel". Otherwise the terms of art are quite different. Thus for "oblique case", instead of *camthuisel* we find *réim* "course, movement, series", but with typical pragmatism, this term is confined to those forms that differ from the nominative (*ainm*). Again, the classification of the various parts of speech departs radically from that of Priscian and other Latin grammarians; Bergin notes (without drawing any definite conclusion) that it "corresponds to that of Arabic grammar, which goes back to the seventh century".

The second type of calque, involving the process known as *Lehnprägung*, is much rarer in Irish, but all the more interesting on that account. We have seen that some examples of it suggested by Professor Campanile are at best doubtful, though *folud* is quite certain. Had I more space I could add a few others. One of the most striking is the noun *dliged* which the scholiasts annexed in order to translate such unfamiliar concepts as "*ratio*, principle, theory", etc. It had already undergone considerable semantic development before it fell into the hands of the glossators, but there can be no doubt that in origin it was an ambivalent legal term meaning right/duty, claim/debt according to the angle from which the relation between the two parties to an *obligatio*, creditor and debtor, was envisaged. Ironically enough the treatment of *dliged* in the R.I.A. *Contributions*, based on the fallacy that the earliest manuscript appearance supplies the "primary" meaning, presents the semantic history of this word in almost complete reverse.

THE EARLIEST BRAN MATERIAL

JAMES CARNEY

Discussion of the nature of the late seventh or early eighth-century *Immram Brain maic Febuil* "The Voyage of Bran, son of Febul" began with the great work of Kuno Meyer and Alfred Nutt.[1] Being the earliest of the Irish Voyage tales a study of *Immram Brain* had relevance to the other examples of the *genre*, including "The Voyage of Mael Dúin" and the *Navigatio Sancti Brendani*. Van Hamel produced a new edition in his *Immrama*.[2] Many other scholars have commented on the problem including Myles Dillon,[3] Gerard Murphy,[4] Proinsias Mac Cana,[5] Hans Oskamp[6] and the present writer.[7] I had laid considerable stress on the Christian elements in the tale; objections were made to these being dismissed as "interpolations", and it was held that the tale as a whole had a Christian allegorical intent, showing Man struggling in the world on his voyage towards Paradise; the possibility of the existence of a version of *Immram Brain* on an oral level before the composition of the text that has come down to us was dismissed.

Here it is proposed to deal with some early material which has not hitherto, it would appear, been given consideration, and which may throw considerable light on an earlier stage in the Bran tradition. There are in all three items. The most important is a Dialogue (*Imbaccaldam*) consisting of eight stanzas, four uttered by Bran's druid, and four by Febul's "prophetess" as they contemplated Loch Febuil (Lough Foyle). The Dialogue is found in two sources: TCD MS. H.4.22, p. 48 cols. *a* and *b* (from which it was printed by Kuno Meyer but without comment or translation),[8] and in Nat. Lib. of

---

[1] *The Voyage of Bran*, vols. i, ii (London, 1895).
[2] *Med. and Mod. Ir. Ser.*, vol. x (Dublin, 1941), pp. 1-19.
[3] *Early Irish Literature* (Chicago, 1948), pp. 104-7.
[4] *Saga and Myth in Ancient Ireland* (Dublin, 1955), p. 25; *Éigse*, vol. 8 (1956-7), p. 162.
[5] "Mongán mac Fiachna and Immram Brain", *Ériu*, vol. xxiii (1972), pp. 102-42.
[6] *The Voyage of Mael Dúin*, (Groningen 1970), pp. 40-2, etc.
[7] *Studies in Irish Literature and History* (Dublin, 1955), pp. 280-95.
[8] *Zeitschrift für Celtische Philologie*, ix (1913), pp. 339-40.

Ireland Gaelic MS. 7 (N), cols. 9 and 10. The first source is sixteenth century; the second is usually described as belonging to the same century. I would suggest here, however, that we should for the moment keep an open mind on the date of the latter, and that an early 17th century date might be possible; in this regard one should note the bookish use of the double hyphen in word-division at the line endings. The two versions, despite the pseudo-archaic orthography of N, are so close that derivation from a common original is to be regarded as probable. H took the verses from a manuscript containing old material, including texts deriving from the lost eighth-century manuscript, the *Cín Dromma Snechta*. This is indicated by the words *asin l. c. nicc*, "from the same book" (the significance of *nicc* is obscure to me) preceding the druid's utterance and *asin l.* "from the book" preceding that of the prophetess; similarly the words *asan .l. c. na* precede the title of the whole piece, which title is curiously given between the two items that constitute the text. The Dialogue follows *Forfess Fer Falgae* and precedes *Immram Brain*; in other words it is sandwiched between two texts which are known to have existed in the *Cín Dromma Snechta*. In N the Dialogue immediately follows *Compert Con Culainn*, a text which also existed in the *Cín Dromma Snechta;* it is to be noted that, as in H, the title is found between the two pieces that constitute the text. The text of both MSS. is printed below. A text normalized somewhat in the manner of the present writer's edition of The Poems of Blathmac[9] follows, together with translation and notes, and a brief discussion of the evidence of the Dialogue with regard to the evolution of the Bran tradition.

The remaining two of the three items referred to are found only in N where they follow immediately after the Dialogue. The first of these is headed *Hosini mac Fint dixit contra filium side for Sruib Brain*, "Oséne, son of Find, said to the Otherworld youth upon Srúb Brain". This is followed by four quatrains with the opening line *Tarnac imbith coult co cnaip*, "I found many hazeltrees with nuts". Oséne goes on to tell the fairy boy of all the hidden treasures he had found in Ireland, amongst them "natural" treasures which makes the piece in some degree a nature poem. The references to Srúb Brain (Stroove, on the western side of Lough Foyle) begin in the second

---

[9] *The Poems of Blathmac son of Cú Brettan*, Irish Texts Society (Dublin, 1964).

couplet of the second stanza, and continue into the third. Pending an edition of the poem (which has a number of difficulties), the relevant lines may be quoted in normalized orthography:

Tarnac-se féin hi Srúib Brain
coícait prímdaire cach saim.
Tarnac -se huaim ina toíb
hi fil arcat — dus-ceil fruích

"I myself found in Srúb Brain fifty main oak-groves every summer.

I myself found a cave in its side in which there is silver — heather hides it" (i.e. the cave).

This poem has no direct relevance to the Bran problem; it is mentioned here because of the possible relevance of a hidden treasure in the neighbourhood of Srúb Bran, and because a scribe or a collector considered it worthy of inclusion in a collection of Bran material.

This poem is followed by the third item, a *"dindshenchus"* or "lore of places" text. A transcript is given here, line for line as in the manuscript; there follows a translation in which placenames have been translated where this seemed possible or useful:

Anmand tire locha

no *maigi febu*il *inso Echdrui*m *.i. cenindaa*
*Liatdrui*m *.i. rind arda siar* 7 na
*hiubracha Roifeth ota finn*tracht
*co haigthi Finn*magna *orintt*
*arda co carric A*enach *fliuchr*=
*aiss isann ascorat orb mac*febu*il fora*
*gai issann a2aqorte mbruigi aign*echa
.i. aigneca Tulach ingabae is de ata gaba
*mac febuil ata erch*omair *maic duilén Loch les*
*ar com*air *ua mac cairthin*n *Crocdr*uim *ar com*air *arda .ii.*
*sairdes Druim dos ar com*air *arda siar do rait fe*buil

"Placenames of Loch Febuil (Lake of Febul) or Mag Febuil (Plain of Febue) this. Echdruim (Horse-ridge), that is, Cenindaa. Liathdruim (Grey Ridge) that is, Rind Ardae (Point of the Height) westwards and Na hIubracha (The Yews). Roifeth (Great sea-calm?) from Findtrácht (Fair Strand) to Aigthe

(Faces). Findmagna (Fair places) from Rind Ardae to Carraig (Rock). Oínach Fliuchroiss (Assembly of Wet Promontary), it is there that Orb, son of Febul, was thrown down upon his spear; there is his commemorative stone(?). Mruigi Aignecha (Flat(?) Grasslands), that is, Aignecha. Tulach in Gabai (The Hill of Gabae); hence the *gabae* of the son (sons?) of Febul facing Mac Duilén (Son of Duilén). Loch Les (Lake of Forts?) facing Uí Maic Cairthinn (Descendants of Mac Cairthinn). Cróchdruim (Yellow Ridge?) facing Ardae (Height) to the south east. Druim Dos (Ridge of Bushes) facing Ardae, westwards of Ráith Febuil (Fort of Febul)".

The above text apparently came into being by the excerpting of a number of placenames from an older text concerning mainly the mythical kingdom of Mag Febuil before it was inundated and became Loch Febuil. The first stage in the process was probably one of glossing, and the present text may thus be regarded as consisting of glossed extracts. The glossator, as we may call him, sought to locate the mythical placenames in relation to known places on or near the borders of Lough Foyle. The text commented upon was from the Old Irish period as shown by the form *mbruigi* (= *mruigi*) while *Na hIubracha* (= O.I. *Ind Iubair*) suggests that the glossator belonged to the Middle Irish period.

Of the placenames *Rind Ardae*, the main geographical point of reference, would seem to be Magilligan Point or Ard Magilligan, in the barony of Keenaght, Co. Derry; Uí Mac Cairthinn is in the same area (Cf. *tar Ciandachta ocus tar h. mac Carthainn ocus tar L. Febuil*).[10] The genuine placenames which, however, cannot at the moment be located precisely, would be Cenindaa, Na hIubracha, Findtrácht, Aigthe, Carraig, Aignecha, Mac Duilén (an abbreviation of Cell Maic Duilén, or some such).

The mythical placenames, all from the older text, would then be Echdruim, Liathdruim, Roiféth, Findmagna, Fliuchross (Cf. Mag Fliuchroiss),[11] Mruigi Aignecha, Tulach in Gabai, Loch Less, Cróchdruim, Druim Doss, Ráith Febuil.

There are some doubts and ambiguities. The form of the name *Cenindaa* is strange; the doubling of the *a* is merely to fill the line, a common practice of the scribe. It may be tentatively suggested that

---

[10] Hogan, *Onomasticon Goedelicum* (Dublin, London, 1910), s.v. *Cianachta*.
[11] Gwynn, *Metrical Dindshenchas* iv (Dublin, London, 1924), p. 268.

we have to do with a false expansion of an archaic abbreviated form of *Cianachta (Cénachta)*.

As to the verbal form *ascorat* (= *as-corath*) the meaning is hardly in doubt but the form calls for comment. It may perhaps be taken as pass. pret. sg. of *as-scara (ess-scar-,* v.n. *escor)*, the vocalism of the root syllable being influenced by the v.n. and by *cor* "a cast", v.n. of *fo-ceird (-cuirethar)*. The form *a2aqorte* is more difficult. The abbreviation 2 is based on the common abbreviation for *est*, for which it is used in the present manuscript in a Latin context; in other sources it can be used for *east, eist, iast, ist, st*.[12] Here, in Irish contexts, it is usually used for *da* on account of its resemblance to the Arabic numeral 2; such a practice could hardly be earlier than the fourteenth century when Arabic numerals came into common use. In our manuscript *q* is used for *cu* or for *c*. It is suggested here that in *a2aqorte* 2 is for Lat. *est* = Ir. *attá* (of which I have no other example to offer) and that *q* stands for *c;* hence the phrase may be transliterated *attá a c[h]ort[h]e* which makes excellent sense. It may be noted that, on the basis of the assumptions made above with regard to an old text and a glossator, this matter referring to Orb son of Febul (as well as the reference to Gaba, son of Febul) would derive from the glossator and not from the old text. In *Crocdruim* (l.10) *Croc* has been taken for *Cróch* "saffron", "yellow"; it might as easily represent *Cruach* "peak", in which case the placename should be translated "Peak-ridge". In the same line in *Arda .ii.* the *ii* has been left untranslated; it could be for *aile, eile* "other" a usage found in MSS. of the fifteenth century and later;[13] in this case we should translate "another place called *Ardae*".

The Dialogue

The following is the text of the Dialogue, line for line, as in the two MSS. H and N. The words *iarndedadail* at the beginning of the piece in H are the last words of the preceding text.

H (p. 48, col. a)

> *iarndedadail. f.i.n.i.t. asin .l.c. nicc*
> *IM bumese imbumé.nadfessed auircdine.*

[12] Ó Ceithearnaigh, *Regimen na Sláinte*, vol. i (Dublin, 1942), p. xlvii.
[13] Ó Ceithearnaigh, *op. cit.*, p. lvii.

níbasi fer fesso bic comaidm form andimbir
ic.Anubimmis idún brain icol isin nuargaim fiadum ne
naisc triunu dialuig mofius coard niul-. Rosaig
mofius tiprait glan hfil sais curi cét mban se
uit inbanchuir- conbith do fiur fudgebad bidmar
frith || ain nusóir fed tuaid no aladí fod sloig
A rit amri intséuit glain file htóib sruibe br
oldom anmᶜ rigi Finit amen finit asan .l.c. na
I Macaldaim an druag brain 7 inn ani banfáitho febuil
hoasloch febuil

(col.b)

asin.*l.*   *respoinndit inbanfáith*

    Febul fortemen graigech
hicoimnu conint gairet ni
basidichóim inbi larig maigi
fuinnside
Aildéi maigi noreithmis
ail di tire noteig mis alai
nd atir adscuirmis alaind
aceol nocluin mis || e ara
Mad frignathu na choin
teistis arndoine inid gl
ass force clochach mag
febuil afindscothach.
Batir aildi buidne ban
oenaig himbimis labr
an ba bind as mberedh
inri citeit tait frithisi. Aedh indu

N (Col. 9)

    cucul- 7 ctera || a aircdine. nipasi fer
    mpamissi[14] impa me. nat fessiuth
    fessa bic. comaidm form ind im=
    airic || argaim fiadúnib nenaisscc
A *nubimaiss indun broin icóol issindu*
    triuna dialluith mufiss cohairdniula
R *asaig mu fiss tipprait glan hifil*

---

[14] = *Impamissi*; room left for an ornate initial.

sáss ch⁻e cet mpan .seuit inpanch⁻i
conbith. da fiur fot ngebat patt
már frith ǁ srúmhe prain nosro=
A *rit amrae intseuit glain fili hi toibh*
  irfed tuaid no aldí foth sloig oldamhan
  m⁻críg[15] *Rispondit inpanfaith ǁ ǁ*[16]
F *eb ÷ forthemen graidech . hi coimna conit*
  (End of Col. 9)

In lower margin: *I Macall- indruad brain 7 na banfatha*
feb⁻ os[17] *loch feb⁻ ind sin tuas*

(Col 10)

ngair ÷ nipa si di choiminbí.la rich mui=
chi fuinsidiu ǁ no tegmiss. aulint hi
A *ildiu ínuchiu norethmiss. alte tiriu*
  tir atscurmiss aulint inceul neo cl=
  uínmiss ǁ isstis ar ndane init glass
M *auth frie gnautha na chóine arate=*
  farciu clochuch mag feb⁻ anfinnscoth-
P *ater aldi pugne pan. aenaich hi mbi=*
  miss lia praun pa bint issmperiutt
  indrí. cia teit taet hifrithisi Hosini m̄

The following edited text relies mainly on H, but occasional better readings are based on N. The title, against both manuscripts, is given at the head of the text.

Imbaccaldam in druad Brain ocus inna banḟátho
Febuil hóas Loch Febuil

    1. Imbu messe, imbu mé
        nad fessed a aircdíne?[18]
        Ni ba-se[19] fer fesso bic
        co maidm form ind imbairic.

---

[15] *m-críg*: an effort has been made to erase *g* but it is still legible.

[16] The pair of oblique parallel lines are line-fillers.

[17] *os*: an effort has been made to erase the *s* but it is still legible.

[18] *aircdíne* is taken as a compound of *argg* "chieftain" and the acc. pl. of the neut. io-stem *díne*, "generation"; for *-rc-* = *rgg* note *force* N, *fairciu* H = *fairrge*, etc.

[19] *Ni bá-se* here and in 5c (*-si* MSS.). This is a very archaic form where the copula is indistinguishable from the substantive verb; the regular O. Ir. form

2. A nu-mbímmis i ndún Brain
oc ool isind úargaim,
fiad doínib nenaisc tríunu
dia lluid mo fius co ardníulu.

3. Ro-saig mo fius tiprait nglan
hi fil sáss cuiri cét mban;
séuit in banchuiri con-bíth[20]
do fiur fod-ngébad bid márfríth.

4. Ar it amri int séuit glain
file hi toíb Srúbe Brain;
no soírfed tuaith no al a dí,
foth slóig olldomuin macc rígi.
Respondit in banfáith

5. Febul fortemen graigech
oc coímnu con-indgaireth;

---

would be *nipsa*. This suggests that the poem should be dated at latest to the
early seventh century. A number of comparable forms are found in the early
text published by Grosjean under the title "S. Columbae Hiensis cum Mongano
heroe colloquium", *Analecta Bollandiana* xlv, pp. 75-83 (Bruxelles, 1927).
Another feature pointing in the same direction is *tiprait nglan* 3 *a* showing
tiprae as a masculine noun. The Contributions have no such example; one is
found, however, in the archaic poem *Ba mol Midend midlaige* attributed to
Lucreth [moccu Chiara], c. 600: *maidm tiprait* (leg. *tiprat*) *mair*, ZCP VIII,
p. 308. In a more general way we may count as archaic in the present poem
the use of the preposition *al*, 4 *c*, *foth*, *d*. There is another highly archaic feature: in 4 *d olldomuin* (*oll* + *domuin*, gs. of *domun*) counts as two syllables.
A rule may be stated thus: in the earliest stratum of Old Irish verse words
of a certain structure which have come to be written as disyllables may be
treated as monosyllabic. These are words where the first syllable ends in a
spirant consonant followed by an apparent syllable ending in *l*, *n*, or *r*.
Examples: *re ndoman dainibh* (*v.l. re ndomuin dóinib*), "before the people of
the world" where four syllables are required, ZCP VIII, p. 198. Similarly note
that in the poem entitled *Verba Scáthaige fri Coin Culaind*, deriving from the
Cín Dromma Snechta, *othar* and *foíbur* must count as monosyllables in *otharligi*
and *faeburamnuiss* (Bergin, Best, Meyer, O'Keeffe *Anecdota from Irish
Manuscripts* V, Halle, 1913, pp. 29-30.). In the poem *A maccucáin sruith in
tlag* the word *credal* (sic leg., *credail* MSS., from Lat. *credulus*) must count as
a monosyllable, rhyming with *derb* and consonating with *psalmb*, *marb*
(*Archivium Hibernicum* IV (Dublin 1915), p. 206. Such words might be expected to be monosyllabic in Welsh (e.g. *dofn*). They are recognisable in Irish
by sometimes showing vowel infection in the first syllable, e.g. *othar*, nom. pl.
uithir, *lebor*, nom. pl. *libuir* (Wl. *llyfr*); *bodar* nom. pl. *buidir* (but note Wl.
byddar).

[20] *Con-bíth*: sg. pret. pass. of *con-ben*, lit. "that was shaped". Formally
con-ben could also be 3 sg. imperf. indic. of a compound of *com* with the substantive verb; this compound, however, has only been found in the verbal
noun *combuith*, *commaid*.

ni ba-se díchoím in bí
la ríg Maige Fuindsidi.

6. Áildi maige no-réidmis,
   áildi tíre no-téigmis,
   álaind a tír ad-scuirmis,[21]
   álaind a céol no-cluinmis

7. Mad fri gnáthu na-choíni
   ara tésstis ar ndoíni
   indid glassfairrce chlochach
   Mag Febuil, a findscothach.

8. Batir áildi buidne ban
   oénaig hi mbímmis la Bran;
   ba bind as-mbered in rí
   "cia téit[22] taít a-frithissi".

Translation

The Dialogue of Bran's Druid and Febul's
prophetess above Loch Febuil

1. Was it I, was it myself that did not know its kingly generations?
   I was not a man of little knowledge until I was defeated in the
   contest.[23]

2. When we were in Dún mBrain drinking in the cold winter, my
   fiss (knowledge), when it went to the high clouds, bound strong
   men in the presence of people.

3. My *fiss* reaches a pure well in which there is the equipment of a
   band of hundreds of (Otherworld) women. The jewels of the
   shapely company of women would be a great find for the man
   who would get it.

---

[21] *Ad-scuirmis.* This verb does not seem to be instanced, and the suggested
meaning "thronged" is based on *tascor*; see Pedersen's comments, *Vergleichende
Grammatik* II, p. 615.

[22] *Téit*: 2 pl. absolute of *téit* "goes"; hitherto only the conjunct *-téit* has
been noted.

[23] The "contest" was probably a learned one, perhaps with the prophetess,
concerning genealogical lore: "its kingly generations" would refer to the traditions of the lost kingdom. The eight stanzas that survive may be a fragment of a much longer composition.

4. For famous are the pure jewels that are beside Srúb Brain: it would ransom a *tuath*, or more than two (*tuatha*), the equivalent of the scions of kingship of the host of the great world.

The Prophetess answers

5. Febul, dark and abounding in studs of horses, herded guardingly — the king of Mag Fuindsidi did not think that I was the ugly one of the stock.

6. Beautiful the plains we rode over, beautiful the lands we came to; beautiful the land we thronged (?), beautiful the music we heard.

7. Well do you bewail to companions that our people should flee seeing that Mag Febuil, the fair flowering place, is a grey stony sea.

8. Beautiful were the bands of women of the assembly in which we were with Bran; sweetly would the king say: "Though you go, come back again".

Conclusions

The combination in the Dialogue of a number of elements enables us to attempt a reconstruction of some of the main parts of the structure of *Echtrae Brain*:[24] These elements are: (1) Bran; (2) Bran's druid; (3) the well; (4) the bejewelled Otherworld women; (5) the prophetess; (6) the inundation of the kingdom and the flight of the inhabitants.

If these elements were presented to a medieval Irish storyteller with instructions to make them into a tale there would be a certain inevitability in the resulting product. The story-teller would immediately and without difficulty relate the elements to well-known story-patterns and to the common concepts underlying Irish saga. Our problem, when faced with the elements of the Dialogue, would be similar to the story-teller's but with certain differences. Our knowledge of story-patterns and the general underlying concepts is necessarily narrow, having been acquired laboriously by scholarly processes, and not assimilated, as it were, with mothers' milk.

---

[24] The term *Echtrae Brain*, "The Expedition of Bran", is used here to denote the tale to which allusions are made in the Dialogue and which preceded the creation of the literary *Immram Brain*.

There is also a difference in that our object is simply to recreate strictly in accordance with the evidence. The medieval story-teller would not feel any such restriction and would allow his imagination free play where evidence as to detail was meagre or completely lacking. We may now consider the elements individually.

(1) Bran. Bran was king of Mag Febuil and presided at assemblies (§ 8). He was the hero of the tale and we are naturally to assume that he was present in Dún mBrain (Bran's Fort) at the winter-night's drinking where the events were set in motion (§ 2). *Immram Brain* also opens at Dún Brain, the placename, according to a common early Irish practice, being implicit in the phrase *a dún*, "his (= Bran's) fort" (*Immram Brain*, § 1). Dún mBrain, as we can deduce from the Dialogue, in common with the rest of the kingdom, was to be covered with water (§ 7). From this we gather that *Immram Brain* is to be conceived of as taking place before the inundation of the kingdom, granted, of course, that the inundation was an old and constant tradition, an assumption for which there is ample evidence. The general nostalgic mood of the *Dialogue* implies that Bran is now dead or at least departed and that his last act was his *Echtrae*. But the *Immram* was also Bran's last act. In other words *Echtrae Brain* and *Immram Brain* are variants of a single important incident in Bran's life, his adventurous and perilous visit to *Tír inna mBan*, the Land of Women. One of these tales, it would seem, must have been developed from the other. It will seem from a number of considerations, including the probable respective dates of the *Dialogue* and *Immram Brain*, the lack of Christian elements in the former, and their predominance in the latter, that *Immram Brain* has been based upon *Echtrae Brain* and not the reverse. This con-clusion throws light on the difficulty with regard to the title referred to above. It also means that although the Dialogue must be regarded as the primary source for the recreation of the incidents of the *Echtrae*, some parts of the *Immram* may have a certain relevance.

(2) Bran's druid. The druid's function is to produce the informa-tion that will give the impetus to Bran's *echtrae*. His *fiss*, "knowl-edge", which might here be better translated "faculty of cognition", flies to the high clouds from where it perceives richly bejewelled women at the bottom of a well (§ 2-4). I know of no parallel to this curious shamanistic visionary procedure in Irish literature. The druid corresponds in function to the Otherworld woman in *Immram Brain*. Each gives the impetus to the action; each points out the

existence of a "Land of Women" and it is the hero's duty, implicit
in the Dialogue, explicit in the *Immram*, to seek it out.

(3) The Well. A well in Irish tradition is a natural entrance to the
Otherworld, as indeed is a cave or the side of a mountain. All stret-
ches of water were worshipped, but the well was particularly holy.
In bishop Tírechán's memoir of St. Patrick (end of the seventh
century) the saint is shown as taking action against the well of
Findmag which from its curative properties bore the name *Slán*
"Health". The druids, we are told, honoured it and sacrificed gifts to
it as to a god: *honarabant magi fontem et immolauerent dona ad illum
in modum dei.*[25] This well was the *Rex Aquarum*, The Lord of the
Waters, who, I suggest, is possibly to be identified with Manannán
mac Lir, the Irish god of the sea. The mixture of adoration and
propitiation of wells evidenced here and elsewhere has continued,
despite Patrick's efforts, in a modified and disguised form up to the
present day. A well was naturally a great source of danger and in the
cases of Loch Ríb (Lough Ree on the Shannon),[26] Loch Riach
(Loughrea, Co. Galway) and Loch nEchach (Lough Neagh) was the
instrument by which Otherworld forces destroyed kingdoms turning
them into lakes. The story of Loch nEchach is particularly relevant
to the material under discussion and should be the subject of a special study. This story is known in two forms which may be referred
to as *Loch nEchach* (A) and *Loch nEchach* (B). *Loch nEchach* (A) is
found in the poem *Ba mol Midend midlaige.*[27] This version (a mere
summary of a current story which incorporated genealogical
theories) may be taken as fundamentally pre-Christian. *Loch
nEchach* (B) is, by contrast, a highly Christianized version of the
story upon which *Loch nEchach* (A) was based.[28] The association of a
spring well (*tipra*) with the flooding of an area or a kingdom in the
cases of Loch Ríb, Loch Riach and Loch nEchach suggests a similar
relationship between the well and the inundation of the kingdom in
Echtrae Brain. Furthermore, the well in *Echtrae Brain* would
correspond with the sea in *Immram Brain*: it is the hazardous

---

[25] Whitley Stokes *The Tripartite Life of St. Patrick* (London 1887), ii, p. 323.
[26] For the story of Loch Ríb see Gwynn *The Metrical Dindshenchas* iii
(Dublin 1913), p. 450; for that of Loch Riach *ibid.*, p. 324.
[27] See above, footnote 19.
[28] "Aided Echach maic Maireda in so" Standish H. O'Grady *Silva Gadelica*
(London 1892), Irish Text, pp. 233-7. "This is the death of Eochaid son of
Mairid", Translation and Notes, pp. 265-9. See also Gwynn *The Metrical
Dindshenchas* iv (Dublin 1924), pp. 62-8.

water through which the hero must pass before reaching the land where the women dwell. With regard to this comparison it should be noted that it will be held below on general grounds that the "Otherworld beyond the sea" is a development and rationalisation of the "Otherworld beneath the water".

(4) The bejewelled women. To reach a company of Otherworld women is Bran's object in the *Immram* and in the *Echtrae*. But there are differences in motivation. In the *Immram*, as in *Echtrae Conli*,[29] reaching the Land of Women is the equivalent of the attainment of immortality. In *Echtrae Brain*, insofar as we can make deductions from the *Dialogue*, the hero seeks out the women for the sake of adventure and enrichment; there is no evidence of sexual motivation. Consideration of the varying sexual attitudes of Otherworld women is necessary in seeking to understand this type of literature. The matter could be treated at some length but, for the moment, a summary of the statements and implications of the principal sources must suffice.

Otherworld women are fully sexual beings and often fall deeply in love with human men; indeed, the attraction is mutual. But Christianized literature, by associating the Irish Otherworld with the Christian heaven, has altered the character of Otherworld women: they either ignore sex, being superior to it, or they express themselves as rigidly opposed to it on principle. It is implied or stated that sex is evil, being the result of the transgression (*immormus*) of Adam. Were it not for Adam's sin the human species would propagate itself by a lustless and presumably unexciting device.

In *Immram Brain*, Manannán, the Irish god of the sea, recognises that all sin in the world comes from Adam's transgression. But he and his people have not been touched by this (*nin táraill int immormus* "the transgression has not touched us"). Consequently there is great purity:

> *fir is mná míni fo doss*
> *cen peccad, cen immarmos,*
> "men and gentle women beneath a bush,
> without sin, without transgression"

---

[29] *Echtrae Conli* has some points of contact with *Immram Brain*. For the most recent comments on this tale see my discussion in "The deeper level of Irish literature", *The Capuchin Annual* (Dublin 1969), pp. 162-5 and that of Hans Oskamp "Echtra Condla", *Études Celtiques xiv* (Paris 1974), pp. 207-28. See further below.

When Manannán assumes human form and lies lustfully (*lúthlige*) with Caintigern, wife of Fiachna, in order to beget his human and historical son Mongán († *c.* 629) the author juxtaposes to this incident a "prophecy" of the Incarnation.

In *Immram Maele Dúin*, a tale of very marked ecclesiastical content, and closely related to the *Navigatio Brendani*, Mael Dúin and his companions come to an island where they meet a woman who treats them with wonderful — one might say Otherworld — hospitality. On the third day they make a presumptuous error that leads to a sudden termination of the visit. There are some textual difficulties but the best translation of the verse passage in question is Murphy's, quoted here with some slight changes making no difference to the general sense:[30] 'When she had been besought to satisfy the leader's wanton desire, she said that she was wholly unacquainted with wicked sin. "What you contemplate, lacking as it does any trace of piety, is not the best of faith."'

In *Tochmarc Étaíne* a poem is put into the mouth of Midir, giving an account of the beauty and happiness of the Otherworld. He says: "fine and flawless are the inhabitants of that land; conception there is without sin or guilt. We see everyone on every side, and no one sees us; it is the darkness caused by Adam's sin which hides us from those who would count us."[31] The statement in this early source that in the Otherworld there is "conception without sin or guilt", coupled with the sexlessness shown in *Immram Brain* raises the question as to what means (in ecclesiastical thinking) the Otherworld folk used to propagate their species. Another way of putting this question would be: By what means would the human race propagate itself if the sin of Adam and Eve had not inflicted upon the human race the evil and degrading act of sex? An answer of a kind to this question is given only in sources that need not be earlier than the fifteenth century. In *Echtra Thaidg mheic Céin* "The Expedition of Tadhg mac Céin"[32] the hero Tadhg in his wanderings comes to Adam's Paradise. There he meets Ueniusa, daughter of Adam, one of four immortal sisters. She tells him that it is she who lured Conle from Ireland, and she points out the beautiful and now immortal youth. "I loved him with a great love", said the maiden, "and I brought him to me into this land. And it is our delight, the two of us,

---

[30] *Early Irish Lyrics* (Oxford 1956), pp. 104-5.
[31] *Ériu* xii, part ii, (Dublin 1938), p. 49.
[32] O'Grady *Silva Gadelica*, Text, pp. 342-59, Translation, pp. 385-401.

to be gazing and constantly looking at each other, and we have no other sexual act or corruption except that." "That is beautiful and strange", said Tadhg (*Is aebda ocus is ait sin*), a phrase paraphrased by O'Grady as "c'est magnifique mais ce n'est pas la guerre".

This idea, that mutual gazing might have been the ultimate in sexual contact, is implied in a poem of perhaps fourteenth or fifteenth century date; but of this poem only a single quatrain survives in The *Irish Grammatical Tracts*, a kind of textbook of sound poetic and grammatical usage. The dove has always been, as it still is, a symbol of purity. The unknown poet writes:

> *Adhaltrus fhear na cruinne*
> *ní hí clann na colaime*
> *clann do dhénuimh fa dheógh dhi*
> *le féghuin an éoin eile.*[33]

> "The intercourse of the people of the world
> is not (like) the family of the dove; she finally
> makes her family by looking at the other bird"

In *Loch nEchach* (A) there is no trace of Otherworld women dwelling beneath the lake. But the element is found in *Loch nEchach* (B), if in an attenuated form: Lí Ban, "Beauty of Women", a daughter of the king, Eochu, from whom the lake was named, survived beneath the lake as a kind of mermaid, half woman, half fish. In this form she lived for hundreds of years until Christianity was firmly established. In the sixth century she was caught in a net by a monk of Bangor, and accepted the Christian faith. She could have lived on, but she chose death in order to attain heaven. By this choice she became a Christian saint. She is doubtless a Christianized form of the Otherworld Lí Ban, wife of Labraid Luathlám ar Claideb in *Serglige Con Culainn*. We may assume that Lí Ban was made into a Christian saint because of being an important cultic figure associated with the lake, and dwelling in it, in preChristian times.

The Otherworld women mentioned above live beneath water or in islands across the sea. All have been given explicit Christian or biblical associations, fitting them, if not very comfortably, into Christian patterns of thought. Where there are no explicit Christian

---

[33] Bergin "Irish Grammatical Tracts", Supplement to *Ériu* viii-x (1915-28), p. 62.

associations the sexual behaviour of the Otherworld women is less inhibited: we are, it would appear, in touch with the older tradition. In both instances given below it may be noted that the dwelling place of the Otherworld women is beneath water and not in islands across the sea. I would venture the opinion, already alluded to above, that "dwelling in islands" is a rationalisation of the more primitive "dwelling under water", an idea found also in other cultures. This rationalisation, if it did not come with Christianity, would have been strongly reinforced by it.

In "The Adventure (*Echtra*) of Laegaire son of Crimthann to Mag Mell"[34] the hero came to the Otherworld by invitation, accompanied by fifty warriors; they reached Mag Mell "The Plain of Delights" by diving into a lake. After some martial adventures Laegaire took to wife Dér Gréine, daughter of Fiachna, and wives were also found for the warriors who had accompanied him. Life in the Otherworld was a superlative version of life in Ireland. There was little that was ethereal or Utopian about it; it was a satisfactory mixture of love, war, and dynastic struggle; and when Laegaire was appealed to by his father to return to Connacht, and to kingship, he refused.

In *Tochmarc Emire* "The Wooing of Emer" a Munster king Ruad, son of Rigdond, while voyaging on the sea was made by a stratagem on the part of nine Otherworld women to come to their land under the sea. He slept with each of them on successive nights, and was rewarded by a gift of nine golden boats. On one of the women he begot a son.[35]

Unfortunately the Dialogue is neutral on the question of whether or not Bran had any sexual adventures in the Otherworld. On one point there is a feature in common with the incident in *Tochmarc Emire*: the Otherworld women are in possession of great treasures which the hero may obtain by fair means or foul.

(5) The prophetess. The prophetess, who like the druid is left unnamed, was probably conceived of as an elderly woman: she had been a lover of Bran's father, Febul (§ 5). She had outlived him and her best memories were of the period of his rule (§ 6); in the latter days of the kingdom she had been present at assemblies where Bran presided as king (§ 8). It is clear that in the reign of Febul the plain which constituted the kingdom would not have been called Mag

---

[34] Jackson *Speculum* xvii (Cambridge Mass. 1942), pp. 377-89.
[35] Van Hamel, *Compert Con Culainn and other stories* (Dublin 1956), pp. 39-41; translation by Jackson, *Celtic Miscellany* (London 1951), p. 163

Febuil; hence another name had to be used, and she refers to it as Mag Fuinnsidi (§ 5). Just as the druid was a participant in the action of the tale it would seem probable that the prophetess also had a part to play.

Prophets or prophetesses are never introduced into the *dramatis personae* of an Irish tale in a casual manner, background figures used as decorative details in an exotic scene. The prophetess's function, similar to that of Fedelm, the prophetess, in Táin Bó Cuailnge would have been to warn that the intended action (that is, seeking out the bejewelled women in the well) would result in disaster.

There is a close parallel to this hypothetical situation in the traditions of the bursting forth of Lough Neagh, with some difference in the social position of the prophet. A prophetess (*banfáith*) is a high-class professional woman with specific training. She could also be called *bandruí*, a female druid, or *banfili*, a female seer or poetess; she would have been more or less a priestess, and part of her function would have been to deliver oracles. In the traditions of Lough Neagh the part is played by a man resembling somewhat the Shakes-pearean fool, a type well-known in early Irish material. In *Loch nEchach* (A) he is Mídend Midlach or Mídend, the witless: he prophesies that the well will burst forth and drown the kingdom. In (B) the part is given to one Curnán Óinmit, Curnán, the witless, who prophesies the same disaster, encouraging the people to hew wood and build boats. It is a characteristic of the prophet, in Irish, as well as other tales, that he knows the terrible truth, cries it abroad, but nobody heeds him. If the hero took the prophet's advice there would be no story. The prophet's function then is to create tension, and to prepare the audience for tragedy.

Inasmuch as the role of the prophet is to discourage action there is a certain parallel between the part that we assume to have been played by the prophetess in *Echtrae Brain* and that of Corann, the druid, in *Echtrae Condli*. The latter tale I regard, not as a traditional story, but as a new creation from a conglomeration of *Echtrae* elements. It is a Christianized type of creation similar to *Immram Brain* and possibly originating in the monastery of Bangor. To discuss this matter closely would widen too greatly the scope of the present article. But the general framework has resemblances both to the hypothetical *Echtrae Brain* and to the existing *Immram Brain*, and like the latter it was one of the texts contained in the *Cín Dromma Snechta*. An Otherworld woman appears to Condle and invites him to a world of peace, happiness and immortality. He wishes to go but his leaving is opposed by the druid Corann. The Otherworld woman, after some lapse of time, presses her case strongly and Condle sets out with her in a crystal boat for *Tir inna mBan*, "The land of Women". There can be no prophecy of disaster since in the view of the composer there is no tragedy in gaining eternal life. The druid's role cannot therefore be that of prophecy, but merely that of an opponent of the influences that draw Condle to eternal life.

(6) Inundation and flight.

When the kingdom of Mag Febuil was destroyed it is clear that some people escaped (§ 7), amongst them Bran's druid and the prophetess; indeed, the latter, knowing the danger in advance would have taken the obvious precautions.

That a great kingdom should be destroyed as a mark of supernatural displeasure is a commonplace, and the obvious biblical parallels come immediately to mind, the Deluge and the destruction of Sodom and Gomorrah. In these too certain people escaped. In the case of Noah the escape is of particular importance, since the calamity makes him a second Adam, an ancestor of the whole human race. A comparison with Loch nEchach (A) and (B) would suggest that *Echtrae Brain* too may have been used as an origin legend for peoples in Ulster, or, indeed, other parts of Ireland. There is not, however, to my knowledge, any substantiation of this.

Echtrae Brain has not survived as a story. One reason for this would be that it has been displaced by *Immram Brain*. There remain, however, a number of allusions to the inundation, all implying the existence of some account of the event. In the *Annals of the Four Masters* the *tomaidm* ("bursting forth") of Loch Febuil is assigned, along with that of nine other lakes, to the reign of Tigernmas and is given as occurring in A.M. 3581. The event is also noted in the *Annals of Inisfallen*. *Tomadmann* ("burstings forth") formed a special category of early Irish narrative and three are mentioned in the lists of sagas, amongst them *Tomaidm Locha hEchach*, "The Bursting forth of Loch Neagh"; in *Lebor na hUidre* this tale is called *Aided Echach meic Maireda*, "The Death of Eochu, son of Mairid". It is possible that the tale which we have called *Echtrae Brain* here had also a double title: *Echtrae Brain ocus Tomaidm Locha Febuil*.

In the sixteenth century Nat. Lib. of Ireland MS. G 1, fol. 66 recto, there is a brief topographical tract dealing, amongst other

matters, with plains that have become lakes. Amongst these is
Magh Fuinnsend forsadá Loch Feabhuil "Magh Fuinnsenn upon
which is Lough Foyle"; this is, of course, the tradition alluded to in
the Dialogue where the name of the plain is Mag Fuinnsidi (§ 5).

The glossed extracts edited above (pp. 180 f.) are apparently from
a tale dealing with the transition of Lough Foyle from plain to lake;
it is possible that in the lemmata we have a few remnants of *Echtrae
Brain*.

In this connection it is important to note the anecdote of Colum
Cille of which the latest edition is by Grosjean under the title
Sancti Columbae Hiensis cum Mongano Heroe Colloquium.[36] This
deals with a mysterious youth who was interrogated by Columb Cille
at Carraic Eolairc on the shores of Loch Foyle. It has much in
common with the Dialogue: the geographical location, the use of a
dialogue form, of Latin phrases such as *Respondit iuuenis*, and of
forms of the 1st person sg. preterite of the copula which are comparable with those found in the Dialogue. The mysterious youth
came to be identified with Mongán mac Fiachna, but I would suggest
tentatively that in the original composer's mind, although preserved
without identification, he probably came out of the water and may
have been a manifestation of Manannán mac Lir. When asked by
Columb Cille about the original form of the lake the youth gave a
description of it from his own experience.

The date of this piece is probably very close to that of the *Dialogue*, and on the basis of certain forms in the latter which have been
mentioned in the textual notes I would suggest a date in the early
part of the seventh century.

In my *Studies in Irish Literature and History*[37] (as already mentioned above) I have held that *Immram Brain* is a thoroughly
Christian composition, that it is allegorical from beginning to end,
and that we cannot expect to find there any clear idea as to what
conception of Bran mac Febuil existed in pre-Christian Ireland;
furthermore, that before its composition as a literary text *Immram
Brain* had no existence on an oral level. I regard the new evidence
presented here as by and large corroborative of this view. *Echtrae
Brain* supplied some background material and certain hints that
were capable of a Christian application and development. But the

---

[36] See above, footnote 19.
[37] pp. 280-95.

two compositions were separated by the cultural chasm that divided pagan and monastic Ireland; the qualities of thought, imagination and poetry found in *Immram Brain* may be regarded as the exclusive contribution of the seventh-century author. Similarly I would regard *Echtrae Conli* as a tale composed with the primary object of inculcating a Christian message; it is in some way closely related to *Immram Brain*, and could, indeed, have been created by the same author.[38]

The strangest feature of *Immram Brain* is the presence there of Mongán son of Fíachna who died in or about 629: he is presented as a "son" of Manannán mac Lir, the Irish sea-god. Manannán, himself, foresees his begetting in future ages. What to us might seem a blasphemous comparison is made when the conception of Mongán is deliberately juxtaposed with the Incarnation. Manannán also foresees that Mongan's life on this earth will be short. But the *drong find*, the fair host (of angels), will take him away and he will be "through eternities of centuries" in a fair kingdom.

Here we must face a difficult question. In recounting the adventure of the ancient pagan Bran who set off in a coracle to find the otherworld why did the author (who was a gifted and subtle individual) burden his tale with the cumbersome insertion of matter concerning Mongán? There is, it seems to me, an explanation to hand that is as obvious as it is daring. Bran is used as a general symbol of the seeker after paradise; Mongán is the particular seeker whom the poet has in mind. This would mean, of course, that *Immram Brain* was composed as a commemoration of Mongán in 629 or shortly afterwards. Making Mongán a son of Manannán need be nothing more than a poetic conceit: Mongán, we may take it, was a sailor, plying on military expeditions between Ireland and northern Britain: the sea was his natural element, and he could poetically be regarded even in his lifetime as a veritable re-birth of the sea-god. Regarding Mongán as central rather than as a peripheral incongruity makes the whole tale comprehensible as a piece of literature. I would hazard the view that the author was an Irish *fili* with a good knowledge of monastic teaching: he is personally involved in the problem of being a Christian, while at the same time retaining as much as possible of his traditional heritage.

---

[38] See above, footnote 29.

LATIN INFLUENCE ON BRITISH: THE PLUPERFECT*

PROINSIAS MacCANA

From the first to the fifth century Latin was the language of the political and cultural ascendancy in Britain and as such it exercised a considerable influence on the evolution of British, that branch of Celtic which was spoken throughout most of Britain at the time of the Roman conquest. The nature and the extent of this influence is obviously related to the question of the relative positions of the two languages in Roman Britain and in this regard, as Professor Jackson has remarked,[1] we find a marked swing of expert opinion since the beginning of the present century. Where formerly it was assumed that Latin was spoken generally throughout the Roman province and that the role of British was correspondingly peripheral, in more recent years the pendulum has swung strongly in favour of British. Professor Jackson, while acknowledging that the pendulum may have swung a little too far, nonetheless confirms the wider currency of British: "Latin was the language of the governing classes, of civil administration and of the army, of trade, of the Christian religion, and very largely (but perhaps not entirely) of the people of the towns. The rural upper classes were bilingual; the peasantry of the Lowland Zone, who constituted the great bulk of the population, spoke British, and probably knew little Latin; and the language of the Highland Zone (apart from the army and its native camp-followers) was to all intents and purposes exlusively

---

* The following abbreviations are used in this article:
MBret   Middle Breton
MCorn   Middle Cornish
ModIr   Modern Irish
MW   Middle Welsh
ModW   Modern Welsh
OW   Old Welsh
PKM   *Pedeir Keinc y Mabinogi*, ed. Ifor Williams (Caerdydd 1930).
RM   *The Text of the Mabinogion ... from the Red Book of Hergest*, ed. John Rhŷs and J. Gwenogvryn Evans (Oxford 1887).
WM   *The White Book Mabinogion*, ed. J. Gwenogvryn Evans (Pwllheli 1907).
[1] Kenneth Jackson, *Language and History in Early Britain* (Edinburgh 1953) 94ff.

British." And yet, however the balance may have been redressed in favour of British in social and spatial terms, the fact remains that there is a very palpable and substantial Latin element within the British languages. So important indeed is this element that, in the view of one of the most recent commentators, Professor David Greene, it presupposes "massive bilingualism on the part of the speakers of British" which, but for the collapse of the imperial power, must eventually have produced a Romance language in Britain.[2]

In this connection attention has tended to be concentrated on the individual words borrowed from Latin into British, some 800 in number by Jackson's rough estimate.[3] These cover a wide range of interest and activity and bespeak an extensive penetration of British language and culture: words like Welsh *pysg* "fish", *braich* "arm", *coes* "leg", *llaeth* "milk" and *plant* "children", supplanting or supplementing more or less synonymous native terms, argue prolonged and intimate contact between the two languages. But other evidences are hardly less impressive. Scholars have adverted to the close analogy between the system of vocalic length which became established in British *c*. 600 and that which emerged somewhat earlier in Vulgar Latin; for Sommerfelt and Greene the British innovation derives from Latin, though Jackson seems to regard the two systems as analogous but causally unconnected.[4] British also parallels Vulgar Latin in its use of compounds of two, or even three, prepositions,[5] and there is general agreement that British is in this instance the borrower. Similarly, the creation of a pluperfect tense, common to the several branches of British Celtic but without counterpart in Irish, can hardly be explained except through Latin influence. Here we begin to touch upon syntax as well as on vocabulary and morphology, and in this area the most notable instance

---

[2] *Christianity in Britain, 300-700*, ed. M. W. Barley and R. P. C. Hanson (1968), 76.

[3] Jackson, *op. cit.*, 77ff.; J. Loth, *Les mots latins dans les langues brittoniques* (Paris, 1892); Sir John Rhŷs, *Archaeologia Cambrensis* (1873-74); Henry Lewis, *Yr Elfen Ladin yn yr Iaith Gymraeg* (Cardiff 1943; despite its title, "The Latin Element in the Welsh Language", it confines itself to individual word borrowings).

[4] Alf Sommerfelt, *Norsk Tidsskrift for Sprogvidenskap* 19 (1960), 300ff.; David Greene, *op. cit.*, 86; Kenneth Jackson, *op. cit.*, 338ff., 270f.

[5] Alf Sommerfelt, *op. cit.*, 304; J. E. Caerwyn Williams, *The Bulletin of the Board of Celtic Studies* 13 (1950), 4.

is that of the noun-initial word-order of the MW prose sentence: this seems to reflect heavy Latin influence on southern British.[6]

In the present essay I had hoped originally to attempt a comprehensive survey of the effects of Latin influence on British, of which the foregoing items are far from constituting an exhaustive catalogue, but exigencies of time and space have obliged me to adopt a much more modest proposal, namely to trace in broad outline within Welsh the evolution of the pluperfect tense which was modelled on Latin.

The British pluperfect was formed by adding the terminations of the imperfect indicative to the preterite stem; thus MW *caru* "to love", preterite stem *carass-*, pluperfect lsg. *carasswn* (MCorn. *carsen*, MBret. *carsenn*). To begin with, it must have fulfilled the same function as the Latin pluperfect, cf. OW (9th. cent.) *di-r-gatisse* (plup.) glossing L. *concesserat*, and this continued to be its normal function in early MW prose:

> *o'r a welsei* (plup.) *ef o helgwn y byt, ny welsei* (plup.) *cwn un lliw ac wynt* "of all the hounds he had seen in the world, he had seen no dogs the same colour as these" PKM 1.20-21; *ny angassei* (plup.) *Uendigeituran eiryoet ymywn ty* "Bendigeidfran had never been contained within a house" 31.12; *yr atteb a diwedyssei* (plup.) *Uatholwch* "the answer Matholwch had spoken" 33.11-12.

But anteriority to past time could also be expressed by a periphrasis comprising the imperfect of the substantive verb and the preposition *gwedy* "after" with verbnoun:

> *yd oed* (imperf.) *yr vnbennes gwedy kyfodi* (vn) "the lady had arisen" WM 171.30-31;
> *a phan yttoedynt* (imperf.) *gwedy gware* (vn) *talym* "and when they had played a while" RM 157.5-6.

The same construction, but with the present tense of the substantive verb, could be used to express the perfect as opposed to the preterite:

> *y mae* (pres.) *gvedy mynet* (vn) *gyd a Gwenhwyuar y hystauell* "she has gone with Gwenhwyfar to herchamber" WM 408.7.

It is true that in neither case does periphrasis occur frequently in MW and I have no instances to hand from the earliest MW prose, scil. *Culhwch ac Olwen* and the Four Branches of the Mabinogi, but

---

[6] Cf. P. Mac Cana, *Ériu* 25 (1973), 90ff.

its use is almost universal in modern spoken Welsh to express perfect and pluperfect and one suspects that, in common with certain other features of morphology and syntax, it may have existed for a long time in the spoken language before receiving recognition in writing. Even today the conservative register characteristic of written Welsh continues to use the synthetic pluperfect forms to mark the pluperfect tense, despite the fact that in the spoken language this function is now discharged by the periphrastic construction.

This displacement of the pluperfect, which is only partly concealed in the written language, must have had its origin in the morphological relationship between imperfect and pluperfect, both of which have the same flexional endings, and in the functional range covered by the historical forms of the imperfect in insular British. One of the notable features of the insular British verbal system is the tendency for the historical present and imperfect to function as future and secondary future/conditional respectively; this development seems to be related to the spread of the periphrastic progressive forms comprising substantive verb and verbnoun in place of historical synthetic forms (cf. ModW *'roeddwn i'n mynd* "I was going" for MW and literary *awn*) and manifests itself not merely in Welsh and Cornish but also in Manx and Scottish Gaelic.[7] The written literary form of Welsh, which is both conservative and selective, understates the functional shift of the present and imperfect forms because it tends to avoid the use of the progressive periphrastic forms for the simple present/imperfect. Yet there are occasional aberrant instances of these in MW texts, e.g.

> *Bychein ynt wynteu, ac* y maent yn symudaw *enweu: moch y gelwir weithon* "But they are small and they change names: they are called *moch* nowadays" PKM 68.20-21,

which suggest that they were already common in the spoken language of the period. In any event, the use of the imperfect as secondary future is well attested in MW:

> *can gwydywn i* (imperf.) *y dout ti* (imperf.) *y'm keissyaw i* "for I knew that you would come to seek me" *Owein* ed. R. L. Thomson (Dublin 1968) 552;
> *diheu oed* (imperf.) *genthi na deuei* (imperf.) *Ereint uyth* "she was sure that Gereint would never come" WM 441.20-21,

---

[7] Cf. Heinrich Wagner, *Das Verbum in den Sprachen der britischen Inseln* (Tübingen 1959) 67f., 84f., 89, 94f.

and its prevalence in all the Celtic dialects of mainland Britain would suggest that it existed from a very early period in spoken Welsh (or regional British). The position in modern spoken Welsh is that the simple historical forms of the present and imperfect function as future and secondary future/conditional, subject to a relatively small number of exceptions.

Now, given that the secondary future/conditional was expressed by the historical imperfect throughout that part of the history of Welsh which is covered by documentary evidence, it might seem almost inevitable that the pluperfect, which had the same endings as the imperfect, should have come to be used in parallel fashion, in other words that the asymetrical pattern

imperfect = imperfect + sec. fut./conditional
pluperfect = pluperfect

should have been filled out by the addition of a perfective sec. fut./conditional. As we shall see, this is in fact what happens eventually.[8] It may even appear to be attested already in OW poetry, if we have regard to such instances of the pluperfect as *barnasswn* "I should have judged", *nys adawsswn* "I should not have left", *carasswn* "I should have liked" (late 6th to 9th cent.),[9] *rit pucsawn* (9th-10th cent.) "I should have desired"(?), which Ifor Williams translates "I should love to".[10] Curiously enough, this modal use of the pluperfect forms, though attested in poetry which is at least as old as the ninth century, does not seem to occur in early MW prose; at least I have noted no instances in *Culhwch ac Olwen* or in the Four Branches of the Mabinogi, texts which in their original written form may be dated very approximately to the early and late

---

[8] In Breton also the pluperfect developed as a conditional even though the imperfect did not evolve in this direction. The history of the Breton pluperfect is probably best explained as analogous to the functional shift which affected the Latin pluperfect in several of the Romance languages. That this explanation will not suffice for the conditional pluperfect of insular British is clear from the way in which it meshes into the Celtic modal system, as I hope to demonstrate in the following pages.

[9] *Canu Aneirin* ed. Ifor Williams (Cardiff 1938), ll. 78, 79, 988, 990, 992. See Ifor Williams' comment, *op. cit.*, 92 n. 78; also Kenneth H. Jackson's translation, *The Gododdin* (Edinburgh 1968), 119, 148.

[10] *The Bulletin of the Board of Celtic Studies* 6 (1933), 218, 224. J. Loth translated this verb as a straight pluperfect: "Je t'avais désiré", *Revue celtique* 29 (1908), 8. Cf. also *adwnswn* "I should have wished" (?), *The Poems of Taliesin*, ed. Sir Ifor Williams and J. E. Caerwyn Williams (Dublin 1968), VIII. 36.

eleventh century respectively. But, if this discrepancy is not merely fortuitous, it may be significant that the early instances of the modal use of the pluperfect occur in poetic diction and that several of the verbs concerned are desideratives.

The filling of the modal/secondary future slot in relation to the pluperfect is best illustrated by the evolution of conditional statements. In early Welsh these do not formally distinguish the pluperfect:

> Betwn (past subj.) dedwyd dianghut (imperf./cond.) "Had I been fortunate, you would have escaped "Canu Llywarch Hen, ed. Ifor Williams (Cardiff 1935), 4.19c;
>
> pei ys gwypwn (past subj.), ny down (imperf./cond.) yma "if I had known, I would not have come here" PKM 32.23;
>
> ac oed (modal imperf.) llessach y'r march, pei ass archut (past subj.) yr meityn "and it would have been better for the horse had you asked earlier" PKM 12.9-10;
>
> A phy na bei (past subj.) ueichawc hi, nis gordiwedut ti (imperf./ cond.) "And had she not been with child, you would not have overtaken her" PKM 64.17.

It will be seen that this holds for the protasis as well as for the apodosis; thus in pei guarandawud uiui "if you would hear me" PKM 17.15 and pei ass archut "if you had asked" 12.9-10 the verbs are both past subjunctive. This corresponds to OI usage, e.g. fulilsain-se (sec. fut.) matis (past subj.) mu namit duda-gnetis (past subj.) "I should have endured (them) if it had been my enemies that did them" Ml. 73d1. In later MW prose, however, one finds the pluperfect replacing the imperf./sec. fut. in the apodosis:

> a phei nat ystyriei (past subj.) yr Arglwyd Duw ohonunt wy, ef a wnaetoed (plup.) oual tra messur udunt "and if the Lord God had not considered them he would have caused anxiety beyond measure to them" Selections from the Hengwrt MSS., vol. ii, ed. Robert Williams and Hartwell Jones (London 1892), 71;

replacing the past subjunctive in the protasis:

> bei buassut (plup.) wrth vy gyghor i, ny chyuaruydei (imperf./ sec. fut.) a thi na thrallawt na gofit "if you had followed my counsel, neither affliction nor trouble would have come your way" op. cit., 123;

with sometimes the same text showing the transition taking place between the earlier and the later manuscript:

> pei as gorchymynnassut (plup.) nys gadwn (imperf./sec. fut.) "if you had given him [into my keeping], I should not have let him go" RM 280.7 = pei as gorchymynnut (past subj.) ... WM 216.11;

yr nas gwelsei (plup.) *eiryoet* "though he had never seen her" RM
102.5 = *kyn nys ry welhei* (past subj. with perfective particle *ry*)
WM 452.22;

and finally encroaching on both protasis and apodosis:

> *A phei buassut ti* (plup.) *deilwng a chyuyawn, ny buasut* (plup.)
> *gyfueillt y delweu mut a bydeir* "If you had been honourable and just,
> you would not have been a friend to dumb and deaf idols" *The
> Bulletin of the Board of Celtic Studies* 10 (1941), 56.27-28 (MS. Pen.
> 14, c. 1325-1350);
> *buassei* (plup.) *well itti bei roessut* (plup.) *nawd y'r maccwy* "it would
> have been better for you had you given quarter to the squire"
> WM 148.14-15.

Here we have clear evidence in written MW for the spread of the
pluperfect in conditional sentences relating to past time. The position thus reached in Late MW texts is substantially that maintained
in modern "literary" Welsh, but modern spoken Welsh presents a
quite different picture: very briefly, whereas written MW saw the
introduction of the pluperfect forms into conditional statements,
modern spoken Welsh treats them as characteristic of conditional
(and modal) statements and indeed confines them to this function.
O. H. Fynes-Clinton, in his *The Welsh Vocabulary of the Bangor
District* (Oxford 1913), 46, observed that the pluperfect forms of the
substantive verb were obsolete as markers of tense in Caernarvon-
shire Welsh and were used only in conditional and modal sentences
and a couple of minor sub-types, such as the "unreal" optative (cf.
perhaps the examples with desiderative verbs cited above from OW
verse), e.g.

> "*taswn* (plup.) "if I had been, if I were";
> "*fel tasa* (plup.) "as it were";
> *fasech chi'n* (plup.) *leicio i mi roi tan ar y lamp*? "would you like me
> to light the iamp?";
> *piti na faswn i* (plup.) *yno*! "I wish I had been there!"

In periphrasis the pluperfect forms may alternate with the imperf./sec. fut. forms before *wedi* + verbnoun,

> *mi fuasen/fydden nhw wedi cysgu* "they'd have slept",

which demonstrates how devoid of temporal distinctiveness the
historical pluperfect has become. The same applies to other verbs,
mutatis mutandis: where the pluperfect forms survive, they are used

in a conditional sense.[11] I am informed by Mr T. Arwyn Watkins of
the University College of Wales, Aberystwyth, that where both
imperfect and pluperfect forms were used by old speakers in Cwm
Tawe, South Wales, they were indifferent as to meaning, e.g.

rhedech chi? and *rhedsech chi* (plup.)? "would you run?"

but that there has been a strong swing to the imperfect, so that the
historical pluperfect forms are now virtually obsolete except in the
verb "to be".

By this point, it would seem, the wheel has turned almost full
circle. Introduced into British apparently as a simple *plus quam
perfectum*, the new category of forms was affected by the shift of
the historical imperfect towards the secondary future, used also
modally or conditionally, and eventually came to function as the
perfective of the latter. The resulting symmetry was a precarious
one, however, because it was in conflict with two inherited tenden-
cies in the spoken language. One was to express the pluperfect tense
by the periphrasis of substantive verb + prep. "after" + verbnoun,
and this resulted in the eventual disuse of the pluperfect forms as
simple markers of tense and their closer identification with the
modal/conditional function. The other was to use the same forms for
modal/conditional verbs whether or not they were perfective in
sense (cf. ModIr. *dhéanfainn é* "I would do it/I would have done it"
depending on the context). This also helped to confirm the pluperfect forms as modals/conditionals without temporal distinction and
the eventual result was that the simple and pluperfect forms were
used virtually in free variation. This means in effect that the pluperfect forms have become otiose; in contemporary spoken Welsh they
are unproductive and tending to disappear, except in the case of the
substantive verb.[12] In short, their history has been that of many

---

[11] Cf. O. H. Fynes-Clinton, *op. cit.*, xxvi f., 141, *et passim*; Morris Jones,
Studia Celtica 4 (1970), 100, where he regards the traditional imperfect and
pluperfect forms of the auxiliary verbs *gwneud, cael, medru, gallu* as being in
free variation; also *op. cit.*, 103f., 142-146.

There is a nice illustration of the displacement of the imperfect/sec. fut.
forms of the verb "to be" in a note by Sir Ifor Williams on the MW phrase
da oedd (imperf.) *gennyf* "I should like" PKM 9.9. "The imperfect," he remarks,
"where one would have the pluperfect today, 'da *fuasai*'".

[12] It is not relevant to my purpose to pursue the nuances and dialectal
variations in the use of the pluperfect forms in modern spoken Welsh, but it
may be useful to refer briefly to one or two examples. First, where the con-

extraneous elements borrowed by the insular Celts, in literature and religion as well as in language: one of progressive assimilation to the functional categories of the native system.

One point that emerges very clearly from our consideration of the evolution of the pluperfect in British and Welsh is the marked disparity between the testimonies of the written and the spoken languages. Such disparity is far from being peculiar to Welsh, but in the present instance its effect, in conjunction with our natural preoccupation with the historical written text, may be to convey an oversimplified impression of the extent and more especially of the permanence of the Latin element in Welsh. For the written and spoken registers of the literate period one may, with due reservations, substitute the learned/official and colloquial registers of the pre-literate period, and on general historical grounds as well as on the analogy of the later period one can reasonably assume that in wide areas of western and northern Britain the impact of Latin was very much less on colloquial British than on the language of prestige. Similarly, one must assume wide regional discrepancies. Elsewhere I have suggested that the noun-initial word-order of MW, which is ultimately of Vulgar Latin origin, was peculiar to South-West British and that its spread in Welsh was secondary, relatively late

---

ditional conjunction survives, even residually, in the spoken language, both the simple and pluperfect conditional forms of the substantive verb may be used in the protasis of a conditional sentence. This applies to the forms *petae o/pe bydda fo* (simple cond.) and *(pe)tasa fo* (plup.) "if he were", which are used commonly in North Wales and in which the conjunction "if" is expressed as *(pe)t-*. The distinct nuances of meaning which may still be conveyed by these two forms (and which I hope to discuss on another occasion) exist on a modal and not on a temporal level. Where however the verbal form is still further reduced and the conjunction completely lost, the only tangible mark of the conditional is the pluperfect suffix (-s-) and ending and consequently the pluperfect form is obligatory, as in South Welsh *se fe* "if he were".

Secondly, as already remarked, the conditional or modal pluperfect remains productive only in the substantive verb, and this is evidenced most clearly in the marked tendency for modern spoken Welsh to replace the conditional (simple or pluperfect) of a given verb by a periphrasis comprising the conditional of the substantive verb and the verbnoun of the verb in question, or if a temporal pluperfect is required, by a periphrasis comprising the conditional of the substantive verb, the prep. *wedi* "after" and the verbnoun of the verb in question; thus:

taswn i'n (plup.) *mynd yno* "if I went/were to go there";
taswn i wedi mynd yno "if I had gone there".

Thus the conditional of the substantive verb, particularly in its historically perfective form, becomes the indicator *par excellence* of hypothetical or conditional statements.

and restricted to the literary register. No doubt the detailed investigation of other individual items of morphology and syntax would confirm the wide social and regional diversity comprehended within the historical reality of the Latin influence on British.

V

TEXTUAL CRITICISM

BANNITA : 1. SYLLABA, 2. LITTERA

BERNHARD BISCHOFF

In einer Miszelle zu Mico von Saint-Riquier, den "die Beziehung zu den Glossen und seine durch diesen Umgang verdorbene Sprache interessant" macht, besprach Ludwig Traube das von diesem als Synonym für "syllaba" gebrachte "bannĭta".[1] Er erwähnte sein Vorkommen mit gleicher Prosodie in einem karolingischen Rätsel[2] und als "bannĭta" mit kurzem Mittelvokal in den "Versus cuiusdam Scoti de alphabeto", deren Entstehung er schon vor Aldhelm für möglich hielt.[3] Eine etymologische Anknüpfung schien ihm allenfalls das gotische "bandwjan" "andeuten, ein Zeichen geben" zu erlauben. Inzwischen hat das Wort mit neuen Belegen, aber mit gleicher Bedeutung im Thesaurus linguae Latinae,[4] im Mittellateinischen Wörterbuch[5] und in der "Revised Medieval Latin Word-list from British and Irish Sources" von R. E. Latham (London 1965)[6] Aufnahme gefunden; eine Klärung seines Ursprungs ist jedoch noch nicht gelungen. Sie soll im folgenden versucht werden. Karolingischen Definitionen zufolge wurde "bannita" als grie-

---

[1] Im Jahre 1889 veröffentlicht, wiederabgedruckt in Traubes *Vorlesungen und Abhandlungen* 3 (München 1920), S. 161f. Was Traube (*MGH Poetae* 3, S. 801) neben dem Beleg aus Micos Vorrede zu dem Florileg (ebd., S. 279,4) noch anführt, stammt aus Dicuils Traktat "De prima syllaba", wie A. van de Vyver, *Revue Belge de philologie et d'histoire* 14 (1935), S. 35ff. nachgewiesen hat.

[2] Das Distichon ist herausgegeben von J. Huemer, *Wiener Studien* 5 (1883), S. 168 und 6 (1884), S. 324. Eine Umformung in zwei Hexameter mit der Schreibung "pannitis" druckt aus Clm 19416 (X. Jh.) Christine E. Eder, *Die Schule des Klosters Tegernsee im frühen Mittelalter im Spiegel der Tegernseer Handschriften* (Münchener Beiträge zur Mediävistik und Renaissance-Forschung, Beiheft: Sonderabdruck aus Studien u. Mitteilungen O.S.B. 83, 1972), S. 136 A.

[3] Nach den Editionen von E. Baehrens, *PLM* 5, S. 375-378 und H. Omont, *Bibl. Ec. Chartes* 42(1881), S. 431-440 (mit dem Kommentar der Hs. von Chartres) neu herausgegeben von F. Glorie in: *CC*, Ser. Lat. 123 A, S. 729-740 (mit dem Komm.), vgl. 123, S. 151.

[4] Neben den "Versus" ist zitiert das Gloss. cod. Casin. 90 (nach E. A. Loew, *The Beneventan Script*, Oxford 1914, S. 343 aus dem XI. Jh.).

[5] Außer Micos Prolog sind angeführt Erchanbert (s. Anm. 10), Dicuil, Prolog zu "De prima syllaba" (nicht Mico, s. Anm. 1) und Abbo von Saint-Germain.

[6] Das von demselben herausgegebene *Dictionary of Medieval Latin from British Sources* enthält das Wort nicht.

chisches Fremdwort betrachtet, wie "syllaba" selbst. Ein kurzer Traktat "De syllaba" in dem jetzt im Faksimile vorliegenden Grammatikercodex Diez. B 66 der Staatsbibliothek Preußischer Kulturbesitz in Berlin, aus der Zeit um 790, beginnt (S. 88, 1ff.): "Syllaba Grecum est, Latine (korr. aus -na) dicitur conprehensio, et quare dicta est syllaba? Ad conprehendendum, eo quod conprehendit litteras. Queritur: si possit (korr. aus posit) alio nomine syllaba vocitari? Potest Greco vocabulo "bannita", quod est in Latina lingua "conglutinatio" vel "circumplectatio", quia conglutinat et circumplectitur ..."[7] Einfacher schreibt der Ire Clemens in seiner am Anfang des IX. Jahrhunderts entstandenen "Ars grammatica": "altero vero vocabulo 'bannita' dicitur, quod Latine 'conglutinatio' interpretatur."[8] Der Kommentar zu den "Versus Scoti de alphabeto", den H. Omont aus einer jetzt verlorenen spätkarolingischen Handschrift von Chartres herausgab, erklärt zu V. 11 des Textes: "bannita vero Grece dicitur syllaba."[9]

Mit einer neuen Bedeutung, nämlich "littera", ist "bannita" in einem etymologischen Versuch des Karolingers Erchanbert versehen, der wahrscheinlich in dem Bischof Erchanbert von Freising (836-854) wiederzuerkennen ist. Auch hinter seiner Erklärung steht unausgesprochen die Anschauung, daß "bannita" griechisch sei. Seine Ausführungen zu "syllaba" beginnt er mit dem Eingangssatz der Definition Isidors (Etym. 1, 16, 1 "syllaba-dicitur") und fährt fort: "Syllaba est nomen compositum ex tribus, si non me traditio magistri fefellit, idest ex sy et lempsis et banniton. "Sy" ponitur saepe pro 'con', sicut dicimus 'synagoga' 'congregatio', 'syneresis' 'conglutinatio'; 'lempsis' 'praehensio', 'banniton' 'litterarum' interpretatur", danach fast wörtlich aus Isidor: "Dicta autem syllaba apo toy syllabannita grammaton, idest conceptione litterarum."[10] "Banniton" ist hier griechisch flektiert wie "grammaton", dessen Sinn es angenommen hat, sodaß die Erklärung Silbe um Silbe aufgeht.[11] Die Wortfolge "apo toy syllabannita grammaton" ist von dem

[7] Sammelhandschrift Diez. B. Sant. 66. Einführung von B. Bischoff (Codices selecti phototypice impressi 42; Graz 1973), S. 30.
[8] Clementis Ars grammatica primum ed. J. Tolkiehn (*Philologus*, Suppl. 20, 3; Leipzig 1928), S. 19, 5f.
[9] Omont (s. Anm. 3), S. 437; Glorie (ebd.), S. 731.
[10] W. V. Clausen, *Erchanberti Frisingensis Tractatus super Donatum* (Diss. Univ. of Chicago 1948), S. 110f.
[11] Huemer, *Wiener Studien* 5 (1883), S. 168 zitiert "bannita .i. grammata" mit Berufung auf Clm 14420 saec. IX (anscheinend irrtümlich).

Herausgeber Wendell V. Clausen als korrupt zwischen cruces gesetzt worden, und er vermutet, daß in "syllabannita" das Wort
"bannita" stecken könnte. Doch nicht erst der Erchanbert-Text ist
an dieser Stelle verderbt, sondern in ihn ist eine ältere Korruptel
des Isidor-Textes eingegangen.

Die griechischen Wurzeln und Etymologien im Werke Isidors, die
in Lindsays Ausgabe korrigiert und griechisch gedruckt sind, sind
in sehr vielen Fällen in den Handschriften mit lateinischen Buchstaben geschrieben und zumeist mehr oder weniger entstellt überliefert, nachdem sie schon im Original nicht immer die klassische
Sprachform zeigten. In Lindsays Text des Kapitels "De syllaba"
stehen als Graeca ἀπὸ τοῦ συλλαμβάνειν τὰ γράμματα und das noch
einmal wiederholte Verbum, aber in der lateinischen Translitera-
tion von συλλαμβάνειν, wie die Handschriften sie bieten, fehlt in
der überblickbaren Überlieferung ausnahmslos das μ. Die Mu-
sterung von 28 vorkarolingischen, karolingischen und spanischen
Isidor-Handschriften ließ weitere Unsicherheiten und Mißverständ-
nisse sowie vergebliche Bemühungen um Korrektur erkennen.[12]
Weitaus die Mehrzahl enthält den Wortlaut "apo tu sillabanin
(syll.) ta grammata". Aber unter den Varianten begegnen: "apo to
(tou) syllabani ta grammata" (London, B.L., Harl. 2686; Reims 426,
hier korrigiert zu: "syllabanninta gr."); "apo to^v syl^{l}abannita grammata" (Wolfenbüttel, Weiss. 64, saec. VIII, mit Korrektur; dazu am
Rand saec. IX: "al. apoty syllabanin TωN ΓΡΑΜΜΑΤωΝ);
schließlich: "ΑΠΟ ΤΟ CYllΑ BANNITA ΓΡΑΜΜΑΤΑ" (Clm 6411),
mit kleinen Zwischenräumen vor und hinter BANNITA. Auch unter
den Lesarten mit dem Genitiv "grammaton" (wie bei Erchanbert)
findet sich: "apo to syllabannita gr." (Sankt Gallen 231; Schaffhau-
sen 42, hier "gr." aus "grammata" verändert).

In mehreren dieser Textformen ist das Gebilde "bannita" in Er-
scheinung getreten, und es ist meine These, daß es durch ein Mißverständnis oder durch eine willkürliche Entscheidung mit der Bedeutung "Silbe" behaftet aus diesem Zusammenhang herausgelöst
wurde und seine selbständige Existenz begann. Ohne andere Mög-
lichkeiten dieses Vorgangs ausschließen zu wollen, möchte ich die

---

[12] Die Auswahl ging von der in der *Revue d'Histoire des Textes* 2 (1972),
S. 288 gegebenen Liste aus. Für die Zusammenstellung der meisten Lesarten
danke ich herzlich Herrn M. Reydellet, für Ergänzungen J. Brown, J. Duft,
W. Hörmann, C. Jeudy, W. Milde, H. Mordek, F. Mütherich, A. Paredi,
Y.-Fr. Riou, Chr. v. Steiger.

folgenden zu erwägen geben. Als das Wort mit dem Genitiv "grammaton" in Verbindung gebracht war, konnte ein des Griechischen ein wenig Kundiger, von "grammaton" ausgehend, in "bannita" den übergeordneten Begriff sehen und ihn sich als Abstraktum mit einer Bedeutung wie "conceptio", bei Isidor der Interpretation von "syllaba", erklären. Aber auch dies wäre denkbar: wenn die schon korrumpierte isidorische Phrase in griechische Schrift umgesetzt wurde, wie es unvollkommen in Clm 6411, einer karolingischen Handschrift mit vielen irischen Symptomen,[13] geschehen ist, folgen einander lateinisch lesbar die Worte: "syllaba dicta est ... BANNITA".

Daß Clemens, Dicuil und der irische Dichter der "Versus de alphabeto" es gebrauchen, spricht für eine Herkunft aus irischem Milieu.[14] Da die datierbaren Belege erst mit der frühkarolingischen Zeit einsetzen, erhebt sich die Frage, wieweit die "Versus" als Zeugnis für ein höheres Alter angerufen werden können.

Während Traube allzu summarisch den zeitlichen Vorrang des Iren vor den angelsächsischen Rätseldichtern postulierte, versuchte Manitius eine genauere Datierung. Er zog dazu den Kommentar der Handschrift von Chartres heran; da die Anspielungen der Verse in diesem zutreffend erklärt sind, sprach er sich für die Abfassung desselben durch den Autor des Gedichts aus. Es war aber wohl überspitzt, in dem Satz: "Karthago est metropolis Affricae" (zu "caput Afrorum", K 3, von Pompeius abhängig) nicht traditionellen Ruhm, sondern eine noch gültige historische Aussage sehen zu wollen.[15] Manitius nahm daraufhin eine Entstehung in der ersten Hälfte des VII. Jahrhunderts an, und mit einer Datierung vor oder in die Mitte desselben ist ihm fast die gesamte Literatur gefolgt.[16] Inner-

---

[13] Zu der Hs. vgl. B. Bischoff in: *Studien zur lateinischen Dichtung des Mittelalter, Ehrengabe für Karl Strecker* (Dresden 1931), S. 9f. und *Die südostdeutschen Schreibschulen und Bibliotheken* I² (Wiesbaden 1960), S. 150. Sie enthält u.a. Etym., B.I mit Auslassungen und Umstellungen.

[14] Bei Annahme einer solchen ist es vielleicht kein Zufall, daß die Erklärung des "griechischen" Wortes "bannita" durch "conglutinatio" der Ausdrucksweise des Virgilius Maro angenähert ist, der die Silben als "glutini litterarum" bezeichnet (*Opera* ed. J. Huemer, Lipsiae 1886, S. 11,5; vgl. auch "cum syllabarum conglutine paulatim gradiatur" sc. littera, ebd. S. 7, 14). Sonst werden "conglutino" und "conglutinatio" von den Grammatikern für andere Operationen und Figuren gebraucht.

[15] Manitius, *LG* I, S. 191.

[16] Kenney; Raby; De Ghellinck; Dekkers-Gaar; Glorie (s. Anm. 3), der freilich auch eine Entstehung nach Aldhelm für möglich hält. Bücheler wollte

halb der Rätseldichtung bestehen neben gedanklichen Berührungen
vereinzelte wörtliche Übereinstimmungen der "Versus" mit Sympho-
sius[17] und Eusebius;[18] wenn bei dem Wortspiel "flumen-lumen"
eine Abhängigkeit vorliegt, kommt dem Eusebius die Priorität zu.[19]
Ein besonders auffälliger Zug der "Versus" ist jedoch das Interesse
des Dichters für die Rolle der Buchstaben in römischen und christlichen Abkürzungen;[20] er scheint die antiquarische Neigung der karolingischen Gelehrten zu teilen, die die alten "Laterculi" wieder
vervielfältigten.[21] Die Überlieferung der "Versus"[22] steht einer
Ansetzung in karolingische Zeit nicht entgegen: sie beginnt — da die
Datierungen gegenüber den Ausgaben z.T. zu berichtigen sind —
mit drei Handschriften, die alle etwa aus dem dritten Viertel des
IX. Jahrhunderts stammen: Oxford, Bodl., Rawlinson C 697 (aus
Nordostfrankreich), Paris, N.B., Lat. 2773 (aus Reims) und Lat.
5001 (aus dem östlichen Frankreich). Der Dichter kann ein auf dem
Festland wirkender Ire gewesen sein. Der Ursprung von "bannita"
aber braucht nicht über das VIII. Jahrhundert zurückzugehen.[23]

Im ganzen gesehen, muß "bannita" in der Karolingerzeit mit
Zurückhaltung aufgenommen worden sein, denn von bekannten
Autoren verwendet außer Grammatikern nur Abbo von Saint-Ger-
main das Wort in dem gespreizten Widmungsbrief seines Epos. Aber
wohl als einen in der Schule gelernten Ausdruck konnte es auch der
Dichter des kleinen Rätsels als bekannt voraussetzen.

Immerhin war das Wort so selten und auffällig, daß es auch in die
lexikographische Literatur einging. Das Glossarium codicis Casinen-
sis 90, saec. XI, bietet "bannita syllaba .i. conglutinatio litterarum
vel temporum" (CGL 5, 562, 33). Das Gleiche, doch ohne den über-

---

die "Versus" in die Nähe des Eusebius stellen (*Rhein. Mus.* 36, 1881, 340);
ihm folgt Teuffel[6].

[17] Vgl. Glorie unter A 2 und H 1; O 2.

[18] Vgl. A 2; K 1.

[19] Vgl. F 3.

[20] Zur römischen Verwendung: D 3 (der Kommentar schmückt aus); G 1;
P 3; R 3; S 1; zur christlichen: G 2; S 2. Die Sigle GḠ für Gregorius ist bei
Lindsay, Notae Latinae, S. 427 zuerst aus dem Moore Beda belegt.

[21] Auch die Schreibung "lauta" für "labda", die "Versus" L 1 voraus-
gesetzt und von den Iren verbreitet wird, scheint erst vom IX. Jh. an belegt
zu sein. Vgl. Glorie zur Stelle; *Poetae* 3,700. Ebenso dringt "lautacismus" für
"labdacismus" in die Überlieferung ein, s. Thes. L.L.; *Aldhelmi Opera* ed.
Ehwald, S. 321 App.

[22] Dazu Ch. E. Finch, *Scriptorium* 28 (1974), S. 275f.

[23] Handschriftlich ist das Wort zuerst in dem rund um 790 im austrasischen
Bereich entstandenen Teil des Cod. Diez. (s. Anm. 7) überliefert.

raschenden Zusatz "vel temporum", findet sich in den "Derivatio-
nes" des Hugutio,[24] und wohl über diesen konnte das Wort noch zu
einem spätmittelalterlichen Lexikographen gelangen: denn der 1477
gedruckte "Teuthonista" oder "Der Duytschlander" des Klever
Offizials Gert van der Schuren, ein lateinisch- niederrheinisches
Lexikon, enthält die Gleichung "bannita (.i. sillaba) silve."[25]

---

[24] Vgl. Omont (s. Anm. 3), S. 437, der die Varianten "banita" und "ban-
niata" anführt.

[25] Bei L. Diefenbach, *Glossarium Latino-Germanicum mediae et infimae
aetatis* (Frankfurt a.M. 1857), S. 67. Über den Autor des "Teuthonista" vgl.
J. van Dam in: Stammler-Langosch, *Verfasserlexikon* 2, 39ff.

DER WIENER PAPYRUSCODEX 2160* (W)

RUDOLF HANSLIK

Da Sie, lieber Freund und verehrter Jubilar, in jungen Jahren die
Anfänge Ihrer so erfolgreichen wissenschaftlichen Tätigkeit als
Assistent Edmund Haulers am Wiener Kirchenvätercorpus der
Österreichischen Akademie der Wissenschaften und an der Hand-
schriftensammlung der Österreichischen Nationalbibliothek begon-
nen haben, glaube ich, daß Ihnen eine kleine Abhandlung über den
Wiener Papyruscodex s. VI des Hilarius De trinitate Freude berei-
ten wird, der damals freilich ein ganz anderes Aussehen hatte als
heute; damals ruhten seine oft schwer lesbaren Blätter und Lagen un-
gebunden in einer Reihe von braunen Umschlägen in einem schach-
telartigen Behälter. Kürzlich wurden sie einer Restauration unter-
zogen und liegen nun wieder gebunden und besser lesbar als "Codex"
Nr. 2160*, mit den Maßen 279 × 195 (215/25 × 135) vor, der den
größten Teil der ersten Hälfte von De trinitate und den Traktat
Contra Arrianos enthält. Leider bietet der Codex den Text nicht so
vollständig wie andere Hss. des Werkes, die aus dem V. oder VI. Jh.
stammen. Als die Blätter noch lose lagen, hat sie irgendjemand mit
großen, schwarzen Ziffern numeriert; diesen Ziffern gemäß hat sie
der Restaurator zusammengefügt, frühere Beobachtungen, daß die
Numerierung falsch sei, blieben unbeachtet. Fol. 1^r bietet den Text
ab B. II col. 56, Z. 16 Mi. Doch die Numierung war bei 7 Blättern
irreführend: der Codex beginnt nicht erst im Buch II, sondern bietet
schon Teile von Buch I. Fol. 30^r bis 36^v beinhalten von Buch I col.
34, 23 Mi. (cum aeternus) bis 43, 26 (non ambigue), der Rest von B. I
und der Anfang von B. II fehlen. In B. II fehlen col. 66, 15 (et
spiritu) bis col. 68, 12f. (universorum), das sind 2 Blätter. In B. III
col. 82, 10 (saxa) bis 83, 17 (ei), das ist 1 Blatt; und col. 92, 30 (non
est) bis col. 95, 11f. (existat), das sind 3 Blätter; in B. IV col. 121, 2
(significationem) bis col. 122, 15 (significationem), wohl 1 Blatt; in
B. V col. 130, 33 (necessitatem) bis 132, 2 (reddiderint), das ist 1
Blatt; col. 139, 14 (euangelicae) bis col. 140, 28 (coepisset), 1 Blatt.
Im B. VI fehlen col. 162, 18 (huius) bis col. 164, 31 (ecclesiae), das
sind 2 Blätter; col. 167, 3 (non series) bis col. 168, 4 (praeparato),
d.i. 1 Blatt; col. 170, 1 (quod) bis col. 172, 4 (ingenito), d.i. 2 Blätter;

col. 179, 2 (hodie) bis 180, 17 (sui), d.i. 1 Blatt. VI col. 187, 13 (sunt portae) bis col. 190, 9f. (praestitisse), d.i. wahrscheinlich 2 Blätter. Der Text endet col. 197, 18 (se). Reste des folgenden Textes stehen noch im Fragment St. Florian, Stiftsbibliothek III 15 B und Vatican, Barb. lat. 9916, ferner ein Frgm. s. Lowe CLA X nr. 1507. Der Codex ist in Süditalien in Halbunziale geschrieben. H. Sedlmayer, "Das zweite Buch von Hilarius de trinitate im Wiener Papyrus", in: *Serta Harteliana* (1896) 177-180 hatte ihn noch für die älteste Hilariushs. gehalten; daß dies nicht der Fall ist, daß C (Paris Bibl. Nat. lat. 8907), V (Verona Bibl. Cap. XIV) und B (Rom, St. Peter) vom J. 509/10 älter sind, ist schon erkannt, s.P. Smuders, "Manuscripts of Hilary De Trinitate", in: *Studia Patristica* III (1961) 129-138. Das Auffälligste an dem Codex ist, daß er in den Büchern I; III-VI im großen und ganzen gleiche oder ähnliche Lesarten bietet wie die anderen Unzial- und Halbunzialhandschriften; in B. II dagegen weicht er gelegentlich von diesen so sehr ab, daß Sedlmayer diesen Codex als erste Ausgabe des Werkes angesehen hatte; das hat P. Smulda bezweifelt. Die Frage steht jedoch noch im Raum. Weiters ist zu klären, wieweit der Codex sonst mit CBVD (= Paris Bibl. Nat. lat. 2360) Beziehung hat, welches seine Sonderfehler sind, und ob sich Nachwirkung in späteren Hss. des IX.-XIII. Jh. findet.

Sedlmayer hat die wesenlichen Divergenzen zwischen W und den übrigen Hss., die sich zu B. II finden, verzeichnet, doch nicht besprochen. Die erste steht col. 57, 39f. Mi; Hilarius führt aus, daß das, was nur Teil ist, von Natur aus nicht die Wesenheit hat, alles zu sein; doch Christus ist perfectus a perfecto (scil. patre): quia qui habet omnia (der Vater), dedit omnia (den Sohn). Dann fährt er fort: neque existimandus est non dedisse quia habeat; vel non habere, quia dederit = man darf nicht meinen, er (d.i. der Vater) habe nicht (zu ergänzen: alles = den Sohn) gegeben, da er (alles) habe (d.h. man dürfe nicht meinen, Christus sei nicht Gottes, des Vaters Sohn, er habe ihn nicht gegeben, da Gott Vater weiterhin alles sei); vel non habere, quia dederit (man dürfe auch nicht meinen, Gott Vater habe jetzt nicht mehr alles, da er den Sohn gegeben habe). Diesen etwas komplizierten Gedankengang hat der Schreiber von W eigenständig simplifiziert, zugleich aber auch im ersten Teil verdorben: neque non dederit ob hoc, quia non habeat; neque non habeat idcirco, quia dederit. Das ist offenkundig Verderbnis des richtigen, nicht verstandenen Textes. — Col. 59, 19f. wird dem Gedanken Raum gegeben, daß sich der Sohn vom Vater in nichts unterscheide; anschließend steht gegen die übliche Lesart: quia vita viventis in vivo est, in W: quia uiuus uiuentis hereditas est. Daß hier die Lesart des Cod. W einen sachlich schlechteren Gedankengang gegenüber dem der übrigen Hss. bietet, ist offensichtlich; er ist dem scharf denkenden Hilarius auch in einer eventuellen Erstfassung nicht zuzutrauen. —

Wenn sich col. 62, 23f. folgende Divergenz findet: tempus enim est spatii non in loco, sed in aetate manentis significata moderatio. et cum ab eo omnia, res nulla non ab eo; et idcirco tempus ab eo est — gegenüber: tempus enim rei nomen est, manentis inspicatio. et cum ab eo omnia, res nulla non ab eo W, so ist hier klar ersichtlich, daß der Lesart des Cod. W Priorität nicht zukommt, sondern daß die Vorlage von W den üblichen Text vor Augen gehabt und selbständig verändert hat. Denn im Hinblick auf das folgende res nulla non ab eo ist der Genetiv spatii durch rei ersetzt worden; der Absicht eines Schreibers, den Text kürzer zusammenzuziehen, entspricht auch das Weglassen des Schlußsatzes. Möglicherweise wollte er manentis als rei manentis verstanden wissen, und hat dann völlig frei zu nomen ein zweites Prädikatsnomen: (rei manentis) inspicatio angefügt. Den Satz hat er so freilich verdorben.——

Eine starke Textdifferenz findet sich B. II 20, col. 63, 18ff.: enarra, quid non sine eo factum sit. *Quod factum est in eo, vita est* (Joh. 1, 4). Hoc igitur non sine eo, quod in eo factum est: nam id quod in eo factum est, etiam per eum factum est. *Omnia* enim *per ipsum et in ipso creata sunt* (Coloss. 1, 16). In ipso autem creata, quia nascebatur creator Deus. Sed etiam ex hoc sine eo nihil factum est, quod in eo factum est, quia nascens Deus vita erat: et qui vita erat, non postea quam est natus, effectus est vita. Demgegenüber: enarra quid non sine eo (factum est *add.* W[2]), quia non sine ⟨se⟩ et sua uoluntate natus est ipse, quem constabat esse in patrem. factum enim uidetur ipsum quod natum est sed uoluntate communi quibus sua perfecta cognitio est. [sine eo factum] est enim in eo facta uitam et deus natus est. neque enim postea quam est natus, effectus est W. Hilarius ging von dem Satz col. 63, 4ff. aus: "*Et sine eo factum est nihil*" und fährt da fort: "Verum confundor et turbor in eo, quod *sine eo factum est nihil*. Est ergo aliquid per alterum factum (die creatio des Sohnes durch den Vater), quod tamen non sit sine eo factum: et si aliquid per alterum, licet non sine eo. Dieses "non sine eo" nimmt er col. 63, 18ff. wieder auf: enarra, quid non sine eo factum sit. Ein euer Gesichtspunkt wird von Hilarius in der Regel

durch ein neues Bibelzitat eingeführt, das dann interpretiert wird.
So geschieht das auch in allen Hss. außer W: *"Quod factum est in eo
vita est* (Joh. I 4). Das "Leben" Christi ist nicht ohne ihn erfolgt. In
W wird dieser Terminus ohne Bibelzitat eingeführt: "est enim in eo
facta uita". Voran geht ein Gedanke, der p. 63,6 angeklungen war:
est ergo aliquid per alterum (durch den Vater) factum, und dieser
wird in W entwickelt: Christus ist im Vater; daher ist seine Geburt
durch einen gemeinsamen Willensakt erfolgt. Hier sah sich also
jemand bemüßigt, den Begriff "per alterum factum" (col. 63,6)
näher zu erklären und das "sine eo factum est nihil" zu modifizieren,
völlig unnötig, da die Einheit von Vater und Sohn auch hinsichtlich
der Menschwerdung dann ohnehin col. 63, 33ff. behandelt und aus-
führlich mit Bibelzitaten belegt wird. Der differente Text in W ist
also gegen die Arbeitsweise des Hilarius eingeführt und stellt inhalt-
lich eine Doppelversion zu col. 63, 33ff. dar: er gehört Hilarius
nicht an. Hat ihn der Schreiber von W erfunden? Jedenfalls: factum enim uidetur ipsum quod natum est sed uoluntate communi
quibus sua perfecta cognitio est entspricht nicht der glänzenden
Diktion des Hilarius. Die Version von W stammt also aus einer
älteren Vorlage, die eigenständigen Text eines Interpolators enthielt.
Er hat auf gleiche ungeschickte Weise unmittelbar hernach den
Text verschlechtert, col. 63, 33ff.: nascens enim a vivente vivus, a
vero verus, a perfecto perfectus, non sine potestate nativitatis suae
natus est, nativitatem videlicet suam non postea sentiens, sed se
Deum in eo ipso quod Deus ex Deo nascebatur, intellegens, gegenüber nascens enim a uiuente uiuus, a uero uerus; non ignorauit ea
quae consensu suo facta sunt natiuitatem uidelicet suam in qua
condebatur intellegens W. Vor allem der Schluß: natiuitatem uidelicet suam in qua condebatur, intellegens ist einem Hilarius nicht
zuzumuten. — Eine große Textdifferenz findet sich im B. II col.
69, 17 bis 70, 10; hier stehen in den Hss. Bibelzitate, die die Existenz
des Hl. Geistes bezeugen, Gal. IV 6; Ephes. IV 30; I Cor. 2, 12; Rom.
8, 9; 11. Diese sind in W ersetzt durch folgenden Text: De quo si
quis intellegentiae nostrae [quaerit per quem, quando, ue(l)
qua[e]lis est in euangeliis legimus ambo, deum a semetipso uni-
genitum a deo ab unigenito omnia proferemus et apostolus eum,
quem in commune legimus, in quo inquid habemus redemptionem
per sanguinem ipsius remissione⟨m⟩ peccatorum, qui est imago dei
inuisibilis, primogenitus omnis creaturae, quia in ipso creata sunt
universa in caelis et in terra, *uisibilia et inuisibilia siue throni siue*

sedes siue principatus siue potestates siue dominationes; omnia per ipsum et in ipso (Coloss. I 16) creata sunt et ipse est ante omnes et omnia ipsi constant. Dieser Text paßt weder zu den vorausgehenden Sätzen über den Hl. Geist, noch zu den folgenden Bibelzitaten über ihn. Er ist ein zusammengeflickter Einschub, eine Randnotiz zum Worte (intellegentiae nostrae) sensum, der in den Text geraten ist.

Eine letzte Differenz ist in B. II bei col. 74, 24 bis 27 zu finden. Nach "ait enim, ut iam superius ostendimus, apostolus: *nos autem non spiritum huius mundi accepimus, sed spiritum qui ex Deo est, ut sciamus quae a Deo donata sunt nobis* (I Cor. 2, 12) setzt der Cod. B (Rom, St. Peter a. 509/10), (aus ihm C² und spätere Hss.) fort: quae et loquimur non in doctrinae (richtig: doctrina, Klosterneuburg nr. 206 s. XII) humanae sapientiae uerbis sed in doctrina spiritus spiritalibus spiritalia comparantes. animalis autem homo non percipit quae sunt spiritus dei. Statt col. 74, 24 bis 27 hat W aus B entnommen: "animalis enim homo non percipit quae sunt spiritus. Spiritalibus enim spiritalia comparamus." —

Das führt zur Frage, ob W zu der Hss.-Gruppe V und B [509/10 in der Schule des auf Cagliari in Sardinien in der Verbannung weilenden Fulgentius von Ruspe geschrieben ist (A. Wilmart, *L'odyssée du manuscrit de San Pietro...*, *Festschrift E. K. Rand*, New York 1938, 293-305)], stärkere Beziehung hat als zu C D, und ob er nicht nur in den aus Buch II aufgeführten Textdifferenzen, sondern auch bei einzelnen Wörtern auffallende eigenständige Lesarten zeigt, nebensächliche braucht man nicht zu beachten. Zum zweiten Problem sei verzeichnet: col. 58, 14f.: sensum unde hauseris] sensum unde auxeris; col. 58, 18f.: qualiter sensum inseras] qualiter sensum auxeris; col. 58, 21: inperitus in tuis] inpeditus in tuis; col. 58, 41: arcano te inopinabilis nativitatis inmerge] a.t.i.n. insparge; col. 59, 32f.: et nefas est mihi] et non licet mihi; col. 61, 6: haerebit in ceteris] reuinceris; col. 62, 12: apud... deum...praedicatur] apud...deum... conlocatur; col. 62, 32f.: reddidisti auctorem] sed didicisti auctorem; col. 62, 34: intellego non solum] intellego et alium; col. 65, 28f.: *clarifica me...ea claritate quam habui*] clarifica me...eo honore quo fui; col. 65, 34f.: nouelli apostolatus, sed ab antichristo praedicatores, omni contumelia dei filium inludentes] arii omni contumelia filii; col. 65, 38: *ego in patre et pater in me* (Joh. 14, 11)] pater in filio et filius in patre; col. 68, 20f.:sic vagitus per angelorum divina gaudia honorantur] sic uagitus per angelorum uocem diuino gaudio honorantur; col. 70, 14: ex quo omnia sunt] ex quo inuisibilia; col. 70, 21f.: quod nominatur Spiritus] quod donatur Spiritus; col. 72, 23: (natura et muneris et honoris) significata est] (natura et muneris et honoris) expressum; col. 72, 25ff.: (adorandi) infinitatem, dum in Spiritu deus Spiritus adoratur] (adorandi) magnitudinem conprehendit; col. 73, 6: significat] conprehendit; col. 73, 32: (intercessionis suae) foedere] (intercessionis suae) solacio. — Ähnliche Sonderlesungen, die einem Hilarius auch in einer ersten Ausgabe nicht zuzutrauen sind, finden sich auch in den übrigen Büchern, etwa in B. I col. 36, 17: temeritatis ingenia] temeritatis audacia; in B. III col. 76, 29: divinarum scripturarum doctrinam] rationem diuinarum scripturarum; col. 76, 31: de cognitis ac familiaribus] de cognitis ac familiaribus rebus; 78, 20: efficientiae] intelligentiae; col. 80, 15f.: nec plenitudo in eo erit] et plenitudo in eo ueritatis; col. 81, 15: syllogismis suis] sinlogis musicorum. Aus B. IV ist signifikant col. 122, 33: constituit] confessio; col. 133, 2: testis] interpres; col. 124, 31: in Bethlehem] in aegyptum usque in bethlem; col. 124, 40f.: reges Tharsis] reges tarsis et insulae; col. 126, 4: distinctione² discretione. Aus B.V: col. 134, 14: dissentientem] dissimilem; col. 135, 9: haeretica intellegentia] haeretica subtilitas.

Diese Beispiele zeigen, daß eine Hand — eher die des Schreibers der Vorlage von W als die des Schreibers von W selbst — sehr eigenwillig in den Text eingegriffen und oft nach freiem Ermessen Wörter durch andere ersetzt, den Text gelegentlich gekürzt und interpoliert hat. Daß col. 65, 34f. die Priorität dem Ausdruck der Masse der Hss: novelli apostolatus, sed ab antichristo praedicatores, omni contumelia dei filium inludentes gehört, daß dieser Passus nicht aus der Fassung von W: arii omni contumelia filii hervorgegangen sein kann, ist evident. Gelegentlich zeigt sich ‚wie in col. 58, 14f. und col. 58, 18f. die ganze Unbeholfenheit dieses für die Wortersetzungen Verantwortlichen, da er statt hauseris und inseras das gleiche Wort auxeris in den Text setzte. Die erst aufgeführten starken Divergenzen von W und die Ersetzungen einzelner Wörter in W liegen auf der gleichen Ebene: sie sind Eingriffe in den ursprünglich von Hilarius geschriebenen Text, nicht erste Fassung des Autors selbst.

Die Beziehungen zwischen den ältesten Hss. außer W sind einigermaßen zu klären: D = Paris 2630 und C = Paris 8907 gehören enger zusammen, desgleichen B = Rom, St. Peter und V = Verona, bibl. Cap. XIV; T = Paris nouv. acq. 1592, das aber erst von Buch VI an erhalten ist, hat enge Beziehungen zu BV. Von den Hss. des IX. (und frühen X.) Jhdts stammt E (Paris 12132) aus D; der cod. F aus Fleury (Paris 1695) und L aus Lorsch (Brit. Mus. Harl. 3115) stammen aus C; cod. A aus der Reichenau (Karlsruhe Aug. CII) ist aus V abgeschrieben. P aus der Bibl. von Thou und Colbert (Paris 1694) und K (Cambrai 436 I) gehören eng zusammen (col. 62, 5: redde Sacramenti] red(sed K) decramenti P¹K; col. 59, 31 hebesco] tabesco PK), desgleichen J (Cambrai 541) und G aus Corbie (Paris 12133). Wem steht nun W nahe?

W steht in der Mitte zwischen der Gruppe BV(T) und der Gruppe CD. Wenn man in Hinblick auf die gelegentlich starken Divergenzen in Buch II vor allem dieses ins Auge faßt, so geht W z.B. mit der Gruppe BV zusammen in col. 68, 22: angelus nuntians] id ipsum (ipsud W¹) angelus nuntians BVAJGW; col. 69, 3: dicere] edicere BVAJGW; col. 73, 13: agnitionem] cognitionem BVAFLPKJGW. Oder W geht bald mit V, bald mit B zusammen; mit V: col. 57, 5: inenarrabilem] incomprehensibilem VAJG¹W; col. 58,9: reuoco] non reuoco VAJGW; col. 59, 26: sibi] *om.* VJGW; transmittuntur saecula] transcenduntur saecula VAKGW; col. 61, 27: numquid audieras VW, fehlt in CDBEFL; col. 62, 20: ergo si] ergo (*om.* si) VAJGW; 63, 2: sollicito] solliciti VJKW — mit B geht W zusammen: col. 60, 9: uixisse] reuixisse BW; col. 60, 21: tempora] saecula BW; col. 69, 3: non] autem non BPKW; col. 69, 13: confessioni] confessione BPG¹W; col. 73, 28: et] ac BJGW; col 74, 4: et rursum] et iterum: Nos autem non spiritum huius mundi accepimus, sed spiritum, qui ex deo est, ut sciamus, quae a deo donata sunt nobis. Et rursum BJGW.

Wenn B (oder V) mit C zusammengeht, bietet W oft gleiche Lesarten: col. 60, 2: conniuere] cohibere C¹LF BW; col. 60, 16f.: ueste uuida pedibus limo oblitus] pedibus limo oblitus (oblitis W) ueste umida CFL BJGW; 61, 33: consequentia] cum sequentia CFL¹BW; col. 62, 31: sit] sunt CF¹LBW (sint VA); col. 63, 5: sine eo] sine illo CFLBW; col. 71, 19: dominus respondit] respondit dominus *tr.* CFLBW; col. 71, 18: traditionum memor] memor traditionum *tr.* CFLBW; beispielshalber auch aus Buch V, col. 130, 18: conniuientis] cohibentis CF(-ntes) LBW(-nti).

Lehrreich ist aus Buch IV col. 114, 26ff.: ne quid tibi hinc liceat mentiri, Sapientia, quam tu ipse Christum confessus es, contrahit] ne quid tibi hinc liceat si ementiri sapientiam quam tu ipse Christum confessus es, contraibit CF¹L¹V ne quid tibi hinc liceat si mentiri

uolueris sapientiam esse Christum contraibit W. Hier hat der
Schreiber von W oder schon der seiner Vorlage einen verderbten,
CV gemeinsamen Text in eine haltbare Konstruktion zu bringen versucht, was freilich so auch nicht möglich war, da das Subjekt zu
contraibit, das Sapientia ist, fehlt.

Gelegentlich geht jedoch W auch mit C allein (ohne BV) zusammen: col. 64, 29: hoc] in hoc CFL¹W; col. 74, 9: sed idem] idem
autem CFLW; In Buch III col. 80,32: et quod infirmum est] et infirmum CFW; col. 81, 26: haeserint] haec erint CFW; col. 81, 24:
stulta mundi elegit deus] stulta mundi elegit deus ut confundat sa-
pientes CFLW. Aus Buch V sei angeführt col. 130, 23: non] om. CW;
aus Buch VI col. 195, 21: confessionis] confessionis orantis CFL¹
PKW.

Von den Hss. des IX./X. Jhdts scheint W starke Beziehungen zu
G zu haben; das war schon aus zuvor angeführten Stellen ersichtlich. Im Buch II gibt es nur in diesen beiden Hss. folgende Sonder-
lesarten: col. 59, 8: ait et filio] et filio WG¹; col. 64, 36: tantum] om.
WG¹; col. 65, 28: apud temetipsum] om. WG¹; col. 66,2: aequalem
se] se aequalem tr. WG; col. 71, 6: legitur] legimus WG¹ (mit anderen Hss.); col. 71, 15: eius qui esset] qui eius esset WG¹. Da G eng
zu J gehört, finden sich W-Lesungen auch in JG: col. 59, 22: et
nefas est mihi] et non licet mihi WJG¹ (und spätere); col. 60,
5 emundatos] mundatos WJG (und spätere); col. 72, 10: qui]
quia WPKJG; col. 74, 10: unicuique autem donatur] unicuique
autem nostrum datur WJG¹; col. 75, 10: hic igitur] igitur hic tr.
WJG.

Auch zwischen W und PK, die Nahverwandtschaft zu C, bez. C²
zeigen, bestehen Beziehungen. Außer schon angeführten Stellen
zeigt das z.B. Buch V col. 136, 3f.: quaestionis] om. WPK; col. 136,
26: diuinitatis] om. WP¹K; col. 137, 34f.: indulgeatur] indigeatur
W indigeat PK; col. 138, 5f.: natio uiperarum] natura uiperarum
WPK; col. 139, 2: non] om. WPK; col. 141, 30: infirmus] infirmis
C¹WPK. In col. 155, 13f. bieten C¹V: quia non est aliunde quod
genitus est; et per hoc non refertur ad aliud, quod in unum (unoV)
subsistit ex uno; in B steht: quia non est aliunde, quod genitus est
neque aliud quam deus est ille qui genitus est; et per hoc non refertur
ad aliud, quod in unum subsistit ex uno: doch C²FK haben:
quia non ex alio genitus neque aliud quam deus est ille qui genitus
est; et per hoc non refertur ad aliud, quod in unum subsistit ex uno;
und in WK steht: quia non ex alio genitus neque aliud quam deus

est ille qui in unum subsistit ex uno. Deutlich zeigt sich, daß W zwischen C¹B steht und daß K enger zu W gehört als P.

Somit ergibt sich: Der Text von W stellt keine Erstausgabe des Hilarius dar; er steht zwischen den Gruppen BV und CD, und zu ihm stehen auch spätere Hss. in Beziehung, vor allem JG.

ALCUIN'S *PRISCIAN*

J. REGINALD O'DONNELL

To the extensive handlist of manuscripts of the *Institutiones* of Priscian published in *Scriptorium*[1] it might be useful to add three more from the Bibliothèque municipale of Valenciennes which have come to us as "le commentaire bien connu d'Alcuin". They are MSS. 391 (374), fols. 1-130 = *A*, 392 (375), fols. 1-17 = *B*, and 393 (376), fols. 1-77 = *C*. *A* and *B* are listed in the catalogue as epitomes of Priscian, but *C* is called the well-known commentary, probably due to the incipit of the text: *Albini in Priscianum incipit liber primus*. Except for lacunae in *B*, the texts are almost identical. All three are from the ninth century. B. Bischoff has dated *C* as early ninth century. At one time these manuscripts belonged to the abbey of Saint Amand, near Valenciennes, but I am not certain they were products of the scriptorium of Saint Amand. The abbey was greatly damaged by the Normans in 883 and all three manuscripts were copied many years before this date.

The texts of Priscian contained in the manuscripts are quite good and very close to the text established in H. Keil's *Grammatici latini*. The most interesting fact, however, is the structure of the work and the manner in which Alcuin excerpted Priscian. He divided the text not into *maior* and *minor*, but into two books of 98 chapters for book I and 93 chapters for book II; the order of the chapters is occasionally mixed up, as, for example, in book I chapter 28 is

---

[1] Margaret Gibson, "Prisciani Institutiones Grammaticae. A Handlist of Manuscripts", *Scriptorium*, 26 (1972) 105-124. See also: André Boutemy, "Le scriptorium et la bibliothèque de Saint-Amand", *Scriptorium*, 1 (1946-7) 6-16. Henri Platelle, *Le temporel de l'abbaye de Saint-Amand des origines à 1340*, (Paris, 1962) pp. 67-8) on *la bibliothèque et le scriptorium*. Bernhard Bischoff, *Mittelalterliche Studien*, I and II (Stuttgart, 1966) p. 217fn. 50, pp. 12ff. L. H. Cottineau, *Répertoire topo-bibliographique des Abbayes et Prieurés*, 2 (Macon, 1937) cols. 2581ff. Heinrich Keil, *Grammatici Latini*, II and III (Georg Olms, Hildesheim, 1961). *Catalogue général des manuscrits des bibliothèques publiques de France*, tome XXV (Paris, 1894) p. 360. I should like to express my gratitude to the director of La Bibliothèque municipale de Valenciennes et Le centre national de la recherche scientifique; centre de documentation for supplying me with microfilms of manuscripts *A*, *B*, and *C*.

missing in *A* and *B*. The text follows that of Priscian quite accurately, but the great amount of Greek in Priscian is left out as also are many of the quotations from Latin authors. Sometimes too a passage from one book of Priscian is supplemented by and conflated with passages from other books.

The chapter headings are given at the beginning of the manuscripts and are numbered from 1-98 and 1-93; these are repeated in the body of the text in rustic capitals. Because the choice of texts from Priscian is both curious and interesting and because it may be of some help to understand what was actually taught in the schools in Alcuin's day, I shall give the chapter headings here with reference to folio and the volume and page of Keil's edition. At the end I shall edit chapter 66 of book I to illustrate Alcuin's method. I shall give only meaningful variants; they are not very numerous, most often being merely the results of scribal carelessness, such as *pessorem* for *possessorem*, *ordine* for *ordinatione* or differences of mood, such as *iungantur* for *iunguntur*, or differences of case such as *nominatiuus* for *nominatiuos*.

I. Diffinitio orationis et quid sit proprium nominis, quid uerbi. 7^vA, 1^vB, 4^vC; Keil II. 53.

II. Quid sit proprium pronominis et quod qualis et talis et similia pronomina non sint. 7^vA, 1^vB, 5^rC; Keil II. 55.

III. Quid sit proprium aduerbii, quid praepositionis. 7^vA, 1^vB, 5^rC; Keil II. 56.

IIII. Quid sit proprium coniunctionis et quid intersit inter coniunctionem et praepositionem et de ordinatione partium orationis. 8^rA, 1^vB, 5^rC; Keil II. 56, III. 108.

V. Quare doctissimi artium scriptores primo loco nomen, secundo uerbum posuerint. 8^vA, 1^vB, 5^vC; Keil III. 116.

VI. Comparatio elementorum uocalium et consonantium ad dictiones. 9^rA, 2^rB, 6^rC; Keil III. 114.

VII. Quare post nomen uerbum, non pronomen ponatur. 9^vA, 2^rB, 6^vC; Keil III. 117.

VIII. Obliquos casus pronominum absolutos esse. 10^rA, 3^rB, 7^rC; Keil III. 118.

IX. Quare participium post uerbum ponatur. 10^rA, 3^rB, 7^rC; Keil III. 119.

X. Participium non solum per obliquos casus utile esse, sed etiam per nominatiuum. 10^vA, 3^vB, 7^vC; Keil II. 553.

XI. Quod quemadmodum coniungitur aduerbium uerbo

sic etiam participio. 11^vA, 4^rB, 8^rC; Keil II. 554.

XII. Ad quid participium inuentum sit uel ad quid sint utiles obliqui eius casus. 11^vA, 4^vB, 8^rC; Keil II. 554.

XIII. Quod post participium pronomen sequi debeat, aduerbium uero post pronomen et post aduerbium praepositio. Post supradicta omnia coniunctio accipiatur. 12^rA, 5^rB, 8^vC; Keil III. 120.

XIIII. Quare interrogatiua dictionum in duas partes orationis solas concesserint, id est, in nomen et in aduerbium et quare non in unum nomen et unum aduerbium, sed in ampliora. 12^vA, 5^rB, 9^rC; Keil III. 121.

XV. Quod de singulis oporteat tractari et de eo quod in loco sumitur uel assumitur et de eo quod assumitur solum. 13^vA, 6^rB, 9^vC; Keil III. 124.

XVI. De constructione diuiduorum. 14^rA, 6^vB. 10^rC; Keil III. 125.

XVII. Qui et quis eandem esse partem orationis et de constructione qui ad nominatiuum uel ad obliquos casus. 14^vA, 6^vB, 10^rC; Keil III. 127.

XVIII. Quod qualis et quantus et quot relatiua per defectionem talis et tantus et to tfrequenter inueniuntur. 15^vA, 7^rB, 10^vC; Keil III. 128.

XVIIII. Quis interrogatiuum posse cuicumque uerbo adiungi et quando altera interrogatione egeat uel quando non egeat. 16^rA, 7^vB, 11^rC; Keil III. 130.

XX. Quod nomini tam substantiua quam uocatiua uerba adiungi possunt; pronomini uero tantum substantiua. 16^{r-v}A, 7^v-8^rB, 11^r-11^vC; Keil. III. 130.

XXI. De nominibus et aduerbiis infinitis uel interrogatiuis uel relatiuis uel redditiuis et de accentibus eorum. 16^vA, 8^rB, 11^vC; Keil III. 132.

XXII. Quare prima et secunda persona pronominum diuersis uocibus non egeant. 17^rA, 8^vB, 12^rC; Keil II. 577.

XXIII. Quid sit inter demonstrationem et relationem. 18^rA, 9^rB, 12^rC; Kiel II. 579.

XXIIII. Pronomen quod est ipse quidam commune existimauerunt, sed non bene. 18^rA, 9^rB, 12^vC; Keil II. 579.

XXV. Ad nomina uel aduerbia interrogatiua quae generaliter omnes in se species comprehendunt, omnes bene posse sibi subiectas species reddi. 18^vA, 9^vB, 13^rC; Keil III. 133.

XXVI. Quod nomini infinito quod est quis appellatiua nomina soleant subiungi. 19^{v}A, 10^{r}B, 13^{v}C ; Keil III. 134.

XXVII. Quando nomina infinita uel aduerbia geminentur uel assumant cumque. 20^{r}A, 10^{v}B, 13^{v}C ; Keil III. 135.

XXVIII. Quod aduerbia quae ad diuersas non pertinent species interrogatiua esse non possint. 20^{v}A, 11^{r}B. 14^{r}C ; Keil III. 138.

XXVIIII. De pronominum constructione. 21^{v}A, 11^{v}B, 14^{v}C ; Keil III. 139.

XXX. Quod apud Latinos pronomina sint discretiua. 21^{v}A, 11^{v}B, 15^{r}C ; Keil III. 141.

XXXI. Quod pronomini accidat relatio in tertia persona. 22^{r}A, 11^{v}B, 15^{r}C ; Keil III. 141.

XXXII. Quod quaedam sint oculorum demonstratiua, quaedam et oculorum et intellectus. 22^{r-v}A, 12^{r}B, 15^{v}C ; Keil III. 142.

XXXIII. De bipertita specie pronominum et de quindecim pronominibus in quibus nulla controuersia est. 23^{r}A, 12^{v}B, 15^{v}C ; Keil II. 577.

XXXIIII. Quod uocatiuum casum aliud pronomen non habeat nisi secundae personae primitiuum et primae possessiuum. 23^{r}A, 12^{v}B, 16^{r}C ; Keil II. 582.

XXXV. Utrum eccum, eccam et similia pronomina sint conposita an aduerbia. 23^{v}A, 13^{r}B, 16^{v}C ; Keil II. 593.

XXXVI. Quid sit inter mei, tui, sui, nostri, vestri genetiuos possessiuorum et primitiuorum. 24^{r}A, 13^{v}B, 16^{v}C ; Keil III. 4.

XXXVII. Quare meus, o mi non o mee faciat uocatiuum et o non esse pronomen nec articulum. 24^v=25^{r}A, 13^{v}B, 17^{r}C ; Keil III. 11.

XXXVIII. Quod quidam male putauerint secundam personam nominatiuum non habere. 25^{r}A, 14^{r}B, 17^{v}C ; Keil III. 12.

XXXVIIII. Quod omnia pronomina apud Latinos absoluta sint. 26^{v}A, 15^{r}B, 18^{r}C ; Keil III. 14.

XL. Quare sui non habeat nominatiuum. 26^{v}A, 15^{r}B, 18^{v}C ; Keil III. 15.

XLI. Quare quis a quibusdam pronomen esse putetur. 27^{r}A, 15^{v}B, 18^{v}C ; Keil. III. 19.

XLII. Quidam falso obiciunt talis et tantus pronomina esse propter demonstrationem quam dicunt propriam pronominis esse. 28^{r}A, 16^{r}B, 19^{r}C ; Keil III. 21.

XLIII. Quod talis et tantus et tot, si ad praesentes dican-

tur, sint demonstratiua; sin autem ad absentes relatiua uel reddi-
tiua tantum. 28^v*A*, 16^r*B*, 19^v*C ;* Keil III. 22.

XLIIII. Quod quidam grammaticorum bene diceret coniuga
esse in personis pronomina; uerba uero inconiuga. 29^r*A*, 16^v*B*, 20^r*C ;*
Keil III. 144.

XLV. Quod inpersonalia uerba siue transitiue siue in-
transitiue proferantur obliquis casibus iungantur. 30^r*A*, 17^r*B*, 20^v*C ;*
Keil III. 148.

XLVI. De constructione pronominum ad uerba et quod
non omnia uerba obliquos desiderent casus nominum uel pronominum, quomodo omnes obliqui casus nominum uel pronominum,
quomodo omnes obliqui casus uerba desiderant. Reading of *A.*
31^r*A*, 18^r*B*, 21^r*C ;* Keil III. 154.

XLVII. Quod sint in quibusdam partibus orationis aliarum
partium intellectus. 32^r*A*, 18^v*B*, 21^v*C ;* Keil III. 155.

XLVIII. Quod inpersonalia uerba cum per se sint infinita
personarum et numerorum additione pronominum diffiniantur.
33^r*A*, 19^r*B*, 22^r*C ;* Keil III. 158.

XLVIIII. Quod frequenter sine additione pronominum pro-
ferantur eadem inpersonalia uerba. 33^r*A*, 19^r*B*, 22^v*C ;* Keil III. 158.

L. De duobus inpersonalibus uerbis, id est, interest et
refert quae cum quinque pronominum diriuatorum ablatiuis construuntur cum alibi genetiuis aliarum omnium casualium applican-
tur. 33^v*A*, 19^v*B*, 22^v*C ;* Keil III. 159.

LI. Quod participia tam nominum quam uerborum
sibi defendant structuram. 34^r*A*, 19^v*B*, 22^v*C ;* Keil III. 159.

LII. Participium et uerbum conparatione penitus carere
quantum in sua uoce, nam adiectione aduerbii posse comparari. 34^v*A*,
20^r*B*, 23^r*C ;* Keil III. 160.

LIII. De constructione coniunctionis si praeponatur uel
casuali uel uerbo. 34^v*A*, 20^r*B*, 23^r*C ;* Keil III. 160.

LIIII. Quod in quadam constructione liceat genetiuis co-
pulare nominatiuos possessiuorum, 35^r*A*, 20^v*B*, 23^v*C ;* Keil III. 161.

LV. Item de inpersonalium duorum supradictorum
constructione quae sunt interest et refert. 35^v*A*, 20^v*B*, 23^v—24^r*C :*
Keil III. 161.

LVI. Quibus partibus praepositio uel per compositionem
uel per appositionem praeponi possit. 36^r*A*, 21^r*B*, 24^r*C ;* Keil III.
164.

LVII. De reciproca constructione quam habent tres personae et de transitiua quam habent prima quidem et secunda ad binas personas, tertia uero ad tres. 36^{v}A, 21^{v}B, 24^{v}C; Keil III. 164.

LVIII. Quod possessiua tribus modis construantur. 37^{r}A, 21^{v}B, 24^{v}C; Keil III. 165.

LVIIII. Quod omnia possessiua in genetiuos primitiuorum uerbis sociata possunt resolui. 37^{v}A, 22^{r}B, 25^{r}C; Keil III. 166.

LX. Quod possessiua pronomina primae et secundae personae siue possessoris sui siue extrinsecus personis bene copulantur. 38^{r}A, 22^{r}B, 25^{v}C; Keil III. 167.

LXI. Quod a tertia persona retransitio in tertiam dubium gignat. 38^{v}A, 22^{v}B, 26^{r}C; Keil III. 169.

LXII. Quod genetiuos quorumcumque casualium cum possessiuis per quemcumque casum prolatis liceat coniungere. 39^{r}A, 23^{r}B, 26^{r}C; Keil III. 170.

LXIII. Quod suus pro uniuscuiusque proprio accipiatur. 39^{v}A, 23^{r}B, 26^{v}C; Keil III. 170.

LXIIII. Item quae sit differentia inter genetiuum primitiui et possessiui mei, tui, sui. 41^{r}A, 24^{r}B, 27^{r}C; Keil III. 173.

LXV. Quare sui quando est primitiuum non habeat nominatiuum 41^{v}A, 24^{v}B, 27^{v}C; Keil III. 175.

LXVI. De inter et inuicem. 42^{v}A, 25^{r}B, 28^{r}C; Keil III. 177.

LXVII. Quod quomodo pronomina finita habent et patria et possessiua ita et quis et qui habeant et patrium et possessiuum. 43^{r}A, 25^{v}B, 28^{v}C; Keil III. 179.

LXVIII. Cur nostras et vestras a plurali tantum modo numero diriuentur. 43^{v}A, 25^{v}B, 28^{v}C; Keil III. 178.

LXVIIII. Pronomina quasdam habere proprias observationes, singula quasdam communes. 43^{v}A, 25^{v}B, 28^{v}C; Keil III. 179.

LXX. Non mirandum diuersas aliquando personas figurate inter se copulari cum etiam diuersi casus aliquando bene coniungantur. 44^{r}A, 26^{r}B, 29^{r}C; Keil III. 181.

LXXI. Quod ad aptam adiunctionem numeri uel genera uel reliqua accidentia ferri debeant. 45^{r}A, 26^{v}B, 29^{v}C; Keil III. 182.

LXXII. De uariis figurationibus accidentium et exempla auctorum. 46^{r}A, 27^{r}B, 30^{r}C; Keil III. 183.

LXXIII. Quod figurae aliae pro aliis poni soleant. 47^{r}A, 28^{r}B, 31^{r}C; Keil III. 193.

LXXIIII. Aduerbia quaedam cum omnibus accidentibus indifferenter poni, quaedam omnibus non posse copulari. 48^{v}A, 28^{r}B, 31^{r}C; Keil III. 196.

LXXV. Item de pronominibus quae coniugata vocantur. 48^{v}A, 28^{v}B, 31^{v}C ; Keil III. 198.

LXXVI. Quod ad explanandas diuersae significationis dictiones constructio sit maxime necessaria. 50^{r}A, 29^{v}B, 32^{v}C ; Keil III 200.

LXXVII. Quod diuersae figurae quamuis quantum ad ipsas dictiones incongrue disposita esse uideantur, tamen ratione sensus rectissime ordinata esse iudicentur. 51^{r}A, 30^{r}B, 33^{r}C ; Keil III. 201.

LXXVIII. Utrum tu sit nominatiuus tantum an tantum uocatiuus an utrumque. 51^{v}A, 30^{r}B, 33^{r}C ; Keil III. 202.

LXXX. De singulorum constructione casuum. 55^{r}A, 32^{v}B, 35^{r}C ; Keil III. 211.

LXXXI. Quas constructiones Stoici dignitates uel congruitates uocarent quas minus quam congruitates et quam incongruitatem nominarent. 55^{v}A, 32^{v}B, 35^{v}C ; Keil III. 211.

LXXXII. Adiunctio nominatiui casus ad genetiuum. 56^{v}A, 33^{v}B, 36^{r}C ; Keil III. 213.

LXXXIII. Quae nomina substantiuo uerbo adiuncta possint tam genetiuo quam datiuo conecti. 57^{r}A, 33^{v}B, 36^{r}C ; Keil III. 213.

LXXXIIII. Quod ea nomina quae laudem uel uituperationem uel accidens ostendunt per nominatiuum possessorem; per genetiuum vero possessionem significent. 57^{v}A, 34^{r}B, 36^{v}C ; Keil III. 214.

LXXXV. Quod Graeci in huiusmodi sensu genetiuo tantum utuntur; Latini vero etiam ablatiuo. 58^{r}A, 34^{r}B, 36^{v}C ; Keil III. 214.

LXXXVI. Quod comparatiua et superlatiua Graeci genetiuo; Latini uero comparatiua ablatiuo; superlatiua uero iungant genetiuo plurali. 58^{v}A, 34^{v}B, 37^{r}C ; Keil III. 215.

LXXXVII. Magis aduerbium non solum positiuo, sed etiam comparatiuo iungi. 59^{r}A, 34^{v}B, 37^{r}C ; Keil II. 94.

LXXXVIII. Utrum prior et primus sit comparatiuus et superlatiuus. 59^{r}A, 34^{v}B, 37^{r}C ; Keil II. 90.

LXXXVIIII. Uerbialia nomina genetiuo iungenda. 59^{v}A, 35^{r}B, 37^{v}C ; Keil III. 215.

XC. Similiter genetiuo adiungi omnia quae obtineri uel desiderari aliquid ostendunt uel contraria his. 60^{v}A, 35^{v}B, 38^{r}C ; Keil III. 218.

XCI. Ea quae sunt ad aliquid eandem constructionem seruare. 61^{r}A, 38^{r}C ; Keil III. 218.

XCII. De adquisitiuis constructionibus et eas datiuo iungi. 61ʳ*A*, 38ʳ*C ;* Keil III. 219.

XCIII. Quid sit inter docilis et docibilis. 61ᵛ*A*, 38ᵛ*C ;* Keil III. 219.

XCIIII. Accusatiuo nominatiuus adiungi figurate quando quod parti accidit, hoc toti redditur. 62ʳ*A*, 38ᵛ*C ;* Keil III. 220.

XCV. Ablatiuum nominatiuo coniungi quando per eum aliquid euenire demonstratur illi qui per nominatiuum profertur. 62ʳ*A*, 39ʳ*C ;* Keil III. 221.

XCVI. Participia cum nomine et pronomine et per se posita constructionem tam uerbi necessario sequi quam nominis. 63ʳ*A*, 39ʳ*C ;* Keil III. 222.

XCVII. Singula participia uerbi ex quo nascuntur constructionem seruare. 63ʳ*A*, 39ᵛ*C ;* Keil III. 223.

XCVIII. Datiuum adquisitiuorum uel effectiuorum cum omni casu solere consociare. 64ᵛ*A*, 36ʳ*B*, 39ᵛ-40ʳ*C ;* Keil III. 224.

Explicit liber primus, incipit liber secundus

I. De uerbo infinito. 64ᵛ*A*, 36ʳ*B*, 40ʳ*C ;* Keil III. 224.

II. Quod nominatiuis adiectiuorum et obliquis eorum pulcherrima figura infinitum coniungatur. 65ʳ*A*, 36ᵛ*B*, 40ᵛ*C ;* Keil III. 227.

III. Quod uerborum omnibus modis et participiis infinita possunt coniungi. 65ᵛ*A*, 36ᵛ*B*, 40ᵛ*C ;* Keil III. 227.

IIII. De inpersonalis uerbi constructione et quod debet aliquando inpersonale accipiatur. 66ʳ*A*, 37ʳ-37ᵛ*B*, 41ʳ*C ;* Keil III. 229.

V. Quae sit differentia inpersonalis uerbi ad infinitum. 67ʳ*A*, 38ʳ*B*, 41ᵛ*C ;* Keil II. 413.

VI. Quid sit inter infinitum passiuum et infinitum quod fit ab inpersonali uenienti a uerbo actiuo. 67ʳ*A*, 38ʳ*B*, 41ᵛ*C ;* Keil II. 413.

VII. Quaedam inpersonalia genetiuo simul et accusatiuo iungi. 67ᵛ*A*, 38ʳ*B*, 42ʳ*C ;* Keil III. 230.

VIII. Inpersonalia passiuam terminationem habentia infinitis non posse adiungi. 67ᵛ*A*, 38ᵛ*B*, 42ʳ*C ;* Keil III. 231.

VIIII. Inpersonalia quae accusatiuo simul et genetiuo copulantur per accusatiuum significare personam in qua fit passio per genetiuum illam ex qua fit. [Infinita quoque necnon gerundia

uel supina uerbi sui constructionem ad casus seruare.] 68ʳ*A*, 42ʳ*C ;*
Keil III. 232. An interpolation on 39ʳ-39ᵛ*B*. Incipit: Haec tibi
dulcis. Explicit: nec iterum flenda committat. Require in alio loco in
istum libellum.

　　　X. Quid intersit inter supina uerba et nomina uerbialia in dus desinentia. 69ʳ*A*, 42ᵛ*C ;* Keil III. 233. *B* omits chapter
heading.

　　　XI. De duabus terminationibus supinorum in um et in
u. 70ʳ*A*, 40ᵛ*B*, 43ᵛ*C ;* Keil II. 411.

　　　XII. Quod ab actiuis et communibus supina uenientia
communem habeant significationem. A neutris uero et deponenti-
bus simplicem et quid intersit inter nomina uerbialia et gerundia.
70ᵛ*A*, 41ʳ*B*, 43ᵛ*C ;* Keil II. 412.

　　　XIII. Expositio uersus aio te Aeacida Romanos uincere
posse. 71ᵛ*A*, 41ᵛ*B*, 44ʳ*C ;* Keil III. 234. See TLL, s.v. Aeacida; also
Keil IV. 221.

　　　XIIII. Infinitum omnibus aliis modis et participiis posse
adiungi. 71ᵛ-72ʳ*A*, 41ᵛ*B*, 44ᵛ*C ;* Keil III. 235.

　　　XV. De indicatiuis. 72ʳ*A*, 42ʳ*B*, 44ᵛ*C ;* Keil II. 421.

　　　XVI. De imperatiuis. 73ᵛ*A*, 42ᵛ*B*, 45ʳ*C ;* Keil II. 423.

　　　XVII. De optatiuis. 74ᵛ*A*, 46ʳ*C*. Chapter heading missing
43ᵛ*B*. Keil II. 424, III. 239.

　　　XVIII. De subiunctiuis. 75ᵛ*A*, 46ʳ*C*. Chapter heading missing 44ʳ*B*. Keil II. 424, III. 241.

　　　XVIIII. Omnibus modis subiunctiuum posse sociari et de
coniunctione si. 76ʳ*A*, 44ᵛ*B*, 46ᵛ*C ;* Keil III. 241.

　　　XX. Esse quando per defectionem si et ut subiunctiua
proferantur. 77ʳ*A*, 45ʳ*B*, 46ᵛ*C ;* Keil III. 247.

　　　XXI. Nunc dubitationem nunc comprobationem nunc
possibilitatem significare subiunctiuum. 77ʳ*A*, 47ʳ*C*. Chapter
heading missing 45ʳ*B*. Keil III. 247.

　　　XXII. Paenitentiam rei non factae per subiunctiuum de-
monstrari. 78ʳ*A*, 47ᵛ*C*. Chapter heading missing 45ᵛ*B ;* Keil III. 252.

　　　XXIII. De praeterito indicatiuo et futuro subiunctiuo.
79ᵛ*A*, 48ᵛ*C*. Chapter heading missing 46ʳ*B*. Keil; III. 260.

　　　XXIIII. De speciebus uerbi. 80ʳ*A*, 48ᵛ*C*. Chapter heading
and part of text missing with an interpolation 47ᵛ*B*. Keil II. 427.

　　　XXV. De desideratiuis (deriuatiuis Priscian). 81ᵛ*A*, 48ʳ*B*,
49ᵛ*C ;* Keil II. 431.

　　　XXVI. Quod apud Graecos soleant quaedam uerba ex

nominibus diriuari; apud Latinos uero nomina ex uerbis. 82ᵛA, 50ʳC; Keil II. 432.

XXVII. Quae genera uel significationes uerborum, quibus casibus construuntur. 83ᵛA, 50ᵛC; Keil III. 267.

XXVIII. De passiuis. 84ᵛA, 51ᵛC; Keil III. 269.

XXVIIII. De communibus. 85ʳA, 51ᵛC; Keil III. 270.

XXX. De absolutis. 85ʳA, 51ᵛC; Keil III. 270.

XXXI. Uerborum alia ad corpus, alia ad animam, alia ad utrumque, alia ad extrinsecus accidentia pertinere. 86ʳA, 52ʳC; Keil III. 272.

XXXII. De contraria significatione. 86ʳA, 52ʳC; Keil III. 272.

XXXIII. De laudatiuis, uituperatiuis, deceptiuis et aliis uarie nuncupatis. 86ʳA, 52ʳC; Keil III. 272.

XXXIIII. Totius uerbi declinationem et participia et supina ad eos casus construi ad quos indicatiuum. 88ʳA, 53ʳC; Keil III. 278.

XXXV. Multa et diuersa auctorum exempla collecta. 88ᵛA, 53ᵛC; Keil III. 278.

XXXVI. Quaedam passiua datiuo posse adiungi. 91ʳA, 55ʳC; Keil II. 374.

XXXVII. Quae proprie neutralia uocentur. 92ʳA, 55ᵛC; Keil II. 377.

XXXVIII. Quaedam deponentia accusatiuum desiderare, quaedam casu non egere. 92ᵛA, 55ᵛC; Keil II. 388-9.

XXXVIIII. Quaedam uerba in alia constructione passiua esse; in alia uero absoluta. 92ᵛA, 55ᵛC; Keil II. 389.

XL. Quod quaedam actiua et passiua uerba soleant absolute proferri. 92ᵛA, 56ʳC; Keil II. 390.

XLI. De uerbis quibusdam quae modo actiuam, modo absolutam, modo passiuam significationem habent. 93ʳA, 56ʳC; Keil II. 393.

XLII. Quod quaedam actiua primae coniugationis transeant in neutra absoluta siue reciproca secundae coniugationis. 93ᵛA, 56ᵛC; Keil II. 397.

XLIII. Quid sit extra ordinem et de multorum uaria constructione uerborum. 94ʳA, 56ᵛC. Chapter heading missing 48ʳB. Keil III. 293.

XLIIII. De addita causa uel adempta et exempla diuersarum constructionum. 95ʳA, 48ᵛB, 57ʳC; Keil III. 310.

XLV. Duplici abnegatione pro simplici in eodem; de participio et uerbo. 95^{r}A, 49^{r}B, 58^{r}C; Keil III. 340.

XLVI. Quod omne nomen a quocumque uerbo natum uel genetiuum uel datiuum casum figurate sequatur. 96^{r}A, 49^{v}B, 58^{r}C; Keil II. 550.

XLVII. Quibusdam philosophis placere nomen et uerbum solas esse partes orationis, sed non bene. 97^{v}A, 50^{r}B, 58^{v}C; Keil II. 551.

XLVIII. Quaedam uerba deponentia antiquos tam actiua quam passiua significatione protulisse. 98^{r}A, 50^{v}B, 59^{r}C; Keil III. 267.

XLVIIII. De facio et fio cum infinito compositis et de eis quae cum coniugatione mutant significationem et de eis quae una uoce et una coniugatione diuersas habent significationes. 99^{v}A,51^{v}B, 60^{r}C; Keil II. 402.

L. Quae sit minima pars constructae orationis. 100^{v}A, 52^{r}B, 60^{v}C; Keil II. 53.

LI. De temporibus uerbi. 101^{r}A, 52^{v}B, 60^{v}C; Keil II. 405.

LII. Gerundia uel participialia tempus non habere. 103^{v}A, 53^{v}B, 62^{r}C; Keil II. 409.

LIII. De cognatione temporum. 104^{v}A, 54^{r}B, 62^{r}C; Keil II. 414.

LIIII. Quod differat praeteritum perfectum a praeterito plusquam perfecto. 105^{v}A, 54^{v}B, 63^{r}C; Keil II. 416.

LV. Unde infinita nominentur. 107^{r}A, 55^{v}B, 63^{v}C.

LVI. De praepositione. 107^{v}A, 56^{r}B, 64^{r}C; Keil III. 24.

LVII. Differentia inter praepositiones et coniunctiones. 108^{r}A, 56^{r}B, 64^{r}C; Keil III. 24.

LVIII. Quid Graeci proprium dicant esse praepositiones. 109^{r}A, 56^{v}B, 64^{r}C; Keil III. 30.

LVIIII. De significatione singularum praepositionum quas accusatiuus sequitur. 110^{r}A, 57^{v}B, 65^{v}C; Keil III. 36.

LX. De praepositionibus quae ablatiuo casui coniunguntur. 113^{r}A, 59^{v}B, 67^{r}C; Keil III. 44.

LXI. De quattuor praepositionibus quae modo accusatiuo modo ablatiuo praeponuntur. 115^{v}A, 61^{v}B, 68^{v}C; Keil III. 53.

LXII. Quod omnes locales praepositiones in temporibus et rebus similem habeant constructionem. 116^{r}A, 61^{v}B, 68^{v}C; Keil III. 54.

LXXXVIII. De completitiuis. 129^rA, 70^vB, 76^rC; Keil III. 102.

LXXXVIIII. Quosdam errasse qui equidem compositam existi-mauerunt. 129^vA, 71^rB, 76^rC; Keil III. 103.

XC. Quoque pro etiam uel et accipi. 129^vA, 72^rB, 76^rC; Keil III. 103.

XCI. Enim quae est causalis pro affirmatiua reperiri. 130^rA, 71^rB, 76^rC; Keil III. 103.

XCII. De ordine coniunctionum. 130^vA, 71^rB, 76^vC; Keil III. 104.

XCIII. Quid sit inter adiunctiuas et proprie causales coniunctiones. 130^vA, 71^vB, 76^vC; Keil III. 95.

Explicit liber A.

LIBRI PRIMI CAPITULUM LXVI
De Inter et Inuicem (Keil III. 177)

Praeterea sciendum quod, quando inuicem actum et passionem alterius in alteram personam uno et eodem casu significamus, frequenter in huiuscemodi constructione accusatiuis (causatiuis A) pluralibus utimur omnium personarum antecedente inter ut uideo amare inter se. Conuersique oculos inter se atque ora tenebant; saepe tamen explanandi causa adicitur inuicem, nec solum hoc in tertia, sed etiam in prima, ut ostendimus, fit et secunda persona plurali; quippe quae possunt diuersas in se colligere personas ut ego et tu nosmetipsos inuicem amatis inter uos. Aliis autem casibus sine inter, quod accusatiuum (causatiuum A, C) exigit, utimur addentes inuicem, ut ego et tu inuicem nostri miseremur; tu et ille inuicem uobis indulgetis; iste et ille inuicem se potiuntur. Quod si non adda-tur inuicem, dubitatio fit utrum per sui passionem singulae in se agant, an altera in alteram, ut si dicam: iste et ille se amant. Et in prima quidem persona licet per conceptionem secundam assumere et tertiam, ut ego et tu legimus; ego et ille scribimus; a secunda uero prima concipi non potest. Tertia uero potest ut tu et ille uosmetipsos laeditis.

No evidence of a precise plan emerges from a study of the excerpts of Priscian made by Alcuin. The great number of chapter headings, both as existed at the beginning of the text and within the text it-self, seems to indicate a ready reference book. The omission of the

Greek texts in Priscian is quite understandable, because few in Alcuin's day could read them. Also, the many omissions of texts from
Latin authors need not surprise us, since, often enough, one example would suffice. Although there is no mention of a *Priscianus
maior* and *minor*, nonetheless there is some evidence that some such
distinction was envisaged because of the proportionately large
amount excerpted from books seventeen and eighteen.

RECHERCHES SUR LE TEXTE ORIGINEL DU
DE HUMILITATE DE CASSIEN (*INST*. IV 39) ET
DES REGLES DU MAITRE (*RM* X) ET DE BENOIT (*RB* VII).*

FRANÇOIS MASAI

Dès le moment où parurent les deux premières études visant l'une, révolutionnaire, à démontrer l'antériorité de la *Regula Magistri* (RM) sur la *Regula Benedicti* (RB),[1] l'autre à défendre intégralement la position traditionnelle de Benoît sur ce que l'on considérait comme une simple paraphrase de son oeuvre,[2] un des meilleurs spécialistes de cette littérature mettait en garde contre tout jugement précipité, estimant "que l'origine de la *Regula Magistri*" constituait un problème "complexe".[3]

Tout en maintenant, pour sa part, l'essentiel de la thèse conservatrice, Dom Bernard Capelle qualifiait d'"aiguës" certaines observations qui avaient conduit Dom Genestout à renverser la chronologie universellement admise pour les deux législations monastiques et, à propos de textes dont nous allons reprendre l'examen, n'hésitait pas à conclure (avec une objectivité justement soulignée par son premier contradicteur) :[4] "à mon avis la généalogie Cassien, Maître, Benoît est d'une parfaite évidence, tandis que se démontre impossible la succession: Cassien, Benoît, Maître."[5]

Divers indices en sens contraire, renforcés par l'absence d'édition critique et sutout par les préjugés de sa génération, empêchèrent malheureusement le pénétrant critique de tirer les conclusions

---

* Ces recherches ont d'abord été entreprises pour la session d'étude des moniales bénédictines, qui s'est tenue à Maredsous du 26 juillet au 3 août 1974. Encouragées par le bienveillant accueil qu'elles y avaient reçues, j'ai tenté de les mettre au point pour les offrir à notre jubilaire. Son amitié les lui fera, j'espère, agréer, malgré sa grande expérience des manuscrits et du travail d'édition.

[1] M. Alamo, *La Règle de saint Benoît éclairée par sa source, la Règle du Maître* (*Revue d'Histoire Ecclésiastique*, 34, 1938, p. 740-755).

[2] J. Pérez de Urbel, *La Règle du Maître* (*Ibid.*, p. 707-739), et la réponse au P. Alamo: *Le Maître et saint Benoît* (*Ibid.*, p. 756-764).

[3] Bernard Capelle, *Cassien, le Maître et saint Benoît* (*Recherches de Théologie Ancienne et Médiévale*, 11, 1939, p. 110-118).

[4] M. Alamo, *Nouveaux éclaircissements sur le Maître et saint Benoît* (*Revue d'Histoire Ecclésiastique*, 38, 1942, p. 332-360).

[5] B. Capelle, *op. cit.*, p. 115.

nuancées qui "ces constatations troublantes" jointes à ses observations non moins sagaces en faveur de l'antériorité du *texte* de RB, auraient pu, dès le début, mettre dans la bonne voie les recherches qui tâtonnèrent trop longtemps et qui font encore partiellement fausse route. On se borna donc, d'un côté à ne voir dans l'avis de Dom Capelle qu'une caution, particulièrement autorisée et rassurante, de l'antériorité de S. Benoît, de l'autre, un malencontreux obstacle aux progrès de la thèse nouvelle. Et ce fut grand dommage à tous égards : généralement les autres spécialistes se désintéressèrent d'un débat jugé clos. D'autre part, l'adhésion de Dom Cappelle à une thèse qu'il faudrait bien abandonner sous la pression des faits, allait faire perdre de vue aux défenseurs tiomphants de la thèse du P. Genestout qu'ils avaient à nuancer leurs affirmations pour faire droit aux faits authentiquement décelés, quoique abusivement utilisés, par le savant abbé du Mont-César.

Des nombreux chercheurs qui, à la génération suivante, voulurent élucider le problème, aucun ne montra plus de tenace persévérance que Dom Adalbert de Vogüé. Il n'est même pas exagéré d'affirmer que ses éditions, ses livres et ses innombrables articles n'ont pas poursuivi d'autre but. Personne, en tout cas, ne pourra contester que l'opinion de Dom Genestout lui doit, plus qu'à tout autre sans doute, d'avoir définitivement vaincu les préjugés séculaires.[6] Et cependant qu'on nous permette d'estimer que Dom Cappelle, n'était pas dans l'erreur lorsqu'il estimait le problème "beaucoup plus complexe". Sans doute sommes-nous d'accord et l'avons-nous toujours été pour donner une priorité chronologique au Maître sur Benoît, mais cela ne nous permet pas d'oublier que le *texte* de RM lu par le législateur du Cassin était certainement plus ancien que celui de tous les témoins du Maître actuellement subsistants et que, par conséquent, Benoît avait à sa disposition un texte du Maître éventuellement (sur certains points tout au moins) *meilleur que le nôtre*

---

[6] Augustin Genestout, *La Règle du Maître et la Règle de s. Benoît* (*Revue d'Ascétique et de Mystique*, 21, 1940, p. 51-112) est le premier et, en somme, le plus complet exposé que l'auteur ait fait de sa thèse. Depuis ces premières études beaucoup d'autres ont paru qu'on trouve répertoriées dans : Bernd Jaspert, *Regula Magistri, Regula Benedicti. Bibliographie ihrer Erforschung 1938-1970* (*Studia Monastica*, 13, Montserrat 1971, p. 129-171). En outre, et singulièrement pour connaître les recherches et les conceptions du P. Adalbert de Vogüé, on consultera surtout ses six vol. (nos 181-186) des *Sources Chrétiennes*, consacrés à l'édition (par Dom Jean Neufville), à la traduction et au commentaire de *La Règle de saint Benoît*, Paris 1971-1972.

et peut-être aussi passablement différent, voire une autre édition. Dom
Capelle avait parfaitement saisi la nécessité d'introduire cette
notion de pluralité d'éditions dans le débat si l'on voulait édifier une
hypothèse générale cohérente évitant les contracdictions entre des
faits de signification opposée. Son seul tort fut de vouloir défendre par
ce moyen la position conservatrice. La faillite de celle-ci ne saurait en-
lever toute pertinence aux observations ni à la mise en garde d'un
spécialiste particulièrement qualifié. Les "constatations troublantes"
relevées en 1939 conservent en fait leur caractère dans la nouvelle
hypothèse comme dans la précédente. Celle-ci est grevée de contra-
dictions insurmontables, si l'on ferme les yeux sur l'évolution, sur la
diversité évidente des états, sur la multiplicité — combien normale
en pareille matière — des éditions anciennes d'un code de législation
monastique.[7]

En réexaminant les passages, déjà signalés et comparés par Dom
Capelle, nous espérons remettre au centre du débat des faits qu'on
n'aurait jamais dû perdre de vue, et démontrer la nécessité d'em-
prunter une voie moyenne entre les excès opposés.

Se méfiant du risque de subjectivisme que court une confrontation
limitée à deux textes, Dom Capelle recherche avec raison un cas où un
troisième texte pourrait servir d'arbitre entre les autres. C'est ce
qui l'amène à comparer Cassien, *Inst.* IV 39, *RM* 10, *RB* 7, et plus
particulièrement les trois passages suivants de ce traité *De humilitate* :

"1. Cassien : Quarto si in omnibus seruet oboedientiae mansuetudinem *patientiaeque constantiam.*

Maitre :… tacite *patientiae constantiam* amplectatur.

Benoit :… tacite conscientiâ *patientiam* amplectatur (le texte de
saint Benoît n'est pas sans poser un problème critique. Il offre un
sens tolérable si *conscientia* est un ablatif mais, même ainsi, la
phrase reste embarrassée : *tacite* et *conscientiâ* semblent faire double
emploi, ce qui est très contraire au génie concis de Benoît…).

---

[7] Il suffit de juxtaposer les textes des témoins conservés pour faire apparaître l'étendue et la nature de leurs divergences. Voir, par exemple J. Neu-
ville, *Règle des IV Pères et Seconde Règle des Pères* (*Revue Bénédictine*, 77,
1967, p. 47-106). Quant aux états de RM-RB, on appréciera les résultats que
donne l'impression parallèle des témoins du seul ch. II : voir ma communication au "Premier Congrès International sur la Règle de s. Benoît, Roma
4-9.10.1971" (*Regulae Benedicti Studia*, 1, Hildesheim 1972) : F. Masai, *Les
Documents de base de la Règle*, p. 111-151, plus particulièrement p. 137-144.

2. CASSIEN:... ad omnia se quae sibi *praebentur*, uelut operarium malum iudicarit [et] indignum.

MAITRE:... ad omnia quae sibi *praebentur*, uelut operarium malum se iudicet et indignum.

BENOIT:... ad omnia quae sibi *iniunguntur*, uelut operarium se malum iudicet et indignum.

3. CASSIEN:... uelut naturaliter incipies custodire, non iam contemplatione supplicii uel timoris ullius, sed *amore ipsius boni*, et delectatione uirtutum.

MAITRE:... uelut naturaliter ex *consuetudine* incipiet custodire, non iam timore gehennae, sed *amore ipsius* consuetudinis *bonae*, et delectatione uirtutum.

BENOIT:... uelut naturaliter *ex consuetudine* incipiet custodire, non iam timore gehennae, sed *amore Christi*, et consuetudine *ipsa bona*, et delectatione uirtutum."[8]

Le critique fait alors les observations suivantes (où des points de suspension remplaceront les formulations résultant des préjugés de l'auteur qui ont été dénoncés plus haut): 1° "Le rapprochement des trois rédactions montre d'abord qu'un travail... est commun au Maître et à Benoît. L'un a donc connu l'autre". 2° "Il montre ensuite que toujours le Maître reste plus fidèle que Benoît à Cassien." 3° "Examinant de plus près, on discerne vite que les corrections que présente le texte de Benoît sont logiques et heureuses." 4° "On ne voit pas pourquoi le Maître aurait changé le texte de Benoît s'il l'avait devant lui, moins encore par quelle divination sa correction aurait reproduit chaque fois, à son insu, le texte de Cassien! Et l'on ne peut supposer — seule hypothèse à première vue tolérable — le Maître revenant consciemment et volontairement à Cassien. Le 3e exemple s'y oppose car le texte qui, chez le Maître, est substitut de l'excellent *amore Christi et consuetudine bona* de Benoît, n'est pas celui de Cassien." 4° "On tiendra donc que, pour les parties communes aux deux règles, *le texte du Maître est source directe du texte de Benoît*."[9]

La deuxième de ces trois confrontations suffirait à établir le bienfondé de cette conclusion: *iniunguntur* est plus cénobitique d'origine

---

[8] B. Capelle, *op. cit.*, p. 113.
[9] *Op. cit.*, p. 114-115.

et manifeste à l'évidence la retouche apportée par l'abbé du Cassin,
à un texte ascétique commun à Cassien et au Maître. Au reste, il y a
d'autant moins lieu d'insister sur les faits soulignés et déjà mis en
évidence par Dom Capelle que l'antériorité du Maître n'est plus à
démontrer de nos jours et que, par suite, l'accord Cassien-Maître
contre Benoît n'a plus rien non plus qui puisse nous étonner. Est-ce
à dire que les préjugés du P. Capelle et de ses prédécesseurs ou con-
temporains ont entièrement disparu? Au contraire, ce dont il importe aujourd'hui de prendre conscience c'est que la majeure partie
de ces préjugés continue d'entraver le progrès de la recherche, bien
que de manière plus insidieuse et, par là-même, plus dangereuse.

S. Benoît avait notoirement vécu tout un siècle après Cassien,
aussi son antériorité par rapport au Maître assurait-elle a fortiori
l'antériorité de Cassien sur ce dernier, même si les faits contrai-
gnaient des savants expérimentés et clairvoyants, comme Dom Capelle, à reconnaître honnêtement la priorité du *texte* de RM sur celui
de RB qui nous est parvenu. La chronologie traditionnelle s'étant
révélée inexacte pour les règles dans leur ensemble et pas seulement
pour quelques passages privilégiés, c'est la succession chronologique
des trois termes qu'il aurait fallu mettre résolument en question et pas
seulement deux d'entre eux. Nous ne *savons plus, en effet, quand a
vécu le "Maître"*, ni d'ailleurs, comme depuis si longtemps j'y insiste,
s'il s'agit vraiment d'un auteur ou seulement de l'*éditeur* d'un code
législatif ou même de moins encore: d'une dénomination commode,
empruntée au *Codex regularum* de Benoît d'Aniane, pour désigner
une partie de la "Regula Patrum" conservée dans le Paris latin
12205[10] et dans le "gemellus" de ce manuscrit qu'a visiblement
utilisé le réformateur carolingien.

Dom Genestout proposait hardiment de placer RM avant Cassien
mais, ce faisant, il n'échappait point, lui non plus, à tout préjugé. Il
admettait *ipso facto* l'unité de RM et, frappé de l'antiquité de certains morceaux qu'on y trouve, soutenait contre toute évidence
l'antériorité de l'ensemble. Il ne faut pas chercher ailleurs, me semble-
t-il, l'absence de toute démonstration ultérieure des datations si

---

[10] Une description détaillée de ce manuscrit a été donnée dans l'introduction à *La Règle du Maître. Edition diplomatique des manuscrits latins 12205
et 12634 de Paris,* par Dom Hubert Vanderhoven et François Masai, avec la
collaboration de P. B. Corbett. Bruxelles-Anvers, 1953 (*Les Publications de
Scriptorium,* vol. III), D'autre part une analyse, limitée au seul "Codex
regularum" conservé dans le Paris latin 12205, a été faite dans la communication déjà citée (voir note 7), p. 111-123.

hardies, avancées dans son premier article. Mais s'ensuit-il que sur ce point son intuition ait été moins sûre que pour la chronologie relative de RM et de RB? Ce n'est pas le coup d'oeil du bénédictin de Solesmes qu'il fallait suspecter, mais les préjugés de ses maîtres en l'étude de la règle bénédictine et que, *à son insu*, il incorporait dans sa réhabilitation du "Maître". Tout en défendant, en consolidant la thèse révolutionnaire de Dom Genestout, ses disciples ont abandonné ce qu'ils ont considéré comme des outrances de pionnier. Ils n'ont pas compris qu'il y avait en réalité à rejeter ces restes d'un héritage séculaire de préjugés!

Une étude attentive comme celle du *De humilitate* entreprise par Dom Capelle est de nature à nous en affranchir complètement, me semble-t-il, car elle peut nous faire pénétrer au coeur des textes qui sont à la base de RM-RB et, par eux, nous faire dépasser Cassien lui-même pour nous donner accès à l'une de ses sources. Pour éviter toute méprise, qu'on me permette de le répéter, je n'affirme aucunement avec Dom Genestout que Cassien a connu et utilisé la *Regula Magistri*. Ce qui n'est nullement déraisonnable c'est de se représenter l'abbé de Marseille lisant déjà, dans le premier tiers du Ve s., un texte plus ancien que le sien et transmis, quoique non sans défauts, par les textes de cet énigmatique code législatif, appelé RM depuis l'époque carolingienne seulement et considéré, au mépris de toute vraisemblance et sans preuve, comme la création homogène d'un seul écrivain.

Renouons donc avec l'entreprise de Dom Capelle, pour essayer de découvrir les conclusions que ses excellentes prémisses lui auraient sans doute permis d'en tirer, sans les "obstacles épistémologiques" qui encombraient le champ de nos études, à l'époque où travaillait l'éminent patrologue.

Après des anomalies et des décalages de degrés ou critères d'humilité entre Cassien d'un côté et nos deux codes de l'autre, sur lesquels aucune explication n'a été jusqu'ici fournie et dont il faut cependant rendre compte à propos de textes si manifestement parallèles, ceux-bi présentent une conjonction soudaine, et d'autant plus remarquacle, sur le quatrième "indicium" (Cassien) ou "gradus humilitatis" (RM et RB) :[11]

---

[11] Le texte des *Institutions* est cité d'après Jean Cassien, *Institutions cénobitiques*. Texte latin revu…, par J.-C. Guy. Paris 1965 (*Sources Chrétiennes*, no 109), ceux de RM et de RB d'après les éditions du P. de Vogüé, mais en tenant compte des leçons consignées dans les apparats, étant donné le refus

Cassien	RM	RB
quarto si in omnibus seruet oboedientiae mansuetudinem	quartum...si in ipsa oboedientia duris et contrariis rebus uel etiam quibuslibet inrogatis iniuriis tacite	= RM sauf:
patientiaeque constantiam	patientiae constantiam amplectatur	conscientia patientiam

Sur un seul point donc les textes de RM et de RB divergent, mais l'accord RM-Cassien cautionne le caractère originel de la leçon *patientiae constantiam*. Dom Capelle a escamoté la difficulté en limitant la comparaison de cette leçon, commune et donc sûre, de RM-Cassien à une partie seulement de la variante de RB (*patientiam*). C'est ce qui lui permet de conclure que ce dernier texte "est plus concis que *patientiae constantiam*, sans que l'idée soit affaiblie".[12] Fondée, une telle assertion n'infirmerait pas, mais renforcerait effectivement son hypothèse de deux éditions attribuables à Benoît. En réalité ce n'était pas le seul mot *patientiam* qu'il fallait mettre en regard de *patientiae constantiam*, mais la totalité des éléments correspondant du texte de RB, à savoir: *conscientia patientiam*. On ne peut plus alors parler de concision. Il suffit au demeurant de se reporter à la page précédente du même article et d'y lire la longue note 10, consacrée précisément à ce passage de RB, pour voir combien celui-ci embarrassait en réalité Dom Capelle. A son propos il se livre même, de façon tout exceptionnelle, à une enquête dans les apparats critiques, en soupesant la valeur des variantes qu'ils offrent, pour finalement s'arrêter à cette singulière distinction entre une "leçon *voulue* par Benoît" mais non consignée par lui et celle qu'on rencontre effectivement parce qu'elle aurait "remplacé par inadvertance" celle qu'il avait dans l'esprit. Et, ne le perdons pas de vue, il s'agirait en l'occurrence d'une retouche de l'écrivain visant à améliorer l'expression de sa pensée! Pis encore: le résultat ainsi obtenu n'offre en fin de compte, de l'aveu même du critique, qu' "un sens tolérable", et à condition d'admettre que "*conscientia* est un ablatif". "Même ainsi, devait-il encore reconnaître, la phrase reste embarrassée... et très contraire au génie concis de s. Benoît". Comment un esprit aussi subtil n'a-t-il pas remarqué la contradiction de

---

de prendre en considération l'existence d'une succession d'états et d'éditions pour ces règles. Voir à ce propos: F. Masai, *L'édition de Vogüé et les éditions antiques de la Règle du Maître* (*Latomus*, 26, 1967, p. 506-517).

[12] B. Capelle, *op. cit.*, p. 114.

tels propos à quelques lignes de distance? N'essayons pas de mesurer la force de préjugés ancrés depuis les débuts d'une vie dans la psychologie d'un savant, moins encore de mettre sa droiture en question. En tout état de cause un fait est bien évident: la leçon de RB demeure inexpliquée et inexplicable par l'hypothèse des deux éditions de s. Benoît, proposée par Dom Capelle.[13] Il nous incombe donc de trouver la genèse du texte de RB, que les plus sympathisants de ses interprètes jugent à peine intelligible, tout juste "tolérable".

Un sain réalisme recommande de commencer par se représenter les conditions concrètes où travaillaient le législateur du Cassin (ou son secrétaire éventuel) et tous les copistes du VIe siècle. La connaissance des écritures livresques du temps et les mots sur lesquels s'accordent RM et Cassien nous procurent un point de départ solide en ce domaine: Benoît lisait, naturellement, un manuscrit en *scriptio continua*, un texte portant à cet endroit soit PATIENTIAE-CONSTANTIAM(AMPLECTATUR) soit une transcription altérée de ces mots. Dans le premier cas on ne pourrait rendre compte de l'unanimité des témoins de RB *à ignorer "constantiam" et à introduire* le mot "conscientia" *avant* "patientia(m)". Sur ce premier point, le cas ne présente pas beaucoup de complexité. Le paléographe doit faire appel à un fait fréquemment observé dans toute copie: *l'inversion* de deux mots. Le codex de RM dont se servait Benoît devait présenter CONSTANTIAM écrit avant *patientiae*. Mais le copiste de ce manuscrit de RM ne devait pas s'être borné à cette inversion banale qui n'altérait pas le sens, sinon s. Benoît n'aurait éprouvé aucune difficulté à le comprendre ni essayé de substituer, à un texte aussi clair, l'obscur *conscientia* qu'on lit dans son oeuvre au lieu de *constantiam*.

RB est une édition refondue de RM. En l'établissant son auteur était obligé de fournir un texte au moins "tolérable" de toutes les phrases du texte qui lui servait de base. D'où la nécessité pour Benoît de supprimer ou d'amender les passages qu'il n'arrivait pas à comprendre. Une simple inversion n'avait pas de telles conséquences pour le sens. Il faut donc examiner la possibilité d'un accident survenant *de surcroît* au texte et capable d'en obscurcir la signification. C'est ce que la *scriptio continua* permet aisément dans le cas

---

[13] La stérilité, ici constatée, du recours à l'hypothèse d'une pluralité d'éditions de la Règle bénédictine, n'enlève rien à la pertinence de ce recours pour résoudre d'autres problèmes de la tradition de ce texte, notamment ceux que pose la divergence entre les témoins de son prologue et la comparaison avec la transmission des textes parallèles de RM.

présent. L'inversion susdite pouvait exister dans une famille de mss
de RM, elle peut aussi avoir été introduite uniquement dans le modèle du codex cassinien de RM, mais dans un cas comme dans l'autre,
le scribe de celui-ci avait donc à transcrire :

CONSTANTIAMPATIENTIAEAMPLECTATUR

La plus courante des inadvertances des scribes utilisant pareille
écriture livresque consiste à sauter du même au même, soit d'une
syllabe à une autre, soit même d'une simple *lettre* à une autre, trop
rapprochées entre elles sur la même ligne, c'est-à-dire horizontale-
ment, ou à peu de distance verticalement. Ainsi des portions de
textes, allant d'une seule lettre à des lignes entières se sont perdues
en cours de transcription. Ce fait, bien connu de tous les usagers des
manuscrits, se produisait plus facilement encore dans la copie des
livres en *scriptio continua*. Dans le cas présent, le second A de
PATIENTIAE et l'initiale de AMPLECTATUR n'étant séparés entre eux
que par un seul caractère, la moindre inadvertance du copiste
pouvait lui faire oublier le E du modèle et sauter d'un A au suivant.
En l'occurrence l'altération du texte devenait irrémédiable pour un
lecteur du temps. L'haplographie donnait, en effet, un texte
inintelligible certes, mais *apparemment* facile à reconstituer pour un
lecteur habitué à ce genre d'erreur et connaissant la langue latine.

Lisant CONSTANTIAMPATIENTIAMPLECTATUR dans son exemplaire
de RM, Benoît comprit aussitôt que son codex présentait une
haplographie, mais la malencontreuse forme accusative que celle-ci
avait donnée à *patientia* et l'évidente nécessité de lire ensuite
"*amplectatur*", l'amenèrent tout naturellement à penser que le saut
du même au même avait fait perdre au texte les deux lettres du
début du verbe, soit AM (ou si l'on préfère, le désinence de "patien-
ti*am*"). Il ne pouvait évidemment pas soupçonner qu'il s'agissait de
la perte d'un simple E, désinence du génitif de *patientiae* que rien ne
pouvait plus lui suggérer, à défaut alors de toute méthode d'édition
critique des textes.

Deux accusatifs consécutifs, à cet endroit, auraient rendu le
texte incompréhensible. Encore une fois, comme tout lecteur du VIe
s., Benoît savait que les copistes ajoutaient ou omettaient, sans
aucune raison, un M respectivement à l'abblatif ou à l'accusatif des
substantifs et des adjectifs, *faute d'entendre* encore la différence entre
ces deux désinences classiques. Une telle faute, non moins usuelle
que l'haplographie dans les textes du temps, devait suggérer à
Benoît l'idée d'interpréter une des deux *formes* accusatives comme

un ablatif et, vu le génie de la langue et la présence de *tacite* (autre circonstancielle), c'est *constantiam* qui lui paru être cet ablatif.

Tout cela était logique, allait de soi peut-on dire ; cependant *tacite constantia patientiam amplectatur* ne donnait rien de compréhensible qu'un auteur, ou du moins un éditeur et non un simple copiste, pût maintenir dans le texte qu'il établissait. D'où un effort de correction, de la part de Benoît, pour assainir le passage et le rendre au moins "tolérable" puisqu'il jugeait bon de le maintenir. La ressemblance des mots lui suggéra alors une correction comme on en faisait naguère encore: la substitution de *conscientia* à *constantia*. Le texte de RB se trouvait ainsi désormais constitué. Il demeurait quelque peu bizarre, aussi certains de ses copistes essaieront-ils à leur tour de l'amender en accordant *tacite* avec le *conscientia* voisin. Ce qui est évidemment une *lectio facilior*, et non l'intention restée inexprimée que Dom Capelle imagina d'attribuer à s. Benoît.

L'explication ici proposée paraîtra peut-être un peu compliquée à plusieurs. Mais la nature concrète de ces phénomènes tout simples est seule responsable de cette longue description. En réalité, et cela seul importe, les faits—invoqués et les mécanismes mis en cause sont ceux que rencontrent chaque jour les codicologues, surtout quand ils ont l'avantage de fréquenter des livres de la fin de l'antiquité et du haut moyen âge.

Encore un mot et nous en aurons fini avec l'étude de ce passage, "TACITE" s'est toujours lu dans les manuscrits de RM et même dans les plus autorisés de RB, car il n'y a pas à prendre, avec Dom Capelle, pour une intention non exprimée de s. Benoît la variante *tacita conscientia* qu'on rencontre en plusieurs témoins postérieurs de cette règle. Son caractère de "lectio facilior" en fait le type accompli de la correction médiévale. D'autre part "tacite" fut toujours compris comme un adverbe, comme en témoigne le cas de s. Benoît. A vrai dire, lui ne pouvait guère l'interpréter autrement, l'altération qui avait affecté le texte qu'il lisait, y avait fait disparaître le génitif *patientiae*, sauvegardé en revanche par Cassien comme par le Maître. Un peu de familiarité avec l'orthographe des scribes d'avant Charlemagne permet de savoir que la plupart d'entre eux écrivaient indifféremment *tacite* et *tacitae*. N'est-ce pas cette dernière forme que l'éditeur critique doit ici restituer? En tout cas un adjectif accordé avec *patientiae* donne au passage une clarté et une force particulières. De surcroît ce style concorde pleinement avec celui de plus d'un autre morceau de RM.

Concluons: d'après RM le "quatrième degré" de l'échelle d'humilité est gravi par le candidat à la perfection — je traduis littéralement d'abord — "si lorsque, dans l'obéissance même, on lui impose des choses pénibles et contrariantes, voire des injustices de toute sorte, il saisit, lui, avec empressement la fermeté d'une patience qui sait se taire." Délaissant des figures de rhétorique peu conformes au génie de notre langue, nous traduirions la *pensée* de RM en ces termes: "le quatrième degré d'humilité consiste à obéir sans broncher (*tacitae*), avec fermeté de caractère (*constantiam*) et même avec empressement (*amplectatur*), aux ordres les plus pénibles et les plus vexants (*in ipsa oboedientia duris et contrariis*), voire à toute sorte d'injustices (*quibuslibet inrogatis iniuriis*)." Si s. Benoît s'était, si parfaitement exprimé dans une première édition, jamais, faut-il le dire? il n'eût apporté les modifications, à peine intelligibles, qu'on lit à présent dans RB, censément sa seconde édition.

Une autre idée de Dom Capelle nous a paru mériter plus d'attention: "combien il est difficile, écrivait-il, de déceler par simple comparaison entre deux auteurs lequel a copié l'autre: Est-ce le prolixe qui a interpolé, ou bien le concis qui a écarté les développements inutiles." Trop souvent cette remarque de bon sens fut oubliée dans les démonstrations en faveur de l'antériorité du Maître ou de Benoît. Mais s'applique-t-elle bien à ces textes parallèles de Cassien et de RM? De prime abord on pourrait dire que RM fait figure de prolixe puisqu'il présente trois lignes où Cassien se contente d'une seule, mais ne peut-on soupçonner ici Cassien, à savoir "le concis", de résumer un texte long? Son vague "in omnibus" donne manifestement l'impression de recouvrir les vexations énumérées par RM. Et si effectivement RM ne recule pas devant la prolixité, pourquoi omet-il alors ici la jolie formule de Cassien: "oboedientiae *mansuetudinem*"? Le terme "seruet" de Cassien de son côté est bien banal, vis-à-vis du verbe "amplectatur" de RM, si expressif et si éloquemment placé à la fin de la phrase.

Devant de telles constatations, la vérité est qu'on peut demeurer indécis sur le rapport de filiation qui lie les deux textes. Ne tranchons pas à la légère et voyons plutôt le troisième passage étudié par Dom Capelle. En le soumettant au même examen paléographique que le précédent, peut-être l'hésitation se transformera-t-elle en certitude.

Le troisième des rapprochements opportuns de Dom Capelle peut être présenté en colonnes de la manière que voici (où sont écrits en capitales les éléments qui retiendront plus spécialement l'attention du paléographe):

RB	RM	CASSIEN
sed amore	sed amore	sed amore
CHRISTI	IPSIUS	IPSIUS
ET CONSUETUDINE IPSA	CONSUETUDINIS	
BONA	BONAE	BONI
et delectatione uirtu- tum	et delectatione uirtu- tum	et delectatione uir- tutum

Posé en principe que le Maître était postérieur à Benoît, lui-même certainement postérieur à Cassien, Dom Capelle n'avait pas le choix dans l'interprétation des faits mis en évidence par ces parallèles, malgré son idée si juste de la difficulté de décider entre un développement et un résumé et sa loyale reconnaissance de l'antériorité du *texte* de RM sur celui de RB. Pour lui la leçon *amore ipsius consuetudinis bonae* de RM ne pouvait représenter qu'"une correction", et "maladroite", de Cassien, "car on comprend mieux l'*amor ipsius boni* que l'*amor ipsius consuetudinis bonae:* un homme agit par amour du bien ou par une habitude contractée, plutôt que par amour de cette habitude".[14] Tout cela est hors de conteste. On aurait pu cependant ajouter que RM étant censé nous avoir conservé le premier état de la législation cassinenne, c'est l'auteur de celle-ci, et non l'esprit dépourvu de jugement du "Maître", qui porterait en ce cas la responsabilité d'avoir si sottement modifié le texte, parfaitement compréhensible et profond, de Cassien. On admettra volontiers avec Dom Capelle que s. Benoît, peu satisfait de la formule consignée dans RM, ait éprouvé le besoin de la modifier, mais on consentira difficilement à croire que cette "correction maladroite du texte de Cassien" soit imputable à celui qui ensuite devait la rejeter (ce qu'exige l'hypothèse des deux éditions de RB dont l'une conservée ici par RM). Et s'il se repentait d'avoir malencontreusement modifié Cassien, pourquoi Benoît n'y revint-il pas? Passant un peu légèrement sur toutes ces difficultés, Dom Capelle continue simplement comme suit à commenter les variantes observées: "Benoît *rectifie* en distinguant l'amour du Christ et la *consuetudo bona:* ils influent l'un sur l'autre".

Abandonnons cette hypothèse des deux éditions de Benoît, si malencontreusement invoquée pour résoudre le problème, elle est

---

[14] B. Capelle, *loc. cit.*

d'ailleurs à présent depuis longtemps abandonnée, dépassée, dans l'étude des rapports entre RM et RB. Toutefois n'oublions pas que le manuscrit utilisé par le législateur du Cassin était plus ancien que tous les manuscrits actuellement subsistants de RM. Comme, par ailleurs, de l'accord de ceux-ci avec le texte de Cassien il appert que le codex cassinien devait, lui aussi, posséder la leçon *ipsius*, nous sommes en droit de reconstituer comme suit le texte de RM que lisait s. Benoît: "sed amore *ipsius* et consuetudine bona et delectatione uirtutum". Sur un point l'auteur de la refonte de RM ne pouvait se satisfaire de ce texte: à quoi ou à qui pouvait se rapporter ce génitif du pronom *ipse*? Une correction s'imposait pour supprimer l'obscurité de ce passage; or quel autre amour que celui du Christ pouvait inspirer les actions du moine? Au verset précédent il était au reste explicitement dit que les religieux parfaitement humbles "arrivaient à l'amour du Seigneur" ("ad caritatem illam *Domini* peruenientes..."). La retouche de s. Benoît ne s'en trouve justifiée ni grammaticalement ni paléographiquement, mais elle allait de soi dans l'optique d'un correcteur du temps et surtout dans celle d'un auteur responsable du texte de son *propre* code monastique.

Notre tâche à nous est tout autre, elle consiste à expliquer *génétiquement* l'obscurité du texte que lisait l'abbé du Cassin vers le milieu du VIe siècle. Or, rien n'est plus simple, si l'on observe qu'un siècle plus tôt, Cassien lisait (ou écrivait, ne tranchons pas encore) non pas *bona* mais *boni*. Remplaçons par cette dernière forme celle que Benoît trouvait dans son manuscrit et tout s'éclairera sans peine: nous n'aurons plus besoin de modifier le pronom *ipsius* qui lui faisait difficulté et, d'autre part, il ne sera pas moins aisé d'expliquer l'apparition de la forme *bona* dans son texte. Celui-ci, en effet, dérivait en ce cas de cet autre: "sed amore ipsius et consuetudine ipsa boni et delectatione uirtutum".

Replaçant maintenant cet ensemble dans son contexte, nous constaterons que non seulement tout y est parfaitement en situation, mais que l'idée est exprimée avec une élégance et une force admirables. Seulement avec, en sus, un peu d'affectation dans le style, bien conforme au goût de l'époque mais non sans danger pour la transcription fidèle du texte. C'est là qu'un scribe trébucha, comme il était fatal.

Voici donc le passage en question remis dans son contexte: "Ergo his omnibus humilitatis gradibus a discipulo perascensis, uitae huius in timore Dei persubitur scala et mox ad caritatem illam Domini

peruenientes, quae perfecta foris mittit timorem, per quam uni-
uersa, quae prius non sine formidine obseruabas, absque ullo labore
uelut naturaliter ex consuetudine incipiet custodire, non iam timore
gehennae, *sed amore ipsius et consuetudine ipsa boni* et delectatione
uirtutum."[15] Cette admirable doctrine aurait pu s'exprimer en
précisant qu'il s'agissait de "amore ipsius boni" puis, en répétant ce
mot sous sa forme adjectivale: "et consuetudine ipsa *bona*". Plus
élégamment l'écrivain énonça sa pensée en supprimant l'adjectif,
qui allait de soi, et dans un raccourci qui ne manquait ni de force ni
d'audace linguistique, écrivit "sed amore *ipsius* et consuetudine ipsa
boni". Mais là résidait le danger pour les copistes de la *libraria* du
temps, trop absorbés par une tâche matérielle difficile pour rester
attentifs aux élégances de style ou simplement à la pensée des
auteurs qu'ils transcrivaient, non par phrases entières du reste, mais
par petits groupes de mots, voire de caractères seulement. Le rapprochement voulu mais trop audacieux du féminin *consuetudine*
avec l'adjectif apparent *boni* devait fatalement conduire un copiste
à modifier (consciemment ou non) "bon*i*" en "bon*a*". C'est ce dont
porte témoignage la leçon d'un manuscrit du milieu du VIe siècle,
conservée par RB.

Cette altération d'un texte si exposé aux accidents n'était pas la
seule possible. La prononciation du latin conduisait en certains
milieux les copistes à écrire l'une pour l'autre les terminaisons *i, e, ae*.
En l'occurrence un manuscrit peut donc fort bien avoir porté
"bon*e*" ou même "bon*ae*". Ce qui rendrait compte de la "correction"
indiscutablement "maladroite" que Dom Capelle discernait dans la
vulgate de RM. Mais ce détour n'est même pas nécessaire. Un copiste
ou un correcteur du VIe siècle, moine médiocrement cultivé d'ordi-
naire qui, en outre, ne se sentait pas la responsabilité de s. Benoît,
mieux: qui ne pouvait, comme celui-ci le devait au contraire, prendre une initiative d'*auteur*, avait à recopier le plus fidèlement
possible la *lettre* du texte à reproduire. Tout ce qu'on lui demandait,
en cas d'erreur du modèle, c'était de restituer une exactitude

---

[15] Sauf pour le passage imprimé en italique, qui tient naturellement compte
des résultats de notre reconstitution du texte, celui-ci est repris à l'édition
A. de Vogüé, *La Règle du Maître*, vol. I, p. 438. On se référera aux apparats
pour connaître les variantes des autres témoins, E et A (insignifiantes en
l'occurrence), et surtout pour apprécier les réminiscences scripturaires de
l'auteur (autre contraste avec le texte de Cassien qui, par là encore, donne
l'impression d'une réduction volontaire au minimum requis par l'intelli-
gibilité).

grammaticale, sans souci intempestif, sans vouloir notamment insuffler à l'oeuvre un esprit qui aurait pu paraître lui faire défaut.

Le texte de la vulgate de RM ne peut nous satifaire — Dom Capelle avait raison de le déclarer, — mais il répond parfaitement aux normes exigées des scribes et de leurs correcteurs: il est correct. Voyons à quel prix et comment il l'est devenu; de nouveau cela nous permettra de suivre la genèse de la modification d'un texte, de l'*autre* altération du texte originel. Ne s'estimant aucun droit sur le fond du texte, à la différence d'un abbé législateur comme s. Benoît, le correcteur ne vise qu'à sauvegarder sa forme. Comme il décide de maintenir le génitif *ipsius*, impérieusement exigé par "sed amore" qui précède, il faut, lui semble-t-il, accorder en "cas" le substantif qui suit ("consuetudo") et en "genre" ou en "cas" (selon qu'il lit encore "bon*i*" ou déjà "bon*a*", comme Benoît) ce qu'il prend sûrement pour l'épithète de "consuetudo".

Les leçons divergentes, rencontrées dans les trois témoignages parallèles, se trouvent de la sorte expliquées, toutes et de la manière la plus simple. Reste toutefois encore sans réponse une question que Dom Capelle ne s'est pas et ne pouvait se poser, vu l'idée préconçue qu'il avait de la chronologie respective des trois textes en présence: d'où proviennent les mots "et consuetudine ipsa" qu'ignorent les *Institutions* de Cassien? Mais examiner comme il convient ce problème, c'est entreprendre une nouvelle enquête, vaste et délicate, c'est vérifier si Cassien est bien effectivement la source de RM-RB ou si Dom Genestout avait raison de la faire dépendre de RM ou encore si nos textes parallèles sont les témoins d'un quatrième, insoupçonné jusqu'ici, dont chacun d'eux porterait témoignage de façon propre et, on l'a constaté, complémentaire pour les besoins de l'éditeur.

Quelques brèves observations et réflexions préliminaires sont ici indispensables. On nous les pardonnera sans doute, en égard à l'importance de l'enjeu.

1. Insistons d'abord sur un fait exceptionnel: les "indicia" occupent à peine une ligne ou deux chez Cassien, sans aucune des références habituelles à l'autorité des Ecritures, tandis que les "gradus" correspondant de RM-RB présentent un développement logique complet et une base théologique appropriée; dans la conclusion du traité, en revanche, l'ampleur de Cassien n'a rien à envier à celle de ses concurrents! Des deux côtés le texte est même

pratiquement identique. Ne serait-ce pas un signe que Cassien résu-
mait jusqu'alors et qu'il ne se sentit plus la même liberté de le faire
quand il passa de la simple énumération des critères d'une vertu à la
description finale de l'état de perfection?

2. Si la différence entre les textes parallèles est réduite à presque
rien, elle n'est pourtant pas nulle. Un examen superficiel pourrait
suggérer, pour en rendre compte, une erreur de transmission dans le
texte de Cassien ou, en cas de dépendance, dans celui de l'auteur
qu'il démarquait ici. A ne regarder que le texte litigieux le paléographe pourrait être tenté d'y voir une sorte d'haplographie du
copiste qui, après avoir écrit le mot *ipsius*, en se reportant à son
modèle, n'aurait pas repris le texte où il l'avait interrompu mais
après *ipsa*, qui suit précisément à peu de distance. Ainsi s'explique-
rait conformément à la psychologie, l'omission de *et consuetudine
ipsa*. Pour tentante qu'elle puisse être, cette hypothèse est à écarter.
Un examen du contexte fait apparaître une absence du même mot
consuetudo un peu plus haut *dans la même phrase*. Alors que RM et
RB s'accordent à compléter *uelut naturaliter* par *ex consuetudine*, là
également Cassien ignore cette mention de l'habitude. Il faut donc
renoncer à l'idée d'une omission fortuite, accidentelle. Ou bien Cassien a jugé suffisant d'écrire "*uelut* naturaliter" (l'habitude n'est-elle
pas en effet, de l'aveu de tous, une "autre nature", n'est-elle pas
"uelut natura"?) ou bien son utilisateur a estimé opportun d'interpréter, de gloser ce "uelut naturaliter" par "ex consuetudine". Mais
cette seconde explication, plausible s'il s'agissait de l'absence de la
première mention de "consuetudo" dans le passage, est à son tour
insuffisante comme motif de la seconde, celle-ci n'est plus une glose,
et l'on ne voit pas ce qui aurait pu suggérer une interpolation, si
limitée d'ailleurs, à cet endroit du texte de Cassien! L'hypothèse
de la glose n'a finalement pas plus de vraisemblance que n'en avait
celle de l'haplographie.

3. Somme toute Cassien, qui a visé à une extrême concision au
§ 2, peut avoir voulu tenir à cette concision dans le § 3. Il faut reconnaître qu'en ce dernier la marge autorisée pour les suppressions
était fort étroite, le texte étant, cette fois, d'une densité et d'une
importance exceptionnelles. Voilà qui justifierait le nombre infime
des mots *éliminés*. On peut au reste le vérifier, il s'agit effectivement
de deux expressions pour lesquelles le contexte présentait un équi-
valent suffisant: "uelut naturaliter" dans le premier cas (synonyme),
"et delectatione uirtutum" dans le second ("uirtus" = "habitus").

Irons-nous jusqu'à soutenir que Cassien se seit d'un document préexistant, dont nous n'affirmerions certes pas, avec le P. Genestout, qu'il s'identifie avec RM, mais qu'il est une source *commune* de RM et de Cassien? Devant l'énormité de l'enjeu, on peut encore admettre ici l'hésitation. D'autant plus que l'oeuvre de Benoît s'étant avérée une refonte de celle du "Maître", se fait à nouveau sentir la manque d'arbitrage d'un tiers. Seules, en effet, demeurent en présence les revendications respectives d'un texte concis, Cassien, et celles d'un texte plus long, RM-RB.

Les précautions recommandées par Dom Capelle en pareil cas redeviendraient donc actuelles, si le témoignage même de Cassien n'intervenait ici, à point nommé, pour nous tirer d'embarras. Les chapitres des *Institutions*, en effet, qui intéressent précisément notre propos, se présentent comme la reproduction fidèle d'une autre oeuvre: de celle d'un expert en spiritualité. Le traité des vertus auquel appartient le chapitre sur l'humilité n'est, au dire même de Cassien, qu'un discours emprunté à un abbé égyptien, Pinufius; "exhortationem quam dedit fratri (à l'occasion de la réception de ce novice, précise le contexte)... quia puto ex hac posse instructionis accedere, animus est opusculo huic intexere."[16] Est-ce ici de la part de Cassien, pur procédé littéraire, forme fictive de "reportage" qu'il aurait employée de façon plus systématique dans ses *conlationes*? Sans doute notre écrivain n'a-t-il pas rapporté d'Egypte ni surtout traduit de textes grecs (tous perdus) les discours qu'il attribue aux Pères du Désert. Mais c'est une raison supplémentaire de penser qu'il a dû chercher ailleurs ses sources d'inspiration. Dès lors pourquoi, surtout avec des indices recoupant ses dires, ne le croirions-nous pas quand il déclare reproduire le texte d'un abbé illustre. Nous avons la preuve—il en existe encore—que des textes circulèrent au Ve siècle sous de prestigieux noms d'emprunt: Macaire, Sérapion... Rien n'empêche donc d'admettre l'existence d'un pseudo-Pinufius que Cassien aurait utilisé et même — car il s'y entend — doctrinalement revu.[17]

---

[16] Cassien, *Inst.*, IV, 32.

[17] L'habileté et la signification doctrinale de certains silences ont été finement analysées par Dom M. Cappuyns dans son article *Cassien* du D.H.G.E. (11, 1949, 1319-1348), spécialement col. 1340-1343. Voir aussi J.-C. Guy, *Jean Cassien, Vie et doctrine spirituelle*, Paris, 1961, p. 24ss. Cassien se garde à l'évidence de mentionner par leur nom ceux qu'il désapprouve. C'est pourquoi il faut souligner aussi l'absence de toute mention de s. Martin et de son monachisme dans l'oeuvre d'un auteur vivant dans un

Notre seconde impression, celle d'un *résumé* de la source, n'est pas non plus démunie de fondement objectif. C'est encore un texte de Cassien qui lui fournit son appui. A la fin du ch. 29 de ce même l. IV des *Institutions*, arrivant à parler précisément de l'humilité ("illam Christi humilitatem quae est uera nobilitas"), laquelle ne s'obtient à son avis que par l'exercice de l'obéissance ("per oboedientiae gratiam desiderat obtinere"), Cassien se trouve tiraillé entre deux exigences. D'une part il voit la nécessité de traiter comme il sied de l'obéissance puisque, à ses yeux, celle-ci détient la premier rang parmi les vertus: "oboedientiae bonum, quae inter ceteras uirtutes primatum tenet" (n'oublions pas son propos, qui est de faire accepter aux religieux de Gaule les cadres de l'organisation cénobitique); d'un autre côté, il constate que son IVe livre a déjà pris trop d'ampleur. Il se décidera donc à parler de l'humilité, mais en *abrégeant*, autant que possible, ce qu'il convient d'en écrire: *"coartat nos libelli modus ad finem tendere"*.[18]

Conclure de tout ce qui précède qu'un "Traité du Pseudo-Pinufius" a circulé au début du Ve siècle ne présente rien que de plausible. L'idée d'une *source commune, mais utilisée de façon indépendante* par Cassien et RM, que l'analyse de ces auteurs nous a fait soupçonner, prend une réelle consistance et même une forme concrète, avec cette référence expresse des *Institutions*. Mais sont-ce, malgré tout, des prémisses suffisantes pour avoir le droit de se dire en présence d'une certitude?

Un surcroît de prudence s'impose quand il s'agit d'une conclusion historique pouvant porter à conséquences aussi graves. C'est pourquoi nous suspendrons encore notre jugement: utilisant l'existence de cette source écrite, commune à Cassien et à RM (attribuée ou non à Pinufius, c'est secondaire), comme simple hypothèse de travail que nous allons mettre à l'essai, pour voir si elle peut élucider les obscurités et autres difficultés que présentent le l. IV des *Institutions* et les chapitres correspondant de RM. Peut-être alors, après services ren-

---

milieu qui ne pouvait les ignorer. L'opposition entre les deux orientations discernées par F. Prinz, *Frühes Mönchtum im Frankenreich* (München-Wien, 1965), trouve ici un solide appui. Une comparaison particulièrement éloquente peut être faite entre le miracle rapporté par Sulpice Sévère, *Dialogues*, I, 19, et le récit ramené à ses dimensions naturelles (quoique plus spirituelles) par Cassien, *Inst.*, IV, 24. Cf. à ce sujet Henri Bremond, *Les Pères du Désert*, I (Paris, 1927), p. 254.

[18] Cassien, *Inst.*, IV, 29-30.

dus, l'hypothèse pourra-t-elle être considérée comme suffisamment vérifiée.

Ce traité, cette source commune que, par souci de brièveté, Cassien nous autoriserait peut-être à appeler "le Pseudo-Pinufius", serait donc à l'origine d'une partie de RM-RB comme d'*Institutions* IV, 32-43. Il faudrait admettre alors que, dans ce dernier ouvrage, l'apocryphe ou, pour nous, l'anonyme aurait été utilisé le plus souvent sous forme de résumé ou de paraphrase, rarement démarqué à la lettre, tandis qu'il aurait contribué pour une part beaucoup plus large, et plus littéralement surtout, à constituer RM-RB. Ce qui ne revient nullement à dire que l'ordre de la source y aurait été parfaitement suivi ni jamais farci de textes d'autre provenance.[19]

Pour comprendre la suite de cet exposé, il est maintenant nécessaire de rappeler les conclusions de l'analyse de RM, esquissée dans la communication faite au congrès de Rome sur la règle bénédictine.[20] La "Regula Patrum" que transmet, non dans sa teneur première mais du moins sous une forme encore représentative de sa genèse, le codex Paris latin 12205, résulte de l'union de la "Regula sanctorum patrum Serapionis, Macharii, Paphnutii et alius Macharii" (= RIVP) avec cet écrit que Benoît d'Aniane et la postérité ont appelé "Regula Magistri". Celle-ci, ce manuscrit P le montre encore à l'évidence, a été réalisée par la juxtaposition de plusieurs écrits initialement indépendants et qu'un examen des textes démontre avoir été grossis d'éléments divers et surtout *partiellement fusionnés*. C'est cette fusion, fort incomplète et très imparfaite (d'où son caractère heureusement encore si reconnaissable) des documents de base qui intéresse notre propos actuel.

La redistribution des textes à laquelle procéda l'éditeur du "codex regularum" que, pour suivre l'usage, nous continuons d'appeler RM, affecte entre autres le traité de l'humilité. Or, il est facile de reconnaître dans Cassien des éléments de ces traités, mis en pièces et répartis autrement par le "Maître".

---

[19] Vu l'âge respectif des témoins, on peut *a priori* s'attendre à ce que le *texte* ait été particulièrement bien conservé dans les *Institutions* et plus fidèlement aussi, parfois, dans les *manuscrits* de RB que dans les autres témoins de RM (tous postérieurs à s. Benoît; fait perdu de vue dans le premier essai d'édition critique de RM: jamais RB n'y est appelé à la barre). C'est ce que viennent confirmer, de la façon donc la plus normale, l'excellente leçon *boni* du seul Cassien et la qualité de l'ablatif *consuetudine* de Benoît.

[20] Voir plus haut note 7.

Dans l'étude sur "Les documents de base de la règle", communiqué aux spécialistes réunis à Rome, l'idée d'une confrontation avec le passage de Cassien ne m'était pas venue. Inattention profitable tout compte fait, si l'on veut bien constater que les résultats naguère obtenus alors par l'analyse du seul texte de RM, trouvent maintenant, de façon tout indépendante donc, un précieux recoupement dans l'exhortation de l'abbé Pinufius à un fils spirituel du IVe livre des *Institutions*.[21]

A dire vrai la nouvelle comparaison des textes ne confirme pas toutes les déductions faites à Rome, mais ce n'est pas le lieu de corriger les imperfections de cette première approche. La convergence globale compte seule ici: l'opuscule supposé, et reconstitué alors uniquement par l'analyse interne du premier "document de base" de la règle, dont un explicit interne (!), étrangement maintenu après le ch. X de RM, nous a conservé le titre ("Actus militiae cordis..."), se reconnaît chez Cassien aussi, avec les mêmes éléments, disposés selon l'ordre que cette première enquête avait précisément reconnu.

Il est superflu de relever ici les échos, pourtant perceptibles me semble-t-il, du "Prologus", du "Thema" et même du titre du document dans les premiers chapitres du discours que Cassien prête à Pinufius. Bornons-nous aux rapprochements hors de conteste qu'on a relevés à partir de *Institutions* IV, 39 et de RM VI-X (= RB IV, 78-VII): les thèmes s'y suivent et s'y enchaînent avec un tel parallélisme qu'on a pu y retrouver des expressions et des phrases entières, littéralement identiques.

Première étape du cheminement vers la perfection chrétienne, chez Cassien comme en RM, "timor Domini" qui s'identifie avec une "custodia" (*Inst.* IV, 39, 1) dont les modalités se trouvent complaisamment détaillées en RM VIII et X (comme en RB VII d'ailleurs) pour chacun de nos sens, chacune de nos facultés.

Vient ensuite l'"humilitas" dont *originellement* en RM (cf VII, 1 et X, 42-51), comme présentement encore chez Cassien (IV, 39, 2), les

---

[21] Cette *Exhortatio* ne peut manquer d'évoquer l'*Admonitio*, attribuée à s. Basile et utilisée par s. Benoît pour récrire les premières lignes du "prologus" qu'il empruntait à RM. Cet entrelacs de textes, dont l'un est ignoré du Maître, suffirait à démontrer la dépendance de RB vis-à-vis de RM. Voir les parallèles institués par Eugène Manning, L'"*Admonitio s. Basilii ad filium spiritualem*" et la *Règle de s. Benoît* (*Revue d'Ascétique et de Mystique*, 42, 1966, p. 475-480).

trois premiers degrés sont constitués par autant de progrès dans l'obéissance, c'est-à-dire dans le renoncement à la volonté propre.[22] Par parenthèse, nous comprenons maintenant pourquoi c'est au 4e degré que soudainement se rejoignent Cassien et RM-RB pour ne plus guère se quitter véritablement ensuite. C'est à ce moment aussi qu'ils commencent à s'exprimer de façon équivalente et parfois même en termes identiques.

Quant au sommet de la perfection auquel donne accès cette échelle, ce progrès dans la perfection, il n'y a plus à insister sur la coïncidence des textes. Celle-ci a été relevée depuis longtemps, en particulier par Dom Capelle, et une grande partie du présent article n'a pas eu d'autre but que d'expliquer la genèse des rares divergences qu'on observe sur ce point entre les textes de Cassien, de RM et de RB. L'attention mérite plutôt d'être attirée maintenant sur un autre point, qui semble avoir échappé jusqu'ici aux commentateurs de Cassien.

A propos de la vertu d'humilité qui, chez lui aussi, fait parvenir le religieux à la perfection, Cassien ne parle pas *ex-professo* d'une échelle. Pas question de *scala* ni de *gradus* (échelons) mais, plus vaguement, d'*indicia*. A y regarder de plus près, c'est-à-dire en scrutant le contexte, on découvre cependant que Cassien décrit, lui aussi, les progrès du moine comme une *ascension*. Il lui fait également *gravir des échelons* "(*gradu excelsiore perducet*", 37, 3). Tout l'ensemble du traité est même introduit (fin du ch. 38) par cette phrase où deviennent des plus explicites les idées de progression et d'échelons: "ad quem perfectionis statum his *gradibus* atque hoc *ordine per*uenitur". Le ch. 39 d'ailleurs commence d'emblée par "*Principium...*"

Au § 2 de ce ch. 39 il est traité de l'"humilitas", mais à la réflexion on ne peut manquer de se poser quelques questions à propos des lignes consacrées à cette vertu. Quelle raison y avait-il d'articuler cet exposé, de le détailler, d'aller jusqu'à *chiffrer*, et jusqu'à dix, ces "indicia"? Ne pouvait-on les livrer en vrac? Comment est-on parvenu à en discerner dix si l'on ne s'est pas livré à une longue méditation préalable? Or, celle-ci n'est pas communiquée au lecteur, au

---

[22] On notera combien l'ordonnance du traité des vertus monastiques dans le IVe livre des *Institutions* confirme l'existence d'anomalies et de désordres, dénoncés au Congrès de Rome (cf. *op. cit.*), dans l'utilisation du premier "document de base", à la suite d'une simple analyse des chapitres sur l'obéissance, l'amour du silence et l'humilité dans RM (VII-X) et RB (V-VII).

contraire plus d'un de ces "indices" demeure assez énigmatique dans sa formulation à qui l'examine de près. N'est-ce pas la preuve que ces lignes supposent cette méditation mûrie?

On aperçoit déjà combien on se trouve fondé à soupçonner l'existence d'un travail préalable à celui-ci, d'un véritable traité de l'humilité, dont les lignes de Cassien ne seraient qu'un résumé. N'est-ce pas d'ailleurs à un tel traité, *présenté sous forme d'échelle de perfection*, que Cassien lui-même fait allusion plus loin quand il conclut son IVe livre en ces termes: "Audi ergo paucis *ordinem*, per quem *scandere* ad perfectionem *summam* sine ullo labore ac difficultate praeualeas..." (IV, 43). Peut-on plus clairement faire allusion à une *scala*, à une échelle et à des échelons qui, dans un programme détaillé, auraient expliqué le cheminement vers la perfection?

L'hypothèse d'un écrit de spiritualité, ainsi organisé, qui aurait été utilisé par Cassien comme par RM trouverait, semble-t-il, dans les textes même du premier de ces auteurs un appui solide, si l'on pouvait s'expliquer pourquoi, en cas d'existence d'une telle source, les *Institutions* ne prononcent pas le mot *gradus* à propos de la vertu d'humilité. Pourquoi Cassien aurait-il préféré le terme si vague d'*indicia* s'il avait connu l'expression, si suggestive au contraire, de *gradus humilitatis*, répétée jusqu'à douze fois dans le traité parallèle de RM?

Précisément, un très sérieux obstacle existait dans ce traité qui suffit certainement à expliquer pourquoi l'image des degrés et de l'échelle pouvait déplaire ici à Cassien, alors que — on vient de le constater — il la garde ou du moins la suppose dans le contexte qui précède et suit le traité de l'humilité. Un esprit cultivé comme celui d'un Cassien ne pouvait manquer d'être sensible à des subtilités logiques et stylistiques qui devaient échapper, par contre, aux générations d'un goût moins sûr, plus barbares en somme, qui allaient bientôt suivre. Un auteur attentif à la cohérence du langage, à la justesse des termes et des images, ne pouvait se sentir le droit d'une référence à l'échelle et aux échelons qu'à la condition d'exprimer effectivement une pensée où la gradation était marquée. Or, la logique n'était respectée et les figures cohérentes que du premier degré du traité au septième. Arrivé à celui-ci — notons ce nombre parfait (pure coïncidence?) — le paradoxe annoncé au début était consommé: le comble de l'humilité, de l'abaissement (sens du terme en latin, combien vivace encore en cette période de dure servitude des "humiles") consenti, se confondant avec le sommet de l'élévation morale. Comment en douter, en effet, quand on voit RM charactériser en ces termes, qui sont aussi ceux de Cassien, ce 7e degré d'humilité:

RM	Cassien
Deinde septimum gradum humilitatis in scala caeli ascendit discipulus *si* omnibus *se inferiorem* et *uiliorem non* solum sua ligua *pronuntiet*, sed etiam *intimo cordis credat affectu*.	(octavo) *si se*metipsum cunctis *inferiorem non* superficie *pronuntiet* labiorum, *sed intimo cordis credat affectu.*[23]

Parvenu à cet endroit, le religieux qui recherche l'humilité a nécessairement touché au terme, puisqu'il a atteint le niveau le plus bas de l'abaissement et que, surtout, il estime en toute sincérité que cette place est celle qui lui convient.

Voyons du reste ce qu'on nous présente alors en fait d'étapes ultérieures, d'échelons prétendûment supérieurs encore à ces sept premiers. D'abord ce "8e degré" de RM (devenu 6e chez Cassien, à la suite de certains aménagements de la fin du traité dont nous allons dire quelques mots dans un moment): "... si nihil agat, nisi quod communis *monasterii regula uel maiorum* cohortantur exempla". Après cela ce "9e degré" de RM: "si linguam ad loquendum prohibeat et taciturnitatem habens, usque ad interrogationem non loquatur..."; ce qui correspond à la première partie seulement du 9e "indice" de Cassien: "nono si linguam cohibeat". Le 10e degré de RM et le 10e indice de Cassien se recouvrent entièrement: "si non sit facilis ac promptus in risu". Dans RM se lit alors un "11e degré" qu'on rencontre comme 2e partie de son "9e indice" chez Cassien (les mots soulignés sont identiques de part et d'autre): "si cum loquitur, leniter et sine risu... et *non sit clamosus in uoce*...". RM présente encore un 12e et dernier degré (le nombre 12 étant convenable pour achever dignement une énumération): "... sed et iam non solo (!) corde sed etiam (!) in ipso corpore humilitatem uidentibus (!) se indicet". A ce 12e degré ne correspond aucun "indice" ni partie d'indice dans le raccourci de Cassien. Quoi d'étonnant? Si elle peut être une marque d'humilité, cette attitude ne peut-elle être aussi la démarche du parfait orgueilleux, cachant hypocritement son vice,

---

[23] La numérotation de Cassien ("octauo" en regard de "septimum") trouvera son explication dans la suite de l'exposé. Retenons seulement ici le caractère plus littéraire des termes "cunctis" et "superficie labiorum", par lesquels Cassien rend les idées que RM, c'est-à-dire l'"Actus militiae cordis", exprime respectivement par "omnibus" et "solum sua lingua". Lequel des deux auteurs a retouché la prose de l'autre sinon celui qui offre le style le plus châtié?

bref la caractéristique même de la pire expèce de religieux, de ces "gyrovagues", dénoncés précisément ailleurs par Cassien, qui se font passer pour d'humbles religieux en courbant l'échine seulement, non la volonté propre: "ut humiles intrant hospites *solo capite incli-nati*, deinde *superbi...*", dira du reste le Maître lui-même au ch. I v. 72 là où il s'inspire précisément de la VIIe *Conférence* de Cassien.

A y bien regarder ce "12e degré" ne paraît pas être en réalité dépourvu de tout répondant chez Cassien: c'est lui sans doute que doit viser ou, du moins, y remplacer cette sorte de "et caetera": "talibus namque indiciis et his similibus...". Autre constatation qu'une observation attentive permet de faire, c'est ce singulier rapprochement, qui ne semble guère une simple coïncidence, entre ce dernier mot de Cassien, "indiciis", et celui qui précisément terminait l'énoncé du singulier "12e degré" dans le traité de RM: "indicet". Nous tenons-là apparemment la clef de la double énigme, posée par le raccourci de Cassien. N'est-il pas naturel que l'idée de substituer le mot "indicium" à "gradus" soit venue au vigilant écrivain, au moment où il achevait la lecture de ces "gradus" qui n'en étaient pas? Au moment aussi où se faisait plus impérieusement sentir à lui la nécessité de supprimer ce 12e "degré", équivoque et, en même temps, passablement ridicule. D'autre part, aucune énumération qui se respectât ne pouvait se terminer avec un nombre tel que onze, l'idée devait alors se présenter de réorganier l'exposé relatif à l'humilité en dix points ou "signes" (indicia), la décade étant elle aussi à sa manière un nombre parfait.

Cette question étant réglée, et d'une façon pleinement satisfaisante si je ne m'abuse, une autre demeure, qui revêt une importance encore plus décisive pour éprouver la valeur de notre hypothèse de travail, à savoir celle d'une source commune, antérieure à Cassien comme à RM: comment expliquer la présence des échelons qui actuellement surmontent indûment une échelle de perfection, authentique et admirable si on supprime tout ce qui suit le septième degré?

Rien là de réellement difficile, à condition de se replacer dans l'esprit du temps, d'épouser les préoccupations majeures de ceux qui, au tournant du Ve siècle, avaient la responsabilité des milieux monastiques. Leur grand souci n'était assurément pas d'ordre littéraire, mais concernait la discipline. Aux générations précédentes il avait fallu surtout adresser un rappel des exigences du christianisme authentique, vécu dans la plénitude des "conseils" évangéliques.

C'était un besoin urgent, eu égard au laisser-aller, à la tiédeur qui se généralisait en raison des conditions qui avaient été faites au christianisme après la grande persécution du début du IVe siècle: on entrait en masse dans l'Eglise, et les privilèges dont elle pouvait faire bénéficier ses fidèles n'étaient pas étrangers sans doute aux succès de l'Eglise catholique. Désormais un nouveau besoin, une extension de la "réforme" même, si l'on préfère, se faisait sentir et non moins pressant: il concernait les ascètes chrétiens eux-mêmes. Les indisciplinés, les vagabonds commençaient de foisonner parmi ces chrétiens "voués à la perfection". Plus d'un parmi ces "religieux" était en fait simple similateur ou même charlatan. On songea donc à les encadrer, à les soumettre à des dirigeants compétents et responsables, à constituer des communautés de "cénobites", des monastères sous la direction de moines chevronnés, d'abbés, bref des "abbayes" comme on dira plus tard.

Si l'appel à la perfection avait pu se borner d'abord à ne pas voir au delà du 7e degré de l'humilité, on comprend que les nouveaux besoins de la société chrétienne ait ensuite conduit certains esprits à exiger de nouvelles conditions pour l'exercice de cette vertu comme des autres: la soumission à une règle dans le cadre d'une communauté hiérarchisée. L'image de l'échelle et l'échelle elle-même s'en trouvèrent endommagée, mais le résultat qu'on rencontre, soulignons-le, dans Cassien comme dans RM, répondait bien aux préoccupations qui dominaient plus particulièrement chez les responsables de l'Eglise dans la Gaule du Sud-Est au début du Ve siècle.

Ces échelons ont donc été ajoutés très anciennement à l'échelle de perfection du document de base, en vertu d'un besoin qui continuera de sortir ses effets et qui explique tout le travail ultérieur du Maître sur ce même document de base. Il suffit d'avoir présent à l'esprit cette volonté d'adaptation aux exigences communautaires, pour comprendre les additions des ch. I ("De generibus monachorum"), VII ("De oboedientia" = V de RB) et IX ("De taciturnitate" = VI de RB), sans oublier l'insertion d'éléments tirés du second "document de base", en particulier le premier article ("ordo monasterii", devenu dans la 1ère édition de RM la seconde partie du ch. I comme en témoigne encore la place occupée par ce texte dans le ms Paris latin 12634, et, à sa manière, une partie des mss de RB) et une partie du quatrième article ("gradus", ou "de la hiérarchie") qui constitue l'actuel ch. II de RM comme de RB, c'est-à-dire le directoire du supérieur du monastère, de l'"abbé".

L'"Actus militiae cordis" ne présentait initialement aucune finalité proprement cénobitique, c'était une exhortation à la perfection chrétienne, à la vie religieuse valable pour toutes ses formes ascétiques. Le caractère surajouté de l'orientation communautaire et le fait que ce trait se retrouve aussi bien au IVe livre des *Institutions* (où Cassien en a fait une "Admonitio Pinufii ad filium spiritualem") et dans RM (où le document de base semble bien avoir gardé son titre originel "Actus militiae cordis pro timore Dei, quomodo fugiantur peccata") présentent une importance qu'il ne paraît guère possible d'exagérer. Cela confirme de façon décisive l'existence d'un écrit antérieur à Cassien comme au Maître et leur ayant servi de source commune, de document de base, pour les écrits qu'ils destinaient aux cénobites du bassin du Rhône.

Il est à peine besoin de préciser que cette conclusion ne coïncide nullement avec la thèse de Dom Genestout, faisant du Maître la source de Cassien : ce n'est pas sous la forme aussi gravement altérée dans le sens cénobitique qu'elle présente dans RM, que l'abbé de Marseille a connu ce "Traité du combat spirituel", quoiqu'il eût déjà reçu certaines additions l'orientant dans cette direction.

D'autre part, si Cassien a connu un état plus proche de l'original, n'allons pas supposer que le Maître n'a connu l'opuscule qu'à travers Cassien, qui fut par ailleurs incontestablement l'un de ses maîtres en spiritualité. Trop de preuves existent qu'il a eu personnellement accès au texte de l'"Actus militiae cordis". Il le cite et l'exploite plus servilement, plus abondamment, que ne le fait Cassien.

Ces observations et démonstrations se suffisent sans doute à elles-mêmes et ne paraissent plus réclamer de nouveaux étais. Deux différences pourtant, remarquées en établissant la comparaison entre les traités parallèles de l'humilité chez nos auteurs, peuvent donner à réfléchir, ouvrir sur de nouvelles perspectives. C'est pourquoi il sera peut-être encore utile de les signaler ici.

Dans RM le traité se termine par une référence expresse au modèle inoubliable que Jésus lui-même a proposé de la vertu d'humilité: la prière du publicain. Imagine-t-on Cassien lisant l'évocation de ce célèbre ch. 18 de l'Evangile de Luc et négligeant pareille référence, soit par souci de brièveté, soit parce que mise au service de ce trop discutable "12e degré" relatif à l'attitude *extérieure* du moine? C'eût été méconnaître l'importance et la pertinence de cette référence à l'autorité suprême du christianisme, touchant la conception même que Jésus voulait inculquer par cet exemple. On est donc amené à penser que Cassien ne lisait pas encore cette référence précieuse dans le texte de l'"Actus" dont il disposait et qu'il ne dédaigne pas de citer quelquefois *ipsis verbis*, malgré son désir de concision.

Une autre observation du même genre peut-être faite, mais en sens inverse, c'est-à-dire attestant que le Maître n'a pas connu tous les éléments que Cassien incorpore dans son résumé de l'"Actus militiae cordis". On voit bien que, dans le modèle suivi, le traité de l'obéissance faisait suite à un traité de la "crainte de Dieu" (*timor Dei*), vertu de base parce que première "sauvegarde" (*custodia*) de toutes les autres vertus. Toutefois chez Cassien, malgré son extrême brièveté, nous rencontrons un texte qui se lit entre l'exposé relatif à "timor Dei" et les "indicia" d'humilité. Ce passage mérite d'être cité *in extenso*: "qui (*timor Dei*) cum penetrauerit hominis mentem, contemptum rerum omnium parit, obliuionem parentum mundique ipsius gignit horrorem: contemptu autem ac priuatione omnium facultatum *humilitas* adquiritur" (*Inst.*, IV, 39, 1).

Ici surtout il paraît impossible qu'un législateur comme le "Maître", nullement soucieux de concision mais préoccupé à l'extrême de fonder le cénobitisme, et précisément sur les deux piliers du renoncement à la volonté propre et à la *propriété individuelle*, ait pu négliger une réflexion si admirablement appropriée à son dessein. Cette fois, cela paraît certain, l'idée n'était pas exprimée dans l'état de l'"Actus" dont se servait le Maître. Mais, il faut le confesser, peut-être pas non plus dans l'exemplaire utilisé par Cassien. Celui-ci pouvait évidemment la tirer de son propre fonds et l'insérer dans la texture du traité, à l'endroit jugé par lui le plus propice. Cette divergence entre RM et les *Institutions* ne prouve donc pas que Cassien lisait l'*Actus* dans un exemplaire enrichi d'éléments que le Maître n'aurait pas connus (alors que la réciproque, nous l'avons vu, est au moins probable). De toute façon ces différences confirment, s'il en était encore besoin, que RM ne dépend pas du IVe livre des *Institutions*, en ce qui concerne du moins ses pages sur l'humilité.

Pour l'essentiel, les conclusions auxquelles toutes ces recherches conduisent, semblent donc pouvoir se résumer comme suit:

1. Les *Institutions* de Cassien ne sont pas la source de RM-RB ou, plus précisément, de ce document de base, de ce traité de spiritualité explicitement intitulé par RM: "Actus militiae cordis".

2. Le Maître, c'est-à-dire l'auteur ou l'éditeur de la règle monasti-

que dite "Regula Magistri", en l'un quelconque de ses états, n'a pu être, lui non plus, l'écrit dont Cassien s'est servi pour écrire l'"*Admonitio*" qu'il attribue à l'abbé Pinufius au livre IV de ses *Institutions* (contrairement à ce que pensait Dom Genestout).

3. C'est une source *commune* qu'on trouve à l'origine des deux oeuvres, comme il appert surtout de cette autre évidence:

4. Cette source commune avait déjà subi, avant d'être utilisée par Cassien et par RM, une adaptation aux nouveaux besoins de la vie chrétienne parfaite, à savoir l'encadrement de celle-ci dans des communautés régies par des règles et des abbés.

Ces conclusions ne sont pas un terme: comme il arrive souvent, elles suscitent à leur tour de nouvelles questions, mais il n'est plus indispensable d'y répondre ici. Contentons-nous donc à leur sujet d'une "prospective", au lieu d'une enquête en bonne et due forme.

On devrait maintenant rechercher s'il est possible de jauger, fût-ce de manière aproximative, le temps qui a séparé la première rédaction de l'"Actus militiae cordis" et l'état retouché pour cénobites que déjà l'oeuvre de Cassien suppose. Autres problèmes: dans quel milieu est apparu ce traité de spiritualité chrétienne et où a-t-il commencé de recevoir ses compléments cénobitiques? On trouvera peut-être des éléments de réponse à ces questions dans l'étude qu'il conviendrait d'entreprendre touchant le lien exact qu'entretiennent dans RM l'"Actus militiae cordis" et certains apocryphes et passions de martyrs. La passion romancée de s. Sébastien peut à cet égard nous rendre des services particuliers, car elle montre des attaches à la fois avec Rome, dont elle connaît bien la topographie, et la Narbonnaise sur laquelle elle insiste d'une manière qui n'est certainement pas fortuite non plus. Mais trouvera-t-on une voie conduisant aux sources de RM et de Cassien ou seulement à celles de RM et, dans ce dernier cas, de laquelle de ses éditions?[24] Impossible de le décider sans de nouvelles et prudentes investigations dans les textes.

---

[24] Ce qui a été dit plus haut, note 17, incitera le critique à utiliser, avec plus de circonspection que jamais, l'argument "ex silentio" à propos des textes de Cassien, mais aussi en utilisant RB.

OPTIMIST AND RECENSIONIST:
"COMMON ERRORS" OR " COMMON VARIATIONS"?

LEONARD E. BOYLE O.P.

If an Optimist is a scholar who selects and then edits a *"Codex optimus"* from among the various extant manuscripts of a work, a Recensionist, on the other hand, is one who holds that all the manuscripts, all the extant witnesses, should be reviewed and as a whole should be made to contribute to the edition. Where the Optimist prefers to place his trust in a single "best" or "basic" manuscript, the Recensionist relies on a complete *Recensio*, often accompanied by a *Stemma codicum*, of the relationship between all the witnesses to a text.

The Optimist method is more popular with editors of vernacular texts than with those of texts in the classical languages. The best-known exponent of the method is Joseph Bédier, particularly in an article in 1928 on the manuscript tradition of the *Lai de l'Ombre*.[1] According to Bédier and others of the same persuasion, the sensible thing to do when confronted with a large or even a small number of codices of a work, is to single out for editing that codex which is on the whole the most satisfactory, and then to follow this *"Codex optimus"* through thick and thin, except, of course, where it is obviously defective or unintelligible. A variation on this method prefers to speak of a "basic" rather than of a "best" codex. This codex, to quote one practitioner of the method, is chosen "because it appears the most suitable when the number of its obvious errors and deficiencies is weighed against the character of its spellings, dialect forms and grammar". In order to correct these errors and deficiencies, variants from other manuscripts are compared with the base text, and are used where suitable. With respect to the basic text as a whole, variants from the other manuscripts can be incorporated into it if they are judged by the editor to be more original than what the basic text has to offer. The end-product of this refinement of the Optimist method is therefore a "corrected basic manuscript", which,

---

[1] J. Bédier, "La tradition manuscrite du Lai de l'Ombre. Réflexions sur l'art d'éditer les anciens textes", *Romania* 54 (1928) 162-86, 321-56 (also printed separately, Paris 1929).

when published, is accompanied by a presentation of all the variants, by an indication of the points where corrections have been made, and by a discussion of the evidence.[2]

Sensible though it may seem, the Optimist method has its critics, particularly among editors of classical texts. A. E. Housman has some rough remarks on it in various prefaces and reviews.[3] Ludwig Bieler is far from enthusiastic about it in his "Grammarian's Craft".[4] Alphonse Dain, for whom there is really no such thing as a "best" or "basic" manuscript, is convinced that it is a solution "begotten of sloth".[5]

Optimists, in turn, are no less caustic about the Recensionist method. Bédier showed plainly that it was full of pitfalls.[6] Kane abandoned it as impracticable for his edition of Piers Plowman.[7] Vinaver averred that the method had become as "obsolete as Newton's physics".[8]

Often know as the "Lachmann" or "Common errors" method, the Recensionist method is, in fact, as Timpanaro has well shown, a combination of methods of classification of manuscripts which were used or advocated in the first half of the last century by scholars such as Wolf, Lachmann himself, Madvig, Ritschl, Zumpt and Sauppe.[9] Its most influential modern theorist is Paul Maas, whose overly-schematic work has recently been given a more discursive presentation by Martin West.[10]

---

[2] See *Piers Plowman: The A Text*, ed. G. Kane (London 1960), p. 147.

[3] E.g., preface to Manilius I (1903): "This method answers the purpose for which it was intended: it saves lazy editors from working and stupid editors from thinking" (A. E. Housman, *Selected Prose*, ed. J. Carter, Cambridge 1961, p. 36). See D. R. Shackleton Baily, "A. E. Housman as Textual Critic", in *La critica del testo. Atti del secondo Congresso internazionale della Società Italiana di Storia del Diritto* (Florence 1971), pp. 739-48.

[4] L. Bieler, "The Grammarian's Craft. A Professional Talk", *Folia* 10.2 (1958) 13.

[5] A. Dain, *Les manuscrits* (Paris 1964[2]), p. 171.

[6] See A. Castellani, *Bédier avait-il raison? La méthode de Lachmann dans l'édition de textes du Moyen Age* (Fribourg 1957).

[7] *Op. cit.*, pp. 115-72 ("Editorial resources and methods").

[8] E. Vinaver, "Principles of Textual Emendation", in *Studies in French Language and Literature presented to Mildred K. Pope* (Manchester 1939), p. 351.

[9] S. Timpanaro, *La genesi del metodo del Lachmann* (Florence 1963). A German translation, *Entstehung der Lachmannischen Methode* (Hamburg 1971), has a good bibliography of textual criticism at pp. 153-71. The best general survey of the method as such is in G. Pasquali, *Storia della tradizione e critica del testo* (Florence 1952[2]), pp. 3-12.

[10] P. Maas, *Textual Criticism*, trans. B. Flower (Oxford 1958); M. L. West,

The aim of the Recensionist is to make a complete *Recensio* or review of a given text as it is found in each of its manuscripts or extant witnesses, and this in order to arrive at an overall view of that text as it was before these extant copies were made and put into circulation. We do not know, the Recensionist says, which one of the manuscripts possesses that text in greater or lesser measure, and unless the original text of the author comes to light, we shall never know unequivocally. Assuming that manuscripts that claim to carry an author's text actually do carry it, the Recensionist is convinced that he can disengage and pry loose this common text from these manuscripts, collectively as well as individually. To do this, he argues, one must thoroughly review (*recensere*) the setting and the textual content of each manuscript, and then the codices as a body. What should stand out at the end of this general review is a common denominator that must be the text of the author — not, the Recensionist hastens to add, the text of the author as it came from his pen, but as it is transmitted in common by the manuscript witnesses. Where the manuscripts are at variance, the Recensionist claims that he can sort out the witnesses and decide which manuscript of which block of witnesses to follow. He accomplishes this by plotting "Common errors" and then constructing from the results a *Stemma codicum* which allows him to see beyond the contentious witnesses to the text as it was before the witnesses began to disagree.

Many Optimists feel that there is an undue if not pernicious element of subjectivity in the Recensionist method. They are particularly suspicious of the technique of "Common errors" and of the validity of a *Stemma codicum*. They have good reason. For one thing, Recensionists often construct the *Stemma codicum* in a less than correct fashion. For another, the classification of codices through "Common errors" does not always do justice to the complete codicological tradition of a text.

A *Stemma codicum* is not, as is too easily assumed, a means whereby all of a text is established from a number of manuscripts. Rather it is a means to which one resorts only when the codices are in disagreement, and that in order to solve the disagreements.

Textual Criticism and Editorial Technique (Stuttgart 1973). According to the preface (p. 5), West's volume replaces the *Textkritik* (Leipzig 1957³) of Maas and the *Editionstechnik* (Leipzig 1914²) of O. Stählin in the Teubner *Studienbücher : Philologie.*

Ideally there are three stages in the Recensionist procedure, and a *Stemma codicum* properly belongs to the second. The first stage uncovers the text that is common to all the witnesses. The second tackles the problem of what is not common. The third (with which I shall not deal here) turns the text established in the first and second stages from the witnesses into an edited text which, with the aid of conjecture, emendation, etc., goes beyond them.[11]

In the first stage, the credentials of all the witnesses are examined: date, script, scribe, location, origin, provenance, ownership century by century, gatherings, quire-marks, *peciae*-marks, colophons, ornamentation, and the like. After this, one of the manuscripts (the oldest usually) is transcribed faithfully, completely, flawlessly; and with every cancellation, erasure, gap, correction, inversion, misspelling, filler, grammatical inanity, homoioteleuton and all.[12]

What the Recensionist winds up with at this stage is simply a scrupulously transcribed but utterly unedited text of the chosen first witness. Since this text opens the way to a *Recensio* of the codices as a whole, it may be called a "Recension-text". But it is not a "Collation" or "Basic" text with which the other witnesses are collated, as happens in Optimist circles. It is rather an instrument by means of which all the witnesses are seen in relation to one another on some sheets of paper; and it has no more textual value at this point than any other witness.

With the help of the Recension-text, the other codices may now be recorded on the recension sheets with a certain expedition, for only the variations from codex to codex will need to be set down or transcribed. All the same, each witness must be recorded with the same archeological precision that went into the Recension-text itself — with all the peculiarities, the blemishes, the hesitations. Not to do so is to place the Recension-text on some sort of value-pedestal, as though transcribing it in full had given it some special standing.

---

[11] The more common division is into *Recensio* and *Emendatio* (= *Examinatio*): see K. Lachmann, *Novum Testamentum graece et latine* I (Berlin 1842), p. V; L. D. Reynolds and N. G. Wilson, *Scribes and Scholars. A guide to the Transmission of Greek and Latin Literature* (Oxford 1968), pp. 137-47. But a three-stage procedure, as outlined here, with *Recensio* spread over two distinct stages, seems more helpful, if not more logical.

[12] See in general F. Masai, "Principes et conventions de l'édition diplomatique", *Scriptorium* 4 (1950) 177-93, and Dain, *Les manuscrits*, pp. 76-93, 174-186.

When all the witnesses have been set out in relation to one another on the recension sheets, it is not difficult to see at once what is common to all the manuscripts by way of text (a line here, a paragraph there), and what is not. When the text common to all the witnesses has been established in this way, the first stage of *Recensio* is more or less complete. And if one subscribes to the dictum of Bentley that an author should be "corrected by himself", there is a good opportunity to hand in this common text of absorbing the style and usages of the author in preparation for the editorial work of stage three (conjecture, emendation), and possibly for the task of sorting out the discrepancies between witnesses in stage two. Admittedly, this is only the style of the author as it is transmitted by the witnesses, but if there are no other writings extant of this particular author, it is hard to imagine where else to look. And even if there are other works to hand, this is not a bad place to begin.

The second stage is taken up with what is not common to the witnesses, with, that is, those passages, phrases or words upon which the manuscript-witnesses are not in agreement. In the Recensionist method an editor is not entirely helpless at this point, given that he has made a proper codicological examination of all the witnesses, and has objectively recorded the text precisely as it is found in each witness. For if the first function of *Recensio* is to uncover what is common to all the witnesses — to look for what is in the codices without any interpretation, as Lachmann put it[13] — a useful by-product of this tedious and exacting process is that certain relationships between the codices are also uncovered during the search for what is common.

Since we do not possess the text of the author himself, it is impossible to say, in the quest of a way through the contentious readings, which one of these manuscripts is closest to that original text. But it is possible, the Recensionist claims, to make a start at least by finding out which witnesses depend on or are close to one another. This, the Recensionist says, can be accomplished by examining and tabulating what are usually called "Common errors" but which I shall here term "Common variations".

From a textual point of view, this technique of "Common variations" depends to a large extent on the proven fact that texts

---

[13] "Ex auctoribus quaerere, quod primo loco posui, id quod recensere dicitur, sine interpretatione et possumus et debemus...": *op. cit.*, p. V.

change progressively as copied, whether because of a scribe's failure to understand or read the text he was copying or because of many other factors: conscious alteration of the text, haplography, dittography, homoioteleuton, scribal corrections and free associations, haste, fatigue, spelling by auditive memory, poor light, perhaps a recalcitrant pen.[14]

Hence, the Recensionist holds, if a copy A deviates from the exemplar X that it is copying for one or other of the above or other reasons, the chances are sound that the variations now present in A will be perpetuated in copy B or other manuscripts copied from A. These further copies (B and companions) in turn will pass on both the A variations and their own special variations to any copies made from them (C for example). And so there is a chain-reaction, each copy of C carrying not only the variations peculiar to C and B but also the original variations on X perpetrated by A. In short, variations compound variations. And what was once a fairly undisturbed textual tradition in X (perhaps an autograph or apograph, or some copy not far removed from either) is now wandering all over the world in copies that carry the variations of, for example, A alone, or of A and B together, or of A and B and C all at once.[15]

Because of this phenomenon of "progressive variations", and because of the fact that all witnesses of a textual tradition are held together basically by a bond of common text, it is a Recensionist belief that by observing what variations are in common to what manuscripts and what are not, one can trace retrogressively the path of these common variations, arriving in the end at the source or sources of the different sets of common variations, and, possibly, at the source or sources on which these variations originally were made.

---

[14] There are useful lists of possibilities in Vinaver, art. cit., 351-69, Bieler, art. cit., 19-22, Reynolds and Wilson, *op. cit.*, pp. 151-62, J. Willis, *Latin Textual Criticism* (Urbana-Chicago-London, 1972), pp. 51-161. See also J. Andrieu, "Pour l'explication psychologique de fautes de copistes", *Revue des études latines* 28 (1950) 279-92; B. Axelson, *Korruptelenlehre* (Lund 1967); R. M. Ogilvie, "Monastic corruption", *Greece and Rome*, 2nd series 18 (1971) 32-4. See also the recent volume of S. Timpanaro, *Il Lapsus freudiano. Psicanalisi e critica testuale* (Florence 1974).

[15] See, for example, West, *Textual Criticism*, p. 32: "In the absence of contamination, each copy will contain the same errors that were in the exemplar from which it was made, minus those that the scribe has seen and corrected, plus some additional ones (unless, perhaps, the text is very short). This axiom is the basis of stemmatic analysis". The ABC case above is, of course, a broad illustration.

In a word, what one does is to retrace the path of these variations to the first manuscript or manuscripts that put them on their path from copy to copy.[16] What is also revealed is the relationship (sometimes a quite precise one) of each manuscript to another or others and to the witnesses as a whole. One is thus enabled to assign a value to each witness, according to where it stands on the path or paths made by the variations as they progressed or multiplied.

If the Recensionist wishes at this point, he may plot or make a diagram of these variations. Such a *Stemma codicum*, as it is termed, can be a useful visual aid.[17] With the information provided by the pattern of common variations as summed up in the *Stemma*, an editor is now in a good position to tackle the problem of the conflicting witnesses and to decide which of the witnesses to follow. It may be found, for example, that certain manuscripts are direct copies of others and therefore may be discarded, or that others are so close to one another that they form distinct blocks which may be played off against one another with more or less success.

The procedure, of course, is far from watertight and will not resolve all the conflicts. But it will provide the raw, unedited material for the third or editing stage, when the text established from what is common to the witnesses (stage one) and from what is not common (stage two) is worked on by the editor and turned into an edited text. From the knowledge acquired during stages one and two of the codicological tradition, the textual variations and the style of the author, the editor may indeed be able with the help of palaeography, grammar, conjecture and emendation, to reconstruct the archetype of the extant witnesses and thus to present the text as it probably was before any of the present witnesses were made.[18] But he will

---

[16] Because of various Optimist misgivings, I have avoided "genetic" terminology in describing the process. See further the remarks of Mass, *Textual Criticism*, pp. 48-9, on the concept of "families" or "classes" of manuscripts.

[17] A *Stemma codicum* was first used by Karl Zumpt in his edition of the *Verrinae* in 1831, and then by Franz Ritschl in his edition of the Eclogues of Thomas Magister in 1832. Curiously, although the *Stemma* is so much a part of what is known as the "Lachmann" method, Lachmann himself never used one (Timpanaro, *op. cit.*, pp. 45-51). On the limitations of the stemmatic method, see Reynolds and Wilson, *op. cit.*, pp. 143-5.

[18] See R. Marichal, "La critique des textes", in *L'histoire et ses méthodes*, ed. Ch. Samaran (*Encyclopédie de la Pléiade* XI, Paris 1961), pp. 1247-1366. There are many examples of conjecture and emendation in Willis, *Latin Textual Criticism*, pp. 191-220, etc.

only achieve this with some degree of plausibility if he has respected the codices in their entirety from the very first moment of *Recensio* and has not tampered with them along the way to the final stage.[19]

It is not the intention of the present essay to treat in detail of the whole Recensionist method, but rather to present a statement of stages one and two that attempts to meet certain misgivings of Optimists. If the *Stemma codicum* has been relegated to the second stage of *Recensio* and described not as a prerequisite of an edition but as a useful means towards the solving of textual difficulties, this is because its purpose is often misunderstood by Recensionists and misinterpreted by Optimists. If "Common variations" has been used instead of "Common errors", this is because the latter creates an impression of subjectivity.

It should be understood, however, that the "Common variations" in question are not at all variations on the author's text as such, for at this stage (the sorting out of conflicting witnesses), an editor is as far away from knowing what that text is as he is from knowing what is the total text carried by the witnesses as a whole; all that he is sure of is what the witnesses have in common. Nor should the variations be taken exclusively as variations of the text from witness to witness, although such textual variations are indeed an important part of the whole array of common variations. Above all, these variations are not in any sense variations which the various witnesses have in common against what the editor thinks is or should be the ideal text.

What constitutes a "Common variation" is not whether it is "right" or "wrong" (this we have no means of judging in most cases at this point), but the simple physical fact that two or more witnesses have some feature in common that a third does not have. In this business of sorting out the witnesses in order to break through a

---

[19] Many editors, apparently, are more concerned to arrive as soon as possible at the third, "creative", stage, than to toil over stages one and two. There were no short-cuts for Lachmann: "Ex auctoribus quaerere, quod primo loco posui, id quod recensere dicitur, sine interpretatione et possumus et debemus. Contra interpretatio, nisi quid testes ferant intellectum fuerit, locum habere, nisi de scriptore constiterit, absolvi non potest. Rursus emendatio et libri originis investigatio, quia ad ingenium scriptoris pertinet, tanquam fundamento nititur interpretatione. Quo fit ut nulla huius negotii pars tuto a ceteris separari possit, nisi illa una quae debet esse omnium prima: illam dico quae testium fidem perscrutatur et locupletissimis auctoribus tradita repraesentat" (*op. cit.*, opening paragraph of preface, p. V).

barrier of contentious witnesses, anything that is not shared by all the extant witnesses can be a variation, from a pressmark to a doodle, from a garbled word to a cancelled passage, from a change of ink or a change of hand to word-separation.

What in fact the editor is attempting at the second stage of the *Recensio* is to discover the relationship between the witnesses as such. Codicological variations — marginal notes, colophons, holes, *peciae*marks, inversions, insertions, erasures, fillers, glosses, expunctions, ornamentation, odd forms of abbreviation — are therefore as much a part of "Common variations" as are the truly textual variations.[20] One small example must suffice. A blank in the text of one witness is not necessarily a textual aberration, and may well prove later to have been a discerning erasure. It is, however, a distinguishing feature of that witness, and it could have been the foundation of an everwidening series of common variations among the witnesses of that textual tradition. For witness A, which displays the blank, could have trapped witness B into leaving a blank at this point when copying A; while witness C, when copying A or B, could have hazarded a wild guess at what should fill the blank, and was then copied by D, and by others through D or directly. And even if the blank in A is not found in any other witness, and thus cannot be spoken of as a common variation, it is nevertheless a separative variation, in as much as all the other witnesses are thereby commonly at variance with A.[21]

"Common variations", then, are variations that are common to various witnesses, not simply variations or "errors" that are common to the texts in those witnesses. For manuscripts are not primarily witnesses to a text but to a textual tradition. To look only at the text in a witness is not to see the witness for the text.

The pattern of witnesses that is discovered through the detection of common variations is therefore called a *Stemma codicum* and not a *Stemma textuum*. Most theorists and editors, however, rarely look beyond the text and what "scribal errors" they find there when setting up *Stemmata*.[22] Whether or not this means (as some Optimists

---

[20] On, for example, the importance of fillers, see C. Jeudy, "Signes de fin de ligne et tradition manuscrite. Le *De translatione romani imperii* de Marsile de Padoue", *Scriptorium* 27 (1973) 252-62.

[21] The most lucid treatment of separation and conjunction (though restricted to "errors") is still Maas, *op. cit.*, pp. 42-9.

[22] For West, *op. cit.*, the "errors" that go to the making of a *Stemma* are scribal "corruptions and emendations" (p. 32). See Maas, *op. cit.*, p. 41; and

understandably suspect) that these scholars are convinced that they possess some inside knowledge of a text that has yet to be established from the witnesses, it certainly suggests that they are more concerned with variations between the texts in the witnesses than with variations between the witnesses as such. This sort of approach is inevitable, and this sort of impression predictable, if the witnesses are not allowed to speak with a full, codicological voice but only in muffled, "textual" tones. The object of an edition, however, is not solely to recover a text from the witnesses. Rather it is to uncover a textual tradition by which to see beyond the text encased in that tradition to that text as it was before it was launched on the devious path of variation by the present witnesses. This, it hardly need be said, will only be achieved with security if the witnesses are heard out with patience and urbanity both for their textual witness and their witness to the textual tradition.

All in all, the consecrated Recensionist term "Common errors" is as ill-advised as it is restrictive. For it rightly suggests to an outsider, and above all to an Optimist, that somehow or other a Recensionist knows precisely what is right and what is wrong — that he has some sort of archetypal text in the sky — before a text of any kind has been established, not to say edited. To continue to use the term is to condone if not to encourage a deficient methodology and to invite derisive assertions by Optimists (and I quote one) that the "whole classification [of manuscripts] depends on purely subjective choices made before the work of editing begins".[23] This is not far short of the truth if, as frequently happens, editors begin their work by spotting and plotting textual "errors", and then label the result of their pursuit of "Common errors" a *Stemma codicum*.[24]

Although in some cases the use of the term could be interpreted benignly to mean nothing more than "readings which some MSS. have in common against the readings of others", it would be helpful

---

Reynolds and Wilson, *op. cit.*, p. 141: "Of fundamental importance in stemmatics are the errors which scribes made in transcribing manuscripts; for these errors provide the most valid means of working out the relationships of the manuscripts".

[23] F. Talbot Donaldson, *Speaking of Chaucer* (London 1970), p. 107.

[24] See Willis, *op. cit.*, in the chapter "Drawing up the Stemma": "If one collates all the known manuscripts over three or four sections of text scattered through the work, one insures onself fairly well against missing anything of real importance; and manuscripts of particular interest or difficulty can be examined at greater length" (p. 14).

if the term "Common errors" (and the word "errors" itself) were to be jettisoned irretrievably from the Recensionist vocabulary. Then, perhaps, codices would cease to be looked on merely as textual carriers and would recover their rightful position as bearers of a textual tradition.

"Common variations", in any case, is a more neutral and realistic term than "Common errors" to describe the meandering of a textual tradition from codex to codex. Certainly it lacks the somewhat censorious (and to the Optimist, sinister) overtones of the term "Common errors". And it does have the considerable advantage of embracing everything from common textual aberrations to egregious codicological vagaries.[25] The use of the term might serve to remind the Recensionist that there is more to a critical edition than editing a text — and it could help to persuade the Optimist that there is less sleight-of-hand in the Recensionist position than he had been tempted to suppose.

---

[25] "Variations", of course, are not to be confused with "Variants", a term usually reserved for the variant readings which remain after the text has been established from the codices in stages one and two, and between which the editor has to choose at the third or editorial stage proper.

CURRICULUM VITAE

Place of Birth: Vienna (Austria)
Date of Birth: 20th of October, 1906
Married on: 2nd of May, 1939 to Eva née Uffenheimer
Children: Thomas Albert and Elizabeth Mary

Details of Education:
1925 Matura (Leaving Certificate), Vienna
1925-1930 Studied Classics and Comparative Philology at the Universities of Vienna, Tübingen, and Munich
1929 Dr. Phil., University of Vienna, "summa cum laude"
1931 Lehramtsprüfung (Higher Diploma of Education) in Greek and Latin for Austria
1935 Examination for Wissenschaftlicher Bibliotheksdienst (Higher Diploma of Librarianship) including Greek and Latin Palaeography

Professional Employment:
1930-1938 Assistant to "Corpus Scriptorum Ecclesiasticorum Latinorum", Academy of Letters, Vienna
1932-1938 Instructor in Greek, University of Vienna
1935-1938 Assistant Keeper of Manuscripts, National Library, Vienna
1936-1938 Privatdozent (Lecturer) in Classics, University of Vienna
1940-1946 Visiting Lecturer in Palaeography and Early Medieval Latin, National University of Ireland.
1946-1947 Archivist, National Library of Ireland
1947-1948 Assistant Professor of Classics, University of Notre Dame, Indiana (U.S.A.)
1948-1959 Assistant, then Assistant Lecturer, then College Lecturer, University College Dublin
since 1960 Professor of Palaeography and Late Latin, University College Dublin

Professional Associations:
since 1947 Member of the Royal Irish Academy. On Council 1958-1960 and 1965-1968
1968-1975 Secretary of the National Committee for Greek and Latin Studies
since 1954 Member of the Institute for Advanced Study, Princeton.
since 1963 Corresponding Fellow of the Mediaeval Academy of America
since 1964 Mitglied der Österreichischen Akademie der Wissenschaften
since 1971 Member of the British Academy
since 1947 Member of the Royal Dublin Society

Honours, Prizes, Awards:

1970	Litt. D. honoris causa, Trinity College Dublin
1972	Dr. Phil. honoris causa, University of Munich
1975	Litt. D. honoris causa, University of Glasgow

Other Biographical Listings:

1966	Kürschners Deutscher Gelehrtenkalender
1971	Répertoire International des Médiévistes
1973/74	The Academic Who's Who

Hobbies:
Music, Gardening, Hiking

Current Address:

Home:	22 Villiers Road, Rathgar, Dublin 6, Ireland
Office:	Department of Palaeography and Late Latin, University College Dublin, Belfield, Dublin 4, Ireland.

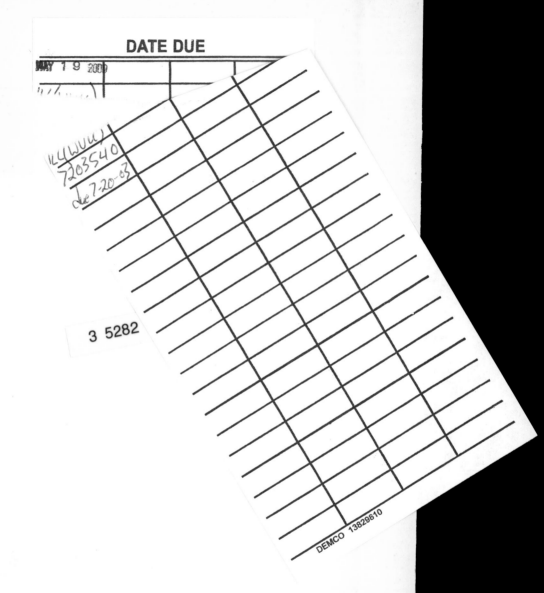